Building Enterprise Projects with Go

Clarity at Scale in Production-Grade Go Systems

Saeed Shahsavan

Apress®

Building Enterprise Projects with Go: Clarity at Scale in Production-Grade Go Systems

Saeed Shahsavan
Vienna, Austria

ISBN-13 (pbk): 979-8-8688-2369-5 ISBN-13 (electronic): 979-8-8688-2370-1
https://doi.org/10.1007/979-8-8688-2370-1

Managing Director, Apress Media LLC: Welmoed Spahr
Acquisitions Editor: Melissa Duffy
Editorial Assistant: Gryffin Winkler

Cover designed by eStudioCalamar

Distributed to the book trade worldwide by Springer Science+Business Media New York, 1 New York Plaza, New York, NY 10004. Phone 1-800-SPRINGER, fax (201) 348-4505, e-mail orders-ny@springer-sbm.com, or visit www.springeronline.com. Apress Media, LLC is a Delaware LLC and the sole member (owner) is Springer Science + Business Media Finance Inc (SSBM Finance Inc). SSBM Finance Inc is a **Delaware** corporation.

For information on translations, please e-mail booktranslations@springernature.com; for reprint, paperback, or audio rights, please e-mail bookpermissions@springernature.com.

Apress titles may be purchased in bulk for academic, corporate, or promotional use. eBook versions and licenses are also available for most titles. For more information, reference our Print and eBook Bulk Sales web page at http://www.apress.com/bulk-sales.

Any source code or other supplementary material referenced by the author in this book is available to readers on GitHub. For more detailed information, please visit https://www.apress.com/gp/services/source-code.

If disposing of this product, please recycle the paper

In the name of God, the Lord of soul and wisdom

Beyond whom no thought can ever pass.

—Ferdowsi

To my father and mother

For your quiet strength, your endless patience,

and the love that shaped every part of who I am.

This book began long before a single word was written;

it began in the home you built,

in the values you planted,

and in the hope you carried for me long before I could carry it for myself.

Thank you for every sacrifice unseen,

every kindness unspoken,

and every belief in me when the path felt uncertain.

Whatever clarity exists in these pages

comes from the light you placed in me.

Table of Contents

About the Author

Saeed Shahsavan is a senior software engineer and software architect with more than 18 years of experience designing and implementing enterprise-scale distributed systems. Over the course of his career, he has worked in ERP, telecommunications, government-to-citizen platforms, and banking.

His expertise includes Go, Java, and React, with a deep focus on search engines, event-driven architectures, and high-performance microservices. He has also served as a project manager, technical lead, and instructor, mentoring teams on writing idiomatic, testable Java and Go code and managing complex enterprise projects.

A lifelong reader of poetry and philosophy, he brings a thoughtful and human-centered perspective to engineering, combining practical skills with architectural vision. He is passionate about clarity, scalability, and performance and aims to help professional developers build maintainable systems while sharing lessons learned from real enterprise projects.

You can connect with him on LinkedIn, linkedin.com/in/saeed-shahsavan/, to follow his activities.

About the Technical Reviewer

Suprakash Dutta is a Senior Solutions Architect at Amazon Web Services, leading strategic cloud transformations for Fortune 500 retailers and large enterprises. He specializes in architecting mission-critical retail solutions, generative AI implementations, and enterprise modernization initiatives that drive measurable business outcomes—including transformations across thousands of retail locations.

A recognized thought leader in cloud architecture and AI innovation, Suprakash has established reference architectures and best practices adopted by cloud practitioners globally. He advances the field through AWS blog contributions, open source frameworks, and technical workshops, while serving as a technical reviewer for leading technology publishers. As a multi-cloud certified professional holding 15+ certifications, he serves as a trusted advisor to C-suite executives on strategic technology investments.

Suprakash is passionate about democratizing AI capabilities and mentoring the next generation of cloud architects through university partnerships and community leadership.

Acknowledgments

First, I thank my supportive parents, my kind sisters, and their wonderful families. Your constant support has been my safe place in every stage of my life. Your encouragement gave me the strength to continue, to learn, and to stay hopeful even on difficult days. This book exists because you stood behind me with love and patience.

This is also the result of 18 years of experience in software engineering and architecture. I want to thank every manager who trusted me, guided me, and gave me space to grow. You allowed me to take different roles, learn new skills, and make mistakes. Each project taught me something that found its way into these chapters.

My sincere thanks to the Apress team, especially Melissa Duffy and Dutta Suprakash, for their kind support and professional guidance. I am grateful for your patience and care.

Finally, I thank you, the reader. You chose this book to grow your skills and to build systems that stay clear, maintainable, and ready for real-world scale. I hope these pages guide you with greater clarity, deeper confidence, and a sense of satisfaction in your work. And if this book makes your path even a little easier, then it has fulfilled its purpose.

Introduction

During the last 18 years, I have worked in many roles in software engineering: developer, database administrator, technical lead, software architect, and project manager. These roles were different on the surface, but all lived in **enterprise projects**—large systems that must withstand real users, real traffic, and real change. If I try to find one shared skill across all those years, it is this: understanding how enterprise systems live, grow, and sometimes struggle.

In each role, I read books related to the work I was doing. And in every team, I saw the same pattern: a **gap** between people in different parts of a software team.

Managers often did not understand the true complexity of technical problems. Developers sometimes did not understand how their code behaved in production or how databases and external systems shaped the real performance of their applications. Teams did not always understand the human side of collaboration—how priorities, communication, and respect can save a project, or quietly destroy it.

For a long time, I wished there was a book that spoke to all of these sides at once; a book that helped developers see beyond code. We often talk about "T-shaped people" in agile methods, but our books don't always teach the horizontal part of that "T."

At the same time, many technical books focus only on tools and syntax. They forget the deeper stories behind engineering: the lessons about patience, design, failure, teamwork, and the quiet art of building something that will live for years. Since childhood, I have loved poetry and philosophy, and throughout my career, I have believed that technical work can also carry beauty, clarity, and a little bit of soul.

From all these motivations, this book was born.

This is a book about **Go**, but it is not only a book about a programming language. It is about how Go becomes a tool for building real enterprise systems—systems where clean code, memory understanding, concurrency, testing, and architecture truly matter. Enterprise projects are different from small hobby programs. They demand clarity, discipline, and careful thinking about performance, boundaries, and long-term growth. In this book, we explore Go with those needs in mind.

You will see code, of course. But you will also see architecture, team roles, real-world concerns, and small moments of reflection. You may even find brief touches of poetry where the topic allows it.

During the preparation of this manuscript, I used AI-assisted refinement. No generative AI was used for content generation, technical insights, or analysis. All technical content, ideas, and usage of design patterns in enterprise projects are my own. Shared experiences are real, and full responsibility for the work rests with me.

I hope you enjoy reading this book. And I hope that, when you finish it, you will feel more confident and more inspired to use Go in your own enterprise projects—with clarity, with good design, and with a little more joy.

PART I

Foundations of Modern Software: Thinking, Design, and Go

CHAPTER 1

Teamwork: The Architecture Behind the Architecture

Before we build systems, we must learn how to build teams.

In enterprise projects, no algorithm, framework, or architecture succeeds in isolation. The hidden foundation of every scalable system is not just clean code or a clever design—it's the team that shapes and sustains it. A well-functioning team multiplies creativity, accelerates delivery, and makes software resilient to change. A dysfunctional team, no matter how talented its individuals, often produces unstable outcomes.

This chapter explores teamwork as a technical discipline. We will examine common traps such as the *Golden Hammer* and *technical dictatorship*, and we'll highlight virtues like humility and shared ownership. You'll see how decision-making structures, cross-functional communication, and mentorship determine whether a team thrives or fractures.

As systems scale from small squads to enterprise-wide programs, teamwork must also scale: from a single conversation in a stand-up to decision-making processes that coordinate dozens of teams. Along the way, leadership must evolve from control to service, empowering engineers to solve problems together rather than enforcing one person's solution.

In short, teamwork is not "soft" compared to architecture—it *is* the architecture behind the architecture.

S. Shahsavan, *Building Enterprise Projects with Go*, https://doi.org/10.1007/979-8-8688-2370-1_1

Philosophy First

In business, we say "Customer first." In software, we say "API first." In life, I say—"Philosophy first."

Almost nine years ago, when I was studying **PRINCE2** as a project manager, one sentence caught my attention:

"A project is a unique and temporary organisation, designed to deliver a tangible output."

—PRINCE2

Out of curiosity, I searched further and found that **PMBOK**—perhaps the most recognized standard in project management—defines it almost the same way:

"A project is a temporary endeavor undertaken to create a unique product, service or result."

—PMBOK

That similarity struck me. Both frameworks agree that a project is **temporary** and **unique**.

As someone who loves both philosophy and poetry, a thought emerged:

If life has a goal, then life itself is the grandest project of all.

"The unexamined life is not worth living."

—Socrates

That quote may sound severe, but it reminds us that reflection gives meaning to creation.

We don't need to drift into metaphysics to see its relevance to software. Every system, every plan, every meeting inherits the values of its builders. Your professional projects are temporary; your principles are not.

Through the years, I've written thousands of lines of code. Many of them are gone—deprecated, replaced, or locked inside corporate repositories I'll never access again. Yet what remained were not the commits, but the **colleagues**: the laughter in code reviews, the quiet resilience during release nights, the friendships that survived migrations and deadlines.

So when you join a project, remember: it is **just one small chapter** in your larger life. Don't let it shrink your humanity. Be honest. Be kind. Be supportive. Let the project serve your life's goal, not replace it.

Persian poet Dr. Jaleh Esfahani once captured this truth in verse:

Life is our unique artistic stage,

Everyone sings their song and leaves.

The stage is everlasting;

Blessed the song that people remember.

That, to me, is the essence of teamwork and architecture alike.

Technology fades. Products end. But how we live and build together—that is what endures.

The Golden Hammer Trap: When Familiarity Kills Innovation

If all you have is a hammer, everything looks like a nail.

—Abraham Maslow

In software teams, the "Golden Hammer" is a cognitive bias: the tendency to apply a familiar tool or technology everywhere, regardless of whether it truly fits the problem. What begins as confidence in a skill can turn into rigidity, slowing the team down and reducing adaptability.

Real-World Examples

- **Oracle Full-Text vs. Elasticsearch**

  In an enterprise project, the team chose Oracle's Full-Text Index to handle large-scale text search. While powerful within the database, it could not match the speed, scalability, or flexibility of dedicated search engines like Elasticsearch or Solr. The result was unnecessary complexity and low performance.

- **Oracle ADF in a Large-Scale System**

  Another team leaned heavily on Oracle ADF because they were comfortable with PL/SQL. This decision reduced flexibility, limited testing capabilities, and locked the team into the Oracle ecosystem. A modern language framework (e.g., Java with its rich ecosystem) would have provided faster development, more adaptability, and stronger scalability.

- **Kafka Misapplied As a Database**

  A colleague once shared an example of using Apache Kafka not just for event streaming, but as a general-purpose database and object store. While Kafka excels at high-throughput event pipelines, using it as storage created bloat and performance issues. This misuse turned a strong event-streaming capability into a source of inefficiency.

How Teams Can Avoid the Trap

- **Evaluate Needs, Not Habits:** Before committing to a tool, clarify the actual requirements. Don't let habit dictate architecture.
- **Stay Flexible:** Teams that allow debate and experimentation are less likely to overfit one solution to every problem.
- **Learn Broadly:** Exposure to multiple technologies prevents over-reliance on a single "hammer."

Enterprise Lesson Golden Hammer choices rarely break systems overnight. Instead, they gradually rigidify the code base, making it harder to scale, test, or adapt to new business needs. In enterprise contexts, where projects live for years, this rigidity multiplies costs and reduces the capacity to innovate.

The best safeguard is not banning specific tools, but cultivating a culture where the team continually asks: *"Is this still the right tool for this job?"*

Technical Dictatorship: When Leadership Turns into Control

Leadership without collaboration is not leadership—it's control.

In software teams, having a highly knowledgeable technical person is often a blessing. Their experience can guide the team through complex architectural decisions. But when that same person monopolizes every decision and silences alternative perspectives, the team slips into what we call **technical dictatorship**.

This form of control usually takes one of two shapes:

- **The Autocratic Technical Manager**: Enforcing decisions without real consultation.
- **The Controlling Senior Developer**: Designing structures that leave no room for alternatives.

Both stifle creativity, motivation, and long-term health of the team.

The Cost of Technical Dictatorship

- **Reduced Creativity:** When ideas are dismissed, teammates stop contributing.
- **Frustration and Silence:** Confidence erodes, and valuable voices go unheard.
- **Higher Turnover:** Talented developers rarely stay where they cannot grow.
- **Declining Quality:** Enforcing one perspective leads to rejecting innovative solutions.
- **Inefficient Collaboration:** Teams lose their learning culture, becoming brittle and slow.
- **Organizational Silence:** Opinions are withheld not for lack of ideas, but fear of rejection.

Stories from the Field

- As a project manager, I once rejected a developer's proposal to use Mockito in favor of my preferred JMockit. The developer later left the team—a clear reminder that rigid tool choices can drive away talent and reduce team resilience. In reality, both options were equally valid, and openness would have served the project better.
- In another case, a senior developer—protected by management—pushed away multiple colleagues through conflict. Many resigned before he eventually left, leaving the system in an unsustainable state.
- A project where Apache Camel was forced instead of Rx-Java resulted in rigid, painful code. The system was so inflexible it eventually had to be rewritten.
- I have also seen ideas reused without attribution, teammates criticized publicly, and leadership tolerating it—all of which led to silence and reduced trust within the team.

These are not abstract risks; they are lived experiences in enterprise teams.

Can It Ever Be Useful?

In rare cases—when a team is inexperienced—strong technical leadership can accelerate delivery. But this should always be **temporary** and aimed at teaching, not control. If dictatorship persists, the organization becomes dangerously dependent on a single person, unable to adapt when they leave.

Building Leadership Without Control

To balance expertise with collaboration:

- **Promote Dialogue:** Meetings should genuinely weigh all ideas, not rubber-stamp decisions.
- **Encourage Prototypes:** Let alternative approaches be tested in small experiments.

- **Create Safety:** Team members must feel safe to say, "I disagree," without fear.
- **Use Clear Criteria:** Define how tools are chosen—based on goals, not personal preference.
- **Adopt Collaborative Structures:** Technical committees and ADRs (Architecture Decision Records) help decisions stay collective.
- **Distribute Responsibility:** Avoid concentrating power in one person's hands.

Enterprise Lesson Technical dictatorship can give the illusion of speed in the short term, but it corrodes creativity, drives away talent, and leaves organizations brittle. Teams thrive when leadership creates space for others to think, experiment, and contribute. True leadership is not about always being right—it's about enabling the team to grow stronger together.

Humility: The Foundation of Collaborative Software Teams

Humility is the open window that lets fresh air into a closed room.

In enterprise projects, humility is more than a personal virtue—it is the foundation of collaboration. Teams that create space for members to say *"I may be wrong"* or *"I'm not sure"* learn faster, avoid repeating mistakes, and discover better solutions. Patrick Lencioni, in *The Ideal Team Player* (2016), calls humility the first of three essential virtues (alongside hunger and people smarts). Without it, ambition becomes destructive, and intelligence turns into manipulation.

When the Loudest Voice Replaces the Truth

Too often, decisions in teams are shaped not by truth but by the loudest voice. Social psychology calls this the **Spiral of Silence** (Elisabeth Noelle-Neumann, 1974): once dominant opinions take over, others fall quiet. Over time, silence suffocates creativity.

A humble leader can break this cycle. By saying *"I might be wrong—let's check together"*, they create psychological safety (Edmondson, 1999), the fertile ground where innovation and learning grow.

A Lesson from Experience

I once worked with a junior colleague who spoke with absolute certainty, dismissing alternative views. At the same time, a senior specialist—deeply skilled and patient—was gradually pushed out because management favored confidence over competence.

Before leaving, that specialist noticed my openness and shared his knowledge with me in private sessions. Those lessons became milestones in my career. Meanwhile, the overconfident junior kept defending flawed paths with misplaced certainty—an example of the **Dunning-Kruger Effect** (1999).

Humility, I realized, is not weakness; it is the doorway to growth.

Practicing Humility in Daily Work

Humility is not reserved for dramatic conflicts; it shows up in small, everyday moments:

- **Code Reviews:** A humble developer says: *"That's a good point—let me improve my code"* rather than defending every line.
- **Pair Programming:** Humility asks: *"What do you think about this approach?"* and stays open to a different solution.
- **Debugging:** Pride says: *"I must solve it alone."* Humility says: *"I've tried this—can someone help?"*

These micro-choices shape culture more than any system design document.

Wisdom Across Cultures

> *"The trouble with the world is that the stupid are cocksure and the intelligent are full of doubt."*
>
> —Bertrand Russell (1933)

Across cultures, the message is constant: pride blinds, humility enlightens.

Humility with Determination

Humility is not passivity. Jim Collins, in *Good to Great* (2001), describes **Level 5 leaders** as possessing "a paradoxical blend of personal humility and professional will." They are "modest and willful, humble and fearless." True leadership, then, lies in balance: open enough to listen, yet determined enough to act. The art is in remaining humble while learning, and resolute while executing.

Exercises for Teams

Practical ways to cultivate humility:

- Give open credit in your next stand-up to a teammate's contribution.
- Say *"I don't know"* once this week and invite others to teach you.
- In code reviews, pair each critique with at least one compliment.
- After presenting work, ask: *"What could I do better next time?"*
- Keep a short **humility log**: once a week, note when humility helped—or when pride got in the way.

Enterprise Lesson Humility is not "soft"—it is a strategic advantage. Teams built on humility learn faster, innovate more, and weather crises better. Arrogant teams may deliver quick wins, but eventually collapse under the weight of their own certainty.

Patrick Lencioni, in *The Ideal Team Player* (2016), notes that if he had to choose just one of the three virtues—humility, hunger, and people smarts—he would choose **humility**, because without it, the others lose their balance. The humble developer is not the one who knows least, but the one who creates space for truth to emerge and for the whole team to grow.

Shared Ownership: Code, Decisions, and Responsibility Belong to the Team

> *When code belongs to no one, it belongs to everyone. When it belongs to "just me," it quickly becomes a liability.*

Enterprise systems often fail not because of bad technology but because of **silos**. A single developer becomes the "owner" of a module, a tester guards their scripts like private property, or an architect makes decisions no one else understands. At first, this may look efficient—specialists move quickly in their comfort zones. But over time, it creates fragility: the **bus factor** drops, bottlenecks form, and innovation slows.

The "Not My Module" Attitude

I've seen teams where bugs raised in one component triggered the dreaded response: *"That's not my module."* Responsibility was fenced in by invisible borders. Work stalled until the "right" person was available, creating delays and frustration. In contrast, high-performing teams treat code, decisions, and outcomes as **shared property**—not private gardens.

Why Shared Ownership Matters

When everyone understands the system and feels responsible for its health, delivery becomes faster, learning becomes natural, and stress becomes optional.

The following principles capture why shared ownership is not just good culture—it's sound architecture.

- **Resilience:** When one developer leaves or is offline, the project continues without paralysis. The system depends on principles, not personalities, and knowledge redundancy becomes part of the design.
- **Collective Learning:** When multiple people touch the same parts of the code base, understanding deepens naturally. Knowledge flows through reviews, refactors, and discussions instead of remaining locked in individual minds.

- **Faster Delivery:** Work doesn't stall waiting for a "module owner." Anyone can pick up a task, guided by tests, contracts, and clear standards. Progress becomes continuous, not calendar-dependent.
- **Higher Quality:** More eyes on the same code reveal more blind spots. Collective inspection sharpens decisions, catches regressions early, and drives consistent architectural judgment.
- **Trust and Morale:** Shared responsibility builds psychological safety. When success and failure belong to the team, not individuals, pride replaces blame and learning replaces fear.
- **Stress-Free Vacations:** When ownership is shared, people can disconnect without guilt. No one checks logs from a beach or dials into stand-ups from airports. A resilient team means its members can rest—and come back stronger.

How to Build Shared Ownership

Shared ownership doesn't emerge by accident—it's engineered through habits, tools, and trust.

The following practices turn good intentions into repeatable behavior, ensuring that collaboration scales with the system itself.

- **Pairing and Rotation:** Rotate pairs and reviewers across modules so that no area becomes a dark corner. Pairing accelerates knowledge transfer, uncovers assumptions, and makes decisions visible. Over time, it also builds empathy—developers see the system through another person's eyes.
- **Transparent Decision-Making:** Record architectural decisions using lightweight tools such as Architecture Decision Records (ADRs). Explain not just *what* was chosen but *why*. Months later, when requirements shift or people change, the reasoning stays alive and prevents history from repeating itself.

- **Shared On-Call:** Operational duty is the ultimate form of ownership. Rotating on-call spreads production knowledge, prevents burnout, and reminds developers that "done" includes running in production. A healthy rotation means no one spends weekends firefighting alone.
- **Agreed Standards:** Consistency is the foundation of shared work. Style guides, continuous integration, automated testing, and code review rules ensure that the system behaves predictably regardless of who last touched it. Strong guardrails enable freedom—engineers move faster because quality is enforced automatically.

Enterprise Lesson Shared ownership doesn't mean chaos—*it means accountability without silos.* It ensures the team, not a single person, carries the responsibility for code, decisions, and delivery.

In practice, this mindset breaks the "bus factor curse" and eliminates the "not my module" excuse. When ownership is shared, resilience grows, and the team builds not just software, but trust.

Cross-Functional Communication: Speaking One Language Across Roles

> *"Great software doesn't come from isolated silos—it comes from shared understanding across disciplines."*

In enterprise projects, success is not the product of developers alone. It emerges from collaboration among business analysts, QA engineers, operations, and product managers. Each role sees the system from a different angle: analysts focus on business needs, developers on implementation, QA on quality, and ops on reliability. When these perspectives don't connect, projects stumble.

When Worlds Don't Overlap

I once worked in a team where business analysts had little awareness of APIs, OpenAPI definitions, or even tools like Postman. They sometimes proposed features that were technically impossible. Meanwhile, developers discussed design choices in technical jargon the analysts couldn't follow. Both sides were competent, but they lived in separate worlds—leading to wasted time, frustration, and even conflict.

This illustrates a common problem: without shared language, teams generate parallel monologues instead of meaningful dialogue.

Why Cross-Functional Understanding Matters

The case for cross-functional communication goes far beyond avoiding misunderstandings:

- **Faster Feedback Loops:** When analysts and testers understand basic technical constraints, feedback flows quickly, without weeks of handoffs.
- **Reduced Rework:** Misaligned assumptions are one of the biggest drivers of wasted effort. Shared vocabulary prevents costly rewrites.
- **Innovation at Boundaries:** Breakthrough ideas often emerge at the overlap of disciplines—like a tester suggesting better monitoring or a developer simplifying a business process.
- **Resilience and Knowledge Sharing:** Teams that understand each other avoid bottlenecks and reduce "bus factor" risks.
- **Trust and Empathy:** When colleagues grasp each other's challenges, they negotiate trade-offs with respect rather than suspicion.
- **Stronger Incident Response:** In outages, shared language across dev, QA, and ops shortens the time to diagnosis and recovery.
- **Business Alignment:** Cross-functional dialogue keeps technical design tethered to business outcomes, eliminating the "us vs. them" dynamic.

Building a Shared Language

Agile methods encourage **T-shaped skills**: each person is deep in one specialty but broad enough to collaborate outside it. A business analyst doesn't need to code APIs, but they should understand what an API is and why backward compatibility matters. A developer doesn't need to master market research, but they should know why a feature matters to users.

Practical steps to bridge the gaps include

- **Shared Learning Sessions:** Schedule short cross-functional briefings where developers explain APIs, analysts clarify business rules, and QA walks through automation flows. Regular knowledge exchange turns roles into partners, not silos.
- **Living Documentation:** Maintain evolving artifacts—OpenAPI specs, ADRs, system maps, and dashboards—that anyone can reference. When documentation lives alongside the code, understanding scales faster than tribal memory.
- **Visual Models:** Diagrams such as user journeys, sequence flows, or context maps align mental models across disciplines. A shared picture often resolves what hours of discussion can't.
- **Role Rotation:** Occasionally, let team members shadow or temporarily swap roles. Watching how another discipline works—whether analysis, QA, or ops—builds empathy and exposes design blind spots.
- **Outcome-Focused Dialogue:** Shift conversations from "implementing feature X" to "helping users achieve Y." Framing work in terms of outcomes reinforces collective purpose and prevents local optimizations from derailing the whole.

Enterprise Lesson Cross-functional communication doesn't mean making everyone interchangeable—it means making everyone *understandable*. In high-performing teams, analysts frame requirements with enough technical awareness to be feasible, developers propose features with business value in mind, QA ensures reliability with an eye on user impact, and ops aligns deployment with both technical and business goals.

When teams learn to speak one language across roles, they accelerate delivery, foster innovation, and strengthen trust. When they don't, silos form—and silos are where great projects quietly fail.

Face-to-Face with Reality: Developers Beside End Users

> *"No amount of documentation replaces a few hours of watching the real work happen."*

In enterprise projects, developers often work far from the people who will actually use the system. They rely on specifications, user stories, or secondhand explanations. But requirements captured in documents are never the full story. Subtle constraints, workarounds, and user frustrations are often invisible until you see them firsthand.

Lessons from the Field

I've seen developers propose technically brilliant ideas that collapsed in practice because they didn't fit the real-world workflow of the end user. Sometimes the limitation was environmental—an unstable network, outdated hardware, or regulatory rules no one mentioned. Sometimes the gap came from users themselves, who couldn't fully explain their needs in a meeting or a ticket.

My best experiences came when I sat next to end users, observing how they actually worked. These sessions revealed details no requirements document ever captured: shortcuts scribbled on paper, unused features that cluttered the UI, or frustrations users never bothered to mention because they had adapted over time. A short face-to-face conversation clarified more than weeks of back-and-forth through intermediaries.

Why Direct Contact Matters

- **Reality Check:** Direct exposure to workflows reveals whether assumptions actually hold. You discover how tools behave under pressure, where users improvise, and which "edge cases" are everyday life.

- **Unspoken Needs:** Many user frustrations are invisible in documentation. People rarely verbalize pain points until someone observes them in action—misclicks, delays, or unnecessary steps that specs never mention.
- **Better Empathy:** Working alongside users builds respect for their craft. Developers understand the constraints, multitasking, and pressure behind every request, which leads to more humane design decisions.
- **Sharper Design:** Context exposes details that no wireframe can capture—screen placement, latency tolerance, accessibility quirks, or workflow interruptions. The difference between usable and delightful often lies in those unnoticed moments.
- **Faster Trust:** When engineers show up, listen, and adapt, users stop seeing IT as a distant function. Mutual trust accelerates feedback loops and makes change less threatening for both sides.

When It's Not Possible

Of course, developers can't always sit beside users: distributed teams, security restrictions, or scale may prevent it. In those cases, alternatives like video shadowing, usability testing sessions, or structured feedback loops can bring some of the same insights. The principle remains: the closer developers get to real user experience, the more grounded their design decisions become.

Enterprise Lesson Face-to-face communication isn't just about being Agile—it's about being accurate. Every layer of abstraction between developers and users introduces risk. Bridging that gap periodically, even briefly, helps teams align technology with lived reality.

Specifications may describe *what users say they want*. Sitting beside them shows *what they actually need*.

Every Step Is a Product: Treating the Pipeline with Equal Respect

"Software is not built in one step—it flows through a pipeline of products."

In many teams, developers are seen as the "final stage," responsible for shaping the end product. But this mindset ignores the reality that development is only one part of a longer pipeline: analysis → requirements → design → deployment → testing. Every stage produces something, and every stage can create value—or debt.

When One Weak Link Breaks the Chain

I've seen projects where analysis produced vague or incomplete documentation. Out of respect, fear of conflict, or just habit, nobody raised concerns. The development team then struggled with unclear requirements, taking more time than planned and delivering late. From the outside, it looked like developers were "slow," but the real issue was earlier in the pipeline.

The reverse also happens: developers write code without proper tests or documentation, and operations teams struggle to maintain it. Pressure builds at the end of the pipeline, while the root cause lies upstream.

A Product Mindset for Every Stage

The best teams treat each deliverable as if it were a product in itself:

- **Requirements Documents:** Would you "buy" this document if you were an external team asked to build from it? Is it clear, testable, and complete enough to be worth paying for?
- **Design Artifacts:** Would another architect find this design coherent, or is it full of hidden assumptions?
- **Code:** If this code were offered as a library, would you choose it over alternatives? Is it clean, tested, and maintainable enough that someone else would pay for it?
- **Tests.** Do they provide confidence and clarity—or would another developer consider them brittle and incomplete?

Asking *"Would I buy this?"* forces a shift from internal convenience to external quality.

Breaking the Silence

Why do weak artifacts slip through? Often it's silence. Out of friendship, respect, or fear of slowing things down, teams accept poor inputs and quietly work around them. But silence only shifts the burden downstream. Healthy teams speak up—not to blame, but to improve the pipeline before problems compound.

Enterprise Lesson Every stage of software delivery is both a consumer and a producer. Analysts produce requirements for developers. Developers produce code for testers and ops. Ops produces stable releases for users. If one product in the chain is weak, the whole system suffers.

By treating each stage's output as a product worth "selling," teams ensure consistent quality throughout the pipeline. This mindset not only reduces pressure on the final stage but also builds trust across roles. In the end, a strong pipeline doesn't just deliver faster—it delivers better.

Lessons Learned: The Architecture of Continuous Improvement

"Every failure recorded is one less repeated."

When I was a child, I often saw the aviation world up close. Once, a few days after a plane crash, I watched a truck carry the wreckage of the aircraft past us—twisted metal, scorched paint, fragments of a story that had ended in tragedy. My father explained something that has stayed with me ever since:

> *"In aviation, when something goes wrong, they don't start by blaming the pilot. They start by understanding the cause."*

In the flight industry, every incident triggers a structured investigation. Teams of engineers, pilots, and safety experts analyze what happened, trace every mechanical and human factor, and document their findings in exhaustive detail. The reports are not secrets; they are shared with manufacturers, airlines, and regulators worldwide. Each failure becomes a lesson—one that makes future flights safer.

From Cockpits to Code Bases

Software projects rarely cost lives, but the principle applies. A system crash, an outage, or a failed release is still an opportunity to learn. In mature teams, post-incident reviews or **"lessons learned"** meetings serve the same purpose as flight investigations: they turn failure into documentation and documentation into safety.

Unfortunately, not every team treats them that way.

Some approach retrospectives as a blame party, looking for a single cause or a person to hold responsible. That mindset is as dangerous in software as it is in aviation. When learning stops at guilt, the same mistakes quietly return.

The healthiest teams treat every failure as a *system event*, not a *personal flaw*. They ask:

- What conditions made this error possible?
- What signals did we miss?
- How can we change the process or design so it never happens again?

This is the cultural heartbeat of **DevOps** and **Site Reliability Engineering (SRE)**. Post-incident analysis is data, not drama. The goal is to improve the *system of work*, not to punish the worker.

The Anatomy of an Effective Lessons-Learned Review

1. **Facts Before Feelings**

   Start with a clear timeline: what happened, when, and how the system behaved. Avoid adjectives. Precision creates safety.

2. **Separate Cause from Blame**

   Blame silences people; curiosity invites truth. Ask *why* at least five times, tracing human errors back to process gaps or unclear assumptions.

3. **Capture and Share Knowledge**

   Write a short, accessible report—what failed, what fixed it, what to change. Store it where everyone can read it. The best organizations treat these reports as part of their documentation.

4. **Convert Insight into Action**

   A lesson is not learned until it changes behavior. Create follow-up tasks, update runbooks, refine alerts, or modify tests based on findings.

5. **Celebrate Transparency**

   Publicly thank those who reported and discussed issues. Recognition reinforces the idea that honesty is part of engineering excellence.

Enterprise Lesson Blameless post-mortems are not softness; they are **discipline**. They replace judgment with data and guilt with growth. In enterprise systems—where hundreds of people contribute to outcomes—root-cause analysis is the only way to scale learning faster than failure.

The aviation industry learned long ago that safety depends on shared knowledge.

Software can learn the same truth: every outage, every defect, every near miss is a chance to refine our flight plan. What matters most is not avoiding mistakes but **documenting them so no one repeats the same crash twice**.

Team Topologies

Products inevitably mirror the nature of the organizations that build them. If you are interested in a deeper exploration of how team structure shapes software outcomes, *Team Topologies: Organizing Business and Technology Teams for Fast Flow* is an excellent resource. But in this book, our goal is not to redesign your organization, nor to prescribe managerial reforms. Instead, we want to briefly show why organizational structure matters to you as an engineer—far more than many developers initially assume.

You might think organizational design is a management concern, separate from writing code. Yet in enterprise software, your system rarely lives in isolation. Large organizations depend on multiple systems operating together, and when you add a feature to your service, hundreds or thousands of users must adapt to it. This is even more critical when the users are not internal staff but customers or citizens.

The complexity grows further when your service integrates with other systems. Those systems must adjust to your changes, implement your APIs, and sometimes redesign their own workflows. And this dependency cuts both ways: you may be progressing calmly when suddenly another team announces that they are changing their service, and you are required to update your own within days.

Worse still is when your system depends on a remote service that fails unexpectedly, causing your own application to behave unpredictably. You cannot simply ignore the failure—because the end user will not. Across teams, technologies, and departments, you are all part of one organism.

In these moments, blaming other teams is tempting but unhelpful. The real solution is an engineering discipline: preparing your system for a dynamic, imperfect environment. Patterns like **feature toggles**, **circuit breakers**, and **graceful degradation** exist for exactly this reason. Their importance may not feel urgent until you experience real-world incidents—then their value becomes obvious.

Let me share one example from my own experience:

In a company, our payment module relied on a specific service provided by a PSP. We assumed the service might occasionally be unavailable, so we implemented a short retry loop. Later, the PSP changed part of its behavior in a way that no longer matched our assumptions. Our retries, running quietly in the background, turned into a storm of repeated calls—effectively a denial-of-service attack. Multiple services at the PSP went offline for a short period.

The first question we asked ourselves afterward was simple:

Wouldn't a circuit breaker have prevented all of this?

This is engineering thinking—focusing less on why another team changed something and more on how your own system can stay resilient. In an environment filled with many interacting systems and diverse user expectations, adaptability isn't optional. It's the only way to survive.

Throughout this book, you will find real examples drawn from my own experience—cases where the patterns we discuss proved essential. I hope they help you navigate the complexity of enterprise-scale systems with clarity and confidence.

Summary

In this chapter, we've seen that teamwork is not a "soft" side note to architecture—it is the hidden architecture that makes all technical choices possible. Teams fail not because they lack tools, but because they fall into traps like the Golden Hammer or technical dictatorship. They succeed when they practice humility, share ownership, and build psychological safety. Cross-functional communication, direct contact with end users, and treating every stage of the pipeline as a product all strengthen the invisible fabric that holds enterprise projects together.

Equally important is how teams handle failure. Mature teams, like those in the aviation industry, treat every incident as data—not drama. They document causes, share lessons, and turn setbacks into safety. In software, adopting the same mindset transforms retrospectives into engines of continuous improvement.

The enterprise lesson is clear: technology scales only as far as teamwork allows. An unstable team produces unstable systems; a resilient team creates software that adapts and lasts. If we learn to build teams with the same care we use to build architectures, we gain not just functioning systems, but sustainable ones.

What's Next

The next chapter, **"Choosing a Programming Language: A Decisive Choice,"** shifts the focus from *team design* to *technical foundation*.

We'll examine why languages are more than syntax—they carry philosophies, trade-offs, and long-term consequences for maintainability, cost, and performance.

You'll learn a structured way to evaluate a language for enterprise systems, avoiding hype and aligning choice with architecture.

By the end, you'll understand why Go, born inside Google to solve problems of scale, often provides the clearest path toward simplicity and sustainability in modern enterprise projects.

CHAPTER 2

Choosing a Programming Language: A Decisive Choice

Languages are not fashion—they are foundations.

Selecting a programming language for a project is much like choosing the right tool to build a house. No architect would attempt to raise a glass skyscraper with a hammer, nor would a builder dig foundations with a spoon. Languages are our instruments of construction, each shaped by its own philosophy, history, and community—and each designed to solve a different class of problems.

One of the most common mistakes I've seen managers and software architects make is treating language selection as a matter of fashion. They follow trends, adopt what looks impressive on a presentation slide, or choose what their peers are using—often without questioning whether it truly fits the project. The result is predictable: frustration, wasted effort, and, eventually, regret. A programming language must be chosen with the same discipline as any other engineering decision—anchored in evidence, context, and long-term consequences.

In modern software, the "tool" is no longer just the syntax or compiler. It includes the runtime, memory model, concurrency primitives, and deployment footprint that determine how the system behaves under real-world pressure—especially in containerized, cloud-native, or distributed environments. A wise choice considers not only the elegance of code but also how that code scales, observes, and sustains itself in production.

S. Shahsavan, *Building Enterprise Projects with Go*, https://doi.org/10.1007/979-8-8688-2370-1_2

From both experience and industry lessons, four major factors consistently determine whether a language will serve a project well:

- **Project Requirements:** Technical fit, scalability, performance, and runtime characteristics
- **Budget:** Total cost of ownership, including hiring, training, and operations
- **Organizational Assumptions:** Alignment with infrastructure, compliance, and existing ecosystems
- **Human Resources:** Skill availability, community maturity, and developer retention

In the sections ahead, we'll use these criteria to examine real-world language trade-offs—eventually contrasting two enduring enterprise ecosystems: one born from decades of maturity, the other from a deliberate pursuit of simplicity.

Project Requirements

The first and most fundamental factor is how well a language aligns with the technical realities of the system you are building. Every project brings its own constraints: how many users it must serve, how quickly it must respond, how much data it must process, and how resilient it must remain under stress. A language that cannot gracefully handle the expected scale soon becomes a bottleneck.

For example, a system handling millions of concurrent connections requires more than raw speed—it needs **built-in concurrency support** that allows tasks to run in parallel without exhausting system resources. Beyond concurrency, performance characteristics still matter: some projects demand ultra-low latency; others emphasize throughput or predictable response times under load.

Equally important is the **toolchain and ecosystem** surrounding the language. Does it provide a mature standard library for networking, cryptography, and data processing, or will your team spend time reinventing these? Are profiling, testing, and observability tools integrated well enough to maintain velocity and quality throughout the release cycle?

Finally, in a world of **containerized and cloud-native deployments**, runtime behavior now matters as much as language syntax. How does it manage memory, scheduling, and garbage collection inside constrained environments? Can it start fast and scale predictably?

In short, the right language is not merely powerful in theory—it must provide the practical abstractions, tooling, and runtime behavior that let a team deliver reliably at scale. Choosing a language without weighing these realities is like picking a tool that looks impressive in the catalog but shatters under the first real workload.

Budget

When evaluating programming languages, cost must be viewed in its broadest sense. It's not only about whether the compiler or runtime requires a paid license—most modern languages are open source—but about the **total financial footprint** a language creates over the lifetime of a system.

Training developers to become proficient, or hiring experts in niche technology, carries a real price tag. Some languages demand specialized skills that are scarce in the market, driving up salaries and extending recruitment cycles.

Operational costs are equally important. A runtime that consumes large memory footprints, relies on heavyweight virtual machines, or requires constant tuning may appear attractive at first but will quietly inflate cloud bills and infrastructure complexity. Conversely, a leaner language that compiles to efficient, self-contained executables can reduce both compute costs and scaling overhead—especially in containerized or serverless environments.

Even **long-term support** has a budgetary dimension: Will the community or vendor maintain active releases, or will you need paid contracts for extended support?

In short, budgeting for a programming language extends far beyond its initial adoption. The true cost is measured in **training, operations, and maintenance over time**—factors that ultimately determine the sustainability and economic viability of the system.

Organizational Assumptions

Beyond technical performance, a programming language must fit into the broader environment of the organization that adopts it. Every company already has established infrastructure, security policies, compliance standards, and operational habits that define the boundaries for technology choices.

For instance, highly regulated sectors—such as finance, healthcare, or government—operate under frameworks like **GDPR**, **HIPAA**, or **PCI-DSS**, which may favor languages with stronger type safety, mature cryptographic libraries, verifiable audit tooling, and long-term vendor or community support.

Infrastructure integration is equally critical. If your entire monitoring, logging, and CI/CD pipeline is built around the **JVM ecosystem**, introducing a language that doesn't interoperate seamlessly with existing tools can create friction, duplicated effort, and hidden costs. Conversely, **cloud-native** organizations often prefer languages that produce small, static binaries, improving startup times and minimizing container image sizes—a decisive factor for scaling microservices efficiently across clusters.

In 2026, many enterprises also weigh **software supply chain security** and **open source licensing** as part of their governance model. Some mandate permissive licenses (like BSD or MIT) to simplify compliance, while others require vendor-backed LTS releases to ensure predictable maintenance cycles.

In short, even the most technically elegant language is not viable if it cannot operate within the **regulatory, infrastructural, and cultural realities** of the organization. Enterprise architecture succeeds not by chasing novelty, but by aligning new tools with established systems and responsibilities.

Human Resources

No matter how powerful or elegant a language is, it becomes a liability if there are not enough skilled developers to work with it. A project's success depends not only on the technology itself but also on the **availability, adaptability, and motivation of the people** who build and maintain it.

If the talent pool is too small, hiring will be slow and costly. If the language requires months of training before new members can contribute effectively, productivity will suffer. The **maturity of the language community** plays an essential role here: an active ecosystem provides documentation, tutorials, forums, and shared experience. It also means a wider selection of reusable libraries and battle-tested design patterns, reducing the burden on internal teams.

Another key dimension is the **learning curve**. A language with clear syntax, consistent tooling, and stable idioms allows developers from other ecosystems to onboard quickly—one reason Go has continued to spread rapidly in enterprise settings despite its relative youth. By contrast, languages with steep or shifting learning curves drain team energy and inflate onboarding costs.

In today's distributed workplaces, team composition has also changed. Hybrid and remote teams rely heavily on clear, uniform code bases and predictable tooling. Languages that enforce consistency—through standardized formatting, integrated testing tools, or opinionated frameworks—reduce cognitive overhead and ease collaboration across time zones.

Retention matters as much as recruitment. Developers tend to stay longer with languages that have **vibrant communities**, visible career prospects, and modern developer experiences—including good IDE support, reliable CI/CD integrations, and even AI-assisted tooling. A stagnant or fragmented ecosystem, no matter how technically sound, risks long-term attrition.

From hiring and onboarding to retention and morale, the human factor can make or break a technology choice just as much as raw performance. The most elegant syntax means little if there's no one left to maintain it.

Case Studies

I've learned that real experiences often teach more than abstract reasons. In the case studies below, you'll see a few situations I've witnessed firsthand—where language decisions succeeded and where they quietly set teams up for failure.

When C Became a Trap

I once observed a project where *performance was treated as the holy grail*. The architects were convinced the "core" of their distributed system had to be written in **C**, because nothing else could deliver the raw speed they envisioned. Their plan was to build a C core for performance-critical logic and integrate it with **Java** modules handling business workflows.

On paper, the hybrid design looked clever. In practice, it collapsed. The team lacked deep knowledge of C's complexities and quickly ran into unsafe memory operations, pointer leaks, and race conditions that were nearly impossible to reproduce. But the real trap wasn't performance—it was **integration**. Connecting C with Java through the **Java Native Interface (JNI)** proved fragile, verbose, and painfully hard to debug. Each boundary between C and Java became a fault line for crashes, undefined behavior, and sleepless nights.

While C itself remains a powerful systems language, the *interop ecosystem* between C and modern enterprise stacks hasn't evolved much. The result was predictable: what started as a performance optimization became a productivity and stability disaster. The project eventually failed—not because C is weak, but because the choice ignored the team's skills, tooling maturity, and long-term maintainability.

If you ask me, this entire system could have been written in **Go**. Go provides a rare balance between *performance, concurrency, and developer productivity*. Even if someone truly needed to squeeze out the final few percentage points of performance, they could have isolated those parts in **Rust**, which offers memory safety without garbage collection, and integrated them through lightweight boundaries like gRPC or FFI.

But truthfully, for most enterprise workloads, Go alone would have been enough. The reasoning isn't just about benchmarks—it's about **human resources, maintainability, and team sanity**. Choosing Go would have kept the system running—and the engineers sleeping.

When Go Was Misunderstood

At the opposite end of the spectrum, I once saw a project fail not because of language limitations, but because the team didn't know how to use the language they chose. The language was **Go**.

The developers approached Go as if it were **Java**—writing verbose code, wrapping everything in unnecessary abstractions, spawning goroutines like threads, and ignoring proper error handling. They hadn't read a single Go book (and, honestly, I doubt they'll read this one either). Their technical lead summed up the culture perfectly: *"I'll keep banging my head against the wall until I break through."* His approach to engineering was brute-force trial and error, not structured learning or research.

The result? A chaotic, brittle code base riddled with anti-patterns. They reinvented dependency injection frameworks, ignored `context.Context` for cancellation, misused channels for shared state, and built a system that looked concurrent but wasn't. Ironically, they might have been better off sticking with **Java**, the language they already understood—at least their bad practices there were predictable.

The real issue wasn't Go; it was the **team's unwillingness to learn and adapt**. They brought an old mental model into a new paradigm and refused to change their habits.

Here's the key lesson: **knowledge matters more than the tool.**

If all you know how to use is a hammer, every problem looks like a nail. This is the *Golden Hammer Syndrome*—forcing familiar patterns onto unfamiliar contexts. Mastery isn't about collecting more tools; it's about understanding the strengths and boundaries of each one.

A team that truly studies its tools will often realize that some "problems" disappear entirely with the right mindset. Go rewards simplicity, discipline, and clarity—but punishes cargo-culting.

So remember: if your team isn't ready to invest in learning, research, and unlearning, stick with the language you already know. A programming language only empowers you when you understand its philosophy. Without that, even the most elegant tool becomes a blunt instrument.

The Expert Who Struggled in Enterprise

I once worked with brilliant developers who could perform wonders in small, low-level projects—especially in languages like **C**. They understood memory layouts, compiler flags, and performance tuning at an astonishing level of detail. In small systems, their precision produced magic.

But when they stepped into enterprise-scale environments, that same focus on micro-optimization became their downfall. They got lost in the details—tuning loops, inlining functions, and chasing nanoseconds—while ignoring the broader picture of **system design, modularity, and long-term maintenance**. Some even resorted to copy-pasting similar logic across the code base to "get things done," trading short-term control for long-term chaos.

This wasn't a failure of talent; it was a failure of adaptation. The skills that make someone exceptional in small projects—control, precision, and low-level mastery—don't automatically translate to success in large systems.

In enterprise environments, the real skill is **architectural thinking**:

- Knowing when to abstract and when to stay concrete
- Designing for clarity rather than cleverness
- Optimizing for readability, change, and collaboration—not just execution speed

Mastery of detail is valuable, but without architectural discipline, it can quietly work against you. In the enterprise world, code longevity, clarity, and composability are the true performance metrics.

Enterprise Lesson Smaller projects often chase raw performance or speed of delivery. Enterprise projects, by contrast, optimize for something deeper: sustainability. Performance still matters—but not at the expense of maintainability, integration, and long-term evolution.

The real question isn't "Which language runs faster?" but "Which language helps the team think clearly, integrate easily, and grow safely over time?"

In the enterprise world, a programming language is more than syntax or benchmarks—it's the **architecture's foundation**. The right choice helps teams manage complexity, avoid reinvention, and build systems resilient enough to survive years of change without losing their shape.

What Makes Enterprise Projects Different?

Not all software projects are created equal. In smaller projects, raw performance or rapid delivery often take priority, and developers may tolerate messy code if it helps ship faster. This is never a best practice—but in small systems, the consequences are usually contained.

Enterprise projects are different. They are designed to *endure*—to run for years, sometimes decades, across changing teams, requirements, and infrastructures. They often involve dozens or even hundreds of developers, distributed across geographies and time zones. Here, the question isn't "Does it work today?" but "Will it remain maintainable, scalable, and secure as it grows?"

Based on experience—and what countless organizations have learned the hard way—enterprise projects differ in several essential ways.

Long-Term Maintainability

Enterprise systems grow over time. Clever one-liners and ad hoc optimizations that impress in small projects often become toxic in large ones. Maintainability comes from **clarity, consistency, and backward compatibility**.

Languages that enforce formatting, predictable idioms, and stable APIs make this easier.

- **Go** enforces consistency with **`go`** `fmt`**`go`** `fmt`, idiomatic simplicity, and strict backward compatibility across versions.
- **Java**, especially since Java 25, continues to evolve while keeping strong LTS guarantees and structured patterns through frameworks like Spring or Jakarta EE.

The goal is longevity: code that can outlive its authors without becoming a burden.

Integration with Tools and External Systems

Enterprise applications rarely live in isolation. They must integrate with databases, message brokers (Kafka, Pulsar, RabbitMQ), observability stacks, authentication services, and often legacy systems that predate the current team.

A suitable language must come with reliable integrations, open standards, and strong protocol support.

- Go's native support for **HTTP, gRPC, JSON, Protobuf, and OpenTelemetry** makes it ideal for microservice and event-driven architectures.
- Java's ecosystem still leads in enterprise connectors and mature libraries across every domain—from security to batch processing to data access.

The ability to "play well with others" often matters more than theoretical speed.

Rich Ecosystem to Avoid Reinventing the Wheel

In enterprise software, writing utilities from scratch is an expensive mistake. Every custom library adds long-term maintenance, testing, and security overhead.

Mature ecosystems—**Maven Central** for Java and **Go Modules** for Go—provide a foundation of well-tested, community-maintained packages. Both ecosystems have embraced **supply chain security** through signed modules and checksum verification (`go.sum`, Maven signatures).

A healthy ecosystem doesn't just save time—it's a force multiplier for reliability and compliance.

Clean Programming Paradigms

Enterprise systems thrive on **clarity of architecture**. Loose coupling, separation of concerns, and composable components prevent chaos in large teams.

- **Go's implicit interfaces** and composition-over-inheritance model promote modular, testable designs with minimal ceremony.
- **Java's explicit interfaces and annotations** (now enhanced with pattern matching and module imports in Java 25) bring predictability and tooling power.

In small projects, these paradigms may feel optional. In enterprise systems, they are the scaffolding that keeps the structure standing as teams and technologies evolve.

Testing and Quality Assurance

Testing in enterprise software is not a luxury—it's a **survival mechanism**. Unit, integration, and performance tests prevent regressions and validate complex workflows.

- Go includes testing, benchmarking, fuzzing, and race detection in its standard toolchain. The new `testing/synctest` package even simplifies deterministic testing of concurrent code.
- Java relies on an extensive testing ecosystem (JUnit 5, Mockito, Testcontainers, JMH), which continues to mature with strong IDE integration and static analysis tools.

What matters most is **testing as part of the language's culture**, not an afterthought.

Observability and Monitoring

Writing code is only half the job; running it is the other half. Enterprise systems require deep **observability**—logs, metrics, traces, and profiles that tell the story of what's happening in production.

- Go's ecosystem naturally fits modern **cloud-native stacks** like Prometheus, Grafana, and OpenTelemetry. Its lightweight binaries make instrumentation and distributed tracing straightforward.
- Java 25 builds on its legacy of introspection with **JFR (Java Flight Recorder)** enhancements, **CPU-time profiling**, and **structured concurrency tracing**.

A language's ability to expose insights into its runtime behavior determines how fast teams can detect and fix problems under pressure.

Security and Compliance

Enterprise systems often handle sensitive data and must comply with strict regulations—GDPR, HIPAA, PCI-DSS, ISO 27001, and more.

- Go's **memory safety and minimal surface area** eliminate entire classes of vulnerabilities—no inheritance hierarchies, no unchecked concurrency primitives. Its modern crypto libraries are easy to use and audit.
- Java 25 continues to lead in **cryptographic standardization**, with native support for PEM encodings, key-derivation APIs, and stronger TLS defaults.

Security is not just about libraries—it's about predictable defaults and frameworks that make the *secure path the easy path.*

Scalability of Teams

Enterprise projects are not built by heroes; they're built by **large, rotating teams**. The language must scale with the organization, not just the CPU.

- **Go** enforces uniformity—`go fmt` eliminates style debates, and simple idioms make code bases readable across teams and cultures.
- **Java** enforces discipline through structure, frameworks, and decades of design conventions that prevent fragmentation.

Both approaches aim for the same goal: team scalability and sustainable velocity.

As AI-assisted development becomes common, team scalability also depends on code clarity. Languages that produce simple, machine-readable patterns (like Go's composition model) integrate better with modern AI tooling and automated refactoring systems.

Enterprise Lesson In enterprise software, success is measured not by how fast you ship, but by how long your system endures.

Enterprise projects differ not in ambition but in **timescale, complexity, and collective ownership**.

They demand languages that promote **discipline, integration, observability, and maintainability**—not just raw speed. The right language decision today becomes the **silent architecture** that sustains a system for years.

Why Choose Go over Java for Enterprise Projects?

For decades, **Java** has been the default choice for enterprise systems—the backbone of banks, telecoms, and governments worldwide. Its vast ecosystem, strong tooling, and deep talent pool have made it nearly synonymous with reliability at scale. Few languages can match its track record of powering critical infrastructure.

Yet the software landscape has changed. Cloud-native architectures, containerized deployments, and the rise of distributed microservices have shifted the definition of "enterprise-grade." In this new world, performance, simplicity, and operational efficiency matter as much as frameworks and maturity.

Go: Originally designed at Google to handle massive, concurrent systems, Go has grown into a credible—and in many cases superior—alternative for modern enterprise workloads. Its design addresses pain points that Java teams have lived with for years: long build times, heavy runtimes, verbose concurrency models, and complex dependency management.

This isn't about replacing Java—it's about **recalibrating architectural priorities**. Java remains a trusted pillar for legacy systems and JVM-based ecosystems. But when enterprises build new systems that demand **speed, scalability, and maintainability**, Go often delivers the same reliability with less overhead and greater clarity.

The sections that follow explore why Go's simplicity, concurrency model, and toolchain make it a natural fit for the next generation of enterprise systems, while Java's strengths continue to serve in well-established domains.

Interfaces: Structural vs. Nominal Typing

In **Java**, interfaces are *nominal*: a class must explicitly declare that it implements an interface, for example, `implements InterfaceX`. This design enforces clarity but also introduces rigidity. As enterprise systems grow, this explicitness often leads to *interface pollution*—classes bloated with multiple `implements` clauses just to satisfy framework or testing requirements. Every declaration ties the implementation to the interface's name rather than its actual behavior, creating unnecessary coupling.

Go takes a radically different path. Its interfaces are *structural* and *implicit*. Any type that satisfies an interface's method set automatically implements it—no extra syntax, no declarations, no ceremony. The focus shifts from *what a type says it is* to *what it can do.*

This simplicity has three profound architectural benefits:

- **Cleaner Design:** Interfaces can live in the consumer package, defined by *needs* rather than dictated by producers. This flips dependency direction and naturally supports the Dependency Inversion Principle.
- **Better Decoupling:** Types remain flexible and composable without tangled inheritance trees or explicit declarations. Systems evolve more freely.
- **Easier Testing:** Creating mocks or fakes requires no external libraries. A test can define its own interface inline—no need for frameworks like Mockito or boilerplate generation.

Here is an example from our transport system. We define the repository interface as follows:

```
type AssignmentRepository interface {
  Save(ctx context.Context, a models.Assignment) (bool, error)
  FindByID(ctx context.Context, id string) (models.Assignment, error)
  FindAll(ctx context.Context, status *string) ([]models.Assignment, error)
}
```

The following struct satisfies the interface simply by implementing its method set—without ever mentioning `AssignmentRepository`:

```
type sqlAssignmentRepository struct {
   db *sql.DB
}

func (r *sqlAssignmentRepository) Save(ctx context.Context, a models.
Assignment) (bool, error) {
      // implement later
}

func (r *sqlAssignmentRepository) FindByID(ctx context.Context, id string)
(models.Assignment, error) {
      // implement later
}

func (r *sqlAssignmentRepository) FindAll(ctx context.Context, status
*string) ([]models.Assignment, error) {
      // implement later
}
```

Because Go uses **structural typing**, any type that implements these methods automatically satisfies the interface. You can therefore pass this repository to any function expecting the abstraction:

```
func Run(cfg configs.ServerConfig, repo ports.AssignmentRepository) error
```

In Java, the same repository would require the implementation to explicitly declare the interface:

```
public interface AssignmentRepository {
    boolean save(Assignment a);
    Assignment findById(String id);
    List<Assignment> findAll(String status);
}

public class SqlAssignmentRepository implements AssignmentRepository {
    private final DataSource ds;

    @Override public boolean save(Assignment a) { /* ... */ }
    @Override public Assignment findById(String id) { /* ... */ }
    @Override public List<Assignment> findAll(String status) { /* ... */ }
}
```

This nominal typing requirement means you **must** modify the implementing class—or create a wrapper—whenever you want to substitute a mock or reuse a class from a library.

For enterprise projects, where abstraction boundaries define system health, Go's *structural typing* encourages lightweight, resilient designs. The result is code that grows organically with the organization—*leaner, more expressive, and less fragile* than the rigid interface hierarchies that often burden large Java code bases.

Compilation Speed and Developer Productivity

In **Java**, source code is compiled to **bytecode**, which the **JVM** executes through *interpretation* or *Just-In-Time (JIT)* compilation. This model enables runtime optimizations, but it adds overhead. Even with incremental builds and modern tools, large enterprise projects often spend minutes compiling and warming up, extending feedback loops and slowing continuous integration.

Recent advances—especially **Project Leyden** and the new **AOT profiling features in Java 25** (JEP 514 and 515)—are steps toward faster startup and predictable performance. Yet these approaches come with trade-offs:

- Building native images via **GraalVM** or Leyden requires lengthy configuration.
- Reflection and dynamic loading become restricted.
- The ecosystem support remains partial.

Go, by contrast, was engineered from day one to eliminate this problem. Its dependency model and build system are intentionally simple and deterministic. When you run **go** `build`, the compiler performs a full **ahead-of-time (AOT)** compilation to a static binary in seconds—no classpath scanning, no build scripts, no intermediate bytecode.

At Google, Go's creators famously joked that the language was born during a *45-minute C++ build wait*. That spirit still defines it. The Go 1.25 toolchain maintains near-instant builds, reproducible outputs, and minimal hidden dependencies—even for large code bases.

For enterprises running extensive **CI/CD pipelines**, these differences translate directly into cost and productivity gains. Faster builds mean shorter feedback cycles, more deploys per day, and less idle developer time. In modern DevOps economics, that makes Go's compilation model not just a convenience—but a **strategic advantage**.

No JVM Required

The **Java Virtual Machine (JVM)** has long been both Java's greatest strength and its enduring constraint. Its portability and mature runtime ecosystem made Java a natural fit for enterprise systems across platforms. However, that same runtime—powerful as it is—carries operational costs that matter in today's **cloud-native era**: larger container images, longer startup times, higher memory footprints, and complex tuning requirements.

Java 25 mitigates some of this. Features like **Compact Object Headers (JEP 519)**, **Generational Shenandoah GC (JEP 521)**, and **Project Leyden's AOT profiling groundwork** make the JVM leaner and more predictable. These are real advances—but the fundamental model remains: Java code runs *inside* a virtual machine that must be booted, managed, and tuned. Even with optimizations, cold-start latency and memory overhead remain visible in microservice and serverless workloads.

Go, on the other hand, eliminates this layer entirely. It compiles directly to a **self-contained static binary**—no runtime, no dependency manager, no separate VM. The program you build is the program you deploy.

The practical results are decisive for modern operations:

- **Smaller container images**, reducing storage and network costs across clusters
- **Instant startup times**, ideal for serverless functions, auto-scaling deployments, and Kubernetes workloads
- **Simplified deployment**, with no JVM, classpath, or environment-specific runtime to manage
- **Predictable resource usage**, thanks to Go 1.25's container-aware runtime, which automatically adapts `GOMAXPROCS` to CPU limits

In cloud-native systems, these operational differences add up quickly. While Java remains an excellent choice for stable, long-running enterprise services, Go's static binaries and lightweight runtime deliver a **cleaner operational model**—one that scales naturally in the distributed, containerized world enterprises now live in.

Concurrency: Goroutines vs. Threads and Virtual Threads

Concurrency has always been one of the defining differences between **Go** and **Java**. It is where Go's philosophy of simplicity meets the realities of distributed, high-throughput enterprise systems.

Java: Heavy Threads to Structured Concurrency

Traditionally, Java's concurrency model was built on **operating system threads**—powerful but heavyweight structures that consumed significant memory and kernel resources. Frameworks like **Vert.x**, **Akka**, and **RxJava** tried to bridge the gap with event-driven and reactive models. These solutions improved scalability, but often introduced steep learning curves, complex debugging, and callback-heavy, non-intuitive code.

With **Project Loom**, now integrated into **Java 25**, this picture has changed. Loom introduces **Virtual Threads**—lightweight, user-mode threads that map efficiently onto OS threads. Combined with **Structured Concurrency (JEP 505)** and **Scoped Values (JEP 506)**, Java finally supports writing concurrent code in a more structured and readable style. This is a major leap forward for the JVM ecosystem.

However, Loom and Structured Concurrency still operate *on top of* the JVM. They depend on the runtime scheduler, lack decades of performance tuning in production-scale deployments, and require ecosystem updates in frameworks and libraries to fully realize their potential. Java's concurrency is evolving—but it is still *catching up to the design simplicity Go has had from day one.*

Go: Concurrency by Design

In **Go**, concurrency is a *first-class language feature*, not an afterthought. **Goroutines** are lightweight green threads managed by Go's runtime scheduler using an efficient **M:N model**—mapping millions of goroutines onto available OS threads. Each goroutine starts with only a few kilobytes of stack space, growing and shrinking automatically.

Communication happens through **channels**, following Tony Hoare's **Communicating Sequential Processes (CSP)** model. Instead of explicit locks or shared state, goroutines exchange messages. This model is both **simple and safe**, making it natural for developers to reason about concurrency without introducing race conditions or deadlocks.

Go 1.25 further refines this model:

- The runtime is now **container-aware**, adjusting `GOMAXPROCS` dynamically based on CPU limits.
- The experimental **GreenTea garbage collector** improves GC performance in high-concurrency workloads by optimizing cache locality and reducing contention.

Enterprise Lesson For enterprise systems handling millions of simultaneous connections, simplicity is performance. Go's goroutines and channels let teams scale effortlessly—no reactive frameworks, no configuration sprawl.

By embedding concurrency into the language itself, Go transforms parallelism from an architectural challenge into a natural workflow. In high-throughput, distributed environments, this built-in design achieves what many JVM stacks still pursue: **lightweight scalability without the weight of complexity.**

Testing and Tooling

In enterprise software, testing is not an optional phase—it's the **safety net** that keeps systems evolving without fear. The right language and toolchain should make testing not only possible but natural, fast, and repeatable across teams.

Java: Mature But Modular

In **Java**, testing excellence has long relied on an ecosystem of external frameworks: **JUnit 5**, **Mockito**, **AssertJ**, and increasingly **Testcontainers** for integration testing in containerized environments. These tools are powerful and flexible, but they require setup, dependency management, and maintenance. As projects grow, test configurations and CI pipelines often become as complex as the systems under test.

The **Java 25 ecosystem** continues to refine this space. Tools like **JFR Method Timing and Tracing (JEP 520)** and **CPU-Time Profiling (JEP 509)** now provide deep observability for performance testing. Combined with modern CI tools and Gradle or Maven's incremental builds, Java's testing story is robust—but also **dependent on many moving parts**. The modularity is a strength, but the setup overhead can slow iteration cycles, especially in polyglot teams.

Go: Testing Built into the Language

Go takes the opposite approach. From its earliest releases, testing was treated as part of the **core toolchain**, not an external layer. With a single command—**go** `test`—developers gain

- Unit testing, benchmarks, and coverage analysis built-in.
- Race detection and fuzz testing, integrated since Go 1.18.
- And as of Go 1.25, the new `testing/synctest` package enables precise and deterministic testing of concurrent code by virtualizing time and goroutine behavior. This is a major step forward for reliability in high-concurrency systems.

Go's testing design philosophy is simple: *no dependencies, no excuses.* There's no need for mocks frameworks or external runners. Tests are first-class citizens, run with the same speed and simplicity as the build itself.

Enterprise Lesson In Go, testing isn't something you assemble—it's something you inherit.

By making tests, benchmarks, and race detection part of the language itself, Go turns validation into a daily reflex rather than a framework to configure.

For enterprise teams, this built-in discipline shortens feedback loops, simplifies CI/CD, and strengthens confidence in every release. Testing is no longer a separate activity—it's woven into the act of building software.

Memory Model and Garbage Collection

Memory management defines how a language behaves under real-world load. In enterprise systems—where uptime, latency, and cost converge—the difference between a *tuned runtime* and a *predictable runtime* can determine architectural success.

Go: Predictable Memory, Minimal Tuning

Go's memory model was designed for simplicity and performance.

- **Value-Oriented Design:** Structs can embed arrays and other values directly, avoiding the extra indirection common in heap-heavy languages. This yields tighter, cache-friendly layouts and more deterministic behavior.
- **Escape Analysis:** The compiler automatically places short-lived values on the stack, reducing garbage collection pressure without manual effort.
- **Interior Pointers and Safe References:** Developers retain fine control over data access while preserving type and memory safety.

Go 1.25 introduces an **experimental GreenTea GC**, focused on improving locality and CPU scalability for small-object workloads. Early benchmarks show a 10–40% reduction in GC overhead for services that generate many short-lived allocations—exactly the pattern seen in cloud-native APIs. Combined with Go's already low-latency concurrent GC, these improvements reinforce its "configure once, scale anywhere" ethos.

For operations teams, this means predictable performance: Go services rarely need tuning flags, heap analysis sessions, or pause-time management. The runtime simply keeps pace with the workload.

Java: Powerful But Complex

Java's garbage collectors remain among the most sophisticated in the industry—but they demand understanding.

- **Generational Shenandoah (JEP 521)** adds young/old-generation separation, drastically improving throughput and pause-time stability.
- **ZGC** and **G1** continue to evolve, offering near-pause-less collection for heaps into the hundreds of GB.
- **Compact Object Headers (JEP 519)** reduce per-object memory overhead, a welcome gain for microservice deployments. Yet this power comes with complexity: tuning heap sizes, choosing algorithms, and balancing latency vs. throughput remain common production tasks. Java 25's new **JFR Method Timing and CPU-Time Profiling** tools (JEP 509, 520) make diagnosis easier, but tuning is still part of the operational lifecycle.

Enterprise Lesson The contrast is philosophical as much as technical.

- **Java's Approach:** Optimize for maximal throughput, assuming expert operators and dedicated performance teams.
- **Go's Approach:** Optimize for predictability, assuming lean DevOps pipelines and minimal manual tuning.

In production environments—where microservices scale dynamically and memory budgets are tight—Go's simplicity often translates to **lower operational cost and more consistent latency**.

In short, Java's GC can deliver astonishing performance *after* tuning; Go's GC delivers *sufficiently high* performance *without* it. For many enterprise workloads, that distinction means fewer late-night incidents and more reliable scaling curves.

Dependency Management and Jar Hell

In enterprise systems, dependency management isn't just a build concern—it's a **trust problem**. Knowing *what* your system depends on and *which version* is running in production is critical for security, reproducibility, and compliance.

Java: From Classpath Chaos to Modular Order

Historically, **Java** developers have wrestled with *Jar Hell*—conflicting versions of libraries scattered across the classpath. Tools like **Maven** and **Gradle** have greatly improved dependency resolution, but version conflicts, transitive upgrades, and runtime mismatches still occur.

Java 25 moves a step further with **Module Import Declarations (JEP 511)**, allowing explicit module-level imports directly in code. This improves readability and helps tooling infer dependencies more accurately. Combined with **Gradle's version catalogs** and **dependency locking**, modern Java projects are more reproducible than ever—but the ecosystem still relies heavily on manual discipline and careful CI/CD governance to maintain consistency across environments.

Go: Determinism by Design

Go takes a radically simpler path. With **Go Modules**, introduced years ago and refined through Go 1.25, dependency management is **fully deterministic**:

- **Minimal Version Selection (MVS)** ensures that every build picks the same versions, regardless of indirect dependencies.
- **`go.sum` files** store checksums to verify integrity, creating a built-in **supply chain safeguard**.
- The new **`go` `mod ignore` directive** in Go 1.25 even allows excluding directories from dependency resolution, improving control in monorepos and complex workspaces.

In Go, if your project compiles, you can be confident that every dependency—and its checksum—is exactly as declared. No hidden surprises, no classpath ambiguity, no runtime drift.

Enterprise Lesson Dependency determinism isn't just a developer convenience—it's a compliance requirement. Enterprises need to reproduce builds months or years later, validate open source provenance, and audit every external artifact.

Go achieves this **by construction**, while Java achieves it **through tooling discipline**. For teams building cloud-native platforms where trust and repeatability are non-negotiable, Go's model turns dependency management from a liability into a strength.

Simplicity As a Feature

In enterprise engineering, simplicity is not naivety—it is *strategy*. Complex systems rarely fail from missing features; they fail from excess.

Java: Power Accumulated Over Decades

Java has evolved continuously for nearly three decades. Each release adds expressive power—generics with type erasure, annotations, lambdas, streams, and more recently records, pattern matching for primitives (JEP 507), flexible constructor bodies (JEP 513), and module import declarations (JEP 511).

These advances have made Java an incredibly capable language, but they've also expanded its conceptual surface area. Modern Java code often mixes multiple paradigms: functional, object-oriented, and reactive. While that flexibility enables precision, it also increases the cognitive load for teams maintaining large systems. Enterprise developers must now understand dozens of interacting features, frameworks, and annotations just to reason about a single service.

This accumulated complexity isn't a flaw—it's a cost. Java's strength lies in its **breadth and compatibility**, but every new construct lengthens onboarding time and makes code reviews harder to reason about at a glance.

Go: Deliberate Minimalism

Go took the opposite path. With **only 25 keywords** and minimal syntactic sugar, it enforces a discipline of clarity. Instead of adding new abstractions each release, Go focuses on refining its toolchain, runtime, and libraries. The language has remained stable from 1.0 to 1.25—a rare feat in modern software ecosystems.

Features often requested by other communities—inheritance, macros, operator overloading, default parameters—remain deliberately absent. Their omission is philosophical: to ensure every Go developer, from intern to principal engineer, writes code that looks and feels the same.

This uniformity is Go's hidden superpower. In large enterprises, where teams span continents and code bases persist for years, **readability outlives cleverness.** A Go function written today will likely compile—and be understandable—a decade later.

Enterprise Lesson Go was born inside Google, not academia—designed to survive millions of lines of code, thousands of contributors, and continuous deployment. Its simplicity is not aesthetic minimalism but operational discipline: fewer ways to express ideas mean faster builds, easier reviews, and code that endures.

In modern enterprises, where clarity and evolution matter more than syntax or novelty, Go's simplicity becomes a **scaling strategy**, not a limitation.

Summary

Selecting a programming language is not a stylistic choice—it is a **strategic act of architecture**. The decision shapes how teams think, collaborate, test, deploy, and sustain systems over the years.

This chapter showed that sound language selection rests on four foundations: **project requirements**, **budget realities**, **organizational constraints**, and **human capability**. It illustrated how mismatched choices—like over-engineering in C or misusing Go as Java—can sink projects not through code, but through misunderstanding.

Enterprise software brings its own demands: long-term maintainability, seamless integration, rigorous testing, observability, security, and scalability across both systems and teams. Within this context, language design becomes policy.

Java remains a proven foundation for ecosystems rich in legacy and compliance, but Go has matured into a pragmatic alternative—offering speed, simplicity, deterministic builds, and concurrency by design. Its minimalism is not restraint; it is **clarity engineered for scale**.

In the end, the best language is the one that aligns with your architecture's purpose and your team's reality. Choose it with discipline, and it will reward you with systems that endure, adapt, and stay understandable long after the original authors have moved on.

What's Next

In this chapter, we learned how choosing a language is an act of architecture—one that shapes scalability, maintainability, and team effectiveness. Next, we turn theory into practice. **Chapter 3** explores the philosophy and design of Go itself: why it was created, how it simplifies concurrency, and what makes it uniquely suited for modern, cloud-native systems. You'll set up your environment, write your first Go program, and begin to see why Go's simplicity isn't a limitation—it's the very foundation of lasting software.

CHAPTER 3

Introducing Go: The Architecture of Simplicity

Simplicity is not a lack of power; it is the foundation of lasting systems.

Go was born from impatience with slow builds and avoidable complexity. It bets that clarity, fast compilation, and built-in concurrency beat ever-growing feature lists. In this chapter, we'll meet Go as it is used today—Go 1.25—so you can see why enterprises choose it for services that must scale, start fast, and stay readable. By the end, you'll know what Go is, why it exists, and how to run your first program.

Why Use Go

Go exists in a very deliberate space in the landscape of modern programming languages. It does not try to be the most powerful, the most expressive, or the most abstract language. Instead, it focuses on something far more valuable in enterprise systems: *reliable simplicity at scale.*

Modern languages like Go and Rust share an important shift in design philosophy. They encourage **small interfaces defined by the consumer**, not by the provider. When interfaces are narrow and owned by the caller, systems become more modular, easier to reason about, and far more resilient to change. Go embraces this idea naturally. Interfaces emerge where they are needed, not where they look elegant. As a result, Go code bases tend to feel *solid*: fewer hidden dependencies, fewer surprises, and clearer boundaries between components.

S. Shahsavan, *Building Enterprise Projects with Go*, https://doi.org/10.1007/979-8-8688-2370-1_3

Solid by Design

Go favors clarity over flexibility. There is usually one obvious way to model a concept, one obvious way to wire components together, and one obvious way to read the code six months later. This is not a limitation—it is a constraint that protects large teams.

In long-lived enterprise systems, complexity rarely comes from algorithms. It comes from human coordination: onboarding new developers, reviewing code, debugging production issues, and evolving systems without breaking contracts. Go's small language surface, explicit error handling, and uniform formatting lead to code bases that look and feel consistent, even when written by many teams over many years.

Performant Where It Matters

Go is also designed to be fast in practice, not just in benchmarks. Its concurrency model is a key reason for this.

Goroutines are lightweight execution units managed by the Go runtime, not the operating system. They require very little memory and can be created in large numbers without the overhead associated with OS threads. This allows Go programs to handle high levels of concurrency—network calls, I/O, background tasks—without complex infrastructure.

Combined with pointers, value semantics, and a runtime optimized for modern CPUs, Go enables developers to write systems that are both readable and efficient. You can reason about performance without fighting the language. Most importantly, performance-critical decisions remain *visible in the code*, not hidden behind abstractions.

No Middleware, No Waiting

There are two classic ways to build portable software:

1. Ship one artifact that runs on a shared middleware (such as the JVM).
2. Ship a native artifact for each target platform.

Go chooses the second approach. A Go program compiles into a single, self-contained native binary for its target platform. There is no runtime dependency like a JDK, no interpreter, and no startup tax. The result is simple deployment, fast startup, and predictable behavior in production environments.

This model fits modern infrastructure extremely well. Containers become smaller. Cold starts become cheaper. Operational complexity drops.

When platform-specific behavior is required, Go handles it cleanly at compile time using build tags. Platform concerns remain explicit and isolated, rather than leaking into runtime logic. The same code base can support Linux, Windows, macOS, or specialized environments without compromising clarity.

Easy, But Not Naive

Go is not the only language that offers safety, performance, and modern design. Rust, for example, provides stronger compile-time guarantees and more control over memory. However, that power comes with a cognitive cost.

Go makes a different trade-off. It is intentionally easier to learn, easier to read, and easier to use correctly under pressure. Teams become productive faster. Code reviews focus on behavior instead of language mechanics. Architectural discussions stay at the system level instead of drifting into compiler theory.

For enterprise development, this matters. Software is written once, but read and maintained for years. Go optimizes for that reality.

A Practical Choice

Go's continued adoption across cloud platforms, infrastructure tooling, and back-end systems is not an accident. It is the result of a language that respects both machines and humans.

Go does not promise perfection.

It promises *progress without friction.*

And in large systems, that promise is often the one that matters most.

History of Go

Go's creation was driven by the need for a better programming tool for large-scale systems. It was designed at Google in 2007 by **Robert Griesemer, Rob Pike, and Ken Thompson**—all experienced systems engineers. At the time, Google's code base was enormous, and existing languages (like C++ and Java) were struggling to provide fast builds and simple concurrency for the new multicore era. The Go team wanted to improve developer productivity in an era of multi-core processors, large code bases, and networked services. In particular, the designers were frustrated with the complexity and slow compilation of C++ in Google's code (they even joked that Go started as an experiment while waiting for a C++ program to compile). The goal was to create a language that retained the good aspects of languages in use (e.g., the performance of C and the readability of Python) while eliminating unnecessary complexity. This included having static typing and efficiency like C, but with higher-level ease of use, and providing built-in concurrency support to better utilize multicore CPUs. In short, they wanted a **simpler, faster-to-build language** for writing Google's servers—and their dislike of C++'s complexity was a major motivating factor.

Google **open-sourced Go in November 2009**, releasing it publicly so the community could contribute and use it. Over the next few years, Go evolved rapidly but carefully. **Go 1.0** was released in **March 2012** as the first stable version. With Go 1, the developers established a strong commitment to backward compatibility—known as the "Go 1 promise." Code written for Go 1.0 would continue to compile and run on Go 1.x versions, a policy that has helped the ecosystem remain stable and avoid fragmentation. Since 2012, the Go team has put out regular releases (roughly two per year, numbered as 1.1, 1.2,...up to the current 1.25) with incremental improvements, but without breaking older code.

Over the last decade, several milestones marked Go's growth. In 2015, Go 1.5 moved the compiler and runtime entirely to Go (from C), and improvements in garbage collection and performance in versions 1.6/1.7 helped boost Go's adoption in production. In 2018, Go introduced a new module system for dependency management (replacing the old GOPATH approach), making it easier to manage packages in large projects. A long-awaited feature, **generics** (parametric polymorphism), was **finally added in Go 1.18 (March 2022)**, allowing developers to write type-safe reusable code containers like lists and maps. This addressed one of the few major criticisms of the language's early design (which initially omitted generics). Throughout, the core philosophy of Go has remained intact—*keep the language simple, efficient, and oriented toward real-world software engineering problems.* As of 2026, Go is **mature (18+ years old)** and is at version **1.25**, with new releases focusing on performance tuning, better developer tools, and telemetry, all while maintaining backward compatibility and not introducing gratuitous complexity. The result is a language that has steadily "Stood the test of time"—widely adopted in industry and still true to its original ideals of simplicity, speed, and reliability.

What Kind of Language Is Go?

Go is a **compiled, statically typed, garbage-collected, concurrent, and imperative** programming language. It was designed to feel as simple and productive as a scripting language, yet deliver the speed, safety, and deployment advantages of a compiled one. Its design emphasizes readability, fast compilation, and built-in concurrency—bridging the gap between low-level control and high-level ease of use. Its defining characteristics are as follows:

- **Compiled:** Go source code is translated directly into native machine code, producing fast, self-contained binaries—no virtual machine or external runtime required.
- **Statically Typed:** Every variable and expression has a known type at compile time, allowing the compiler to catch errors early and optimize execution.
- **Garbage-Collected:** Go's runtime automatically reclaims unused memory through a concurrent garbage collector, freeing developers from manual memory management.
- **Concurrent by Design:** Goroutines and channels are built into the language, enabling lightweight concurrency and safe communication without complex locking or external frameworks.
- **Imperative and Procedural:** Go programs are organized into packages, functions, and types. You express intent through explicit, ordered instructions that the computer executes step by step.

Is Go Object-Oriented?

This question often arises, especially among developers coming from Java or C++. To answer it clearly, let's revisit the four classical principles of object-oriented programming (OOP) and see how Go approaches each one.

- **Encapsulation: Bundling Data and Behavior, Hiding Internal Details**

  ☑ Go supports encapsulation through **structs** and **methods**.

  A struct holds data, and methods can be attached to any named type (not just structs). Visibility is controlled at the package level: identifiers starting with a capital letter are **exported** (public), while lowercase names remain **unexported** (private). This simple rule replaces the complex access modifiers found in many OOP languages.

- **Abstraction: Exposing Only Essential Features, Hiding Implementation Details**

  ☑ Go supports abstraction via **interfaces**.

  An interface defines a set of method signatures. Any type that implements those methods **implicitly satisfies** the interface—no explicit declaration is required. This encourages programming to behavior rather than to specific implementations, allowing flexible substitution and clear boundaries between components.

- **Inheritance: Reusing Code Through Class Hierarchies**

  ✕ Go deliberately omits inheritance.

  There are no classes and no "extends" keyword. Instead, Go promotes **composition**—embedding one struct or interface inside another to reuse functionality. Composition avoids the tight coupling of inheritance hierarchies and enables developers to build systems from small, composable parts that can evolve independently.

- **Polymorphism: Treating Different Types Uniformly When They Share Behavior**

  ☑ Go supports polymorphism, but through interfaces rather than class hierarchies.

  If a type implements the required methods, it automatically fulfills the interface contract. This **structural typing** provides polymorphism without the boilerplate of explicit `implements` declarations or virtual method overrides. The result is flexible and decoupled polymorphism—behavioral, not hierarchical.

Why Go Isn't "Classical" OOP

Go deliberately omits **classes** and **inheritance**, so it doesn't fit the traditional mold of an object-oriented language. There are no `extends` clauses or base-class hierarchies. Instead, Go applies object-oriented ideas in a lean, compositional way:

- **Data** → Structs
- **Behavior** → Methods
- **Reuse** → Composition
- **Polymorphism** → Interfaces

This design leads many to describe Go as *"object-oriented without classes."* It still provides **encapsulation**, **abstraction**, and **polymorphism**, but replaces inheritance with a simpler and more adaptable model.

The absence of inheritance was not a limitation—it was a **philosophical choice**. The Go designers intentionally avoided the complexity of deep class trees, virtual method resolution, and fragile base classes that often hinder large systems. Instead, Go encourages developers to **compose small, focused types** that work together through interfaces.

In practice, Go preserves the benefits of OOP—structured organization, reusable behavior, and polymorphic design—while avoiding one of its biggest pitfalls: the tight coupling that grows from inheritance chains.

The result is object-oriented thinking, executed with compositional clarity and modern simplicity.

Download and Install

This book keeps setup short and practical—no lengthy walkthroughs you can find elsewhere.

To install Go, simply visit the official guide at `https://go.dev/doc/install`, and follow the steps for your operating system. The instructions are clear, current, and maintained by the Go team itself.

With Go installed and your path configured, you're ready to run your first program.

Choosing an Editor

Go works well with any modern text editor, but two environments consistently stand out for professional development:

- **Visual Studio Code:** Lightweight, fast, and free, with the **official Go extension** maintained by the Go team. It supports integrated debugging, testing, code navigation, and real-time linting through `gopls`, the Go language server.
- **JetBrains GoLand:** A full-featured commercial IDE offering advanced refactoring, static analysis, profiling, and deep integration with the Go toolchain. Ideal for large enterprise code bases.

Both environments provide features such as **auto-completion, go-to-definition, inline documentation, and integrated `go test` support**. Choose the one that best fits your workflow—VS Code for a fast, extensible setup and GoLand for an all-in-one engineering suite.

Once **Go 1.25** is installed and your editor is configured, you're ready to write and run your first Go program.

Enterprise Tip Add your workspace binaries ($HOME/go/bin on Linux and macOS, or `%USERPROFILE%\go\bin` on Windows) to your system PATH. This ensures that any tools you install with `go install` are available everywhere on the command line.

Hello World in Go

As a quick example, here's a simple "Hello World" program in Go. First, you need to create a Go module with this command:

```
go mod init example.com/transport
```

This command creates a **go.mod** file, which serves as the module's manifest. **go.mod** records the module path you chose, the Go version your project targets, and—later on—any external dependencies your code imports. Even for very small examples, starting with a module mirrors real-world Go development and ensures your project builds reproducibly across machines.

Now create a file named **main.go** with the following content:

```
package main

import "fmt"

func main() {
   fmt.Println("Hello, World!")
}
```

If you don't want to set up anything, you can copy this code into the official **Go Playground** at go.dev/play and run it directly in your browser.

When you run this program, it will print:

```
Hello, World!
```

Let's break down the code.

- The first line `package main` declares that this file is part of the `main` package—which is a special package name indicating an **executable program** (as opposed to a library package). Every runnable Go program must have a `main` package and a `main()` function as the entry point.
- Next, the `import "fmt"` line brings in Go's **formatting library** (from the standard library). The `fmt` package provides formatted I/O functions; here we use `fmt.Println` to print a line of text to standard output.
- The `func main()` is the function where execution begins.
- Inside `main`, we call `fmt.Println("Hello, World!")` which prints the string to the console followed by a newline.

This simple program illustrates Go's minimalist structure—no class or method definitions are required around the `main` function, and printing to the console is as straightforward as calling a single function. (In case you're curious, `fmt.Println` is analogous to `printf`/`println` in C or System.out.println in Java—it's part of Go's standard library for formatted output.)

Compile and run this program by executing `go run main.go` (or build it with `go build` to produce a binary). You should see the output "Hello, World!" printed on your terminal. With just a few lines of code, we've written and run our first Go program!

One of Go's most practical advantages is its fast compilation. Even small projects compile almost instantly. For example, running

```
time go run ./cmd/vehiclectl/main.go
```

Produces output such as

```
Hello, Go! The transportation system is starting...

real    0m0.452s
user    0m0.233s
sys     0m0.148s
```

Building the same program by running this command:

```
time go build ./...
```

Produces output such as

```
real    0m0.096s
user    0m0.098s
sys     0m0.052s
```

I created the same "Hello World" program inside a small Java Gradle project and measured its build time for comparison:

```
gradle build

BUILD SUCCESSFUL in 1s
2 actionable tasks: 2 up-to-date

real    0m1.318s
user    0m1.736s
sys     0m0.156s
```

These numbers naturally vary by machine, but they illustrate a core part of Go's design philosophy: **fast builds encourage fast iteration**, which is especially valuable in enterprise-scale development.

Quick Overview of the go Command

One of Go's strengths is its unified toolchain. Go provides a single command, go, which acts as the entry point for various build and development tasks. This go tool streamlines compiling, running, testing, formatting, and managing dependencies in Go projects. Below is a quick overview of the most commonly used subcommands of go (as of Go 1.25), along with their purpose and basic usage syntax:

- **`go run`:** Compiles and **runs** a Go program in one step, without saving an output binary. This is handy during development. For example, `go run main.go` will build and execute the program defined in *main.go* immediately.
- **`go build`:** Compiles the packages and dependencies listed (typically the current directory/package) into an **executable binary** (or library). By default, `go build` writes the output as an executable file in the current directory (for the main package). It uses only the information in the source files (no separate Makefiles are needed).

  Example: **go** `build .` will compile the current package, and **go** `build -o app.exe ./cmd/app` builds the package in `cmd/app` and names the output binary `app.exe`.
- **`go install`:** Compiles and **installs** a package binary into your Go workspace's bin directory (so you can run it from anywhere). Essentially, **go** `install` is like **go** `build`, but it places the resulting executable in `$GOBIN` or (if that's not set) in the default `$GOPATH/bin` location. It's often used to install command-line tools or your own programs for system-wide use. For example, **go** `install example.com/myapp@latest` will fetch the module and install the `myapp` binary into your `$GOPATH/bin`.
- **`go fmt`:** Automatically **formats** your Go source code according to the standard style guidelines. Running **go** `fmt ./...` (the `./...` means "all files in this directory and subdirectories") will reformat all code files in the project to adhere to Go's official style (which is enforced by tools like `gofmt`). This helps keep code style consistent. Most IDEs/runbooks have this step integrated. (In fact, **go** `fmt` is essentially a wrapper around the `gofmt` tool.)

- **go test:** Runs the test suites for your Go packages. Go has a built-in testing framework, and any file with a name like `*_test.go` containing `Test...` functions will be picked up by **go** `test`. Running **go** `test` in a package directory compiles and executes the unit tests (and any benchmarks or examples) for that package. You can add the `-v` flag for verbose output or specify specific test functions. This makes it straightforward to integrate testing into your development cycle.
- **go mod:** Manages Go's **modules (dependency modules)**. This subcommand is used to initialize new modules, add or update dependencies, and maintain the `go.mod` file which tracks your project's requirements. For instance, **go** `mod init <module-path>` creates a new module in the current directory, **go** `mod tidy` cleans up unused dependencies, and **go** `mod download` fetches the modules. Essentially, **go** `mod` helps with **fetching, adding, or adjusting dependencies** and overall module maintenance. (Since Go 1.16+, modules are enabled by default, replacing the old GOPATH-based dependency management.)

These commands are all part of the standard Go toolchain, and they work together seamlessly. For example, when you run **go** `test`, it automatically formats and builds the code before executing tests. The Go CLI's design emphasizes convention and convenience—with a few simple commands, you can handle the full development lifecycle (edit, format, compile, test, install) without needing external build systems or complex scripts. This makes Go a very **approachable** language for newcomers and contributes to the efficiency of Go development workflows.

Each of the topics above will be expanded in later chapters, but this introduction gives you a taste of what Go offers. In summary, Go provides a powerful mix of **simplicity, speed, and robust tooling**. It was born to address real-world software engineering problems (like fast builds, easy concurrency), and over the years, it has matured into a language of choice for cloud services, systems programming, and many other areas. Now that you have set up your Go environment and run a basic program, you're ready to dive deeper into Go and start comparing how things are done in Go vs. Java in the upcoming sections.

Happy coding with Go!

Summary

Go was born out of frustration with existing languages and has grown into one of the most practical tools for modern software engineering. Its **simplicity, speed, concurrency model, and powerful standard library** make it especially appealing for building reliable systems and services. From its beginnings at Google in 2007 to its current maturity in version 1.25, Go has remained faithful to its design philosophy: cut through complexity, and let developers focus on solving problems, not wrestling with the language.

With a minimal "Hello World," a fast compiler, and a unified toolchain, you've already seen how Go lowers the barrier to entry. At the same time, it scales to power critical infrastructure like Kubernetes, Docker, and countless cloud services. This dual nature—simple yet capable—is what continues to attract developers from Java, Python, C++, and beyond.

Exercises

1. Go is often described as "simple, fast, and built for concurrency." In your own words, explain what makes Go different from Java or Python in terms of compilation and concurrency.

2. Try running the Hello World program either locally with `go run main.go` or online in the Go Playground (`https://go.dev/play`).

   - What happens if you remove the `import "fmt"` line?

   - Why does the compiler complain?

3. Classical OOP has four principles: encapsulation, abstraction, inheritance, and polymorphism.

   - Which of these does Go *not* support?

   - What mechanism does Go use instead, and why did the language designers make that choice?

What's Next

In the next chapter, we'll step into the essential concepts of Go programming. We will learn how a Go project is organized—its workspace, modules, and packages. By the end, you'll build and run a small "Hello, World" program and take your first confident step into the language itself.

CHAPTER 4

Structuring Go Projects: Modules, Packages, and Boundaries

"If the architect lays the first brick askew the wall will rise crooked even to the heavens."

—Saeb Tabrizi

In Go, those first bricks are the **module** and the **project structure**. Many beginners rush into functions and variables. Professionals pause. They ask: *"Where will this code live? How will it grow? How will it be reused?"*

That pause is discipline—the quiet art that prevents future chaos. So before we even talk about variables, let's lay the foundation: **modules**, **project layout**, and **package structures**.

Packages and Modules: Two Levels of Organization

A **package** is a *local unit of organization*—a folder of `.go` files that share the same package name.

For example, every file under `internal/vehicle` belongs to `package vehicle`.

Executables, by contrast, must live in `package main` and include a `func main()`—the program's single entry point.

In Go, a **module** is more than a folder with code. It's the **unit of versioning and distribution**. A module is what you publish, with a version (`v1.2.3`), and consume in other projects.

S. Shahsavan, *Building Enterprise Projects with Go*, https://doi.org/10.1007/979-8-8688-2370-1_4

Packages live *inside* modules, but the module is what the outside world sees.

Think of it this way:

- **Package = The room** in a building
- **Module = The whole building** (with its address and ownership)
- **Import path = The street address** others use to find you

When Do You Create a Module?

A module defines ownership and evolution.

It marks where your code begins to live a life of its own—versioned, documented, and released under its own name. You create one not out of habit, but out of necessity.

- **New Project/Service:** Every independent service or application should be its own module. Example: a `transport` service in a microservices system.
- **Reusable Library:** If you have logic that *could* be reused by other projects (inside or outside your company), put it in its own module (e.g., `github.com/acme/datetime`).
- **Independent Lifecycle:** Modules have lifecycles. If a piece of code needs its own versioning, release notes, or backward-compatibility promises, it deserves to be a module.

When *Not* to Split into Modules?

Not every package deserves independence. Splitting too early multiplies complexity and breeds dependency chaos.

- Don't create a separate module for every package—this adds dependency hell.
- Avoid premature splitting. Keep related packages together in one module until they *must* evolve independently.
- If code is only ever used inside one system, keep it as `internal/` packages inside the main module

Rules of Thumb for Enterprise Architects

1. **Keep it monolithic until it hurts.** Start with one module; split later when reuse/versioning is unavoidable.
2. **Domain boundaries, not folders.** Create a module when a subsystem has a different release rhythm (e.g., `transport-core` vs. `transport-cli`).
3. **Hide the unstable.** Put "experimental" packages under `internal/`. Only promote them to the public API after they stabilize.
4. **Respect import paths.** Use realistic paths from day one (e.g., `github.com/company/transport`), even before publishing, to avoid painful renames.
5. **Use tools:** `go mod tidy` (clean deps), `go mod graph` (inspect deps), `go mod why` (find why a dep is needed).

Create Your Module

Let's start a fresh project for our **Transportation System** examples.

```
# 1. Create a new folder
mkdir transport && cd transport
# 2. Initialize a module (use your GitHub path if real project)
go mod init example.com/transport
```

This generates a `go.mod` file:

```
module example.com/transport
go 1.25.1
```

That's your **identity card**:

- `module` defines the import path.
- `go` pins the Go version.
- As you add dependencies, `require` and checksums (`go.sum`) will appear.

Enterprise Tip Commit both `go.mod` and `go.sum`. They guarantee deterministic builds.

The `go.mod` File in Short

The `go.mod` file is the **manifest** of your Go module. It declares the module's **path**, the **Go version** it targets, and the exact **dependencies (with versions)** it requires.

It ensures that builds are **reproducible** across machines and over time—everyone compiles against the same dependency set, guaranteeing consistency and traceability.

Think of it as your project's **contract with the outside world**:
what you **provide** (the module path) and what you **depend on** (its requirements).

Suggested Project Layout

Good Go systems are **composed**; bad ones are **entangled**. Structure buys you velocity later—especially because Go **forbids circular imports**. Let's design to win that constraint.

Here's a minimal layout for Go System that you can grow into an enterprise code base:

```
transport/
  cmd/
     vehiclectl/
        main.go              # CLI (executable)

  internal/
    models/          # domain model & logic (no main)
    app/             # application services / orchestrations
  go.mod
  go.sum
  README.md
```

There is no standard go structure like Java projects, but there are some naming conventions.

The `cmd/` is the conventional folder for executables.

- Each subfolder (e.g., `vehiclectl`) produces **one binary**.
- Code here should be as thin as possible—ideally just wiring (flags, config, calling into libraries).
- Always `package main` with a `func main()`.

Why? Because enterprise projects often need **multiple binaries** built from the same core logic. All share the same **internal libraries**, but each has its own `main.go`. This avoids duplication while keeping responsibilities clear.

The `internal/` Package: Private Libraries

- `internal/` is a Go convention: any code inside it is **invisible to external modules**.
- This enforces boundaries. If you put your business logic into `internal/vehicle`, no other module (outside `transport`) can import it.
- This is perfect for enterprise projects, where you want to publish a clean public API but keep messy details private.

Inside `internal/`, create subpackages for each **domain or bounded context**. example:

- `internal/vehicle` → Logic about vehicles

This enforces **clean layering**: executables call internal packages; internal packages may depend on each other in a DAG (Directed Acyclic Graph), but never in a cycle.

Circular Dependencies (Why Structure Matters)

Go **does not allow circular imports**. If `package A` imports `package B` and `package B` imports `package A`, the compiler stops you. This is intentional: it forces clean architecture.

Example of a **bad design**:

- internal/vehicle imports internal/role.
- internal/role imports internal/vehicle.

This is a circular dependency. Over time, such tangling makes systems unmaintainable.

How to avoid cycles?

1. **Separate shared types** into a new package (e.g., `internal/model`). Both `vehicle` and `role` import `model`, but not each other.
2. **Depend on interfaces, not concrete types**. For example, `vehicle` defines an interface `RoleProvider`, and `role` implements it.
3. **One-directional dependencies**. Decide the layering: domain → service → adapter. Never let lower layers depend on higher ones.

Best Practices for Enterprise Go Project Layout

- **Keep `main.go` Thin**

  It should do only three things: parse configuration, wire dependencies, and delegate to library code. Nothing more.

- **Business Logic in `internal/`**

  This protects your domain from leaking into other modules or external consumers.

- **Avoid pkg/ Dumping Ground**

  Many projects use pkg/ for "shared" code, but it quickly turns into a kitchen sink. Prefer **domain-driven** packages instead.

- **Keep Packages Cohesive and Small**

  A package should feel like a single concept. If a package does too many things, split it.

- **Explicit Dependencies**

  If package A needs package B, **import it directly**. Don't hide relationships behind "utility" or "common" layers.

- **Review Imports Regularly**

  Use tools like

  ```
  go list -f '{{.ImportPath}}: {{.Imports}}' ./...
  ```

  to detect creeping dependencies, before they grow roots.

First Hello World

It's time to breathe life into our project. Let's build the simplest program possible: **a vehicle control CLI that just says hello**.

Create a file `cmd/vehiclectl/main.go` with the following content:

```go
package main

import "fmt"

// main is the program's entry point.
// Every Go executable *must* have a main package and a main() function.
// Later we'll break down functions, variables, and packages in detail.
func main() {
    fmt.Println("Hello, Go! The transportation system is starting...")
}
```

Breaking It Down

- **`package main`**

  This tells the Go compiler: *"This package builds into an executable."*

  Any other package name produces a library, not a binary.

- **`import "fmt"`**

  We're importing the **formatting package** from the Go standard library. It contains printing functions like `Println`.

  Imports always use **quoted paths**. Standard library packages like `fmt` need no prefix.

- **`func main()`**

  The `main` function is the entry point. When you run your program, execution starts here.

  Every runnable Go program must have this. Without it, you just have a library.

- **`fmt.Println(...)`**

  Calls the `Println` function from the `fmt` package.

  In Go, names that **start with a capital letter** are *exported*—i.e., visible to other packages. That's why we can call `Println`, but not internal helpers like `fmt.doPrint`.

Run It

From the project root, run the following command:

```
go run ./cmd/vehiclectl
```

Output

```
Hello, Go! The transportation system is starting...
```

What Just Happened?

1. The Go tool looked for a `main` package in the folder `cmd/vehiclectl`.
2. It compiled the code into a temporary binary.
3. It executed that binary, which ran the `main()` function.

If you want to keep the binary around:

```
go build -o bin/vehiclectl ./cmd/vehiclectl
./bin/vehiclectl
```

This creates a reusable binary under `bin/`.

Quick Practice

1. Change your module path in `go.mod` to `github.com/<yourname>/transport` and run `go mod tidy`. What changes? Why?
2. Add a second executable under `cmd/garage/` and run it.

Summary

A solid Go project begins with a solid structure. In this chapter, we explored modules as units of ownership and versioning and packages as the building blocks that shape how code is organized and reused. We looked at practical guidelines for deciding when to create new modules, how to keep internal boundaries clean, and how Go's import rules protect us from accidental coupling. By designing a thoughtful layout and building our first executable, we set the foundation for a code base that can scale gracefully as features, teams, and services grow.

What's Next

In the next chapter, we leave structure behind and study the raw materials of Go itself—its primitive types. You'll see how integers, floats, booleans, and strings shape correctness, memory usage, and performance at scale.

CHAPTER 5

Core Language Elements: Types, Variables, and Operators

"Types are the first line of defense against bugs."

—*Martin Odersky*

Before we design structures or craft algorithms, we must understand the raw materials our programs are made of. Go's primitive types are small in appearance but vast in consequence: they shape memory usage, performance profiles, and even the correctness of enterprise workloads. By choosing the right type at the right moment, we give our systems a foundation that remains reliable as data grows and complexity rises.

Primitive Types

Primitive types are the **atoms** of Go. Everything you build—from vehicles in our transport system to fleets spanning thousands of records—rests on these simple data forms.

Choosing the right type is not just a syntactic detail. In enterprise applications, it matters for

- **Memory Usage:** Imagine millions of records stored with a larger type than necessary—wasted bytes become wasted gigabytes.
- **Consistency:** Wrong types (like a signed int for a field that should never be negative) introduce subtle bugs.

S. Shahsavan, *Building Enterprise Projects with Go*, https://doi.org/10.1007/979-8-8688-2370-1_5

- **Interoperability:** APIs, databases, and network protocols often expect fixed-width values (`int32`, `uint16`, etc.).
- **Correctness and Clarity:** A `bool` conveys intent better than using `0` or `1`.

Let's explore each primitive type carefully, always tying back to enterprise use.

Integers

Go provides both **signed** and **unsigned** integers, each with fixed sizes. These types differ in

1. **Memory size** (how many bytes they use)
2. **Value range** (minimum and maximum values they can store)
3. **Use cases** (enterprise correctness, memory optimization, interoperability)

Signed Integers

Table 5-1 summarizes the signed integer types in Go along with their sizes and value ranges.

Table 5-1. *Signed integer types in Go*

Type	Size (Bytes)	Range
int8	1	-128 to 127
int16	2	-32,768 to 32,767
int32	4	-2,147,483,648 to 2,147,483,647
int64	8	-9,223,372,036,854,775,808 to 9,223,372,036,854,775,807
int	4 or 8	Machine-dependent (at least -2^31 to 2^31-1)

- Use `int` for everyday counters and loops—it scales with the architecture.
- Use fixed sizes (`int32`, `int64`) when you must align with external systems.

- Avoid `int16`/`int8` unless you're optimizing tight memory (millions of rows, sensor data).

Unsigned Integers

Table 5-2 summarizes the unsigned integer types in Go, along with their sizes and value ranges.

Table 5-2. *Unsigned integer types in Go*

Type	Size (Bytes)	Range
uint8	1	0 to 255 (alias: byte)
uint16	2	0 to 65,535
uint32	4	0 to 4,294,967,295
uint64	8	0 to 18,446,744,073,709,551,615
uintptr	4 or 8	Big enough to store a pointer value

- Unsigned types double the positive range (e.g., `uint8` goes to 255 instead of 127).
- They're perfect when negatives make no sense (wheel count, manufacture year).
- But beware: mixing signed and unsigned in expressions can cause tricky conversions.
- `uintptr` is special—for low-level pointer arithmetic, not business logic.

Go also defines two special type aliases that make code more expressive: **`byte`** and **`rune`**. These are not new types but just alternative names for existing integer types. Their purpose is to improve readability and communicate intent, especially in enterprise applications where handling both raw data and multi-language text is common.

The byte Type

`byte` is an alias for `uint8`. While you could use `uint8` for any small integer, the name `byte` signals that the value represents **raw binary data**. This convention makes code easier to read and maintain. In enterprise systems, you'll encounter `byte` when dealing with file contents, network packets, or database blobs. By using `byte`, developers immediately understand that the variable holds binary information, not just a numeric counter.

```
data := []byte{0xF0, 0x9F, 0x9A, 0x8C} // UTF-8 bytes for 🚌
fmt.Println(string(data))             // Output: 🚌
```

Here, `data` is defined as a slice of bytes. Converting it to a string reveals the human-readable text. Using `[]byte` is the idiomatic way in Go to represent raw data buffers.

The rune Type (Alias for int32)

`rune` is an alias for `int32`, intended for representing a single **Unicode code point**. Unlike `byte`, which focuses on raw storage, `rune` emphasizes **human-readable characters**. This is particularly important in enterprise systems where applications must support multiple languages, special characters, and even emojis. Since Go strings are UTF-8 encoded, some characters may require more than one byte—but each is represented as a single rune.

```
var symbol rune = '🚍' // Unicode bus emoji
fmt.Println(symbol)    // Prints 128653 (the code point)
```

By using `rune`, you make it clear that your variable holds a character, not just an integer. This improves clarity when building internationalized systems where names, routes, or tickets may include non-ASCII characters.

Why So Many Types?

Go does not just give you "int" and walk away. Instead, it provides multiple integer types: `int8`, `int16`, `int32`, `int64` (and their unsigned counterparts). At first, this can feel overwhelming—but it's a strength, not a weakness. Here are some reasons.

1. **Memory Control:** You don't always need 8 bytes for every number. A passenger count that fits in 0–255 (`uint8`) wastes memory if stored as `int64`. On large datasets, this choice adds up.

2. **Value Range Enforcement:** By picking `uint16` for a manufacture year, you guarantee no negatives. By picking `int16`, you enforce a max range of ~32k. Types are *guardrails*, not just storage.

3. **Interoperability:** Databases, network protocols, and binary formats often require fixed-width integers (`int32`, `int64`). Matching the type ensures consistent behavior across systems.

4. **Portability:** The plain `int` adapts to your machine's word size: 32-bit on 32-bit systems, 64-bit on 64-bit systems. This makes code portable without micromanaging sizes—but it also means you must know the environment.

Enterprise Lessons Use int for counters, loops, and indexes unless you specifically need a fixed width.

Use fixed-size ints (int32, uint16, etc.) when you're interfacing with databases, binary protocols, or APIs where size must match.

Use unsigned types only if negative values are logically impossible.

```go
package main

import "fmt"

func main() {
    var totalVehicles int = 35000           // fits typical counters
    var manufactureYear uint16 = 2020       // year is never negative
    var maxPassengers uint8 = 255           // capacity fits in a
                                            single byte

    fmt.Println(totalVehicles, manufactureYear, maxPassengers)
}
```

Floating Points

Go supports **floating-point numbers** that follow the IEEE-754 standard. These types represent real numbers with a fractional part—unlike integers, they trade exactness for a wider range and convenience in calculations. In enterprise systems, floating points are used for **measurements, averages, and scientific data** where perfect precision isn't required, but they must be used carefully.

In older enterprise stacks like Java, developers faced two recurring pitfalls with floating-point numbers. The first was the **confusion between `float` (32-bit) and `double` (64-bit)**. A `float` was often chosen for memory savings, but its limited precision caused subtle rounding errors when values grew large or required more than ~7 digits of accuracy. Go eliminates this trap by making **`float64` the default**: any literal like `88.5` is automatically treated as a 64-bit float, and you must explicitly request a `float32` if you want one. The second issue was Java's **floating-point arithmetic in financial or critical calculations**. Because binary floating points can't precisely represent decimal fractions, developers often had to rely on `BigDecimal`, which is slower, verbose, and awkward to use. Go doesn't "fix" the nature of floating-point math (IEEE-754 limitations still apply), but its type system and defaults encourage a cleaner split: use `float64` for measurements, averages, and scientific data, and use **integers for exact values like money**. This approach avoids the painful `float` vs. `double` ambiguity and the heavy `BigDecimal` workaround, while keeping code both safe and performant.

Floating-Point Types

Table 5-3 summarizes the floating-point types in Go, along with their sizes and value ranges.

Table 5-3. *Floating-point types in Go*

Type	Size (Bytes)	Approx. Precision	Range
float32	4	~7 decimal digits	±1e−38 to ±3.4e38
float64	8	~15 decimal digits	±1e−308 to ±1.8e308

- **float32** uses less memory and is faster on some architectures, but only gives about seven digits of precision.
- **float64** is the default in Go and should be your choice for most calculations, offering about 15 digits of precision.

Example in the Transportation System

```
package main

import "fmt"

func main() {
    averageSpeed := 88.5                  // inferred as float64
    var fuelConsumption float32 = 12.7 // liters per 100km
    fmt.Println(averageSpeed, fuelConsumption)
}
```

Here:

- averageSpeed uses float64, the safer default for calculations.
- fuelConsumption is stored as float32, which is enough when you know the value won't require extreme precision.

Summary

- Use **float64 by default**. It avoids subtle rounding issues and is the standard for serious numeric computation.
- Consider **float32** only when memory usage is critical and precision requirements are modest (e.g., storing millions of sensor readings where two to three decimals are enough).
- Always document why you chose float32 over float64 so future developers understand the trade-off.
- When precision is critical in your application, consult Go's math/big/Float implementation and its RoundingMode settings.

Important Warning

Floating points are excellent for **measurements**, where a tiny rounding error is acceptable. But they are **not suitable for values that must be exact**—like prices, balances, or ticket counts. The reason is mathematical: IEEE-754 binary floats cannot precisely represent many decimal fractions. Over thousands or millions of operations, these tiny errors accumulate and can corrupt financial data.

The safe strategy in enterprise projects is to **store values in the smallest indivisible unit as an integer**. For money, that unit is usually **cents** instead of euros/dollars. For inventory, it might be **pieces** instead of boxes. This way, every operation is exact, because integer arithmetic has no hidden rounding.

```
fareCents := int64(1575) // represents $15.75 exactly
fmt.Println("Bus fare:", fareCents, "cents")
```

Here, the bus fare is stored as `1575` cents rather than `15.75` euros. The representation is simple, consistent, and precise. When you need to display it, you can divide by 100 and format it as `"15.75"`.

This principle is critical in enterprise systems where **trust and correctness are non-negotiable**. Imagine billing millions of passengers—even a fraction of a cent lost per ride adds up to a massive financial discrepancy. By modeling money (and other exact counts) as integers in their smallest units, you protect your system against silent corruption.

Quick Practice

1. Define a variable `averageSpeed` as a `float64` and set it to 72.35. Why is `float64` a safer default than `float32`?
2. Suppose your system stores millions of short-term fuel sensor readings with only one decimal place (e.g., `12.7`). Would you use `float32` or `float64`? Why?
3. Represent a train ticket price of $42.10 correctly in Go. Why is this safer than using a floating-point type?

Complex Numbers

So far, we've worked with numbers you already know—integers and floats. But Go also supports **complex numbers**, a mathematical concept that includes both a **real part** and an **imaginary part**.

A **complex number** looks like this:

```
a + bi
```

- a is the **real part** (a normal number).
- b is the **imaginary part**, which is multiplied by `i`.

The symbol `i` is special: it's defined so that $i^2 = -1$. While you won't see imaginary wheels on a bus, the concept is very real in fields like engineering, physics, and data science.

Why the Imaginary Part Matters

The imaginary part lets us represent values that describe **two-dimensional phenomena** in a single number. For example:

- In **signal processing**, the real part may represent the amplitude of a wave, while the imaginary part encodes its phase.
- In **electrical engineering**, complex numbers represent resistance (real part) and reactance (imaginary part) in circuits.
- In **control systems**, complex numbers simplify the math of oscillations and feedback loops.

So, the imaginary part is not "unreal"—it's a tool to model real-world systems that naturally have two components.

Complex Number Types in Go

Table 5-4 summarizes the complex number types in Go, along with their sizes and value ranges.

Table 5-4. *Complex number types in Go*

Type	Size (Bytes)	Components
complex64	8	float32 real + float32 imag
complex128	16	float64 real + float64 imag

- **complex64:** Smaller, less precise (about seven digits per component).
- **complex128:** Larger, more precise (about 15 digits per component). This is the default when you write a complex literal.

Example

```
package main

import "fmt"

func main() {
    c1 := complex(2, 3)  // 2 is the real part, 3 is the imaginary part
    c2 := 1 + 4i         // shorthand for complex number
    sum := c1 + c2

    fmt.Println("c1:", c1)                  // (2+3i)
    fmt.Println("Real(c1):", real(c1))      // 2
    fmt.Println("Imag(c1):", imag(c1))      // 3
    fmt.Println("c2:", c2)                  // (1+4i)
    fmt.Println("sum:", sum)                // (3+7i)
}
```

Here, `c1` represents `2 + 3i`. The **real part** is `2`, and the **imaginary part** is `3`. The built-in functions `real()` and `imag()` let you extract them separately.

Where They Matter

In everyday enterprise software (like our transportation system), you probably won't use complex numbers directly to track vehicles or fares. But if your project integrates with **sensor data**, **radar systems**, or **scientific simulations**, complex numbers suddenly become essential. Go includes them as first-class citizens, so you don't need external libraries to handle such workloads.

Imagine analyzing a radar signal for buses: the **real part** of the complex value might represent the signal's strength, while the **imaginary part** represents its phase shift. Together, they let you model the full signal in one number instead of juggling two.

Quick Practice

1. Define a complex number `5 + 2i` and print its real and imaginary parts separately.
2. Create two numbers, `3 + 4i` and `1 + 2i`, multiply them in Go, and check if the result matches your manual calculation.
3. In your own words: how could the real part and imaginary part of a complex number represent two different properties of the same phenomenon? Give an example (signal, circuit, or something from daily life).

Booleans

A **boolean** is the simplest type in Go: it can only hold one of two values—`true` or `false`. Yet, this simplicity makes it one of the most important types in enterprise software.

In some languages, developers rely on "truthy" or "falsy" conventions—where `0` means false, non-zero means true, or an empty string counts as false. This can create subtle bugs when code behaves differently than expected. Go avoids this ambiguity entirely. In Go:

- `0` is an integer, not false.
- `""` is a string, not false.
- Only the literal `true` or `false` are valid boolean values.

This explicit design makes enterprise code more predictable, easier to read, and less error-prone.

Example in the Transportation System

```
package main

import "fmt"

func main() {
    var busOperational bool = true        // the bus is in service
    var maintenanceMode = false           // the bus is not under maintenance
```

```
    fmt.Println("Operational:", busOperational)
    fmt.Println("Maintenance:", maintenanceMode)
}
```

Output

```
Operational: true
Maintenance: false
```

Here, the intent is crystal clear: there is no guessing whether `1` means operational or not. Anyone reading this code knows immediately what the variables represent.

Why Booleans Matter in Enterprise Systems

In large-scale applications, clarity is priceless. Using `bool` instead of numbers or strings for state flags:

- **Prevents Misinterpretation:** `isEmergencyVehicle := true` is more obvious than `emergency = 1`.
- **Improves API Contracts:** When exposing data as JSON, a field like `"active": true` is universally understood.
- **Encourages Self-Documenting Code:** Variable names combined with `bool` values often read like plain English.

Memory Usage of Booleans

In Go, a `bool` occupies **1 byte (8 bits)** of memory. Only one bit is technically needed to represent `true` or `false`, but Go (like most modern languages) uses a full byte for alignment and simplicity. This keeps boolean variables predictable in size and efficient to use in data structures.

However, in enterprise applications, there are times when **two states aren't enough.** You may need to represent

- `true` → Explicitly set to yes
- `false` → Explicitly set to no
- *undecided/not provided* → No value yet

A simple `bool` cannot capture this third state. There are two common approaches in Go:

1. **Boolean Pointer (`*bool`)**

    - `nil` = No value yet
    - `true` or `false` = Explicitly set
    - ☑ Clearer in meaning (distinguishes between "not filled" and "set to false")
    - ✕ Uses more memory (a pointer is 4 or 8 bytes, depending on architecture)

    Example

    ```
    var approved *bool // nil means not decided yet
    yes := true
    approved = &yes      // set explicitly to true
    ```

2. **Small Integer (e.g., `int8`)**

    - `0` = Not decided.
    - `1` = True.
    - `2` = False.
    - ☑ Uses a single byte (efficient).
    - ✕ Less clear—the meaning of each number must be documented, and mistakes are easier.

    Example

    ```
    const (
        Unknown int8 = iota
        Yes
        No
    )
    var approved int8 = Unknown
    ```

Summary

- **Use `bool` for pure yes/no states.** Don't substitute integers or strings when two values are enough. A `bool` communicates intent directly and is the most efficient choice.
- **Name booleans clearly.** Good names read like a question or state: `isOperational`, `hasPassenger`, `inService`. Avoid vague names like `flag`, `status`, or `value`.
- **Don't overload a boolean.** If a field requires more than two states (e.g., *Operational, Maintenance, Decommissioned*), model it explicitly with an `enum` (`const` + `iota`) instead of forcing it into a `bool`.
- **For three-state logic (true/false/undecided):**
- Prefer a pointer to bool (`*bool`) when clarity is more important than memory efficiency. This is common in APIs, JSON payloads, and user forms, where "not provided" is distinct from `false`.
- Use a small integer with constants (e.g., `int8` + `iota`) when you need compact storage for high-volume data and still require a third state.
- **Be explicit.** Whether you use a pointer or an enum, make the third state visible in the type system instead of hiding it behind a "special meaning" of a normal `bool`.

Quick Practice

1. Define a boolean `isEmergencyVehicle` and set it to `true`. Print it with a clear message.
2. Write a program that toggles a variable `doorOpen` from `false` to `true` and prints both states.
3. Suppose your system needs to represent three states for a bus: *Active, Inactive,* and *Under Maintenance*. Why is a boolean insufficient? What Go feature (already learned in the "Integers" section) could solve this?

Strings

A **string** in Go is more than just text. Technically, it is an **immutable sequence of bytes**, always encoded as UTF-8. That immutability is a design choice: once a string is created, it cannot be modified. If you build a new string, Go allocates new memory. This gives safety and predictability in large systems but has performance implications you must be aware of.

In enterprise projects, strings are everywhere—user names, API payloads, JSON messages, file paths, and database queries. Because they are so common, understanding how Go stores and handles strings is critical for both **correctness** and **performance**.

Where Strings Live in Memory

- A string value in Go is represented internally as a **pointer to a byte array** plus its length.
- Short-lived string literals may live on the **stack**, but most strings (especially those created at runtime or passed between functions) are stored on the **heap**.
- Because strings are immutable, multiple variables can safely reference the same underlying bytes without risk of accidental modification.

This design makes strings cheap to copy (only the pointer + length are copied), but expensive to modify (any change creates a new allocation).

Interpreted Strings (Double Quotes " ")

Interpreted strings process escape sequences like `\n` (newline), `\t` (tab), `\"` (quote), and Unicode escapes (`\uXXXX`).

```
s1 := "Bus line:\n\"Express-42\""
fmt.Println(s1)
```

Output

```
Bus line:
"Express-42"
```

This style is best for **user-facing text**, log messages, or anywhere you need to embed escapes for formatting.

Raw Strings (Backticks ` `)

Raw strings span multiple lines and do **not** process escape sequences. Everything between backticks is taken literally.

```
s2 := `{
  "vehicle": "Bus",
  "role": "PublicTransport"
}`
fmt.Println(s2)
```

Output

```
{
  "vehicle": "Bus",
  "role": "PublicTransport"
}
```

Raw strings are invaluable in enterprise projects: they make it easier to embed **SQL queries**, **JSON samples**, or **multi-line configuration values** without worrying about escape characters.

Performance Considerations

- **Immutability:** Modifying strings creates new allocations. For heavy manipulation, use `strings.Builder` for efficiency.
- **Slicing:** Taking a substring does not copy bytes immediately—it reuses the underlying array. Be careful: holding a small slice of a very large string can keep the entire large string in memory.
- **Interop:** Converting between `string` and `[]byte` copies the data. Avoid unnecessary conversions in performance-sensitive code (e.g., JSON processing at scale).

Summary

By now, you've seen how Go offers a small but precise set of primitive types: integers, floats, complex numbers, booleans, and strings. The real skill of a professional Go developer is not just knowing the syntax, but **choosing the right type for the right job**. In enterprise systems, the wrong type can waste memory, introduce subtle bugs, or make your APIs harder to understand.

The first lesson is about **size and efficiency**. Always pick the *smallest safe type*. If you need to track up to 60,000 passengers, `uint16` is plenty. Using `int64` for the same field wastes 6 extra bytes per record. That may seem trivial, but over millions of records, it becomes gigabytes of unnecessary memory. Small types scale better when your data volume grows.

Second, **model your domain rules directly in the type system**. If something can't be negative—like a vehicle's manufacture year or passenger capacity—use an unsigned integer (`uint16`, `uint32`). This way, the compiler itself prevents invalid values from even entering your system. Correctness enforced by types is far stronger than correctness enforced by comments.

Third, **don't misuse floats**. They are perfect for measurements such as average speed or fuel consumption, but dangerous for money or counts that must be exact. A bus fare of `$15.75` should be stored as `1575` cents in an `int64`, not as `15.75` in a float. Precision in financial data is business-critical, and integer arithmetic guarantees it.

Fourth, **use strings only for text**. Strings are immutable UTF-8 byte sequences—great for names, routes, and JSON payloads—but they are memory-heavy compared to integers. Don't encode IDs, numbers, or enums as strings unless there is a real need. An integer is faster to compare and smaller to store.

Finally, **use booleans for binary states instead of conventions**. `isOperational := true` communicates intent immediately, while `status := 1` forces every reader to guess what `1` means. In APIs, booleans also produce self-documenting contracts: `"active": true` is unambiguous across languages and systems. If you need more than two states, don't stretch a boolean—model an explicit enumeration with constants and `iota`.

Quick Practice

1. Why is choosing `uint16` for `manufactureYear` better than `int`? What would go wrong if you allowed negatives?

2. Represent a $2.50 bus fare as `int64` cents. Why is this safer than `float32`?

3. Define a `bool` named `isEmergencyVehicle` and set it to `true`. What does it communicate better than `int isEmergency = 1`?
4. Write an interpreted string with a newline and quotes. Then write a raw string with multi-line JSON. Compare outputs.
5. Imagine storing ten million vehicle records. Why would picking the smallest safe integer type matter for memory usage?

Variables and Constants

Before we can act on data, we must give it a home.

Variables and constants are the containers of Go programs. They define where data lives, how long it lives, and whether it can change. Choosing the right form (mutable variable, immutable constant, or pointer reference) is essential in enterprise systems where clarity and correctness matter.

Declaring Variables

In Go, you declare variables with the `var` keyword or with the short declaration operator `:=`.

```
var platformName string = "GoServices" // explicit type
var totalVehicles int                  // declared, zero value assigned
totalVehicles = 100                    // assigned later
isOperational := true                  // short declaration, type inferred
```

- **`var`**: Can be used anywhere (package or function scope), with or without an initializer
- **`:=`**: Declares and initializes in one step, type inferred, but only valid inside functions

Zero Values

In Go, variables are always initialized—if you don't give a value, they receive the **zero value** for their type.

- Numbers → `0`
- Booleans → `false`
- Strings → `""` (empty string)
- Reference types (pointers, slices, maps, channels, funcs, interfaces) → `nil`

This design avoids "uninitialized variable" bugs that plague other languages.

```
var fleetSize int
var active bool
var route string
fmt.Println(fleetSize, active, route) // 0 false ""
```

Constants and iota

Constants in Go are declared with the `const` keyword. Unlike variables, constants are evaluated at compile time and **cannot change at runtime**. This has two major implications in enterprise applications:

1. **Performance:** Because constants are embedded directly into the compiled binary, no memory is allocated at runtime. A `const` does not consume heap or stack space the way a variable does. This reduces memory pressure and avoids needless lookups.

2. **Correctness:** Constants make your intent explicit. By marking a value as constant, you signal that it is fundamental to the system and should never change during execution.

   ```
   const DefaultCountryCode = "US"
   ```

Here, the compiler substitutes `"US"` everywhere the constant is used. There is no variable stored in memory, just a literal baked into the program.

Enterprise Tip You can't take the address of a constant using &, since constants don't occupy memory—they're replaced with literal values at compile time.

Enumerations with iota

Go provides the identifier `iota` to simplify constant definitions. It starts at `0` in each `const` block and increases by `1` for each new line. This makes it perfect for enums:

```
const (
    RolePublicTransport = iota // 0
    RoleEmergency              // 1
    RolePrivateUse             // 2
)
```

These values are assigned automatically: `0, 1, 2`. This avoids manual numbering and keeps your code clean.

Going Beyond 0,1,2

`iota` isn't just a counter—it's a powerful tool for generating related constants programmatically. Each time a new constant is declared within a `const` block, `iota` increases by one, but you're not limited to using it as a plain number. Because `iota` can be part of expressions, you can derive more meaningful patterns—such as bit flags, scaled units, or enumerations with custom offsets—directly at compile time.

This makes your constant definitions cleaner, less error-prone, and easier to maintain as the system evolves.

Bit Flags (Powers of Two)

Bit flags are a classic way to represent multiple boolean states within a single integer.

Instead of using separate variables or fields for each feature, each bit in the integer acts as a switch—**1** for "on" and **0** for "off."

Because each flag is defined as a distinct power of two, they don't overlap when combined.

```
const (
    FeatureGPS = 1 << iota // 1 << 0 = 1  → binary: 001
    FeatureWiFi            // 1 << 1 = 2  → binary: 010
```

```
    FeatureCamera              // 1 << 2 = 4  → binary: 100
)
```

You can **combine** multiple features using the bitwise **OR (|)** operator.

It turns on every bit that's set in either operand:

```
mask := FeatureGPS | FeatureCamera // binary: 001 | 100 → 101 (decimal 5)
```

Now mask holds 101 in binary—meaning *GPS* and *Camera* are on; *WiFi* is off.

To **check** if a feature is enabled, use the bitwise **AND (&)** operator. It keeps only the bits that are set in *both* operands:

```
fmt.Println("Has WiFi?", (mask&FeatureWiFi) != 0) // false
```

In this example, the variable mask represents a device that has GPS and Camera enabled, but not WiFi. The & operator checks whether a specific bit is set, and the | operator merges multiple flags into one value.

Tip Bit flags are common in enterprise systems, especially when representing permissions, feature toggles, or configuration states efficiently.

Units and Scaling

iota can also generate scaled constants like kilobytes, megabytes, and gigabytes. Because binary systems operate in powers of two, a left shift (1 << n) is an efficient way to express these multipliers.

Each shift moves the bit one place to the left—doubling its value every time.

```
const (
    KB = 1 << (10 * iota) // 1 << 10 = 1024
    MB                    // 1 << 20 = 1,048,576
    GB                    // 1 << 30 = 1,073,741,824
)
```

This is common in enterprise code when defining buffer sizes, memory limits, or storage quotas.

Custom Offsets

By default, `iota` starts from 0 within each `const` block. However, sometimes 0 doesn't make sense as a valid value—for example, in cases where 0 should mean "unset", "unknown", or "not yet initialized". In such cases, you can **shift the starting point** by adding an offset.

```
const (
    StatusActive = iota + 1 // 1
    StatusInactive          // 2
    StatusMaintenance       // 3
)
```

Here, we added +1 to avoid having 0 as a valid status—useful when 0 should mean "unset" or "unknown."

Enterprise Lessons Use plain **`iota`** for sequential enums like roles, statuses, or categories.

Combine with shifts (**<<**) for bit flags when you need compact boolean combinations.

Use formulas for units, offsets, or scaled constants.

Be cautious with persistence: once stored in a database or API, never change the order of `iota` constants, or you'll silently break old data.

Why Constants Improve Performance and Clarity

- **No Allocation:** Constants live in the compiled code, not in runtime memory. Accessing a constant is effectively free.
- **Immutable by Design:** Prevents accidental reassignment. A configuration like `MaxPassengers = 50` should never become 51 mid-flight.

- **Safer Than Magic Numbers:** Using `const TimeoutSeconds = 30` communicates meaning, avoids duplication, and prevents mistakes when the same value appears in multiple places.
- **Stronger Contracts:** Enums with `iota` give your code a clear, typed vocabulary instead of relying on arbitrary integers or strings.

Example: Constants in the Transportation System

```
const (
    VehicleStatusOperational = iota
    VehicleStatusMaintenance
    VehicleStatusDecommissioned
)

const DefaultMaxPassengers = 60

func main() {
    fmt.Println("Default capacity:", DefaultMaxPassengers)
    fmt.Println("Maintenance code:", VehicleStatusMaintenance)
}
```

Here:

- `DefaultMaxPassengers` is baked into the binary, so checking it at runtime has zero memory overhead.
- `VehicleStatusMaintenance` provides a stable, readable code for APIs and databases.

Enterprise Lessons Use `const` for values that should never change (e.g., defaults, units, timeouts).

Use `iota` to model enums (statuses, roles, categories), but be careful when persisting them.

Replace "magic numbers" or hard-coded strings with named constants to improve readability and maintainability.

Prefer constants to variables for compile-time values to save memory and prevent accidental reassignment.

Scope and Shadowing

Scope and shadowing are not only about naming; it also has other aspects; take it seriously.

Scope

In Go, **scope** defines where a variable is visible and usable in the source code. Variables can be declared in several places, and their scope depends on where they are introduced:

- **Package Scope:** A variable declared outside any function is visible to all functions in the same package. If the name starts with a capital letter, it's also exported and visible to other packages.

```
package main
var platformName = "Transport System" // package scope
```

- **Function Scope (Local Variables):** Variables declared inside a function are visible only within that function. These are the most common and usually the most efficient, since they often stay on the stack.

```
func main() {
    var fleetSize = 100 // visible only inside main
    fmt.Println(fleetSize)
}
```

- **Block Scope:** Variables declared inside a block (`if`, `for`, `switch`, `{ ... }`) are visible only within that block.

```
if true {
    status := "operational" // visible only inside this if
    fmt.Println(status)
}
```

- **Function Parameters:** Parameters are local variables whose scope is limited to the function body.

```
func addVehicles(count int) int {
    return count + 10 // 'count' is scoped to this function
}
```

- **Struct Fields:** Fields of a struct are not variables in the same sense, but they have scope tied to the struct. They are accessed through the struct instance.

  ```go
  type Vehicle struct {
      ID     string // field scope inside Vehicle
      Active bool
  }
  ```

If you want to grow into a senior enterprise-level developer, you must think not only about correctness but also about **memory usage** in every decision—including how and where you define variables. The shorter the scope of a variable, the shorter its lifetime, and the less work the garbage collector must do. Defining variables in the smallest possible scope is not just stylistic; it is a technical optimization that keeps systems fast and lean.

For example:

```go
var cache = make([]byte, 10<<20) // 10 MB
```

A package-level variable like this will stay in memory for the entire lifetime of the program, even if only one function ever needs it. If instead you define it inside the function that uses it, Go can reclaim it when the function ends. In enterprise applications, careless scope choices like this accumulate into **memory leaks**—not because Go forgets to free memory, but because your variables are kept alive longer than necessary.

- **Short-lived variables (function scope)** are typically allocated on the **stack**, which is fast to allocate and automatically freed when the function ends.
- **Long-lived variables (referenced outside their scope)** may escape to the **heap**, which has a higher allocation cost and must be garbage-collected later.

Shadowing

In Go, variables follow **lexical scope**, meaning their visibility is determined by where they are declared in the source code.

When a new variable with the same name is declared inside a narrower scope (such as inside a function or block), it **shadows**—or hides—the variable from the outer scope.

```
var status = "global"

func check() {
    status := "local"     // shadows the global status
    fmt.Println(status)  // prints: local
}
```

Inside `check()`, a new `status` variable is created that exists only within the function. The global `status` remains unchanged and inaccessible within this scope. This behavior is sometimes useful for isolating state, but it can also lead to **subtle bugs**—especially when := is mistakenly used instead of =.

Enterprise Tip Use go vet or linters like staticcheck to detect accidental shadowing.

As a best practice, prefer = when you intend to update an existing variable and reserve := for new declarations.

Avoid reusing variable names across scopes unless it significantly improves readability.

Enterprise Impact

- **Performance:** Unnecessary heap allocations slow down programs and increase GC load. Keeping variables scoped tightly inside functions often avoids escapes and improves performance.
- **Memory Usage:** Variables at package scope or heap-allocated values live much longer. Use them only when truly needed; otherwise, prefer local scope.
- **Clarity:** Avoid shadowing—in large enterprise codebases, it confuses readers and leads to costly bugs. Use clear, distinct names that match their scope.

Pointers

A **pointer** is a variable that stores the address of another variable. Instead of holding the value itself, it "points" to where the value lives in memory. Pointers are a fundamental tool in Go for controlling data sharing, avoiding expensive copies, and expressing optional values.

In Go, two operators define pointer behavior:

- **& (address-of):** Retrieves the memory address of a variable
- *** (dereference):** Accesses or modifies the value stored at that address

```
package main

import "fmt"

func main() {
    x := 10
    p := &x       //p is of type *int, points to x
    *p = 20       // modifies x through the pointer
    fmt.Println(x) // prints 20
}
```

Here, `p` doesn't contain `10` directly—it contains *the location of* `x`. When you write `*p = 20`, you're saying: *go to that address and update the value there.* This lets multiple parts of your program work with the same data efficiently.

Key Rules in Go

- **No Pointer Arithmetic**

  Unlike C or C++, Go doesn't allow expressions like `p + 1`. This eliminates a whole class of memory corruption bugs and helps keep Go **memory-safe by design**.

- **Nil Pointers**

  A pointer can hold `nil`, meaning it points to nothing. This is useful when modeling optional or unset values.

- **Pointer Types**

  The type *T means "pointer to a value of type T". For example, *int and *string are distinct pointer types—you can't mix them.

Enterprise Tip Use pointers when you need to modify data inside a function, share large structures without copying, or represent optional or unset values. However, avoid using pointers by default—Go favors **clarity over cleverness**, and unnecessary indirection often makes code harder to reason about.

Why Pointers Matter in Enterprise Systems

In enterprise software, performance and data consistency matter just as much as correctness. Pointers play a crucial role in achieving both. They allow different parts of a system to share and modify the same data without unnecessary copying—essential when working with large domain models, network payloads, or concurrent components. Pointers make it possible to mutate data in place, pass lightweight references across layers, and design APIs that operate efficiently on shared state.

Mutating Data

By default, Go passes arguments **by value**, which means every function call receives a copy of its input.

For small types like integers or booleans, this is fine. But for large structs—such as configuration objects, database entities, or network messages—copying can be both **costly** and **error-prone**.

Passing a pointer avoids that overhead and lets you update the original object directly.

```go
type Vehicle struct {
    ID     string
    Active bool
}
```

```go
func Activate(v *Vehicle) {
    v.Active = true // modifies original
}
```

Here, `Activate` receives a pointer to a `Vehicle`. When it sets `v.Active = true`, the change is reflected in the original variable—no copy, no extra memory, no wasted time.

Enterprise Tip Use pointers when your function's goal is to modify an object's state or when you're passing large data structures around frequently. For simple data or immutable patterns, prefer value semantics—they're safer and easier to reason about.

Avoiding Expensive Copies

Copying large data structures—such as slices or maps containing thousands of records—can quickly become a performance bottleneck. Every copy consumes memory bandwidth and CPU time, both of which scale poorly as datasets grow. By using pointers, you pass **references** instead of entire objects, allowing multiple components to work with the same data in memory.

This approach reduces allocation overhead, minimizes garbage collection pressure, and keeps enterprise systems responsive under heavy load.

Optional Values

A plain bool or int cannot represent "not provided." But *bool can be nil, giving you three states: true, false, or "unset." This is common in APIs where a missing field must be distinguished from an explicit value.

```go
var approved *bool // nil = undecided
yes := true
approved = &yes
```

Method Receivers

In Go, methods can be defined on either value receivers or pointer receivers. The choice determines whether the method works on a copy of the struct or on the original value.

- **Value Receiver (`func (v Vehicle)`)**: The method operates on a **copy** of the struct.

  Changes inside the method do **not** affect the original value. Best for small, immutable types or when the method only reads data.

- **Pointer Receiver (`func (v *Vehicle)`)**: The method operates on a **pointer** to the struct. This allows the method to modify the original value and avoids copying large structs, improving performance.

Performance Considerations

Pointers influence not just how data behaves—but also how efficiently your program runs.

Understanding the trade-offs between **stack**, **heap**, **copying**, and **garbage collection (GC)** helps you write faster and more predictable enterprise Go code.

- **Stack vs. Heap:** Local variables are typically allocated on the **stack**, which is fast and automatically freed when the function returns. However, if you take the address of a local variable and store it elsewhere (e.g., return it or assign it to a global), Go must **promote** that variable to the **heap**, where it's managed by the garbage collector. Heap allocations are slower and add GC overhead.

- **Copy vs. Reference:** Copying large structs consumes memory and CPU time. Passing pointers avoids these copies but introduces shared mutable state, which can make code harder to reason about or debug. Choose pointer passing deliberately, not by habit.

- **GC Pressure:** Every heap allocation increases the garbage collector's workload.

- In high-performance systems—such as servers processing thousands of requests per second—this can translate into noticeable latency. Prefer stack-allocated, short-lived values whenever possible, and reserve heap allocations for data that truly needs to persist or be shared.

Summary

Pointers are a tool of precision. Used wisely, they make enterprise Go systems both efficient and expressive; used carelessly, they introduce subtle bugs and unnecessary complexity.

- **Use pointers to**
  - Mutate data across functions or methods.
  - Avoid copying large structs.
  - Represent optional or nullable fields.
- **Use value types for**
  - Small structs and immutable data.
  - Simple, self-contained values where copying is cheap and intent is clear.
- **Avoid overusing pointers.**

  For primitive types like `int` or `bool`, prefer values unless you explicitly need `nil` as a third state. Excessive pointer use increases indirection and cognitive load.
- **Always check for `nil` before dereferencing** a pointer in production code to prevent panics.
- **Use pointer receivers** when a method needs to modify its receiver or when the struct is large enough that copying it would be costly.

Balancing stack use, heap allocation, and pointer sharing is a cornerstone of high-performance Go design. Profiling tools such as `go test -bench`, `pprof`, and `go build -gcflags="-m"` can help you detect hidden allocations, measure GC pressure, and tune performance before scaling up.

Quick Practice

1. Write a function `deactivate(v *Vehicle)` that sets `v.Active = false`. Call it and show that the change persists.
2. Define a pointer to an `int`, set it to `nil`, and check for `nil` before dereferencing.
3. Create a function `increment(n *int)` that adds 1 to its argument via pointer. Why is this more efficient than returning the new value and reassigning?

Operators

Once you've chosen the right types, the next question is how to *act* on them. Operators are the **verbs of Go**—concise, composable, and predictable. They define how values interact, from arithmetic and comparison to pointer manipulation and bit-level operations that drive high-performance systems.

In enterprise code, operators matter less for novelty and more for **precision and clarity**. They embody Go's philosophy: *no surprises, no implicit conversions, no hidden cost.* Every operator has well-defined behavior, strict type rules, and performance you can reason about.

Table 5-5 summarizes Go's major operator categories and the role each category plays in everyday computation and program control.

Table 5-5. *Categories of operators in Go*

Category	Operators	Purpose
Arithmetic	+, -, *, /, %	Perform basic mathematical calculations such as addition, subtraction, multiplication, division, and remainder.
Comparison	==, !=, <, <=, >, >=	Compare values for equality or ordering to make decisions based on their relationships.
Logical	&& , || , !	Combine or invert boolean conditions to control program flow through logical evaluation.
Bitwise	&, |, ^, &^, <<, >>	Manipulate individual bits for efficient flag handling, state encoding, and low-level data operations.
Assignment shorthands	+=, -=, *=, /=, %=, &=, |=, ^=, &^=	Update variable values in place while reducing repetition and improving code clarity.
Address/ dereference	& (address-of), * (pointer dereference)	Access or modify values indirectly through their memory addresses.
Postfix increments	i++, i--	Increase or decrease a variable by one as a standalone statement for concise counter updates.

Let's explore them with examples relevant to enterprise systems.

Arithmetic and Comparison

Arithmetic and comparison operators form the backbone of all decision-making in software. They **transform data**, while comparison operators **give it meaning**—allowing systems to reason, react, and enforce business rules.

```go
package main

import "fmt"

func main() {
    vehicleCount := 3
    vehicleCount += 2 // now 5
```

```
    fmt.Println("Total vehicles:", vehicleCount)

    fmt.Println("Fleet big enough?", vehicleCount >= 5)
}
```

Here, we increased the vehicle count and then checked if the fleet is large enough. In enterprise code, such comparisons drive business logic: Is the bus full? Has the quota been exceeded?

Logical Operators

Logical operators evaluate boolean expressions and determine how conditions combine, invert, or short-circuit.

In enterprise systems, they form the backbone of decision-making—from service readiness checks to complex access policies.

```
package main

import "fmt"

func main() {
    isOperational := true
    hasDriver := false
    inMaintenance := false

    if (isOperational && hasDriver) || !inMaintenance {
        fmt.Println("Bus cleared for temporary service")
    } else {
        fmt.Println("Bus not ready")
    }
}
```

In this example, the bus runs only if

- It is operational **and** has a driver (&&).
- **Or** it is **not** in maintenance (`!inMaintenance`).

Table 5-6 provides an overview of Go's logical operators and how they behave in boolean expressions.

Table 5-6. *Logical operators in Go*

Operator	Meaning	Description	Example
&&	Logical AND	Returns true only if **both** operands are true.	isOperational && hasDriver
||	Logical OR	Returns true if any of the operands are true and false if both are false.	isOperational || hasDriver
!	Logical NOT	Inverts a boolean value; turns true to false and vice versa.	!inMaintenance

Enterprise Lesson Go's logical operators use short-circuit evaluation to improve efficiency and safety:

&& stops evaluation as soon as one condition is false.

|| stops as soon as one condition is true.

This prevents redundant or unsafe operations—particularly important when conditions trigger API calls, database lookups, or external checks.

Bitwise Operators

Bitwise operators work at the level of individual bits. While rare in business logic, they are extremely powerful for **feature flags**, **permissions**, and **system-level programming**.

```go
const (
    FeatureGPS = 1 << iota // 0001
    FeatureWiFi            // 0010
    FeatureCamera          // 0100
)

mask := FeatureGPS | FeatureCamera // 0101

fmt.Println("Has GPS?", (mask&FeatureGPS) != 0)
fmt.Println("Has WiFi?", (mask&FeatureWiFi) != 0)
```

Here, we represent vehicle features using bit flags. Instead of storing multiple booleans or strings, one integer stores all features compactly. Checking if a feature exists is just a single bitwise operation—fast and memory efficient.

Address and Dereference

Go also lets you work with memory addresses directly. Using & gives the address of a variable; * dereferences it.

```
x := 10
p := &x    // p holds the address of x
*p = 20    // update x through the pointer
fmt.Println("x is now:", x)
```

You'll use this pattern often when working with structs, passing values into functions, or when you need to avoid copying large data. You can go deeper into pointers in the "Pointers" section of this chapter.

Postfix Increments

Go supports i++ and i--, but unlike C or Java, they are **statements only**—they cannot appear inside expressions. This makes code less error-prone and easier to read.

```
counter := 0
counter++ // valid
// fmt.Println(counter++) // invalid: not an expression
```

Summary

- **Use arithmetic and comparison naturally**—Go performs integer division by discarding any fractional part (it **truncates toward zero**).
- **Logical operators** keep code readable when combining multiple conditions. Prefer clear variable names (`isOperational && hasDriver`) over cryptic checks.

- **Bitwise operators** shine in performance-sensitive code. Use them for flags or permissions, but document the meaning of each bit clearly.
- **Pointer operators** (`&`, `*`) are essential for memory control and passing references efficiently.
- **Avoid clever tricks.** Go's philosophy favors readability over terse operator-heavy code.

Quick Practice

1. Write a small program that increments a `passengerCount` variable using both += and ++. Print the results.
2. Define three bit flags for vehicle roles: `PublicTransport`, `Emergency`, `PrivateUse`. Combine them in one integer, and check if a given vehicle is marked `Emergency`.
3. Why does Go forbid using `i++` inside an expression (e.g., `fmt.Println(i++)`)? How does this improve clarity compared to languages like C or Java?

Collections: Arrays, Slices, and Maps

Go provides three core collection types: **arrays, slices, and maps**. Unlike some languages where these structures are abstracted away, Go makes their design explicit. This forces you to think about memory layout, growth strategy, and reference semantics—the kind of details that make you a professional developer.

Arrays

An **array** in Go is a fixed-size sequence of elements. Its size is part of its type.

```
a := [3]string{"Bus", "Car", "Bike"}
```

- `[3]string` means an array of exactly three strings.
- Arrays have **value semantics**: assigning one array to another makes a full copy.

```
a := [3]string{"Bus", "Car", "Bike"}
b := a
b[0] = "Truck"
fmt.Println(a[0], b[0]) // Bus Truck
```

Here, a remains unchanged because arrays are copied by value.

When to use arrays in enterprise projects:

- When working with fixed-size binary formats (network packets, hashes, cryptographic keys)
- When you must guarantee the size at compile time

Enterprise Tip Arrays are less common in everyday Go. Most real-world code uses **slices** for flexibility.

Slices

A **slice** is a dynamic, flexible view over an array. Internally, a slice is a small struct with three fields:

- A pointer to the underlying array
- A length (number of elements it sees)
- A capacity (how many elements can fit before reallocation)

```
s := make([]string, 0, 4)    // len=0, cap=4
s = append(s, "Bus", "Car")
t := s[:1]                   // sub-slice of s
s[0] = "Train"               // visible through both s and t
fmt.Println(t)               // [Train]
fmt.Println(len(s), cap(s)) // 2 4
```

Key Properties of Slices

- **Reference Semantics:** Multiple slices can view the same backing array.
- **Capacity Growth:** When capacity is exceeded, Go allocates a new array (usually doubling capacity), and append returns a new slice pointing to it.

Always reassign append:

```
s = append(s, "Bike") // never ignore the return value
```

Performance Tips Use `make([]T, len, cap)` when you know the approximate size to avoid repeated allocations.

Avoid repeatedly appending single items in hot paths; preallocate capacity when possible.

A tiny benchmark makes this difference concrete. The following code compares appending to a slice without preallocation vs. preallocating the exact size:

```
import "testing"

const n = 100_000

func BenchmarkAppendNoPrealloc(b *testing.B) {
   for i := 0; i < b.N; i++ {
       var s []int
       for j := 0; j < n; j++ {
           s = append(s, j)
       }
   }
}

func BenchmarkAppendPrealloc(b *testing.B) {
   for i := 0; i < b.N; i++ {
       s := make([]int, 0, n)
```

```
        for j := 0; j < n; j++ {
            s = append(s, j)
        }
    }
}
```

You can run this benchmark using the following command:

```
go test -bench=. -benchmem
```

Depending on your environment, you can see similar output like this:

```
goos: linux
goarch: amd64
pkg: example.com/transport/samplecode
cpu: Intel(R) Core(TM) i7-4702MQ CPU @ 2.20GHz
BenchmarkAppendNoPrealloc-8  741   2892743 ns/op  4101410 B/op  28 allocs/op
BenchmarkAppendPrealloc-8    4042  467746 ns/op   802827 B/op   1 allocs/op
```

The benchmark report lists each benchmark, how many times it ran, and key metrics per operation:

- BenchmarkAppendNoPrealloc-8 ran 741 iterations across 8 goroutines; each took ~2.89 ms, allocated ~4.1 MB of memory, and triggered 28 allocations.
- BenchmarkAppendPrealloc-8 ran 4,042 iterations; each took ~0.47 ms, allocated ~0.8 MB, and only 1 allocation.
- The preallocated version runs significantly faster (about 6×) and uses roughly one-fifth the memory, with only a single allocation because the capacity is known upfront.
- The PASS line shows all benchmarks completed successfully, and the module's entire benchmark suite finished in ~4.24 seconds on your machine.

You will learn more about test and benchmarking later in this book.

Slice ↔ Array Conversion (Go 1.20+)

Go treats **arrays** and **slices** differently: an array is a fixed-size value ([N]T), while a slice is a lightweight *view* over an array ([]T). Go 1.20 made it easier to move between them in **two distinct ways**—a **safe copying conversion** and an **advanced reinterpretation via pointer conversion**. Knowing which is which (and why) matters for both **correctness** and **memory usage**.

Safe Copy Conversion (Slice → Array): Makes a New Array

You can convert a slice to a **pointer to an array** (not an array value) as long as the slice has **at least N elements**. This **does not copy**; it reinterprets the first N elements of the slice as an array.

```
s := []byte("ROLE")          // len=4, cap≥4
ap := (*[4]byte)(s)          // reinterpret first 4 bytes; no copy
(*ap)[0] = 'H'
fmt.Println(string(s))       // "HOLE"  (same backing storage)
```

When to use it: only in **performance-critical code** that must avoid copying and you control the lifetimes. It's powerful but sharp: both names now **share the same underlying memory**.

Memory caution: Because this keeps referencing the original backing array, **holding ap (or the slice) can keep a large array alive**. If you only need a small prefix and the original array is huge, prefer a **copy** to avoid retaining megabytes of unused memory.

- Tip []T, [N]T, and [...]T: What the brackets mean.
- []T—**Slice Type**: Dynamic view over an array (pointer, length, capacity).
- [N]T—**Array Type**: Fixed-size N is part of the type (value semantics).
- [...]T{...}—**Array Literal with Inferred Length**: The compiler counts elements for you.

Examples

```
// Slice type and literal
var ids []string                    // nil slice
ids = []string{"BUS-001", "BUS-002"}
```

```
// Array types and literals
var a1 [3]int                 // zero-initialized array of length 3
a2 := [3]int{10, 20, 30}      // explicit length
a3 := [...]int{10, 20, 30}    // length inferred as 3

// Convert slice -> array (copy) when len matches
s := []int{10, 20, 30}
a := [3]int(s)                // copies 3 elements into new array value

// Convert slice -> *array (no copy) when len >= N
p := (*[3]int)(s)             // reinterprets first 3 elements;
                              shares storage
```

Rule of Thumb

- Use **`[N]T(s)`** when you **want a separate array** and are okay with copying.
- Use **`(*[N]T)(s)`** only when you **must avoid copying** and you can guarantee safe lifetimes (both names mutate the same bytes).

Slice Operators

Go provides concise syntax for working with slices and arrays through the **slice operator** `[low:high]` and its **three-index variant** `[low:high:max]`.

```
s := []string{"Bus", "Car", "Train", "Bike"}

a := s[1:3]     // elements 1-2 → ["Car", "Train"]
b := s[:2]      // from start → ["Bus", "Car"]
c := s[2:]      // from index 2 to end → ["Train", "Bike"]
d := s[1:3:3]   // low=1, high=3, max=3 (capacity capped to 2)
```

Parameters

- **`low`**: Starting index *(inclusive)*
- **`high`**: Ending index *(exclusive)*
- **`max`**: Optional capacity bound; limits how much the new slice can grow via `append`

The slice operator creates a **new slice header** (pointer, length, capacity) referencing the same underlying array. No elements are copied—slicing is an **O(1)** operation in both time and memory.

Key Concepts

- **No Copy by Default**

  Slicing creates a new *view* over existing data. Both views share the same memory, so changes in one are visible to the other.

- **Capacity Control with `[low:high:max]`**

  The three-index form limits how far the new slice can grow, preventing accidental overwrites of unrelated data when appending.

- **Bounds Safety**

  All indices must satisfy `0` ≤ `low` ≤ `high` ≤ `max` ≤ `cap(s)`—otherwise, Go panics.

  This runtime check eliminates the unsafe pointer arithmetic common in C.

```
s := make([]int, 0, 5)
t := s[:3]     // len=3, cap=5
u := s[:3:3]   // len=3, cap=3 → appending to u won't overwrite s
```

Practical Uses of the Slice Operator

The slice operator is more than a way to "view data." It's a precision tool for controlling how collections grow, shrink, or split in production systems. Below are common, real-world patterns and the reasoning behind them.

1. Splitting Data
   Use slicing to divide a collection into parts—for example, distributing work across goroutines or servers.

   ```
   left, right := s[:n], s[n:]
   ```

   This creates two independent slices referencing the same underlying array. Each can be processed concurrently without copying data, as long as you don't mutate shared elements.

2. Trimming Processed Elements

   As data flows through a pipeline, you can drop the already-processed prefix or suffix efficiently.

   ```
   s = s[1:]            // remove first element
   s = s[:len(s)-1]     // remove last element
   ```

   This doesn't allocate or copy memory—it simply advances the slice's view. Useful for stream processing, queues, or rolling-window algorithms.

3. Deleting Elements

   Go doesn't have a built-in "delete from slice" function, but combining slicing and `append` achieves it cleanly:

   ```
   s = append(s[:i], s[i+1:]...)
   ```

   This pattern removes an element at index `i` while keeping order intact. Under the hood, it reuses the same backing array when capacity allows.

4. Restricting Growth

   When passing sub-slices between components, you may want to prevent them from growing into unrelated memory regions. The three-index form `[low:high:max]` enforces a hard cap on capacity:

   ```
   s = s[:n:n]  // len = n, cap = n
   ```

   Appending to `s` now triggers a reallocation, isolating it from the original backing array—crucial for memory safety in concurrent code.

5. Copy: Clone Slice Data

   `copy(dst, src)` duplicates elements from one slice to another:

   ```
   copied := make([]string, len(vehicles))
   copy(copied, vehicles)
   ```

   Only the smaller length among the two slices is copied. This operation is often used in enterprise systems for **snapshotting** in-memory data safely without mutating the original slice during concurrent reads.

6. Segmenting Arrays

   Slices also work directly on arrays. You can create views or chunks from a fixed array just as you would from a slice:

   ```
   arr := [6]int{10, 20, 30, 40, 50, 60}
   segment := arr[2:5] // [30, 40, 50]
   ```

This is useful in data processing or binary protocols, where arrays serve as static buffers and slices provide flexible access layers.

Enterprise Lesson The slice operator is one of Go's quiet superpowers. Used well, it enables large-scale data handling with minimal allocations and predictable performance. But sub-slices keep references to their backing arrays—so copy out what you truly need to avoid memory leaks. Preallocate with `make` when possible, and use `[low:high:max]` to control growth and isolate concurrent writes.

Maps

A **map** in Go is a built-in hash table that associates keys with values—your primary tool for efficient lookups, counting, and grouping in enterprise code. Maps can be defined as follows:

```
var m map[string]int
```

In this code, map is the go keyword, string is the key type, and int is the value type. Maps offer **O(1) average-time access**, making them ideal for large-scale systems that rely on quick data retrieval—such as caching, indexing, or tracking session state.

Map Operations

Go keeps its map operations minimal and explicit. Each one is fast, readable, and directly tied to Go's design philosophy: **simplicity with performance awareness**.

- Create/Initialize

  You can create a map with the built-in `make` function or a literal:

  ```
  m := make(map[string]int, 100)
  ```

The second argument to make provides an initial capacity hint, reducing rehashing during growth. Alternatively, you can use the following syntax:

```
m := map[string]int{"A": 1, "B": 2}
```

This syntax initializes a map literal with predefined entries.

- Insert/Update

  Adding or updating entries uses simple assignment syntax:

  ```
  m["BUS-001"] = 42
  ```

  If the key doesn't exist, it's created; if it already exists, its value is replaced. This operation runs in **O(1)** time—fast enough for real-time lookups in high-volume systems. **Worst-case complexity** can degrade toward **O(n)** if many keys hash into the same bucket.

- Retrieve (Read)

  Accessing a key returns its value or the **zero value** of the map's value type if the key is missing:

  ```
  v := m["BUS-001"]
  ```

  For int maps, that's 0; for strings, it's ""; for pointers or interfaces, it's nil.

- Existence Check (Comma-ok Idiom)

  To distinguish between a missing key and a zero value, use the **comma-ok** form:

  ```
  v, ok := m["TRAIN-123"]
  ```

Here, ok is true only when the key exists. This small feature prevents subtle logic bugs, especially when zero values carry meaning in business logic (e.g., "zero seats left" vs. "unknown train").

Delete

The built-in delete function removes an entry safely:

```
delete(m, "BUS-001")
```

Deleting a non-existent key does nothing, which keeps cleanup logic simple and idempotent.

Performance Tips

- Preallocate maps with `make(map[K]V, size)` when you know the expected size—this reduces rehashing.
- Maps are not safe for concurrent writes. Use synchronization (e.g., `sync.Map` or explicit locks) in multithreaded enterprise code.
- Don't rely on iteration order: Go intentionally randomizes it.

Using Maps As Sets

In Go, there's no built-in `set` type, but a **map with dummy values** gives you everything you need: insert, delete, membership, and size. The idiomatic choice for a set is

- **`map[K]struct{}`**—the value carries **no information** (presence is enough).
- Avoid **`map[K]bool`** unless you truly need both states (`true`/`false`) for keys already present.

Basic Set Operations

Once you understand that a map can stand in for a set, the actual operations are refreshingly minimal. Adding, checking, and deleting elements all use the same familiar map syntax—no helper library or wrapper type required. Each action translates directly to a simple hash lookup or update, giving you predictable O(1) performance and clear intent. In practice, this makes Go's map-based sets ideal for tasks like tracking active sessions, registered vehicles, or any collection where uniqueness matters more than order.

```
var fleet = make(map[string]struct{}) // empty set

// Add
fleet["BUS-001"] = struct{}{}
```

```go
// Contains
_, ok := fleet["BUS-001"]
fmt.Println("has BUS-001?", ok)

// Remove
delete(fleet, "BUS-001")

// Size
fmt.Println("fleet size:", len(fleet))
```

This is all you need for a fast, idiomatic set.

Why struct{} Instead of bool? (Clarity + Memory)

1. **Clarity of Intent**

   A set represents *presence*, not a true/false payload. With `map[K]bool`, you could accidentally store `false` and later misread "key exists but false" as "key not in set". With `map[K]struct{}`, the value is unambiguous: if the key is present, it's in the set.

2. **Memory Efficiency**

   a. `struct{}` is a **zero-sized** type in Go.

   b. `bool` occupies **1 byte** (and may incur alignment effects inside buckets).

You can verify the value sizes:

```go
import "unsafe"

fmt.Println("size of struct{}:", unsafe.Sizeof(struct{}{})) // 0
fmt.Println("size of bool    :", unsafe.Sizeof(true))       // 1
```

While Go's map has its own bucket overhead (for hashes, keys, and metadata), using a **zero-sized value** means the map **doesn't store any per-element value payload**. With `bool`, every entry stores a value byte (plus potential padding). Across millions of entries, that extra byte per key—and its alignment—adds up, affects cache locality, and increases memory traffic during resizes.

Enterprise Tip If the value conveys no information, don't pay to store it. `map[K]struct{}` is both clearer and leaner.

When Not to Use struct{}

The idiomatic `map[K]struct{}` works perfectly when *existence alone* defines membership. But sometimes your logic needs more nuance—such as distinguishing between an enabled and a disabled element. A common mistake is to overload the set and use a `map[K]bool` to represent both membership and state:

```
enabled["BUS-001"] = true   // active
enabled["BUS-002"] = false  // disabled?
```

At first glance, this looks compact, but it hides a trap. When you read from the map:

```
v := enabled["BUS-002"]
```

And `v` is `false`, you can't tell whether the key **doesn't exist** or the key **exists but is explicitly disabled**. Both return the same value (`false`), and without using the **comma-ok idiom**, you lose information about presence entirely. This leads to silent bugs in production, especially in stateful systems where "not found" and "disabled" mean very different things.

Clean Alternatives

1. **Two Disjoint Sets**—one for each state:

   ```
   enabled  := map[K]struct{}{}
   disabled := map[K]struct{}{}
   ```

   Presence in one of the two maps makes intent explicit. This separation is easy to read and keeps lookups O(1) in both directions.

2. **A Single Map with Richer Payload**—if the value itself carries meaningful data:

   ```
   map[K]time.Time                          // when the key was added
   map[K]struct{ AddedBy, Note string } // metadata for audits or
   tracking
   ```

   By modeling the additional meaning directly, you avoid ambiguous flags and improve type clarity.

Quick Practice

1. Convert a `[]string` of vehicle IDs into a `map[string]struct{}` set and print its size.
2. Given two slices `inService` and `underMaintenance`, build two sets and compute:
    - Vehicles that are in service **and not** under maintenance (difference)
    - Vehicles in **both** (intersection)
3. Estimate memory: for five million keys, how many extra bytes do you avoid by using `map[string]struct{}` vs. `map[string]bool`? Explain your reasoning and assumptions.

Common Collections Functions

Go provides a small set of **built-in functions** that work uniformly across its major collection types—**arrays**, **slices**, and **maps**. Instead of adding separate APIs or utility packages, Go favors a minimal, predictable core. This design keeps collections composable and easy to reason about across any scale—from a few records in memory to millions of entries in a service cache.

Below are the most commonly used built-in functions you'll encounter when working with collections:

- `len`: Length of a Collection

    The `len` function returns the number of elements currently stored in a collection:

    ```
    n := len(m)
    ```

    - For **arrays**, it returns the fixed size of the array.
    - For **slices**, it returns the number of accessible elements (which may be smaller than the underlying capacity).
    - For **maps**, it returns the number of key/value pairs currently stored.

len always runs in **constant time (O(1))**, even for large maps or slices, because Go stores size metadata internally. It's evaluated directly by the compiler, not through iteration or function calls.

- cap: Capacity of a Slice

The cap function returns the total storage capacity of a **slice**:

```
capacity := cap(slice)
```

For slices, this is the number of elements that can be stored without triggering a reallocation. Understanding capacity is essential when preallocating large slices for ingestion or streaming pipelines—especially in microservices that process high data volume. For maps, cap is **not defined**; maps grow dynamically under the hood, and the runtime handles resizing automatically.

- make: Allocate and Initialize

make is used to create slices, maps, and channels with their internal memory initialized and ready for use:

```
m := make(map[string]int, 1024)
s := make([]string, 0, 256)
```

Unlike new, which returns a pointer to a zero value, make returns the actual initialized data structure. For maps and slices, preallocating with make improves performance by reducing runtime resizing and garbage collection churn.

Summary

Arrays: Use when size is fixed and known (e.g., cryptographic keys, protocol fields).

Slices: Default choice for ordered collections. Preallocate when possible, watch out for sub-slice memory leaks.

Maps: Best for key/value lookups. Always check existence with comma, ok. Don't rely on iteration order.

Conversions: Use cautiously. Prefer explicit copies to avoid hidden memory retention.

Quick Practice

1. Start with `s := []int{1, 2, 3}`. Keep appending and print `len` and `cap` each time. What growth pattern do you see?
2. Build a `map[string][]string` where the key is a vehicle ID and the value is a slice of roles. Insert at least two vehicles with multiple roles.
3. Convert `[]byte("ROLE")` to `[4]byte` using Go 1.20 slice → array conversion. Print the array.
4. Create a sub-slice of a 10 MB slice, and explain why keeping it alive might leak memory. How would you fix it?

Type Conversion

Go enforces type boundaries strictly. There are no silent promotions, coercions, or implicit casts between types. This design choice is deliberate: it makes every transformation explicit and visible at the call site—a key to reliable enterprise code.

Why Go Demands Explicit Conversion

In many languages, expressions like `int` → `float` or `byte` → `string` may convert implicitly. Go rejects this to protect correctness and performance. When you convert, you are signaling *intent*: you know that a copy, truncation, or reinterpretation is about to happen.

This explicitness gives Go code a rare form of safety—one that scales gracefully in enterprise systems with many hands touching the same codebase.

The General Rule

To convert between types, wrap the value in the target type's name.

```
var i32 int32 = 100
var i64 int64 = int64(i32)     // explicit widening
var f   float64 = float64(i64) // numeric → floating-point
```

This pattern works consistently:

- `float64(i)` converts an integer to a float.
- `int(f)` converts a float to an integer (fractional part is truncated).
- `string([]byte{65,66,67})` converts bytes into `"ABC"`.
- `[]byte("ABC")` converts a string into its UTF-8 byte representation.

There's no hidden magic—**you must always write the conversion explicitly**, and that makes enterprise code safer.

Slice ↔ Array (Go 1.20+)

Go 1.20 added conversions between slices and arrays:

- a := [3]int(s) makes a copy if len(s) == 3.
- ap := (*[3]int)(s) reinterprets the slice header as an array pointer if len(s) >= 3. This does not copy—mutations affect both views.

```
s := []int{1, 2, 3}
a := [3]int(s)       // copy
ap := (*[3]int)(s) // no copy, pointer to same backing array
a[0] = 10
(*ap)[1] = 20
fmt.Println(s)       // [1 20 3]
```

Strings and Bytes

Strings are immutable, but conversions are explicit:

- `[]byte("Go")` makes a fresh copy of the string as bytes.
- `string([]byte{'G','o'})` makes a fresh copy as a string.

These conversions are common at API boundaries (e.g., network data as bytes, business logic as strings).

Summary

- Always document your conversions: they often imply copies (memory cost) or truncations (logic cost).
- Never rely on implicit widening/narrowing—Go won't let you, but other languages do, and this explicitness is part of Go's strength.
- For high-volume data, know whether your conversion copies (e.g., `string([]byte)`) or aliases (e.g., slice → array pointer).

Quick Practice

1. Convert `[]byte("ABC")` to string and back. What changes?
2. Safely convert a `[]int` of length ≥ 4 to `*[4]int`, and mutate the second element through the array pointer—what happens to the slice?
3. Convert a `float64` to `int`. What happens to the fractional part?

Summary

In this chapter, we explored Go's core building blocks—primitive types, variables, and operators—and saw how they shape correctness, performance, and memory behavior in enterprise systems. We learned why choosing the smallest safe type matters, how floats differ from integers in precision and intent, and when to use booleans, enums, or strings to model real domain rules. We examined pointers, scope, and shadowing to understand how data moves through memory and how to avoid unnecessary allocations or shared-state bugs. Collections like slices and maps revealed Go's explicit, efficient approach to data handling, along with the pitfalls of sub-slice retention and map iteration order.

What's Next

With Go's types, variables, and operators firmly in place, the next step is learning how to combine these building blocks into meaningful behavior. In the next chapter, we turn to functions exploring return values, error handling patterns, variadic parameters, and the method model that powers enterprise-scale design. This transition moves us from shaping data to expressing behavior, preparing the foundation for structs, methods, and larger architectural patterns ahead.

CHAPTER 6

Modeling Behavior: Functions, Methods, and Interfaces

"Simplicity is Complicated"

—Rob Pike

Before architecture scales, behavior must be expressed clearly. This chapter explores how Go models behavior—through functions, methods, structs, and interfaces—and how control flow shapes the decisions your system makes.

These constructs are simple by design, yet they form the backbone of large, evolving enterprise code bases.

Functions

Functions are the building blocks of Go programs. They encapsulate behavior, enable reuse, and make intent explicit. Go's function model is deliberately simple yet powerful: a function can return zero, one, or multiple values; it supports named parameters and variadic arguments; and methods attach functions to types to express domain behavior.

```
func Add(x, y int) int {
    return x + y
}
```


S. Shahsavan, *Building Enterprise Projects with Go*, https://doi.org/10.1007/979-8-8688-2370-1_6

Return Values in Go

A function in Go can return **zero, single, or multiple values**. This flexibility makes functions more expressive while keeping error handling explicit and predictable.

Zero Returns

Some functions exist only for their side effects, similar to "procedures" in some other languages:

```
func Log(msg string) {
    fmt.Println(time.Now().Format(time.RFC3339), msg)
}
```

Log does not return anything—its purpose is to print a message with a timestamp.

Single Return

The most common case: a single value, like a mathematical operation:

```
func Square(x int) int {
    return x * x
}
```

Multiple Returns

Go's real power appears when functions return multiple values. The most common and idiomatic pattern is **result + error**:

```
func Divide(dividend, divisor int) (quotient, remainder int, err error) {
    if divisor == 0 {
        return 0, 0, fmt.Errorf("division by zero")
    }
    return dividend/divisor, dividend%divisor, nil
}
```

Idiomatic Go avoids exceptions; instead, functions return explicit errors and leave the calling code in charge of handling them. This design makes error paths **visible, predictable, and safe**—crucial for enterprise systems where silent failures are unacceptable.

Named Return Values

Go functions can assign names to their return values in the function signature. This makes the purpose of each result explicit and sometimes reduces boilerplate inside the function.

```
func SplitRouteID(id string) (prefix string, number int) {
    parts := strings.SplitN(id, "-", 2)
    prefix = parts[0]
    if len(parts) > 1 {
        n, _ := strconv.Atoi(parts[1])
        number = n
    }
    return // returns prefix, number
}
```

Here, the return values `prefix` and `number` are declared up front. Inside the function, you assign directly to them, and a plain `return` statement returns the current values.

Enterprise Tips

- **Clarity:** For multiple returns, especially when types are the same (`int, int`), names document what each value represents.
- **Error Handling:** Functions that return (`result, err`) don't need named results—the convention is already clear.
- **Small Functions Only:** Naked `return` (without arguments) is fine in short functions where the meaning is obvious. In longer functions, it can hurt readability because it's harder to see what is being returned.
- Be explicit. In critical business logic, prefer `return prefix, number` instead of a naked `return`. It avoids confusion when the function grows over time.
- Treat named return values as a documentation tool, not as a shortcut. Misusing them can lead to hidden or unintended behavior.

Variadic Functions

Sometimes you don't know in advance how many arguments a function should take. Go solves this with **variadic parameters**—a clean way to accept "zero or more" values.

```
func SumAll(nums ...int) int {
    total := 0
    for _, n := range nums {
        total += n
    }
    return total
}
```

Here, nums behaves like a slice of int. You can call the function in two ways:

```
SumAll(1, 2, 3, 4)       // direct arguments
SumAll(mySlice...)       // expand an existing slice
```

Variadic parameters are powerful, but remember:

- Only the last parameter in a function can be variadic.
- At the call site, variadic arguments are packed into a slice—there's no special magic type.
- Use them when they improve readability (e.g., formatting, aggregation). For general cases, prefer passing a slice explicitly, which makes intent clearer.

Rules to Know

- The last return value is conventionally error if one is needed.
- Named return values can make intent clearer but should be used sparingly; avoid "naked returns" except in very short functions.
- Functions are values: you can assign them to variables, pass them as arguments, or return them.

- Short, focused functions are easier to test and compose. If a function grows beyond ~20 lines, consider extracting helpers.
- Variadic parameters are slices; prefer explicit slices unless variadic style improves readability.

Summary

- Avoid unnecessary heap allocations: pass large structs by pointer instead of value when performance matters.
- Avoid function parameters of type `interface{}` unless generic flexibility is required; prefer well-defined types or Go 1.18+ generics for type safety.
- Keep functions cohesive: a single responsibility per function improves maintainability and reduces bug-prone branching.

Structs in Go

> *"Bad programmers worry about the code. Good programmers worry about data structures and their relationships."*
>
> —Linus Torvalds

Why Structs and Not Classes?

In Go, there are no classes. This often surprises developers from Java, C++, or Python. Instead, Go deliberately separates *data* and *behavior*. A `struct` defines only the data, while behavior comes from functions and methods you attach to it.

Why this design? Go's creators wanted to avoid the pitfalls of classical inheritance. Classes in other languages tightly couple data and methods, and inheritance chains often become brittle.

James Gosling (Java's inventor) was asked, "If you could do Java over again, what would you change?" He replied: *"I'd leave out classes."*

Go takes that advice seriously. By giving us `struct` for data and `interface` for behavior, Go enforces composition over inheritance. This makes code bases more maintainable, reduces hidden dependencies, and avoids the "gorilla holding the banana and the entire jungle" problem described by Joe Armstrong.

So: Go calls them **structs**, not **classes**, to remind us that they are simple containers for fields and that behaviors are composed explicitly, not inherited implicitly.

Declaring Structs

A **struct** in Go is a composite data type that groups related fields together under one name, forming a lightweight record or object. It's the primary way to model real-world entities and compose behavior through embedding instead of inheritance.

```
import "time"

type VehicleID string
type RouteID   string

type Position struct {
	Lat      float64
	Lon      float64
	EpochMs int64 // Epoch milliseconds from devices
}

type Vehicle struct {
	ID       VehicleID
	Plate    string
	Capacity int16
	Active   bool
	LastSeen time.Time
	Position Position
}
```

Initialization Styles

Go gives you several expressive ways to initialize structs, depending on what you need—zero-value safety, readability, or shared mutability. Each style has its own trade-off in clarity, allocation, and ownership semantics. Let's look at them through our `Vehicle` example:

```
// 1) Zero value: safe defaults; all fields take their zero value.
var v1 Vehicle

// 2) Named fields (best for clarity).
v2 := Vehicle{
      ID:       "V-1001",
      Plate:    "WU-123AB",
      Capacity: 24,
      Active:   true,
      Position: Position{Lat: 48.2082, Lon: 16.3738},
}

// 3) Pointer for sharing/mutation.
v3 := &Vehicle{ID: "V-1002"}

// 4) new(T): allocates zeroed T and returns *T.
v4 := new(Vehicle)

// 5) Positional literal: order must match struct definition.
v5 := Vehicle{
            "V-1001",
            "WU-123AB",
            24,
            true,
            time.Now(),
            Position{Lat: 48.2082, Lon: 16.3738},
      }
```

Enterprise Tip Favor **named-field composite literals** over positional ones. They make your code self-documenting—each field name shows intent—and protect you from subtle bugs when struct definitions evolve. When a new field is added, old initializations won't silently break, and version control diffs stay clean and readable.

Exercises

1. Add a `Kind string` to `Vehicle` with a default empty value.
2. Create `Route` with `ID RouteID`, `Stops []Position`, `Active bool`. Initialize two routes.
3. What's the zero value of `time.Time` and why is it useful?

Constructor Functions in Go

A `constructor` in Go is simply a **regular function** that returns a properly initialized instance of a type. Its purpose is to **enforce invariants**, **apply defaults**, and **shield callers** from invalid or incomplete state.

Constructor functions are crucial in enterprise systems where consistency and safety outweigh brevity. They centralize initialization logic, make future changes easier, and document what it means for an object to be "ready for use."

Naming Conventions

- **NewT:** Primary constructor: `NewVehicle(...)`.
- **NewTFromX/ParseT:** Build from another form: `NewVehicleFromJSON`, `ParseRoute`.
- **newT:** Unexported helper for internal use.

Examples

```
package transport

import (
	"errors"
	"strings"
	"time"
)

type VehicleID string

type Position struct{ Lat, Lon float64 }
```

```
type Vehicle struct {
	ID       VehicleID
	Plate    string
	Capacity int16
	Active   bool
	LastSeen time.Time
	Position Position
}

// NewVehicle validates and applies defaults.
func NewVehicle(id VehicleID, plate string, capacity int16) (*Vehicle,
error) {
	id = VehicleID(strings.TrimSpace(string(id)))
	plate = strings.ToUpper(strings.TrimSpace(plate))
	if id == "" {
		return nil, errors.New("id is required")
	}
	if capacity < 0 {
		return nil, errors.New("capacity cannot be negative")
	}
	return &Vehicle{
		ID:       id,
		Plate:    plate,
		Capacity: capacity,
		Active:   true,
	}, nil
}

// Small, copy-friendly types can return values.
func NewPosition(lat, lon float64) Position {
	return Position{Lat: lat, Lon: lon}
}
```

Summary

- Prefer (*T, error) to report invalid input; avoid panics on request paths.
- Return **pointers** for large/identityful structs; **values** for tiny, copy-friendly types.
- If a type must be constructed via NewT, keep crucial fields **unexported** and expose read-only getters.

Exercises

1. Add NewRoute(id string, stops []Position) that rejects empty id and requires at least two stops.
2. Make Assignment fields unexported and provide NewAssignment(v VehicleID, routeID string) (Assignment, error) plus read-only accessors.
3. Decide which should return a value vs. pointer: Position, Vehicle, Route. Justify in one line each.

Methods and Receivers

Go takes a simple, explicit view of methods. A method is not a special construct—it's just a **function with a designated receiver**. This design keeps behavior separate from data, yet allows you to "attach" functionality to any named type when it makes sense.

For example:

```go
func (v *Vehicle) UpdatePosition(p Position) {
	v.Position = p
	v.LastSeen = time.Now()
}

func (v Vehicle) IsEmpty() bool { // value receiver
	return v.Capacity == 0
}
```

Here, `UpdatePosition` modifies the receiver's state and therefore uses a **pointer receiver** (`*Vehicle`), while `IsEmpty` only inspects the value, so it can use a **value receiver** (`Vehicle`). Behind the scenes, there's no magic. The Go compiler simply rewrites a method call like this:

```
v.UpdatePosition(pos)
```

into

```
(*Vehicle).UpdatePosition(v, pos)
```

So the receiver is just an implicit first argument. This is why choosing between pointer and value receivers matters: It controls whether Go **copies the receiver** (value semantics) or **passes its address** (reference semantics).

Value receivers are great for small, immutable structs. Pointer receivers are preferred when the method needs to mutate the value or when the type is large enough that copying would be inefficient.

Nil Pointer Receivers

An interesting property of Go is that you can call a method on a `nil` pointer receiver. As long as the method body does not dereference fields of the receiver, it works fine.

```
func (v *Vehicle) IsActive() bool {
	// safe: we don't touch any fields
	return v != nil
}

func (v *Vehicle) UnsafeCheck() bool {
	// unsafe: panics if v is nil
	return v.Active
}

func ExampleNilReceiver() {
	var v *Vehicle // nil
	fmt.Println(v.IsActive())    // prints: false
	fmt.Println(v.UnsafeCheck()) // panics: nil pointer dereference
}
```

This behavior is by design. Methods are just functions with a receiver argument, and Go allows `nil` to be a valid pointer argument. It becomes dangerous only when the method tries to access the underlying struct.

Enterprise Tip `nil` receiver methods are handy for "zero-safe" APIs, especially in large systems where constructors aren't always used. For example, a function might return a `nil *Vehicle`, but calling `v.IsActive()` won't crash. Be deliberate, though: once you start dereferencing, nil is no longer safe.

Guidelines

- **Pointer Receivers:** Use them when mutating the receiver, when the struct is large, or when the struct embeds synchronization primitives.
- **Value Receivers:** Use them for small, read-only, immutable-ish types.

Enterprise Tip Be consistent. Mixing pointer and value receivers on the same type makes interface satisfaction confusing and may cause unexpected copies.

Exercises

1. Add `Activate` and `Deactivate` methods using pointer receivers.
2. Why would `func (v Vehicle) Activate()` be a bug?
3. Create a method `SafeID()` on `*Vehicle` that works even if the receiver is `nil`. What should it return?

Composition and Embedding

Instead of classes and inheritance, Go gives us two powerful tools: **composition** and **embedding**.

```
type Bus struct {
	Vehicle   // embedding
	Doors int8
}
```

With embedding, the Bus gets Vehicle's fields and methods "promoted." You can write bus.ID instead of bus.Vehicle.ID. This feels like inheritance, but it isn't—there is no hidden type hierarchy, just compile-time field promotion.

Embedding vs. Composition

- **Embedding**

  Embedding is a special Go shortcut for composition. It allows one struct to promote another struct's fields and methods into its own namespace. Think of it as syntactic sugar for delegation. Use embedding when

  - You want to reuse behavior (e.g., a Bus is a kind of Vehicle in the domain model).
  - You want to expose the embedded struct's API directly without extra boilerplate.

- **Composition**

  Composition is the more general pattern: holding a struct as a named field.

  ```
  type Bus struct {
  	Vehicle Vehicle  // composition, explicit
  	Doors   int8
  }
  ```

  Here you must access fields as bus.Vehicle.ID.

  Use composition when

- You want clarity that Bus *has a* Vehicle, rather than *is like* a Vehicle.
- You want to control what is exposed, avoiding accidental name conflicts.

Both solve the same problem—reusing code without inheritance—but embedding trades some explicitness for convenience.

Enterprise Tip Limit embedding to one to two levels. Beyond that, the mental model gets muddy, and conflicts are hard to debug. Use explicit composition for deeper relationships.

A Lesson from the Real World

In one enterprise project, I saw a team that didn't know the principle of **composition over inheritance**—and didn't read any books about Go. As Go doesn't support inheritance, they thought the only way forward was copy-paste. They duplicated common fields across every type: `Car`, `Bus`, `Train`...even APIs were duplicated. Imagine a system where there was no central `Vehicle` struct and every type redefined `ID`, `Plate`, `Capacity`, and `Active`.

The result?

- Multiple bugs from inconsistent logic
- Extra work every time a field changed
- APIs diverging in subtle, dangerous ways

This is exactly what DRY—**Don't Repeat Yourself**—warns us against. Code duplication may feel harmless at first, but in large systems, it multiplies complexity. In enterprise contexts, a single mistake replicated across dozens of copy-pasted structs can cascade into production outages.

Embedding and composition in Go are the antidotes: they let us reuse logic cleanly without inheritance and without repetition.

DRY in Enterprise Go Project

DRY doesn't mean abstracting everything; it means capturing *true* duplication of knowledge.

- **Good DRY:** Factor out `Vehicle` so all transport types share `ID`, `Capacity`, and `Active`.
- **Bad DRY:** Over-abstracting into a "God type" with fields nobody uses.

The sweet spot is explicit, small, reusable types (like `Position`, `Vehicle`, `Route`). They keep code maintainable, testable, and scalable.

Enterprise Tip Duplicated code multiplies quietly: a copied entity breeds duplicate APIs, tests, and rules. Soon, every change means fixing the same bug in five places. DRY isn't polish—it's containment. Prevent one clone today to stop a swarm tomorrow.

Exercises

1. Refactor `Vehicle` to embed `Position` so `v.Lat` compiles.
2. Add `Truck` embedding `Vehicle` with `MaxLoadKg int`.
3. What happens if two embedded structs both define `Start()`? How would composition help?
4. Identify a place in your transportation model where duplication could creep in. Refactor it with composition or embedding.

Equality and Comparability in Go

In Go, the == operator has **strict, type-dependent** rules. Whether two values can be compared (and how) depends entirely on their types. This rigidity means comparisons are **predictable**—but it also means some types can never be directly compared (except to `nil`). Understanding Go's rules is essential to avoid bugs and to write correct, performant code.

What Does == Mean in Go?

Go's == checks for **value equality**, but exactly *what* is compared depends on the kind of type. The Go **specification** defines comparability per type category:

- **Booleans:** Two booleans are equal if they are both `true` or both `false`.

- **Integers:** All integer types (`int`, `int8`, `uint64`, etc.) are comparable. They compare in the usual numeric way.
- **Floating-point:** Floats are compared per IEEE-754 rules. For example, `+0.0 == -0.0`, but `NaN != NaN` (a NaN is not equal to anything, even itself).
- **Complex:** Complex numbers are comparable: `a == b` if both `real(a)==real(b)` and `imag(a)==imag(b)`.
- **Strings:** Compared **byte-by-byte**, not locale-aware. Two strings are equal if they have the same length and the same sequence of bytes.
- **Pointers** (including `*T` and `unsafe.Pointer`)**:** Two pointers are equal if they point to the *same* memory location or if both are `nil`.
- **Interfaces:** Two interface values are equal if **both** their dynamic types and their dynamic values are equal. Concretely, if `x` and `y` are interfaces, `x==y` only holds when they have the **same concrete type** and that underlying value compares equal.
    - This leads to a common pitfall: an interface holding a typed-nil (e.g., a `*MyError` that is nil) is **not** equal to `nil` because its dynamic type (`*MyError`) is non-nil.

```
package main
import "fmt"
type MyError struct{}
func (e *MyError) Error() string { return "something went
wrong" }
func maybeError(bad bool) error {
        if bad {
                return &MyError{} // return a real error
        }
        var e *MyError = nil
        return e // ⚠ typed-nil: *MyError type, nil value
}
```

```
func main() {
        err := maybeError(false)
        fmt.Println("err == nil ?", err == nil) // prints: false
        if err != nil {
                fmt.Println("This branch still runs -- even though
                it's a nil pointer!")
        }
}
```

- It happens because an interface in Go holds **two things**: a dynamic **type** and a **value**. Even if the value is `nil`, the interface itself isn't nil as long as its type (`*MyError`) is set. So `err` has a nil pointer value but a non-nil type—making `err == nil` evaluate to false.

- **Arrays:** An array is comparable if its element type is comparable. Two arrays compare equal if they have the same length and all corresponding elements compare equal.
- **Structs:** A struct is comparable if *every field* is comparable. Two structs compare equal if all their corresponding fields compare equal (in field declaration order).

In summary: **Basic scalar types, pointers, interfaces, arrays, and structs (with comparable fields)** all support == as value equality. The comparisons are deterministic: e.g., floats use IEEE-754 (so NaN never equals itself), strings compare by raw bytes, and struct/array comparisons work element-by-element.

Types *Not* Directly Comparable

Some types in Go **cannot** be compared with == (except to `nil`). Specifically, **slices, maps, and functions** are *uncomparable types*. The language forbids `x == y` if x and y are slices, maps, or functions (unless you are explicitly comparing to `nil`). For example:

```
var a, b []int = []int{1,2}, []int{1,2}
_ = (a == b) // compile-time error: slice can only be compared to nil
```

If a struct contains any slice, map, or func field, **the whole struct is uncomparable**. For instance, in a transportation domain, you might define:

```
type Route struct {
    ID   string
    Path []string  // slice -> makes Route not comparable
    Cost int
}

r1 := Route{ID: "R1", Path: []string{"A", "B"}, Cost: 5}
r2 := Route{ID: "R2", Path: []string{"A", "B"}, Cost: 5}
fmt.Println(r1 == r2) // compile error: invalid operation: r1 == r2 (struct
                         containing []string cannot be compared)
```

The compiler prevents this: you'll see an error like *"invalid operation: r1 == r2 (struct contains []string) cannot be compared"*. In effect, **anything involving slices, maps, or functions can only be compared to `nil`**, not to another value.

Implications: Map Keys and Switch Cases

Because map keys in Go must be of a comparable type, you **cannot** use a slice/map/func (or a struct containing one) as a map key. For example, `map[[ ]byte]int` is invalid. In a transport system, if you tried `map[Route]int`, it fails for the same reason. If you need a map keyed by route, use a comparable key (like a string or an integer ID), or compute a hash key.

Similarly, `switch` statements rely on ==. The switch expression type itself must be comparable, and each `case x:` is evaluated as `x==switchValue` which must be valid. In practice, this means you can only switch on comparable types, and each case value must be a valid comparison to the switch expression (otherwise, the compiler errors). The Go spec explicitly states: *"The switch expression type must be comparable"*, and each `x == t` in a case must be valid.

Comparing Values Safely

When a type isn't comparable (or you want custom semantics), you must use other means:

1. **Write an `Equal` method.** The idiomatic approach is to implement a method that explicitly compares fields. For example, two `Route` values could be equal if `ID` and `Cost` match, and their `Path` slices have the same content. In code:

   ```
   func (r Route) Equal(other Route) bool {
       if r.ID != other.ID || r.Cost != other.Cost {
           return false
       }
       if len(r.Path) != len(other.Path) {
           return false
       }
       for i := range r.Path {
           if r.Path[i] != other.Path[i] {
               return false
           }
       }
       return true
   }
   ```

   - This manual loop stops at the first difference. A field-by-field `Equal` is clear, fast, and under your control (no hidden surprises).

2. **Use `slices.Equal` (Go 1.21+).** The standard library's `slices` package provides `slices.Equal(a, b []T) bool` to compare two slices element-wise. It handles lengths and contents for you. According to the docs, it returns `true` if the slices have the same length and each element compares equal; *empty and nil slices are considered equal.* For example:

   ```
   import "slices"

   func (r Route) Equal(other Route) bool {
       return r.ID == other.ID &&
              r.Cost == other.Cost &&
              slices.Equal(r.Path, other.Path)
   }
   ```

3. **Use `reflect.DeepEqual`.** This is the simplest code-wise: `reflect.DeepEqual(a,b)` does a deep recursive comparison. It handles slices, maps, arrays, structs, etc. However, it has caveats: it is slower, and it treats `nil` vs. empty differently. For example, `reflect.DeepEqual([]string(nil), []string{})` is `false`. If that distinction matters, be aware. For byte slices, prefer `bytes.Equal` instead of converting to string or DeepEqual. Be aware of `bytes.Equal` official document: "*Equal reports whether a and b are the same length and contain the same bytes. A nil argument is equivalent to an empty slice.*"

Performance and Pitfalls

In enterprise systems, the method of comparison matters. You need to be aware of these points:

- **`reflect.DeepEqual` is slower.** Recursive functions are by nature slower for a large number of records, and DeepEqual is a recursive function.
- **Nil vs. empty.** As noted, `reflect.DeepEqual` distinguishes `nil` from empty slices, whereas `slices.Equal` does not. This can cause subtle bugs if you expect them to be equal. Decide on the semantics you need: often treating nil as empty (length zero) is fine, but if your data model differentiates them, handle that case explicitly.
- **Interface comparisons can panic.** The spec warns: "*A comparison of two interface values with identical dynamic types causes a runtime panic if that type is not comparable. This behavior applies not only to direct interface value comparisons but also when comparing arrays of interface values or structs with interface-valued fields.*" In other words, `x == y` when `x` and `y` are interfaces will panic if their underlying type isn't comparable. For example:

```
var a any = []int{1,2}
var b any = []int{1,2}
_ = (a == b) // runtime panic: comparing uncomparable []int
```

    - The compile-time check doesn't catch this because interfaces *are* comparable in the type system, but at runtime, Go tries to compare the dynamic slice values and crashes.

- **Pointer identity.** Remember that comparing pointers (`p == q`) checks identity, not object equivalence. If you store objects by pointer (e.g., `map[*Station]bool`), == only matches the exact same pointer, not two different `*Station` with equal fields. This is not a comparability issue, but a logic one: if you expect structural equality, you need to compare contents, not pointers.

- **`nil`-checks.** Slices, maps, functions, and channels can always be compared with `nil`. It's idiomatic to check for `nil` before use. For instance:

```
if r.Path == nil {
    // treat it as empty path, or initialize it
    r.Path = []string{}
}
if m == nil {
    m = make(map[string]int)
}
if ch == nil {
    // channel not created yet
}
```

Checking `len(s)==0` also works for slices, but sometimes you *want* to treat a nil slice differently (e.g., in JSON marshaling).

Summary

In an enterprise project, clarity and consistency are key:

- **Document your equality semantics.** If you write an `Equal` method or use `slices.Equal`, document whether it treats `nil` as empty, how it orders comparisons, etc. Make sure your team agrees on what "equal" means in each domain type.

- **Avoid surprises.** Be very careful when storing pointers or interfaces in data structures or when returning interfaces (especially `error`). Review code for unintended typed-nil returns or comparisons.
- **Write tests.** For any custom `Equal` logic, add unit tests covering corner cases (nil vs. empty, large slices, unordered elements if needed, etc.).
- **Performance tests (if needed).** If comparisons happen in a hot path, benchmark a few approaches. Generally, a simple loop or `slices.Equal` is quite fast; avoid using reflection in tight loops.

Interfaces in Go

The more a system is decoupled by design, the longer it survives change.

As you can read in other parts of the book as well, decoupling is one of the most important things in my experience. If we can find behaviors that we need and define them as decency, then we can have minimum coupling. That's exactly what interfaces in Go can do.

Why Interfaces Matter in Enterprise Go

Interfaces in Go give *behavior* a voice. They let your code depend on **what something can do**, not **what it is**. This seemingly small distinction changes everything in an enterprise project: it enables polymorphism without inheritance, decoupling without frameworks, and testability without effort.

Think of a large transport system. You might have

- A **real-time GPS tracker** streaming live coordinates
- A **simulation replayer** reading from archived logs
- A **diagnostic emulator** feeding synthetic data for tests

Each one can report a `Position()`. They differ in *how* they get it—but their *behavior* is identical.

```
// VehicleTracker defines the ability to report position.
type VehicleTracker interface {
    Position() Coordinate
}
```

Any component that can return a Coordinate through Position() fulfills this role. This is the essence of **interface-driven design**: depend on what a type *does*, not what it *is*.

Enterprise Tip Interfaces let large teams evolve modules independently. One service can change its storage, protocol, or vendor SDK without breaking others—as long as the interface contract remains stable.

What Is an Interface?

An interface in Go defines a **method set**—a list of function signatures that represent a behavior. Any type whose methods match this list **implicitly** satisfies the interface. There's no inheritance, no implements keyword, no shared base class. Satisfaction is *structural*, not *nominal*.

```
type Locator interface {
  CurrentPosition() Position
}

type Vehicle struct {
  ID VehicleID
  Position Position
}

func (v Vehicle) CurrentPosition() Position {
  return v.Position
}
```

Vehicle automatically satisfies Locator. This is structural typing: if it walks and quacks like a duck, it *is* a duck—at compile time.

Consumer-Defined Interfaces

In classical OOP, interfaces usually live with the **provider**. A class declares that it *implements* some interface, and consumers must import that interface to use it. In Go, the relationship is inverted: **interfaces belong to consumers**, not providers. This simple inversion has profound architectural outcomes. It means that the team using a behavior—not the team providing it—decides *how much* abstraction is necessary.

```
// Good: define the interface where it is used, not where it's implemented.
type Mover interface {
    Move(to Position) error
}
```

The package that needs to move vehicles defines the interface. The implementation—perhaps `Vehicle`, `Drone`, or `Forklift`—only needs to provide a matching `Move` method.

```
type Vehicle struct {
    ID       VehicleID
    Position Position
}

func (v *Vehicle) Move(to Position) error {
    v.Position = to
    return nil
}
```

No `implements` keyword. No imports. No dependency cycle. `Vehicle` remains blissfully unaware that `Mover` exists—yet it fully satisfies it. Contrast this with the **anti-pattern** common in enterprise frameworks:

```
// Bad: defined in the provider's package "just in case"
type Mover interface {
    Move(to Position) error
    Stop() error
    Reset() error
}
```

This "preemptive abstraction" pollutes the API and locks consumers into fat, provider-owned contracts they may not even need.

Enterprise Tip Define interfaces **as close as possible to where they are used**—in the consumer package or even inside a single test. That keeps contracts narrow, prevents circular dependencies, and empowers each package to express exactly the behavior it needs.

Interface Composition

Go doesn't have inheritance, but it has something better: **composition**. Where classical OOP languages build hierarchies, Go builds behaviors like Lego blocks. An interface in Go can **embed** other interfaces, forming larger contracts without duplication. Each embedded interface contributes its method set to the new one.

```
type Metadata interface {
   ID() string
   Type() string
}

type Trackable interface {
   Locator
   Metadata
}
```

Now `Trackable` combines both abilities—it can locate itself *and* describe itself. Any type that implements all methods of `Locator` and `Metadata` automatically satisfies `Trackable`.

```
type Vehicle struct {
    IDValue   string
    TypeValue string
    Position  Position
}
```

```
func (v Vehicle) ID() string           { return v.IDValue }
func (v Vehicle) Type() string         { return v.TypeValue }
func (v Vehicle) CurrentPosition() Position { return v.Position }
```

Because `Vehicle` already satisfies both `Locator` and `Metadata`, it also satisfies `Trackable`—no extra declaration required.

Enterprise Lesson Composition scales better than inheritance. When systems grow, rigid hierarchies crumble under competing requirements. By composing small, orthogonal behaviors, you gain the freedom to extend functionality without refactoring existing code.

The Empty Interface

The **empty interface**—written as `interface{}` or, since Go 1.18, the alias `any`—is special. It means "no requirements." Every type satisfies it because every type has *at least zero methods*. In practice, this makes it Go's **universal container type**—used when a function must accept *any* value.

```
func PrintAny(x any) {
    fmt.Println(x)
}
```

Here, `PrintAny` can receive anything: a string, struct, int, even another interface. This is how packages like `fmt`, `encoding/json`, and `log` accept arbitrary data without knowing its type at compile time. Under the hood, the empty interface still holds two words—**type** and **data**—just like any other interface. When you pass a concrete value into an `any`, Go boxes it together with its runtime type information so it can be recovered later via reflection or type assertion.

Testing with Interfaces

Interfaces make **dependency injection** and **testing** effortless in Go. They let you replace real components—like message brokers, APIs, or databases—with lightweight stand-ins that behave predictably during tests.

Imagine a Scheduler service that publishes vehicle coordinates to a message bus. In production, it uses Kafka or Pulsar; in tests, we want to verify behavior *without* running those systems.

```
// Publisher represents the ability to publish vehicle coordinates.
type Publisher interface {
    Publish(coord Coordinate) error
}

// Scheduler depends on a Publisher but doesn't care which one.
type Scheduler struct {
    pub Publisher
}

func (s *Scheduler) Dispatch(c Coordinate) error {
    return s.pub.Publish(c)
}
```

Here, Scheduler only depends on *behavior*—Publish()—not a concrete implementation. That makes it trivial to test.

Writing a Stub for Tests

In Go, you rarely need heavy mocking frameworks. You can write a tiny **stub** or **fake** that satisfies the same interface and record its usage.

```
// StubPublisher is a test double that records Publish calls.
type StubPublisher struct {
    called bool
    last   Coordinate
}

func (s *StubPublisher) Publish(c Coordinate) error {
    s.called = true
    s.last = c
    return nil
}
```

Now you can test Scheduler in isolation:

```
func TestScheduler_Dispatch(t *testing.T) {
    stub := &StubPublisher{}
    sched := Scheduler{pub: stub}

    coord := Coordinate{Lat: 48.2, Lon: 16.37}
    _ = sched.Dispatch(coord)

    if !stub.called {
        t.Fatal("expected Publish to be called")
    }
    if stub.last != coord {
        t.Fatalf("expected coordinate %v, got %v", coord, stub.last)
    }
}
```

No external services, no mocking libraries—just plain Go.

Why It Works

Go's interfaces empower the **consumer** to define its own testing seams. Each interface represents exactly what the unit under test depends on—no more, no less. This keeps tests clean, fast, and focused.

Summary

- Small interfaces (one to three methods) are *easy to fake.*
- Tests remain simple and decoupled from infrastructure.
- You gain reliable CI pipelines that don't rely on external systems.

Rule of Thumb: Define interfaces for *collaboration points*—where your code interacts with the outside world. Every interface you can stub in a test is a sign your architecture is modular and well-designed.

Interface Evolution

Once an interface is exported, it becomes part of your public **contract**—and in Go, contracts are sacred. Adding even a single method to an interface **breaks every existing implementation**, because those types no longer satisfy it. That's why interfaces, once published, are considered **immutable**. This immutability may sound restrictive, but it's one of the reasons Go libraries remain stable for years. The key is to plan for extension **without** changing existing interfaces.

Strategy for Safe Evolution

When new functionality is needed, **define a new interface** that embeds the old one, rather than modifying it directly. Then, use **type assertions** to detect and use the extended behavior at runtime.

```
// The original behavior: reporting a simple status.
type Reporter interface {
    Report(id string) error
}

// New version adds richer reporting without breaking old implementations.
type ReporterV2 interface {
    Reporter
    DetailedReport(id string) string
}

// Code using Reporter can detect newer implementations safely.
func HandleReport(r Reporter, id string) {
    _ = r.Report(id)

    if v2, ok := r.(ReporterV2); ok {
        fmt.Println(v2.DetailedReport(id))
    }
}
```

Existing types that only implement `Report` continue working. New implementations can opt into `ReporterV2` by adding the new method.

Real-World Example

Go's own standard library uses this approach extensively. For example, `io.Reader` has never changed since 2009, but new capabilities—like `io.ReaderAt`, `io.ReadCloser`, and `io.ReadSeekCloser`—were added as **compositional extensions**. This lets old code keep compiling while new code gains richer features.

Summary

- **Design from the consumer side.** Define interfaces where they're used, not where they're implemented.
- **Keep them small.** One to three methods is ideal; small contracts compose better and test easier.
- **Favor composition over inheritance.** Build new behaviors by embedding, not extending.
- **Interfaces are contracts.** Once exported, treat them as immutable; evolve safely via new versions.
- **Avoid premature abstraction.** Don't invent interfaces "just in case." Start concrete; abstract when patterns repeat.
- **Test through interfaces, not frameworks.** Small interfaces make mocks and stubs trivial.
- **Use any only at system edges.** Keep core logic type-safe and explicit.

Exercises

1. Define a `Mover` interface with `Move(to Position)`, and implement it for `Vehicle`. Write `RelocateAll([]Mover, Position)`.
2. Write a `Logger` interface, and implement it with both a console logger and a slice-backed mock.
3. Why is "accept interfaces, return structs" preferred in API design? Give an example using a `RouteService`.

4. Compare an interface holding a typed-nil pointer with `nil`. Write a test to prove it.
5. Refactor a `VehicleRepository` interface into three focused interfaces. Apply them across your transport services.

Conditions in Go

Every program needs to decide between different paths. In Go, those decisions come through `if` and `switch`. They look simple, but their details matter a lot when building clean, scalable enterprise systems.

if Statements: Asking a Question

The `if` statement checks a condition and executes its block only if that condition is true. Unlike some languages (e.g., JavaScript or Python), Go does **not** allow "truthy" values. Conditions must be strictly boolean.

```
if vehicle.InService {
      fmt.Println("Vehicle is currently in service")
}
```

If the condition is false, the block is skipped, and execution continues after the `if`.

Enterprise Tip Don't abuse nested ifs. For clarity and maintainability, use **guard clauses**—exit early on error or invalid states. This keeps business logic flat and readable.

```
func AssignVehicle(v *Vehicle, r RouteID) error {
      if v == nil {
            return fmt.Errorf("cannot assign: vehicle is nil")
      }
      if r == "" {
            return fmt.Errorf("cannot assign: empty route ID")
      }
```

```
        v.Route = r
        return nil
}
```

if-else: Choosing Between Two Paths

When two outcomes are possible, `if-else` captures both:

```
if v.Assigned {
        fmt.Println("In service")
} else {
        fmt.Println("Idle")
}
```

If the `if` condition is false, Go will run the `else` block.

Enterprise Tip Don't make `else` blocks unnecessarily long. If logic diverges significantly, separate into helper functions. This avoids "fat" functions that are difficult to test.

---

if-else if Chains: Multiple Options

Sometimes you need to compare more than two possibilities:

```
if v.Speed == 0 {
        fmt.Println("Stopped")
} else if v.Speed <= 50 {
        fmt.Println("City driving")
} else if v.Speed <= 120 {
        fmt.Println("Highway driving")
} else {
        fmt.Println("Overspeeding!")
}
```

Performance Note Long `if-else if` ladders are less efficient than a `switch` when cases are simple equality checks. Go compilers often optimize `switch` into jump tables, which can be faster.

if with Initializer: Scoped Variables

Go allows declaring and initializing variables *inside* the `if`. The variable exists only within that block.

```
if route, ok := routes[r]; ok {
      fmt.Printf("Assigned to route: %s\n", route.Name)
} else {
      fmt.Println("Route not found")
}
```

Here, `route` and ok only live inside the `if/else`. This reduces variable clutter in wider scopes.

Enterprise Tip Always prefer this scoped form when dealing with lookups. It prevents accidental reuse of variables outside the condition.

The Comma-Ok Pattern: Idiomatic Go

Many Go operations return two values: the result and a boolean indicating success. This is called the **comma-ok idiom**. This is a way to safely test outcomes of operations like map lookups, type assertions, or channel receives. It returns two values—the actual result and a boolean (ok) showing whether the operation succeeded. This eliminates exceptions and keeps error handling explicit, simple, and predictable.

With Maps

```
if assignment, ok := assignments[v.ID]; ok {
      fmt.Println("Assignment found:", assignment)
} else {
      fmt.Println("No assignment")
}
```

With Type Assertions

```
if bus, ok := v.(Bus); ok {
      fmt.Println("Bus capacity:", bus.Seats)
}
```

With Channels

```
msg, ok := <-ch
if !ok {
      fmt.Println("Channel closed")
}
```

Enterprise Tip Never ignore the ok. In enterprise projects, skipping it can lead to panics (nil dereference on missing map entry, closed channel reads, etc.).

---

switch: Cleaner Multi-way Decisions

The **`switch` statement** in Go provides a clean, readable way to handle multiple conditions without deep nesting. It evaluates expressions top to bottom, executing the first matching case. Unlike many languages, Go's `switch` automatically breaks after each case—no `break` keyword required.

```
switch v.Type {
case "bus":
      fmt.Println("Large capacity vehicle")
case "taxi", "car":
      fmt.Println("Small passenger vehicle")
```

```
default:
	fmt.Println("Unknown type")
}
```

- **Default Case:** Executes if no other case matches. If you omit `default` and no case matches, nothing happens—the switch block just ends.
- **Multiple Matches:** Cases can be grouped (`"taxi", "car"` above).
- **No Break Needed:** Go automatically stops after the first matching case—unlike C or Java.

The fallthrough Keyword

The **`fallthrough`** keyword lets control flow continue into the next `case` block, even if the current one matches. It's useful for intentional grouping of related logic (e.g., categorizing thresholds), but it ignores case conditions—execution always proceeds to the next block.

```
switch v.Capacity {
case 1:
	fmt.Println("Single seat")
	fallthrough
case 2:
	fmt.Println("Small vehicle")
}
```

Use it sparingly: while occasionally expressive, excessive `fallthrough` makes switch statements harder to reason about and less idiomatic in Go.

Switch Without Expression

A **`switch` without an expression** acts like a streamlined `if-else` chain—each `case` is a boolean condition evaluated in order. It stops at the first true case, improving readability when comparing ranges or complex expressions.

```
switch {
case v.Speed == 0:
	fmt.Println("Stopped")
case v.Speed > 0 && v.Speed <= 50:
	fmt.Println("City driving")
case v.Speed > 50:
	fmt.Println("Highway driving")
}
```

This style is common in Go for concise decision logic, especially in configuration, validation, or threshold checks.

Type Switch: Safe Polymorphism

A **type switch** provides safe, readable polymorphism when working with interface values.

It inspects the *runtime type* of an interface and executes the matching case block—no unsafe casting needed.

```
func PrintRouteID(id any) {
	switch v := id.(type) {
	case string:
		fmt.Println("Route code:", v)
	case int:
		fmt.Println("Route number:", v)
	default:
		fmt.Println("Unknown type")
	}
}
```

This avoids unsafe casting and makes enterprise systems resilient to varied inputs (e.g., mixed IDs from APIs).

Enterprise Tip Use type switches at the **boundaries of your system** (parsing JSON, reading from message queues) to validate input types. Inside your core domain, prefer strong types to avoid overusing `any`.

Summary

- **Guard clauses keep code shallow**: Handle errors early, return fast.
- **Switch beats long ladders**: Improves readability and may compile into faster instructions.
- **Use `default` consciously**: In mission-critical systems, a missing `default` might silently skip logic.
- **Don't abuse `fallthrough`**: It makes maintenance harder. Prefer explicit grouped cases.
- **Always check the second value in comma-ok**: Ignoring it leads to production bugs.
- **Scope wisely**: `if` initializers reduce memory footprint and accidental leaks in enterprise projects.

Exercises

1. Write a function `VehicleCategory(v Vehicle) string` using a `switch` on `v.Type` that returns `"Bus"`, `"Car"`, `"Bike"`, or `"Unknown"`. Add a `default` case. What happens if you remove the `default` and `v.Type` is `"Truck"`?
2. Using the comma-ok idiom, write a function that checks if a route exists in a `map[string]Route`. If found, print "Found: <route>", else `"Missing route"`.
3. Implement `SpeedLabel(speed int) string` using both `if-else if` and `switch`. Benchmark them with Go's `testing.B`. Which one is clearer? Which one is potentially faster?

Loops in Go

Every journey has steps, and in Go, those steps are expressed with `for`. Unlike many other languages, Go has **just one loop keyword**: `for`. But this single tool is flexible enough to cover `while`, `do-while`, `foreach`, and traditional counting loops.

By mastering `for`, you master all looping in Go.

The Classic Counting Loop

The most common loop structure is counting up or down with an index:

```
for i := 0; i < 5; i++ {
	fmt.Println("Step:", i)
}
```

- **Initialization** (`i := 0`) runs once.
- **Condition** (`i < 5`) is checked before each iteration.
- **Post statement** (`i++`) runs after each iteration.

It runs an initializer once, checks the condition before each cycle, and executes the post statement afterward. This structure is ideal for tasks with known bounds—such as indexing arrays, iterating slices, or batching jobs—and remains the most performant loop for tight, deterministic workloads.

While-Style Loop

In Go, there's no separate `while` keyword. A **while-style loop** in Go is just a `for` loop without initialization or post clauses:

```
i := 0
for i < 5 {
	fmt.Println("Step:", i)
	i++
}
```

It runs as long as the condition remains true, making it perfect for scenarios like waiting on input, polling, or streaming data.

Enterprise Tip While-style loops often indicate "loop until a condition is met." Use this when waiting for external signals (e.g., reading from a network socket). Always ensure there's a termination condition—**infinite loops without exit strategies cause leaks and outages in production**.

Infinite Loop

When you omit everything, you get an infinite loop. An **infinite loop** runs endlessly until explicitly stopped:

```
for {
	processNextVehicle()
}
```

It's the backbone of servers, background workers, and message consumers that must stay alive.

Enterprise Tip In enterprise projects, always pair infinite loops with safe termination logic—`break`, `return`, or context cancellation—to avoid runaway goroutines and uncontrolled CPU consumption.

Breaking and Continuing

The **break** statement immediately exits the nearest loop, while **continue** skips the current iteration and proceeds to the next. They give you fine-grained control over iteration flow, helping filter or short-circuit logic efficiently.

```
for _, v := range vehicles {
	if v.OutOfService {
		continue // skip broken vehicles
	}
	if v.ID == targetID {
		fmt.Println("Found vehicle:", v)
		break // exit loop early
	}
}
```

Enterprise Tip Exiting loops early with `break` avoids wasted CPU cycles in large datasets. In enterprise-scale systems, this can save milliseconds per request, which adds up to millions of requests per day.

Iterating Slices and Arrays with range

The **range** keyword offers a concise, safe way to iterate over slices and arrays in Go. It yields both the index and the element value on each iteration, making the code readable and less error-prone.

```
for i, route := range routes {
        fmt.Printf("Index %d: %s\n", i, route.Name)
}
```

- The first value (`i`) is the index.
- The second value (`route`) is the element.
- If you don't need one, use _ to ignore it.

```
for _, v := range vehicles {
        fmt.Println("Vehicle:", v.ID)
}
```

Enterprise Tip Iteration over slices copies the element value by default. If elements are **large structs**, prefer iterating by index (`for i := range slice`) and using pointers (`&slice[i]`). This avoids unnecessary copies and improves memory efficiency.

Iterating Maps with range

Maps in Go are **unordered key/value collections**, optimized for fast lookups rather than predictable traversal. When you iterate over a map using `range`, each iteration returns a key and its corresponding value—but the order is **intentionally randomized** every run.

```
for id, vehicle := range vehicleMap {
      fmt.Printf("Vehicle %s: %+v\n", id, vehicle)
}
```

This randomization is not a bug; it's a deliberate design choice to ensure that developers never accidentally depend on iteration order. Each iteration walks through the map's internal hash buckets, and since hash seeds are randomized at runtime, you'll see different sequences each time the program runs.

Understanding Why Order Isn't Guaranteed

Maps are implemented as **hash tables**—their efficiency comes from computing a hash for each key to determine where its value is stored. Rehashing, resizing, or even adding new elements can change how data is laid out in memory, which means that order would be impossible to guarantee without sacrificing performance.

This trade-off is critical for scalability: it allows Go maps to handle millions of entries efficiently while keeping lookup and insert operations near O(1) time complexity.

Getting a Deterministic Order

In cases where deterministic output matters—such as generating reports, logging, or producing consistent JSON—sort the keys explicitly:

```
keys := make([]string, 0, len(vehicleMap))
for k := range vehicleMap {
      keys = append(keys, k)
}
sort.Strings(keys)
for _, k := range keys {
      fmt.Println("Ordered vehicle:", vehicleMap[k])
}
```

This approach separates **data organization** (sorting) from **data storage** (map structure), keeping your logic predictable without hurting map performance.

Iterating Strings with range

In Go, strings are sequences of **bytes**, not characters. However, when you use `range` on a string, Go automatically decodes each **UTF-8–encoded rune** (Unicode code point) for you. This means that every iteration yields the index of the **first byte** of each rune and the rune value itself.

```
for i, r := range "Rüti" {
        fmt.Printf("Index %d: Rune %q\n", i, r)
}
```

Output will be

```
Output:
Index 0: 'R'
Index 1: 'ü'
Index 3: 't'
Index 4: 'i'
```

Notice how the ü occupies two bytes, so the index jumps from `1` to `3`.

Why This Matters

Understanding this behavior is crucial when working with **internationalized text**. Many European, Asian, and Middle Eastern scripts use multi-byte characters, meaning byte-based indexing can easily corrupt strings if you slice or count them incorrectly. The `range` loop shields you from this by automatically decoding Unicode, ensuring that your logic aligns with human-readable characters rather than byte offsets.

If you need **raw performance or binary accuracy**, such as computing hashes or serializing data, you can still iterate over bytes directly:

```
for i := 0; i < len(s); i++ {
    b := s[i] // single byte
    ...
}
```

This approach avoids decoding and is faster for low-level operations, but unsafe for text manipulation.

Enterprise Tip When processing international data (e.g., city names in a transport system), always use runes for correctness. If you need raw binary performance (e.g., hashing IDs), iterate by bytes.

Iterating Channels with range

Channels can also be looped until closed:

```
for msg := range messages {
	fmt.Println("Received:", msg)
}
```

This pattern is idiomatic in concurrent Go: the loop ends when the channel is closed.

Enterprise Lessons Use `range` over strings when processing **user-facing text**, file names, or multilingual data to handle Unicode correctly.

Iterate by bytes (`for i := 0; i < len(s); i++`) only for **binary-level tasks** such as hashing, compression, or checksums.

Always clarify your intent: **runic correctness** for people, **byte precision** for machines.

Nested Loops

Go allows you to **nest loops**, which is common when processing related collections—such as routes and their assigned vehicles. However, the control statements `break` and `continue` only apply to the **innermost** loop by default.

If you need to exit multiple levels of nesting, Go provides **labels** that let you break or continue an outer loop explicitly.

```
outer:
for _, r := range routes {
	for _, v := range vehicles {
```

```
            if v.Route == r.ID {
                fmt.Printf("Match: %s -> %s\n", r.Name, v.ID)
                break outer // exit both loops
            }
        }
}
```

This pattern is rare but occasionally useful—for example, when searching for the first matching record across multiple datasets or stopping early once a condition is met.

How It Works

A label (like `outer:`) marks a specific loop. When you call `break outer`, Go terminates that labeled loop directly, skipping everything below it. Similarly, `continue outer` jumps to the next iteration of that outer loop instead of the inner one.

While powerful, labeled loops should be used with **discipline**—they can quickly obscure program flow if overused.

Enterprise Tip Labels are rare in Go—only use them when absolutely necessary. Overuse makes code harder to follow.

Common Pitfalls in Go Loops

Go's `for` loop looks simple—but beneath that simplicity lie design decisions that trade convenience for **performance, safety, and control**. These choices give developers precision, but they also introduce subtle pitfalls that can surprise even seasoned engineers.

Let's unpack the key ones every professional Go developer must understand.

Taking the Address of Loop Variables

In a `for ... range` loop, iteration variables (`k`, `v`) are **reused** across iterations. They're not reallocated each time for efficiency.

If you take their **address**, every pointer will reference the same underlying memory location.

```
m := map[string]int{"a": 1, "b": 2, "c": 3}
var ptrs []*int

for _, v := range m {
        ptrs = append(ptrs, &v)
}

fmt.Println(*ptrs[0], *ptrs[1], *ptrs[2])
```

Output (Surprising)

```
3 3 3
```

All three pointers point to the *same* `v`, which after the final iteration holds the last value.

Fix: Create a new variable per iteration:

```
for _, v := range m {
        vCopy := v
        ptrs = append(ptrs, &vCopy)
}
```

This allocates a new slot for each value, giving each pointer its own address.

Concurrent Map Iteration

Go maps are **not concurrency-safe**. Iterating a map while another goroutine writes to it triggers:

```
fatal error: concurrent map iteration and map write
```

This panic is intentional—it protects you from race conditions that can corrupt memory.

Fixes

- Use `sync.Mutex` or `sync.RWMutex` to guard reads and writes.
- For high-read, low-write patterns (e.g., caches, routing tables), prefer `sync.RWMutex`: many readers, one writer.
- For dynamic concurrent access patterns, use `sync.Map`, which offers built-in safety at some performance cost.

Enterprise Tip In routing tables, caches, or service registries, a `sync.RWMutex` often strikes the best balance. It allows many readers simultaneously, while writes stay exclusive.

Why These Happen: Memory Model Insight

- In `range`, iteration variables are **reused** for efficiency (Go avoids unnecessary allocations).
- That means addresses or closures tied to them all point to the same underlying slot.
- Maps are **not synchronized** by design—Go forces developers to choose the right concurrency model explicitly.

Summary

- **Never take loop variable addresses directly.**
- **Never assume map order;** sort keys when you need determinism.
- **Never iterate a map concurrently with writes.**
- **`range` over slices is safe, but may copy large values.** Optimize with indices for large structs.
- **Avoid unnecessary nested loops** in enterprise code. They scale poorly ($O(n^2)$). Consider maps or indexes instead.

- **Map iteration order is undefined**—never rely on it. Always sort if order matters.
- **Infinite loops need exits**—tie them to contexts in distributed systems.
- **Use guard conditions inside loops** (`continue`) to keep the main path uncluttered.

These pitfalls are not flaws in Go, but **deliberate design trade-offs**: they prioritize speed and explicitness, leaving responsibility in the developer's hands.

Exercises

1. Write a loop that assigns route IDs `"R1"..."R5"` to the first five vehicles in a slice.
2. Write a function of `PrintAssignments(assignments map[string]Route)` that prints vehicles in **sorted key order**.
3. Write a function that counts the number of runes in `"Straße"` and explains why it's not equal to its byte length.
4. Benchmark iterating a slice of 1,000,000 large structs by value vs. by pointer. Which one uses less memory and runs faster?

Error Handling in Go

> *"The first step in solving a problem is recognizing there is one."*
>
> —Will Rogers

In Go, errors are **ordinary values**, not extraordinary events. Unlike exceptions in languages such as Java, C#, or Python, an error in Go doesn't throw you into an alternate universe of stack unwinding and catch blocks. Instead, it appears in your hand—returned as a value, right alongside the successful result—demanding that you decide what to do next.

This design makes error paths visible in the same way traffic lights are visible on a road: you can't drive forward without acknowledging them. In enterprise projects, this explicitness is a superpower. It keeps failure handling **testable**, **maintainable**, and—most importantly—**predictable**.

Errors vs. Exceptions: Two Philosophies

Exceptions assume that errors are "exceptional"—rare, unpredictable, and worthy of halting normal control flow. They bubble up through stack frames until someone decides to catch them. This can simplify code in the small (no `if err != nil` everywhere), but it complicates code in the large:

- Did this function handle the exception, or is it still bubbling up?
- What kind of exceptions might this library throw? Checked or unchecked?
- What happens if an exception slips through the cracks?

In contrast, **Go's errors are plain values**. Nothing mystical happens when a function fails—it simply returns an `error`. The caller must check it explicitly:

```
r, err := LoadRoute("R-17")
if err != nil {
    return fmt.Errorf("failed to load route: %w", err)
}
```

This has consequences:

- **Visibility**: You see every possible failure right at the call site.
- **Control**: You choose immediately—wrap it, retry, log it, or propagate it.
- **Predictability**: The function does what it says: it computes a result or it doesn't. No hidden stack gymnastics.

Why Go Chose Errors over Exceptions

When Go's creators designed the language at Google, they wanted something engineers could use safely in **large, long-lived code bases**. Exceptions were deliberately rejected for several reasons:

1. **Simplicity:** Go's error model is trivial to explain—`error` is just an interface with an `Error() string` method. No special compiler rules, no hidden stack tracing machinery.
2. **Readability:** In enterprise teams, code is read far more often than it is written. By forcing explicit checks, Go makes error paths visible to reviewers and maintainers.
3. **Testability:** An error is a value, which means you can store it, compare it, wrap it, or fake it in tests. You don't need a special "mock exception."
4. **Predictable Control Flow:** Stack unwinding in exceptions can make performance profiles unpredictable. Go prefers control flow you can reason about directly, which is crucial in systems where latency budgets are measured in milliseconds.

A Life Lesson in Software Form

Errors in Go embody a life philosophy: face problems directly instead of pretending they are exceptional.

- In life, if your car breaks down, you don't pretend it's a one-in-a-million cosmic event. You step out, diagnose, and fix it.
- Exceptions hide failure until it bursts upward like an explosion. Errors in Go force you to stop and check the dashboard after every turn.

It may feel tedious at first, but it's the difference between ignoring warning signs and building resilience. As Marcus Aurelius says: *"The impediment to action advances action. What stands in the way becomes the way."*

In large-scale enterprise systems—handling payments, controlling transport fleets, managing medical records—errors are not exceptions. They are daily companions. Go's philosophy is: don't deny that. Handle it.

The Shape of Errors

Go functions typically return a `(T, error)` pair. If `error` is `nil`, the operation succeeded; otherwise, it failed.

```
func LoadRoute(id string) (Route, error) {
	if id == "" {
		return Route{}, fmt.Errorf("empty route id")
	}
	// ... fetch from storage
	return Route{ID: id, Name: "R-42"}, nil
}

func main(){
	r, err := LoadRoute("R-42")
	if err != nil {
	  // handle
	}
}
```

Styling Error Messages

In Go, error messages are designed to be **concise, consistent, and readable**—they're part of your program's API, not prose for humans. Follow these core conventions to keep your errors idiomatic and helpful:

- **Start with a Lowercase Letter**

  Error messages are usually printed mid-sentence (e.g., `"failed to connect: timeout"`)—not capitalized like logs.

  ☑ `"empty route id"`

  × `"Empty route ID"`

- **No Trailing Punctuation**

  Errors are values, not sentences. Avoid ending them with a period unless part of quoted data.

☑ `"invalid vehicle state"`

× `"invalid vehicle state."`

- **Describe the Symptom Clearly**

  Tell what went wrong, not what was tried.

  ☑ `"missing configuration file"`

  × `"could not load configuration file"`

- **Add Actionable Context Where Useful**

  Combine the operation and the cause:

  ```
  fmt.Errorf("assign vehicle %s to route %s: empty route
  id", v.ID, r.ID)
  ```

This message is specific, traceable, and helpful in distributed logs.

Early Returns (Guard Clauses)

Go favors **clarity and flat control flow**. Instead of nesting logic deeply, handle errors or invalid states **immediately**, then return. This pattern—called a *guard clause*—keeps the "happy path" at the lowest indentation, making functions shorter, safer, and easier to read.

```
func AssignVehicleToRoute(v *Vehicle, r RouteID) error {
	if v == nil {
		return fmt.Errorf("vehicle is nil")
	}
	if r == "" {
		return fmt.Errorf("empty route id")
	}
	v.Route = r
	return nil
}
```

Each guard checks a precondition and exits early when something's wrong. As a result, the main logic (`v.Route = r`) remains visually simple and free of nested `if` blocks.

Why It Matters

Early returns are not just about style—they're about **maintainability** and **reliability**.

- They make it immediately clear which inputs are invalid.
- They reduce indentation, improving readability for code reviews.
- They minimize the cognitive load during debugging or incident response, when clarity saves time.

This approach aligns perfectly with Go's philosophy: **explicit checks, minimal nesting, clear flow**.

Wrapping Errors with Context

Go encourages you to **add context, not noise**, when propagating errors. Rather than returning raw errors, you should wrap them with meaningful details about *what* your code was trying to do when the failure occurred. This provides a full breadcrumb trail from the root cause to the operation that failed.

```
func PersistAssignment(store Store, v *Vehicle) error {
	if err := store.SaveAssignment(v.ID, v.Route); err != nil {
		return fmt.Errorf("persist assignment (vehicle=%s route=%s):
		%w", v.ID, v.Route, err)
	}
	return nil
}
```

Here, the `%w` verb wraps the original error—preserving its identity while adding context. The result is both **human-readable** and **machine-inspectable**:

Developers see the business context in logs, while tools can still unwrap and classify the underlying error type.

Unwrapping and Handling

At the system edge (e.g., your HTTP or gRPC layer), you can inspect errors using `errors.Is` and `errors.As` to make intelligent, consistent decisions:

```
err := PersistAssignment(store, v)
switch {
case errors.Is(err, ErrRouteNotFound):
      // return 404 in HTTP layer
case errors.Is(err, context.DeadlineExceeded):
      // translate to 504, emit a timeout metric
case err != nil:
      // 500 and alert
}
```

This pattern connects **business semantics** (e.g., route not found) with **technical realities** (timeouts, I/O failures) without losing precision.

Sentinel Errors vs. Typed Errors

In Go, **errors are values**, not exceptions—and not all errors carry the same purpose. Some merely **signal a well-known condition** (like "end of input"), while others must **convey structured context** (like which vehicle failed a capacity check). Understanding when to use **sentinel errors** vs. **typed errors** is key to building maintainable, observable, and scalable enterprise systems.

Go's error model deliberately supports both styles:

- **Sentinel Errors:** Simple, shared constants representing universal states.
- **Typed Errors:** Rich, structured types that carry actionable domain details.

Sentinel Errors: Simple and Shared

A **sentinel error** is a **predefined variable** that represents one specific, well-known condition. It's the simplest form of signaling failure in Go—no struct, no metadata, just a shared constant value.

```
var ErrRouteNotFound = errors.New("route not found")
```

Functions use sentinel errors to express clear, universal outcomes:

```
func LoadRoute(id string) (Route, error) {
	route, ok := routes[id]
	if !ok {
		return Route{}, ErrRouteNotFound
	}
	return route, nil
}
```

At the call site, you can detect this specific failure using `errors.Is`:

```
r, err := LoadRoute("R-404")
if errors.Is(err, ErrRouteNotFound) {
	fmt.Println("Route not found, returning 404")
}
```

Advantages

- **Cheap and Simple:** A sentinel error is just a shared variable; there's no struct allocation or extra metadata. This makes it memory-efficient and perfect for lightweight signaling.
- **Easy to Check:** Works seamlessly with `errors.Is`, so callers can test for the condition without fragile string comparisons.
- **Readable and Self-Documenting:** A named error like `ErrRouteNotFound` immediately communicates intent, turning a generic failure into a clear, domain-specific signal.

In short, sentinel errors offer a fast, low-ceremony way to represent *well-understood, context-free conditions* in both internal and cross-package APIs.

Disadvantages

- **Brittle Across Packages:** Two packages can both define `ErrNotFound`, but unless they point to the exact same variable, they're not equal. This makes cross-package comparison fragile and error-prone.

- **Not Expressive:** Sentinel errors carry no structured data. You can't embed useful context such as which route, vehicle, or operation failed. Debugging often requires additional logs or wrapping.
- **Risk of Proliferation:** It's easy to scatter dozens of sentinel errors across a large code base, each slightly different in meaning. This "error sprawl" creates confusion and weakens the system's contracts.

Enterprise Tip Use sentinel errors only for universal, context-independent conditions (e.g., `io.EOF`, `context.Canceled`). They're best for signaling "one obvious meaning" across the ecosystem.

Typed Errors: Rich and Structured

When you need more than a simple "what went wrong," use **typed errors**. A typed error is a custom type that implements Go's `error` interface by defining an `Error()` method.

This lets you return errors that **carry structured data**, not just messages—making them far more useful for diagnostics and decision-making.

```
type CapacityError struct {
        VehicleID string
        Needed    int
        Available int
}

func (e *CapacityError) Error() string {
        return fmt.Sprintf("vehicle %s capacity %d < needed %d",
                e.VehicleID, e.Available, e.Needed)
}
```

Here, the error describes *why* the failure occurred and *which vehicle* caused it. It's still a valid `error`, but with machine-readable context for callers to inspect.

Using Typed Errors in Practice

Here you can see an example of a typed error.

```
func AssignPassengers(v *Vehicle, count int) error {
	if count > v.Capacity {
		return &CapacityError{
			VehicleID: v.ID,
			Needed:    count,
			Available: v.Capacity,
		}
	}
	return nil
}
```

At the call site, you can recover structured information using `errors.As`:

```
err := AssignPassengers(v, 50)
var capErr *CapacityError
if errors.As(err, &capErr) {
	fmt.Printf("Vehicle %s overloaded: need %d, have %d\n",
		capErr.VehicleID, capErr.Needed, capErr.Available)
}
```

This allows your code to branch intelligently based on the **error's meaning**, not its text—making error handling reliable, testable, and expressive.

Why Typed Errors Matter

Typed errors turn your error model into a form of **domain modeling**: they let you describe failures as *first-class data structures* that your system can reason about. This is invaluable in enterprise contexts where you need to decide whether to retry, escalate, alert, or degrade gracefully.

They're also ideal for **logging and observability**—you can extract structured fields directly into JSON logs or telemetry without parsing error strings.

Advantages

- **Carries Rich Context:** You can embed structured details such as IDs, limits, and timestamps, turning an error into actionable information rather than a vague message.
- **Enables Programmatic Handling:** Callers can use `errors.As` or type assertions to branch logic intelligently (retry, fallback, alert, or log structured data).
- **Scales Across Enterprise Domains:** Typed errors make large systems more predictable by clearly modeling business failures—far more expressive than plain strings.

Disadvantages

- **Adds Boilerplate:** Each type requires a struct definition and an `Error()` method, which can feel verbose for simple conditions.
- **Risk of Over-engineering:** Defining too many specialized error types can clutter APIs and overwhelm maintainers.
- **Limited Interoperability:** Typed errors are **package-scoped**; other packages must import the type to check for it, which can create coupling.

Enterprise Tip Use typed errors selectively—only when consumers need to understand and act on the details. For transient or context-free conditions, sentinel errors are simpler and clearer.

Summary

Treat **sentinel errors** as *stop signs*—clear, universal signals that everyone in your system recognizes instantly.

Treat **typed errors** as *incident reports*—they don't just stop the process; they explain *what failed, where, and why.*

In enterprise Go, wisdom lies in choosing the right level of detail: use sentinel errors for simple, shared truths, and typed errors when teams, services, or systems need structured context to act intelligently. Mastering that balance turns error handling from noise into knowledge—and systems from reactive to resilient.

Unwrapping and Joining

Go's error handling model is **compositional**—errors can be **wrapped**, **unwrapped**, and even **combined** into chains that preserve full context across layers. This allows higher-level code to see both *what failed locally* and *why it failed originally*, without losing information.

You can use these functions to achieve these goals:

- `errors.Unwrap(err)`

  Retrieves the next error in the chain—essentially peeling one layer off a wrapped error. This enables you to inspect the underlying cause directly when needed.

- `errors.Is(err, target)`

  Returns `true` if *any* wrapped error matches the target. This is how sentinel errors remain useful even when wrapped with extra context.

- `errors.As(err, &out)`

  Assigns the first matching concrete type into `out`, allowing typed error inspection.

- `errors.Join(e1, e2, ...)`

  Go 1.20 introduced `errors.Join(e1, e2, ...)`, which combines several errors into one composite error—useful when multiple cleanup or shutdown steps fail together.

```
func closeAll(cs ...io.Closer) error {
	var errs []error
	for _, c := range cs {
```

```
            if c != nil {
                if err := c.Close(); err != nil {
                    errs = append(errs, fmt.Errorf("close:
                    %w", err))
                }
            }
        }
        return errors.Join(errs...)
    }
```

This pattern ensures no error is lost: all issues are collected, yet callers still see a single error value they can unwrap or inspect.

Don't Log and Return (Double-Logging)

One of the most common sources of noisy logs in large systems is **double-logging**—when both a library and its caller log the same error. In Go, the rule is simple: **library code returns errors; application edges log them.**

Your libraries shouldn't know *how* or *where* an error is reported—they just describe *what went wrong*. It's the caller's responsibility (e.g., CLI, HTTP handler, or worker) to log, correlate, and convert that error into a user-visible response.

```
// Library function: return, don't log.
func ReadRoute(db DB, id string) (Route, error) { /* ... */ }

// HTTP edge: log + translate to status code.
func (h *Handler) getRoute(w http.ResponseWriter, r *http.Request) {
    route, err := ReadRoute(h.DB, "R-1")
    if err != nil {
        // log once here with request id
        http.Error(w, "route not found", http.StatusNotFound)
        return
    }
    _ = json.NewEncoder(w).Encode(route)
}
```

Double-logging creates confusion during incident response: you see the same error twice—once deep in the library, once at the edge—with different timestamps and no clear source. This inflates logs, breaks alerting thresholds, and hides the *first* place the problem occurred.

Timeouts, Cancellation, and Context

In enterprise projects, **timeouts aren't edge cases—they're normal error paths**. Every service call, database query, or API request must have a clear time boundary to prevent runaway latency. That's why Go's `context.Context` is designed to flow through your entire call chain, carrying **deadlines, cancellation signals, and request scope**.

Always **accept** a `context.Context` as the first argument in any function that performs I/O or blocking work. Then, use `context.WithTimeout` or `context.WithDeadline` to enforce a bound, and call `cancel()` when finished.

```
func (s *Service) Fetch(ctx context.Context, id string) (Route, error) {
      ctx, cancel := context.WithTimeout(ctx, 300*time.Millisecond)
      defer cancel()

      route, err := s.repo.Get(ctx, id)
      if err != nil {
            return Route{}, fmt.Errorf("repo get %s: %w", id, err)
      }
      return route, nil
}
```

Here, if the repository call takes too long or the client disconnects, the context automatically cancels the operation—preventing wasted resources and hanging goroutines.

Use `errors.Is(err, context.DeadlineExceeded)` and `errors.Is(err, context.Canceled)` to differentiate timeout vs. client-cancel.

Defer and Error Handling (and Close Hygiene)

Go's `defer` statement is one of its most elegant safety tools—it guarantees cleanup actions execute when a function returns, no matter which path the code takes. This is invaluable for managing resources like files, network connections, and locks.

However, when combined with error handling, it requires precision and discipline to avoid subtle bugs and leaks. A deferred function runs **only when the surrounding function returns**, not on every loop iteration. This makes it ideal for final cleanup or error augmentation at the function scope.

```
func loadConfig(path string) (_ *Config, err error) {
	f, err := os.Open(path)
	if err != nil {
		return nil, fmt.Errorf("open %s: %w", path, err)
	}
	defer func() {
		if cerr := f.Close(); cerr != nil {
			// prefer to surface both
			if err != nil {
				err = errors.Join(err, fmt.Errorf("close %s: %w",
				path, cerr))
			} else {
				err = fmt.Errorf("close %s: %w", path, cerr)
			}
		}
	}()

	// ... parse
	return &Config{}, nil
}
```

Here, `defer` ensures the file is closed even if parsing fails. The deferred function also *amends* the return value `err` to include both the primary error and any close failure—preserving diagnostic value without losing the root cause.

Enterprise Tip Don't `defer f.Close()` inside large loops; close explicitly each iteration to avoid FD (File Descriptor) leaks.

Panics and Recover: Use Sparingly

Go's **panic/recover** mechanism exists for *catastrophic failures*, not for normal control flow.

A **panic** signals that something is fundamentally wrong—such as a corrupted state, violated invariants, or a bug that makes further execution unsafe.

While Go recovers gracefully from most errors via `error` values, panics bypass that system entirely, unwinding the stack until a `recover()` is found.

Enterprise Tips

- **Do not** use `panic` for ordinary errors.
- Panic is for **programmer bugs** or **corruption** (invariants violated).
- Library code should avoid panicking; app edges may **recover** to prevent a process crash.

```
// Safe HTTP wrapper to prevent a bad handler from crashing the server.
func withRecover(h http.Handler) http.Handler {
	return http.HandlerFunc(func(w http.ResponseWriter, r
	*http.Request) {
		defer func() {
			if rec := recover(); rec != nil {
				// log with correlation id; return 500
				http.Error(w, "internal error", http.
				StatusInternalServerError)
			}
		}()
		h.ServeHTTP(w, r)
	})
}
```

This pattern isolates programmer bugs, allowing the service to recover gracefully while still alerting engineers.

Widely accepted "must panic" pattern is a `template.Must(...)`-style initialization where failing early is correct.

```
tmpl := template.Must(template.New("page").ParseFiles("page.html"))
```

If a template can't parse at startup, it's better to fail fast than to continue in a half-initialized state. This "fail early, fail loud" approach ensures the application starts only in a valid configuration.

In enterprise Go, panics are for **bugs**, not **business logic**—reserve them for the truly unrecoverable.

Summary

- Panics are **nuclear options**—use them for **impossible states**, not runtime errors.
- Library code should **never panic**; let callers decide how to handle failure.
- App edges (servers, workers) should recover from panics to protect uptime, log the failure, and continue serving.
- For resilience, always combine panic recovery with **structured logging** and **request correlation IDs** to aid postmortem analysis.

In enterprise Go, panics are for **bugs**, not **business logic**—reserve them for the truly unrecoverable.

Exercises

1. Implement a function that returns `errors.New("db error")` so it wraps with operation context and route/vehicle IDs using `%w`. Verify with `errors.Is`.
2. Open two files and a network connection; ensure all are closed, collecting any close errors with `errors.Join` while preserving the main error.
3. Add a 200ms timeout to a repository call. Simulate a 500ms sleep inside the repo, and assert that callers see `context.DeadlineExceeded`.
4. Write a middleware `withRecover(next http.Handler)` that converts panics to 500, logs once, and keeps the process alive

Summary

In this chapter, we explored how Go expresses *behavior*: through functions, methods, structs, interfaces, and the control-flow constructs that govern decisions in real systems.

We saw how Go favors clarity over cleverness—multiple returns, guard clauses, and explicit error values—giving enterprise teams predictable execution paths and testable behavior.

We learned how structs model data without inheritance, how embedding and composition prevent duplication, and how small, consumer-defined interfaces keep dependencies clean and systems modular.

We examined control flow and loops not as syntax, but as tools for writing safe, scalable logic—from type switches at system boundaries to loop patterns that avoid hidden performance traps.

Finally, we treated errors as values, not exceptions, using wrapping, typed errors, and context to build systems that fail clearly, recover gracefully, and remain maintainable at scale.

What's Next

In the next chapter, we move from building software to proving it works. After learning Go's structural grammar, we'll now learn how to build trust in that structure through testing. You'll see how Go makes testing a first-class citizen, not a framework bolted on later.

We'll start with fundamentals like naming conventions, `_test.go` files, and `*testing.T`, then grow into enterprise-grade techniques: table-driven tests, subtests, parallel execution, fuzzing, and benchmarks. Along the way, we'll anchor every idea in real transport system examples, showing how Go's simple testing model scales to complex, concurrent systems.

If this chapter taught us how to *speak Go correctly*, the next one teaches us how to *verify that what we say is true.*

CHAPTER 7

Testing in Go: Building Confidence Through Code

"As tests accumulate, you gain confidence in the behavior of the system."

—Kent Beck

Several years ago, I was working on an enterprise project. It had millions of users and thousands of concurrent online users. One day, we had to release a new feature quickly; this system did not have any tests. After deployment, we started seeing serious issues. One bug in the new code caused the entire system to crash. In production, with thousands of users online, we had no choice but to restart the system every few minutes just to keep it running.

The development team had to work under extreme stress. Since there were no tests for the changes, every fix had the risk of breaking something else. We ended up releasing several versions every hour, trying to stop the system from failing. This chaos continued for almost a week. I still remember the final night. I was talking to the system administrator on the phone. We had fixed most problems. When I was happy, I suggested an improvement! Renaming an index to make things easier to maintain. He agreed. I renamed it. A few seconds later, he told me the logs were full of errors. Then he said something terrifying: "The table is gone." In my exhaustion, I accidentally renamed the table instead of the index.

That mistake happened because of stress. And that stress came from a missing safety net: automated tests. If we had tested our code properly from the beginning, none of this would have happened.

S. Shahsavan, *Building Enterprise Projects with Go*, https://doi.org/10.1007/979-8-8688-2370-1_7

Enterprise Lesson Delivering a product is not just about building features. It is about making sure each feature does not break others. Automated testing is a reliable way to protect your system as it grows.

Enterprise systems are always changing. Teams get larger or smaller. Deadlines move. Code that worked well yesterday might stop working tomorrow. Under pressure, new features are often added quickly. Old logic might break quietly, without warning. In the middle of all this, one thing becomes critical: confidence. Not the belief that everything is perfect, but the trust that your system still behaves as expected. And if something breaks, your team should notice it right away.

In Go, testing is not an extra tool or an optional step. It is a built-in part of the language and toolchain. Just like you use `go build` to compile your code, you use `go test` to check if your code behaves correctly. You do not need to install third-party test runners or write complex setup scripts. Testing in Go is simple, fast, and ready from day one.

This design is not only helpful for beginners. It is a long-term advantage. It helps new team members become productive quickly. It gives large teams a shared testing approach. And it encourages a testing culture that keeps systems healthy as they grow.

This mindset—treating correctness as part of your daily routine—is one of Go's most powerful ideas. It is also one of the main reasons why experienced engineers choose Go when working on systems that need to be stable, safe, and reliable.

Why Testing Is First-Class in Go

In many programming languages, testing is treated as something extra. Developers often use third-party libraries, plug-ins, or complex tools to set up testing. It is common to see testing added only after the main code is complete. In those cases, testing feels like a side task, not part of the core development process.

Go is different. From its very first release in 2009, testing was part of the standard toolchain. You do not need to install anything. The `go test` command is as natural as `go build`. It is built on the same ideas: fast feedback, simple tools, and clear structure.

The goal behind this design is practical. A program that compiles is not always correct. Syntax can be checked by the compiler. Behavior must be checked by tests. Go makes this easy by including testing in the language itself.

As I shared before, skipping tests in a real-world project caused serious problems. A single bug in a new feature brought down an entire system. Fixes made under stress created new issues. The team lost valuable time and trust. That painful experience shows how important testing is in real enterprise projects.

Go's built-in testing tools help teams avoid this kind of risk. They allow developers to test early, test often, and test with confidence. When testing is easy, it becomes a habit. And when testing becomes a habit, quality improves across the whole system.

Enterprise Lesson Testing should not depend on extra tools or a complex setup. It should be part of your workflow from the beginning. Go makes testing simple, fast, and reliable—exactly what enterprise systems need to stay healthy over time.

Built-in Toolchain

In Go, you do not need to install any special tools to write tests. Testing support comes with the language. From the moment you install Go, the full test toolchain is ready.

The `go test` command runs tests automatically. It looks for files ending in `_test.go` and for functions that start with `Test`, `Benchmark`, or `Fuzz`. You do not need extra configuration files or special folders. Just follow simple naming rules, and Go will handle the rest.

The standard `testing` package gives you the core types you need:

- `*testing.T` for writing unit tests
- `*testing.B` for writing performance benchmarks
- `*testing.F` for fuzz testing (added in Go 1.18 and still improving)

Go also includes powerful built-in options:

- `-cover` measures how much of your code is covered by tests.
- `-race` detects data races in concurrent programs.
- `-cpuprofile`, `-memprofile`, and other flags help you profile CPU and memory usage.

In Go 1.25, new testing helpers have been added to the standard library:

- The `testing/synctest` package helps you test concurrency patterns by detecting goroutine leaks and checking proper shutdowns.
- The `testing/slogtest` package lets you test structured logs written with the new `log/slog` API.
- These packages are optional, but they give you stronger tools for writing safe, clear tests in complex systems.

All of this works out of the box. You do not need to download third-party libraries, write configuration files, or learn custom DSLs (domain-specific languages). There is no vendor lock-in, and nothing hidden behind paid tools or frameworks.

This simplicity becomes even more valuable in enterprise teams. New developers do not need to spend days learning a custom test setup. Everyone uses the same standard tools. This creates a shared language and a common structure for tests. It reduces friction, avoids confusion, and helps people contribute faster.

Tests As Documentation

In Go, tests are not only for checking correctness. They also help others understand how your code is supposed to work. This is possible because Go encourages simple, clear test functions. That simplicity is intentional. It turns tests into a form of living documentation.

When a test fails with a line like

```
t.Errorf("got %v, want %v", got, want)
```

It tells future developers what the function was expected to do. The test acts like a written explanation. It shows what input was used, what output was expected, and what actually happened. There is no need to read long comments or external documents. The test itself explains the logic.

Go also supports special test functions called `ExampleXxx`. These are more than just examples. They serve two important roles:

1. They run like normal tests during `go test`.
2. They appear in documentation when someone runs `go doc`.

For example, if you write

```
func ExampleAdd() {
    r := Add(2, 3)
    fmt.Println(r)
    // Output: 5
}
```

This code will be shown in the documentation for the Add function. And the test runner will check that the output is still 5. If the behavior changes, the test will fail. This means your examples are always valid, always tested, and never outdated.

This connection between tests and documentation is powerful. You do not need to repeat yourself. The same code helps both the computer verify correctness and the human understand intent.

Enterprise Lesson Strong teams use tests to communicate, not just to validate. When tests are simple and example functions are included, new developers can understand and trust the code base faster. This becomes even more important when you build code for other teams or external users. Good tests and clear examples help others use your packages safely, without guessing how they work. Senior engineers often begin by reading tests. That habit saves time, avoids confusion, and makes collaboration smoother.

Speed and Determinism

Go was built to give fast feedback to developers. Its compiler is quick, even for large code bases, and the runtime avoids hidden behavior. This makes it easy and practical to run the full test suite many times during the day. For healthy development teams, running all tests before every commit should become a normal part of the process.

But speed is not the only goal. Tests are useful when they are **deterministic**. A deterministic test gives the same result every time for the same input. This kind of test builds trust. If you run it today and again next week, the result should be the same.

Go supports deterministic testing by giving you simple tools and clear patterns. Here are some best practices:

- Avoid using shared or global state between tests.
- Seed `math/rand` with a fixed value during testing to make random behavior predictable.
- Use `t.TempDir()` to create temporary directories that are isolated and cleaned up automatically.
- Prefer in-memory data over real files or network calls to reduce environmental differences.
- In Go 1.25, the `testing/synctest` package helps detect leaks in concurrent code. This is useful when tests start goroutines that must finish before the test ends.

These techniques help your test suite produce repeatable results. You can run all tests on Monday, and again on Friday, and still get the same output. This kind of reliability builds confidence, especially in large teams or distributed systems.

Enterprise Lesson A flaky test is worse than no test at all. It slows teams down, creates doubt, and makes developers stop trusting the suite. Go gives you powerful tools to write deterministic tests, but using them well takes discipline. The reward is a reliable, trusted code base that scales safely with your team.

The Senior Mindset: Design for Testability

In Go, testing is not only about finding bugs. It is about writing code that is easy to understand, easy to change, and easy to test. Senior developers think about testing while they design the code, not after. They plan their code so it stays simple, flexible, and testable.

This way of thinking follows the principles of clean code. Clean code is clear, does one thing well, and is easy to read and test. Tests act as a mirror for your design. If your code is hard to test, it is usually a sign that something needs to be refactored.

Here are a few clean code habits that support better testing:

- **Keep packages small.** Each package should have a single purpose. This reduces dependencies and helps you focus your tests.
- **Define clear boundaries.** Use interfaces or constructor functions to define the edges between components. This lets you replace parts in tests without using real databases or network calls.
- **Use pure functions where possible.** A pure function only uses its input and gives a predictable output. It does not change the shared state or use external systems. These functions are the easiest to test and often the cleanest to maintain.

Go testing tools help enforce these ideas. When you write test functions, the language guides you toward small, reusable units of logic. If your function requires too much setup or has side effects everywhere, it becomes obvious during testing. This feedback pushes you to improve your design.

For example, in our transport system, functions like `IsVehicleAllowedOnRoute(vehicle, route)` or `ValidateSchedule(schedule)` can be tested without a database. These functions work directly with in-memory values and do not require external systems. You give them structured input, and they return a result that can be checked easily in a test. This kind of design supports fast, reliable, and isolated testing. It also leads to simpler code that is easier to maintain over time.

Enterprise Lesson Clean code is testable code. Writing tests often shows where your design is too complex or too tightly coupled. Go helps you keep code clean by making testing a core part of development. When your design is test-friendly, your system becomes easier to understand, extend, and trust. This is how senior engineers build systems that last.

Basics You Must Master

Before you can run with confidence, you must first learn how to stand steady. Just like learning to tie your shoes before taking a long walk, writing tests in Go starts by understanding the basic conventions. These basics are not hard, but they are critical.

Go gives you a powerful testing toolset built right into the language. But to unlock that power, you need to understand how it works. Go testing follows clear patterns for naming, structuring, and running tests. Once you learn these patterns, testing becomes a smooth and natural part of your workflow.

I once saw a team that didn't take the time to learn these basics. They avoided reading Go's documentation and never picked up a proper book. Instead, they quickly added third-party test frameworks, thinking it would save time. But those frameworks ended up slowing them down. They added complexity, hid Go's real testing tools, and even blocked access to useful features like race detection and coverage reporting. At one point, they realized they couldn't use Go's latest test options because the framework didn't support them. The frustration was real.

This experience is a clear reminder: you can only get the full value of Go's testing system if you master the standard tools first. You don't need to wrap them or replace them. You just need to know how to use them well.

In enterprise projects, where systems are large, deadlines are tight, and reliability is critical, knowing the basics is not optional. The difference between "code that can be tested" and "code that is tested every day" starts here. By learning the core testing patterns, you put yourself in a better position to develop software that is safe, clear, and ready for change.

File and Package Conventions

Go does not rely on annotations, decorators, or external configuration to find and run tests. Instead, it uses file names and function names. This makes test discovery simple, predictable, and fast.

Here are the rules you must follow:

- **Test files** must end with `_test.go`. Any file with this suffix is automatically detected by the `go test` command.
- **Test functions** must begin with `Test` and take exactly one parameter of type `*testing.T`.
- For example:

```go
func TestAssignVehicle(t *testing.T) {
    // test logic here
}
```

Go allows two main styles of testing:

- **Internal Testing:** Write your test files in the same package as the code being tested. This gives you access to unexported functions, variables, and types. It is useful for internal logic and low-level behavior.
- **External Testing:** Use a separate test package, such as `mypkg_test`, that imports your package like an external consumer. This forces you to test only what is public. It is good for verifying the external contract and avoiding tight coupling.

Both are useful. In most projects, you will use both. But don't mix them randomly in the same test file. Use same-package tests when you need full access and `_test` packages when you want to test exposed functionality.

Fixtures and Golden Files

In enterprise projects, tests often need data: sample payloads, route lists, schedule templates, and other structured inputs. Go has a built-in pattern to manage this: use a dedicated `testdata/` directory.

This folder is special. The Go toolchain ignores `testdata/` during builds, but test code can still read from it. This makes it a safe and expected place for your JSON, CSV, and text test inputs.

You can also use **golden files**. A golden file is a saved version of the expected output for a test case. During a test, your program generates fresh output, then compares it to the golden file. If they match, the test passes. If not, something has changed.

Golden files are especially useful when

- The output is too large or complex for inline strings.
- You want to track test data changes over time with Git diffs.
- You want reproducibility across machines and teams.

If your test needs temporary versions of these files, use `t.TempDir()` to create a clean space at runtime. This function is built into Go 1.15+ and is still the recommended way in Go 1.25 to isolate file system effects.

Understanding *testing.T

Every test function in Go receives a `*testing.T` value. This is how your test talks to the Go test runner. It helps you report failures, skip tests when needed, create temporary files, and clean up resources.

You can think of `*testing.T` as the control panel of your test. It lets you decide what happens when something goes wrong and how the test should behave in different conditions. You will use it in every test you write.

Here are the most important features of `*testing.T` that you will use in daily work.

Failure Reporting

When a test fails, it should tell you clearly what went wrong. The goal is not just to stop the test, but to explain the problem in a way that helps you fix it quickly.

Go provides two main types of failure reporting through the `*testing.T` value:

1. `t.Error()` and `t.Errorf()`

   These methods report a problem but allow the test to continue running. This is useful when running multiple things in one test. All failures will be reported, not just the first one.

   ```
   t.Errorf("got %v, want %v", got, want)
   ```

   This line means: the test expected a different value. The test keeps running, so you can see if other things also failed.

2. `t.Fatal()` and `t.Fatalf()`

   These methods report a failure and stop the test immediately. Use them when the rest of the test cannot continue without this step working.

   ```
   t.Fatalf("missing required field: %s", field)
   ```

This is a good choice if there is no reason to check anything else if this part of the code failed, for example: the database URL is not present in the configuration.

These reporting tools help make test output useful. When a test fails, you want to know exactly what happened and why. Good failure messages save time and reduce confusion, especially in large systems where many tests run together.

Enterprise Lesson Always include both the actual and expected values in your error message. This makes it easier to understand the difference.

Skipping Tests

Sometimes a test should not run in certain situations. For example, a test might only make sense on Linux, or it might use a feature that is not available in your CI environment.

In Go, you can skip a test by calling `t.Skip()` or `t.Skipf()` inside the test function. Here is a typical example:

```
if runtime.GOOS == "windows" {
    t.Skip("this test does not run on Windows")
}
```

This line checks the operating system and skips the test with a clear message if it is running on Windows.

When a test is skipped:

- It does not run the rest of the code.
- It is shown in the test output as "skipped", not as passed or failed.
- It helps your test suite stay clean and green across different systems.

You can also skip tests based on environment variables, missing files, or any condition that makes the test irrelevant or unstable in that context.

Example: Skip if a config file is not found:

```
if _, err := os.Stat("config.test.yaml"); errors.Is(err, os.ErrNotExist) {
    t.Skip("config file not available for this test")
}
```

Enterprise Lesson Always give a clear reason inside `t.Skip()`. This will help your teammates (and your future self) understand why the test did not run. Use skips to keep your suite portable and reliable, but never use them to hide failing tests. Skipping is a tool, not an excuse.

Helper Functions

In real projects, you often reuse the same logic in different tests. For example, reading a file, creating test data, or checking a common condition. It is a good idea to move that repeated code into a small helper function. But there is one important thing to do when writing a helper: call `t.Helper()` at the top of the function.

This tells Go that the function is just a helper, not the main part of the test. So when an error happens inside the helper, Go will show the failure at the line where the helper was used, not inside the helper itself.

Example

```
func mustReadFile(t *testing.T, path string) string {
    t.Helper() // marks this function as a helper
    content, err := os.ReadFile(path)
    if err != nil {
        t.Fatalf("read error: %v", err)
    }
    return string(content)
}
```

If this helper is used in a test, and the file is missing or unreadable, the failure message will point to the test line, not inside `mustReadFile`. This makes debugging faster and error messages easier to follow, especially when helpers are several lines deep in the call stack.

Why It Matters

- When error messages point to helpers, it wastes time during debugging.
- When messages point to the exact test line, you know where the failure started.

Tip Always use `t.Helper()` in any test helper you write, even if the helper is small. It costs nothing and gives clearer output. Clean test output matters in enterprise projects. One misplaced line number can waste minutes or hours in a busy CI pipeline, especially in a stressful situation.

Cleanup Functions

Some tests need temporary resources. You might create a file, open a connection, or start a background goroutine. When the test ends, you must clean up that resource. If you forget to do this, your test might pass but still leak memory, leave files behind, or affect other tests.

Go gives you a simple way to manage this: `t.Cleanup()`.

This function lets you register a cleanup task. Go will run that task automatically when the test ends, whether it passes or fails.

Example: Clean Up a Temporary File

```
tempFile := createTempConfig()
t.Cleanup(func() {
    os.Remove(tempFile)
})
```

In this example, the file will always be deleted when the test finishes. You do not need to remember to remove it manually.

Use Cases

- Remove temporary files and directories.
- Close open connections or file handles.
- Stop background goroutines or timers.
- Reset environment variables or global settings.

Example: Stop a Goroutine Cleanly

```
done := make(chan struct{})
go func() {
    <-done
    // simulate background work
}()

t.Cleanup(func() {
    close(done)
})
```

This avoids leaks. It ensures the goroutine exits when the test ends.

Go ensures that `t.Cleanup()` works correctly, even in tests that run in parallel using `t.Parallel()`. Cleanup functions are queued and executed after each test finishes, without conflict.

Enterprise Tip Always use `t.Cleanup()` instead of writing custom `defer` chains or `if failed` checks. It keeps your tests clean, safe, and easier to read.

Enterprise Lesson In large systems, even small resource leaks can cause flaky test behavior or slow down CI pipelines. Cleanup is not optional—it is part of writing responsible tests.

Main Differences Between defer and t.Cleanup()

Before we look at the code examples, Table 7-1 summarizes the key differences between `defer` and `t.Cleanup()`—when they run, how they scope cleanup work, and why `t.Cleanup()` is safer inside helper functions and parallel tests.

Table 7-1. *Differences between `defer` and `t.Cleanup()`*

Feature	`defer`	`t.Cleanup()`
When it runs	Immediately before the current function (`TestXxx`) returns	After the test finishes, regardless of how it ends
Scope	Only inside the current function	Works even if the helper function returns early
Best used for	Quick cleanup in the same function	Cleanup that should always run, even if it is in a helper function
Multiple calls	Deferred in reverse order	Cleanup functions also run in reverse order
Integration with `t.Parallel()`	Needs care (runs before the test is marked complete)	Safe with parallel tests; runs after the test ends

Temporary Directories

Sometimes tests need to create files. For example, you might want to test how your code loads a configuration file or writes output to disk. In Go, you should not write files to /tmp or a shared location, because this can lead to conflicts between tests, especially when they run in parallel.

Instead, use t.TempDir().

```
dir := t.TempDir()
```

This function gives you a unique, empty directory for your test. Go will automatically delete this directory and its contents after the test finishes—no matter if the test passes or fails. This behavior makes tests safer and cleaner, especially in large test suites or CI environments.

You can use this temporary directory to safely create files, simulate file input/output, or prepare test-specific data:

```
func TestWriteFile(t *testing.T) {
    dir := t.TempDir()
    file := filepath.Join(dir, "data.txt")

    err := os.WriteFile(file, []byte("example content"), 0644)
    if err != nil {
        t.Fatalf("write failed: %v", err)
    }

    content, err := os.ReadFile(file)
    if err != nil {
        t.Fatalf("read failed: %v", err)
    }

    if string(content) != "example content" {
        t.Errorf("got %q, want %q", content, "example content")
    }
}
```

Enterprise Tip Using `t.TempDir()` makes your tests more reliable, especially in parallel test runs or CI pipelines. It also helps avoid side effects across tests, which is important in large teams.

Running Tests

The `go test` command is more than just a way to run your test files. It supports many useful flags that give you more control, better feedback, and higher confidence in your code.

Here are the most important options every developer should know:

- `-run=Pattern`

  Run only tests with names that match the pattern.

  Example: `go test -run=Assign` runs tests with names like `TestAssignVehicle`.

- `-v`

  Print the name of every test, even if it passes. This helps when you want to understand test flow or debug failures.

- `-failfast`

  Stop the test run after the first failure. Useful during debugging to avoid reading a long list of failures caused by the same root problem.

- `-shuffle=on`

  Run tests in a random order. This helps detect hidden dependencies between tests. Go prints the seed it used, so you can reproduce the order later using `-shuffle=<seed>`.

- `-count=1`

  Force the tests to run fresh by disabling test result caching. Use this when you suspect a test is not running due to Go's cache.

- `-race`

  Enable the race detector. It checks for unsafe concurrent access to memory. This is critical for enterprise projects where many users or goroutines might be running at the same time.

- `-cover`

  Show which parts of the code were executed during tests. Combine it with `-coverprofile=out.cov` to save the report and view it later with tools like `go tool cover`.

Enterprise Tip Always include `-race` and `-shuffle=on` in your CI pipeline. These options help you catch bugs related to concurrency and test order. If your tests pass only when run in a specific order, they are not trustworthy.

When you use these flags regularly, your tests become more useful, more reproducible, and more honest. They tell you what you need to know—not just that something failed, but why and how it failed.

Testing the main Function

One mistake that many developers make in Go is putting real logic inside the `main()` function. In Go, `main()` should be small and simple. It should only do things like

- Load configuration.
- Create services.
- Wire dependencies together.
- Start the application (server, CLI, etc.).

All the real business logic should be placed in separate packages. This makes it testable. You cannot test code inside `main()` easily, but you can test a package function like `StartDispatcher()` or `ValidateSchedule()` with standard tools.

Using TestMain in Special Cases

Sometimes you need to do setup work before running all your tests. For example, you may want to

- Start an embedded message broker.
- Set global config for test mode.
- Connect to an in-memory database.

In these cases, Go provides `TestMain()`.

```go
func TestMain(m *testing.M) {
    setup()           // global setup
    code := m.Run()  // run all tests
    teardown()        // global cleanup
    os.Exit(code)
}
```

This function is run before any test starts. It lets you prepare the test environment once for the whole suite and clean up afterward.

When to Use and When to Avoid

Although `TestMain()` is powerful, you should use it only when absolutely needed.

It has some downsides:

- It makes tests harder to run in parallel.
- It breaks test isolation.
- It adds a global state to your test setup.

Most of the time, you should use `t.Cleanup()` inside each test instead. This keeps setup and cleanup local, clear, and isolated.

Enterprise Lesson Use `TestMain()` only when you truly need shared setup across the test suite, like starting a database once. For all other cases, prefer writing small, independent tests with local cleanup. This leads to faster, more reliable, and more maintainable test code.

Writing Clear, Maintainable Tests

Messy or repeated tests can slow down a team as much as messy production code. When test code is hard to read or extend, developers hesitate to use or trust it. This leads to slower development, more bugs, and weaker confidence.

In the Go community, there are well-known patterns that help us avoid these problems. These patterns make tests easier to read, easier to change, and safer to run at scale. When used well, they help teams grow without losing quality.

Learning and applying these test styles is part of becoming a senior Go developer. They are not tricks or shortcuts. They are habits that lead to better software, stronger teamwork, and fewer surprises.

Table-Driven Tests

One of the most important testing patterns is the table-driven test. This pattern helps you check many different inputs and expected results using just one test function.

You create a list (a slice) of test cases, where each case is a small struct. Inside each struct, you put the input values and the expected result. Then you loop over the list and run each case using `t.Run()`.

This style is simple, clean, and powerful.

Why Use Table-Driven Tests?

- **Less Repetition:** You write the logic once, and use it for many test cases.
- **Easy to Extend:** You can add new cases by adding one more line to the list.
- **Readable Names:** You can give each test a name, so it's clear what it checks.

You will see the power of table-driven tests in your project each time you want to add another business logic to your existing production code. I bet you will love it!

Example: Validate Vehicle Assignment

Let's say we have a business rule: a vehicle can only be assigned to a route if its type matches the route's allowed type. For example, buses can only be assigned to bus routes. This rule needs to be tested clearly and repeatedly.

To do this, we can use a table-driven test. Each test case will check one situation: valid assignment, invalid type, or other logic we may add later. This is a super simple example of how to write clean and scalable tests.

Before using the test, imagine we have this simple function:

```
func AssignVehicle(v Vehicle, r Route) error {
    if v.Type != r.Allowed {
        return fmt.Errorf("type mismatch")
    }
    return nil
}
```

Now, here is how to write the table-driven test for it:

```
func TestAssignVehicle(t *testing.T) {
    tests := []struct {
        name    string
        vehicle Vehicle
        route   Route
        wantErr bool
    }{
        {
            name:    "valid bus assignment",
            vehicle: Vehicle{ID: "V1", Type: "bus"},
            route:   Route{ID: "R1", Allowed: "bus"},
            wantErr: false,
        },
        {
            name:    "wrong type",
            vehicle: Vehicle{ID: "C1", Type: "car"},
            route:   Route{ID: "R1", Allowed: "bus"},
            wantErr: true,
        },
    }
```

```
    for _, tt := range tests {
        t.Run(tt.name, func(t *testing.T) {
            err := AssignVehicle(tt.vehicle, tt.route)
            if (err != nil) != tt.wantErr {
                t.Errorf("AssignVehicle(%v → %v) error = %v, wantErr %v",
                    tt.vehicle.ID, tt.route.ID, err, tt.wantErr)
            }
        })
    }
}
```

Each test case has its own name, which is used in `t.Run()` to show which case is running. This is important because when a test fails, the test output will include the case name. That makes debugging faster and easier.

You can add more cases to the `tests` slice as your business logic grows. For example: test with a missing route ID or an empty vehicle type. No need to change the logic in the loop—just add new items to the list.

Enterprise Lesson If your test fails when the order changes, that is a design warning. It usually means your test has a hidden state or depends on something shared. Try using `map[string]case{}` instead of a slice to make the order unpredictable, or use `-shuffle=on` to reveal the problem early.

Subtests with t.Run

Go makes related test cases easy to organize using subtests. You can create them simply like this:

```
t.Run(name, func(t *testing.T))
```

Each subtest has its own name, setup, and result. This gives you more control and makes failures easier to understand.

Benefits of Using Subtests

- **Filterable:** You can run just some subtests by name.

  Example:

  ```
  go test -run=TestAssignVehicle/wrong_type
  ```

- **Isolated Failures:** If one subtest fails, others still run. This helps you find all problems in one run.
- **Better Output:** You see exactly which case failed, with clear names.

We already used subtests in the previous table-driven example. Each case was run with

```
t.Run(tt.name, func(t *testing.T) { ... })
```

This gives you clean and useful test output, especially when a test fails.

Enterprise Lesson Subtests are a best practice in Go. Use them often to separate cases and help your team debug faster.

Parallel Tests with t.Parallel

Go supports parallel testing with almost no extra work. This is very helpful in large test suites, especially in enterprise projects where speed matters. You can run subtests at the same time by calling `t.Parallel()` inside each subtest. Go will handle the scheduling and make sure the tests run safely.

Here's an example that checks if different route IDs are valid:

```
func TestRouteValidation(t *testing.T) {
    tests := []struct{ id string }{
        {"R1"},
        {"R2"},
        {"R3"},
    }
```

```
    for _, tt := range tests {
        tt := tt // capture the loop variable
        t.Run(tt.id, func(t *testing.T) {
            t.Parallel() // allow this subtest to run in parallel
            if !IsValidRoute(tt.id) {
                t.Errorf("route %s should be valid", tt.id)
            }
        })
    }
}
```

Important Tips When Using Parallel Tests

- **Isolate Shared State:** Do not use global variables that can be changed by more than one test. Each test must work with its own data.
- **Use `t.Cleanup()` for Safety:** If your test starts background goroutines or opens files, make sure you clean them up. `t.Cleanup()` ensures clean shutdowns, even if a test fails.
- **Capture Loop Variables:** Always rebind your loop variable (`tt := tt`). If you forget this step, your tests may behave randomly and fail in strange ways.

Enterprise Tip Parallel tests reduce total build and test time. But if you write them carelessly, they become flaky and hard to trust. Write each parallel test as if it runs alone, without shared state.

Go 1.25 introduced updates that help teams write safer, cleaner **concurrent tests.** When used properly, parallel tests let you scale your test suite while keeping confidence and speed.

- **Improved Goroutine Tracking in Test Logs:** The testing framework now includes better reporting for leaked goroutines and stuck tests. If a subtest forgets to stop a goroutine, Go 1.25+ surfaces this more clearly at the end of the test run.

- **Stronger Integration with the Race Detector:** The `-race` flag works more consistently across `t.Parallel()` subtests, especially when combined with `t.Cleanup()`. If your test leaves shared memory in a bad state, the race detector can now catch it earlier.
- **Cleaner `t.Cleanup()` Sequencing:** In Go 1.25+, cleanup functions are always run in reverse order of registration. This makes cleanup predictable and safe, even when multiple cleanups are registered across nested subtests.
- **Better Stack Traces on Test Failure:** If a parallel test fails, the error message and stack trace now point more reliably to the exact location of the failure, even across concurrent test executions. This improves debuggability and speeds up diagnosis.

These updates reduce hidden side effects, improve test hygiene, and give teams stronger confidence in concurrent test behavior.

Beyond Unit: Benchmarks, Fuzzing, and Example Tests

Writing tests that check for correctness is important, but it is not enough. In real-world systems, especially at scale, we care about more than just "does it work." We also need to ask: Is it fast? Does it fail safely? Is it easy to understand and use?

Go's standard testing tools support all of these goals. Alongside unit tests, you can write

- **Benchmarks** to track performance and memory usage
- **Fuzz tests** to explore unexpected input combinations
- **Example tests** that double as documentation

These tools are part of Go's core. You do not need third-party libraries to use them.

Benchmarks with *testing.B

Unit tests help us check correctness, but benchmarks help us track performance. They are important when speed and resource usage matter—especially in back-end systems, real-time services, or high-traffic APIs.

Go makes benchmarking simple with built-in support. You do not need special tools or extra libraries. Just use the standard `testing` package and follow a naming pattern.

Benchmark Function Signature

To create a benchmark in Go, you define a function using this pattern:

```
func BenchmarkXxx(b *testing.B)
```

- The function name must start with `Benchmark` so the Go test tool can find and run it.
- The parameter `b *testing.B` gives access to benchmarking tools provided by Go.

Inside the function, you must write a loop that runs the target code `b.N` times:

```
for i := 0; i < b.N; i++ {
    // code you want to measure
}
```

The value of `b.N` is set automatically by the Go test runner. It increases until the result is stable enough for accurate measurement.

This loop ensures that the code is measured under repeatable conditions and helps avoid noisy or misleading results from single runs.

Enterprise Tip Only include the part you want to measure inside the loop. Keep setup code like test data creation outside the loop so it does not affect the results.

Extra Benchmark Tools

Go provides additional tools inside the benchmark function to help you collect more useful performance data.

- `b.ReportAllocs()` tells the benchmark to track memory allocations. This is useful when you want to watch for unexpected memory usage or compare allocation efficiency between implementations.
- `b.SetBytes(n)` lets you tell the benchmark how many bytes are processed in each iteration. This is helpful when testing the performance of functions that handle data, like encoders, file readers, or network processors. It allows Go to calculate and display the throughput (bytes per second) in the benchmark output.

These tools give more insight than just measuring time. They help you write benchmarks that catch slowdowns or memory problems before they reach production.

Example: Benchmarking Route Lookup

This example measures the performance of the FindRoute function when searching through a list of 1000 routes. It also tracks memory allocations to help detect performance regressions.

```
func BenchmarkFindRoute(b *testing.B) {
    routes := generateRoutes(1000)    // prepare test data

    b.ReportAllocs()                  // show allocation stats

    for i := 0; i < b.N; i++ {
        _ = FindRoute(routes, "R500") // run target function
    }
}
```

This benchmark will run FindRoute many times. The number of repetitions is set automatically by the Go test runner using b.N. This helps you measure performance under repeated load, not just once.

To run the benchmark and see time and memory results, use:

```
go test -bench=BenchmarkFindRoute -benchmem
```

The output shows useful metrics like nanoseconds per operation and memory allocations per call. These numbers help you decide if your function is fast and efficient enough for production use.

Enterprise Tip Save your benchmark results and watch for changes over time. If a small code change causes 10× more memory use or a slower response time, you will see it immediately. This protects performance in the long term.

How to Run the Benchmark

To run your benchmark and see useful output, use this command in the terminal:

```
go test -bench=. -benchmem
```

This runs all benchmark functions in the current package. The output shows how long each benchmark takes and how much memory is used per operation.

You can also run a specific benchmark using part of its name:

```
go test -bench=FindRoute -benchmem
```

This makes it easy to test only the part of the system you are working on.

Enterprise Tip In growing systems, benchmarks are not just about speed—they are safety checks. They act like contracts that define how fast and memory-efficient a function must be.

If a change causes `FindRoute` to run five times slower or use more memory, it should be caught early. CI systems should treat such changes as warnings or even failures. Benchmarks help you detect these regressions before users feel the impact.

Fuzzing with *testing.F

Fuzzing is a powerful way to test your code against unexpected or random inputs. Instead of writing fixed test cases, you let the test engine explore many combinations for you. This helps catch bugs that are easy to miss in normal testing.

Fuzzing became part of Go's standard library in version 1.18. It works like property-based testing in other languages but is integrated with the Go test tool.

Function Signature

A fuzz test in Go starts with a specific function format:

```
func FuzzXxx(f *testing.F)
```

This naming pattern is required so the go test tool can find and run the fuzz test. Inside this function, you follow two steps:

1. **Add seed inputs** using `f.Add(...)`. These are sample values that the fuzz engine uses to start. They should represent typical or boundary inputs for your function.
2. **Define the fuzz logic** with `f.Fuzz(...)`. This block takes a `*testing.T` and one or more input parameters. The test engine will run your code with both the seed values and many new inputs it generates by changing, combining, or mutating the seeds.

Go will continue running different inputs until the test is stopped or it finds a failure like a panic, crash, or logical mistake.

Fuzz tests help you explore cases you might not think of yourself. They are especially useful for input validation, string parsing, or complex formats.

Example: Fuzzing Route Code Parsing

The goal of this test is to make sure that parsing a route code never returns an empty result when there is no error. We want to verify that if `ParseRouteCode` returns `nil` as the error, then the returned route must contain a valid `ID`.

```
func FuzzParseRouteCode(f *testing.F) {
    f.Add("R-12A") // seed input that looks valid

    f.Fuzz(func(t *testing.T, code string) {
        r, err := ParseRouteCode(code)

        // If parsing did not fail, the ID must not be empty
        if err == nil && r.ID == "" {
            t.Errorf("parsed %q into empty ID", code)
        }
    })
}
```

This test starts with one known-good input: "R-12A". Go's fuzzing engine will automatically create many variations based on that seed. Some inputs might be longer, shorter, use symbols, or include invalid characters. The test checks each one for logic problems.

If Go finds an input that causes a failure, it saves that input automatically in a file inside `testdata/fuzz/`. This saved input is reproducible. The next time you run `go test`, the engine will replay it before generating new ones. This makes bugs easy to debug and fix.

How to Run a Fuzz Test

To start fuzzing, run this command in your terminal:

```
go test -fuzz=FuzzParseRouteCode
```

This tells Go to find the `FuzzParseRouteCode` function and begin fuzz testing. Fuzzing is most useful when testing code that works with user input, strings, file formats, or protocols. It helps you catch problems that regular test cases may miss.

Enterprise Tip Fuzz tests run fast and generate lots of input. Avoid calling real services like databases, queues, or external APIs. Instead, keep fuzz logic isolated. Test only pure functions or parts of the code that use in-memory data. This keeps the tests safe, repeatable, and efficient.

Example Tests for Documentation

Go supports a special kind of test called an example function. These are not just ordinary tests. They serve two powerful roles at once: they verify that your code works correctly, and they show others how to use your code in practice.

This is especially helpful for new developers joining a team or for anyone using a shared package or library. Instead of guessing how to call a function or what values to pass, they can simply read the example. It shows real inputs, expected behavior, and output—all in working code.

Unlike regular documentation comments, example tests never go out of date. They are compiled and run by `go test`, so if something breaks or changes, you'll know immediately. This makes them a trusted source of truth, not just a helpful note.

Example functions are also rendered by `go doc` and visible in godoc.org and pkg.go.dev. Anyone viewing your package documentation can see real usage code that compiles, runs, and passes.

For developers in enterprise systems, this is especially useful when designing packages meant for other teams or services. Example tests show exactly how to use your APIs—without the need for extra guides or long README files.

Function Signature

An example test in Go must follow a specific pattern so that the `go test` tool can find and run it. The function name must start with `Example` and follow this format:

```
func ExampleXxx() {
    // some code
    // Output: expected printed result
}
```

The comment starting with `Output:` tells Go what the printed result should be. If the actual output is different, the test fails. This makes the example not just readable, but also verified.

If the output order does not matter, you can use a suffix like `_unordered`, for example: `ExampleListRoutes_unordered`.

These functions are compiled and tested automatically whenever you run:

```
go test
```

Example

Showing How to Assign a Vehicle

```
func ExampleAssignVehicle() {
    v := Vehicle{ID: "B1", Type: "bus"}
    r := Route{ID: "R1", Allowed: "bus"}
    err := AssignVehicle(v, r)
    fmt.Println(err == nil)
    // Output: true
}
```

This example shows how to use the `AssignVehicle` function. It creates a bus and a route, then checks if the assignment is valid. The output must match the string `"true"`, otherwise the test fails.

Because this is a real test, it cannot go out of sync. It always compiles, runs, and confirms the behavior is correct. This helps future developers understand how the function works, with confidence that the example is accurate.

Enterprise Practices That Scale

In small projects, informal or incomplete tests might be enough. But at enterprise scale, where teams are large, code bases are complex, and deployments happen frequently, test discipline becomes critical. The way you design and organize your tests will determine whether your CI/CD pipeline builds trust—or causes confusion and delay.

Go's standard tools give you a solid foundation, but scaling that into a reliable test strategy requires more than just writing tests. It requires habits and practices that keep the suite stable, fast, and meaningful over time.

In the following sections, we'll explore techniques that make Go test suites strong and maintainable in large systems. You'll learn how to avoid flaky results, isolate side effects, test concurrency safely, and structure your test code to support growth.

These are not advanced tricks. They are fundamentals that senior teams rely on every day to deliver dependable software.

Flaky Test Prevention

A flaky test is a test that passes sometimes and fails other times, even when the code has not changed. In small projects, it is annoying. In enterprise systems, it is like cancer! When developers lose trust in test results, they stop relying on them—and that breaks the feedback loop.

Common causes of flakiness and how to fix them in Go:

- **Random Values:** If your test uses `math/rand`, always call `rand.Seed(n)` with a fixed number. We want the test to behave **deterministic**.
- **Time-Related Logic:** Avoid `time.Now()` in tests. Instead, inject a clock interface or use a fixed timestamp.

- **External Services:** Never call real APIs in unit tests. Use `httptest.NewServer` to create a local test server.
- **File System Paths:** Do not write to `/tmp` or fixed locations. Use `t.TempDir()` to create a clean, temporary directory for each test.

Here is an example from our transport project. Instead of calling the real scheduling service, we start a local in-memory HTTP server:

```
srv := httptest.NewServer(http.HandlerFunc(func(w http.ResponseWriter, r
*http.Request) {
    w.Write([]byte(`{"status":"ok"}`))
}))
t.Cleanup(srv.Close)
```

You can then configure your function under test to call `srv.URL` instead of the real endpoint.

This technique helps to avoid network flakiness and keeps tests fast, stable, and safe to run in parallel or CI environments.

Enterprise Lesson A flaky test does more harm than a missing one. It adds noise, breaks trust, and hides real bugs. Go provides the tools to eliminate most sources of flakiness—use them from the beginning.

Reproducibility and Debuggability

A senior-level test suite must allow developers to **replay failures easily**. When something goes wrong, we need to find it, repeat it, and fix it quickly—without guessing.

Go provides several built-in test flags to support this:

- `-shuffle=on` randomizes the order of tests to expose hidden dependencies. If a failure happens, Go prints the random seed used. You can re-run the same order with `-shuffle=<seed>`.
- `-run=TestName` allows you to run just one test or subtest. This saves time when debugging.

- `-count=1` disables test result caching. Use it to force Go to rerun tests even if nothing changed.

These tools help you **reproduce the exact failure** and remove noise during debugging.

Enterprise Lesson Your test failures must speak clearly. Avoid vague messages like `expected false`. Instead, write output that shows the context and intent, such as

```
t.Errorf("AssignVehicle(%s → %s) failed: %v", bus.ID, route.
ID, err)
```

This way, the developer immediately sees the test case, the actual error, and the expected behavior.

```
Clear messages + replayable tests = faster fixes and stronger confidence.
```

Testing Concurrency Safely

Go is designed for concurrency, and many enterprise systems use goroutines and channels heavily. But concurrency also brings hidden risks. Bugs like race conditions, goroutine leaks, or timing issues can go unnoticed—unless you test for them carefully.

Follow these best practices to test concurrent code safely:

- Always enable the race detector in CI using the `-race` flag. It checks for shared memory conflicts and is essential for trustable results.
- Use bounded concurrency. When launching goroutines in tests, use `sync.WaitGroup` or buffered channels to control the number of active workers.
- Always set timeouts in tests that wait for channels or completion. This prevents tests from hanging forever:

```go
select {
case <-done:
    // success
```

```
case <-time.After(time.Second):
    t.Fatal("timeout: worker did not finish")
}
```

- Clean up properly using `t.Cleanup`. If your test spawns background goroutines or temporary servers, make sure they are stopped when the test ends.

Structuring Large Code Bases

As your Go project grows into dozens or hundreds of packages, a clear test organization becomes essential. Without structure, your test suite will become hard to maintain, slow to run, and difficult for new developers to understand.

Here are the best practices that help teams write scalable and maintainable tests:

- **Integration Tests:** Keep fast, isolated tests separate from slow, external tests. Use Go's build tags to mark integration tests:

  ```
  //go:build integration
  ```

  This lets you exclude heavy tests from your default test runs and run them only when needed. You can run integration tests using the following command:

  ```
  go test -tags=integration ./...
  ```

- **Test Helpers:** If you have shared test functions, place them in a common helper directory like `internal/testutil`. This prevents test-only code from leaking into production and keeps it reusable across packages.
- **Black-Box Tests:** For public APIs, write tests in a separate package using `mypkg_test`. This makes sure your test only interacts with exported symbols, just like an external user would. This is useful for validating public behavior without relying on internal details.
- **Internal Tests:** There are some private functions in your project that contain heavy business logic and need to be fully covered using tests. In such cases, you can cover tests using internal tests. Internal

tests are implemented in the same package as production code, and in this way, they have access to private methods. The point is if you implement so much internal tests, it will add more coupling and make changes in production code difficult.

- **Consistent Naming:** Use clear and predictable file names like `vehicle_test.go` for unit tests or `route_integration_test.go` for integration tests. This helps readers quickly understand what the file is for.

This separation helps each test stay focused, fast, and relevant to its layer.

Enterprise Lesson Structure is not just a style preference—it impacts clarity, speed, onboarding, and correctness. A well-organized test suite grows with your code base instead of slowing it down.

Interpreting go test Output

In the previous section, you saw the most important `go test` flags. Now we will do something more practical: we will run some real commands and learn how to read their output.

This is not about memorizing every flag. It is about understanding what `go test` is saying so you can use it with confidence in your daily work and in CI.

Running a Single Test with -run

To save time and effort, you need to be able to test and debug specific tests; running tests can be selective with a regular expression; here, you can see how to use a regular expression to run specific tests.

```
go test -run ^FuzzLoadConfigEnvOverrides$
github.com/yourname/transport/ride/configs
ok      github.com/yourname/transport/ride/configs      0.004s
```

What this does:

- `go test` runs tests in the given package.
- `-run ^FuzzLoadConfigEnvOverrides$` tells Go to **only** run tests whose name matches this regular expression.

- The pattern is a regular expression that matches test names like `TestLoadConfig`, `TestXYZ`.
- The ^ and $ anchor the regex, so only this exact name matches.

How to read the output:

- `ok` means all matching tests passed.
- `github.com/yourname/transport/ride/configs` is the package path.
- `0.004s` is the total time to build and run tests in this package.

Running All Tests in All Packages with ./...

Running tests with ./... means you want to run all tests in this package and sub-packages

```
go test ./...
?       github.com/yourname/transport/ride/cmd  [no test files]
ok      github.com/yourname/transport/ride/configs      0.005s
```

What this does:

- `./...` means "all packages under the current module directory".
- Go walks the folder tree and runs tests in each package it finds.

How to read the output:

- ? github.com/yourname/transport/ride/cmd [no test files]
- ? means "no test result".
- `[no test files]` means this package has no `_test.go` files. It is not an error; Go just has nothing to run there.
- `ok github.com/yourname/transport/ride/configs 0.005s`

The configs package has tests, and they all passed in 5 ms.

Timeouts and Build Tags for Integration Tests

Sometimes running tests takes longer than the default timeout. If you want to run such tests, you need to increase your timeout.

```
go test -timeout 90s -tags=integration_test ./...
?       github.com/yourname/transport/ride/cmd  [no test files]
ok      github.com/yourname/transport/ride/configs      0.005s
ok      github.com/yourname/transport/ride/internal/adapters/
repository 33.410s
```

What this does:

- `-timeout 90s` sets a **maximum time** for each test binary (package) to run.

  If tests in a package run longer than this, Go panics with the message `panic: test timed out after 90s`.

- `-tags=integration_test` enables build tags for files that start with

  `//go:build integration_test`

  Only then these tests are included.

How to read the output:

- `ok .../configs 0.005s`: Fast unit tests.
- `ok .../internal/adapters/repository 33.410s`: Repository package tests took ~33 seconds, which is normal for integration tests that start containers or talk to real databases.

We will discuss integration tests in its own chapter.

Running with the Race Detector

With Go, you can find race conditions before going to production. Race conditions are not easy to find in production; believe me, you can waste a lot of time, effort, money, and reputation without it.

```
go test ./... -race
ok      github.com/yourname/transport/ride/configs      1.025s
```

What this does:

- `-race` turns on Go's race detector. It looks for unsafe concurrent memory access.
- Tests will run slower, because Go watches your memory accesses.

How to read the output:

- If there are no data races, you only see plain ok lines.
- If a race is found, Go prints a detailed report showing the conflicting goroutines, file and line numbers, and stack trace. The test run ends with `FAIL` and a non-zero exit code.

Enterprise Lesson Always run your full suite with -race in CI. It catches concurrency bugs that are almost impossible to find manually.

Running Benchmarks and Understanding the Numbers

Go gives the possibility of running benchmarks without any extra packages.

```
go test -benchmem -bench=. example.com/transport/samplecode
goos: linux
goarch: amd64
pkg: example.com/transport/samplecode
cpu: Intel(R) Core(TM) i7-4702MQ CPU @ 2.20GHz
BenchmarkAppendNoPrealloc-8 1030 1127118 ns/op   4101415 B/op  28 allocs/op
BenchmarkAppendPrealloc-8   6283 160660 ns/op    802827 B/op   1 allocs/op
BenchmarkSetBool-8          5    244990804 ns/op 63922275 B/op 404048 allocs/op
BenchmarkSetStruct-8        6    188179349 ns/op 62588629 B/op 337389 allocs/op
PASS
ok      example.com/transport/samplecode        11.148s
```

What this command does:

- `-run=^$` tells Go to run **no regular tests** (the regex never matches). Only benchmarks run.
- `-bench=.` tells Go to run benchmarks.
- `-benchmem` adds memory metrics (`B/op` and `allocs/op`).

How to read the header:

- `goos`, `goarch`: Operating system and architecture used for the run.
- `pkg`: The package being tested.
- `cpu`: CPU model used. Useful when comparing runs.

How to read one benchmark line:

```
BenchmarkAppendNoPrealloc-8   1030   1127118 ns/op   4101415 B/op   28 allocs/op
```

- `BenchmarkAppendNoPrealloc-8`: Benchmark name. The `-8` shows `GOMAXPROCS` (here, eight logical CPUs used).
- `1030`: How many times Go ran the benchmark loop. Go chooses this to reach a stable measurement.
- `1127118 ns/op`: Average time per operation (per loop iteration) in nanoseconds.
- `4101415 B/op`: Average bytes allocated per operation.
- `28 allocs/op`: Average number of memory allocations per operation.

Compare it with

```
BenchmarkAppendPrealloc-8   6283   160660 ns/op   802827 B/op   1 allocs/op
```

- Fewer nanoseconds per operation → much faster
- Far fewer allocations (`1 alloc/op` vs. `28 alloc/op`)

Enterprise Lesson Benchmarks are not only about time; they are about time + allocations. In high-traffic systems, fewer allocations usually mean lower GC pressure, lower latency, and lower cost.

Forcing Tests to Rerun (Cache and -count)

Go caches successful test results. If neither the code nor the tests changed, Go may reuse the previous result to save time.

This is usually good, but sometimes you need a fresh run:

- When tests depend on environment variables
- When tests read files that have changed

Two useful tools:

Disable cache for this run:

```
go test ./... -count=1
```

`-count=1` means "run tests exactly once, do not use cached results".

Clear the test cache completely:

```
go clean -testcache
```

After that, the next go `test` run will rebuild and rerun everything.

Exercises

1. Write a failing unit test for `AssignVehicle(bus, route)` before implementing the logic. Then implement the function until the test passes.
2. Convert your `AssignVehicle` test into a table-driven test with at least three cases.
3. Wrap each case in a `t.Run` subtest. Run a single case with

   `go test -run=AssignVehicle/wrong_type.`
4. Write a benchmark for `FindRoute` with `b.ReportAllocs()`. Run it with

   `go test -bench=. -benchmem.`
5. Add a fuzz test for `ParseRouteCode`. Let it run and record any failing inputs as regression tests.

Summary

Testing in Go is not an optional step—it is an integrated part of how professional software is written and maintained. This chapter demonstrated how Go's standard testing tools provide fast, deterministic, and scalable support for writing tests that are easy to maintain. You learned how clear, table-driven tests reduce duplication, how subtests and parallel execution improve structure and speed, and how fuzz tests and benchmarks uncover hidden bugs and performance regressions. With enterprise-ready practices like `t.Cleanup`, `t.TempDir`, `httptest.NewServer`, and proper test structuring, you can build test suites that remain reliable as your team and code base scale. Above all, the chapter reinforced a core engineering lesson: in Go, good tests are not just checks—they are living documentation and an investment in long-term software health.

What's Next

In the next chapter, you'll learn how Go's memory model works under the hood. You'll explore the stack, the heap, and how escape analysis decides where your data lives. This foundational knowledge will help you write faster, leaner, and more efficient code.

CHAPTER 8

The Architecture of Memory: Foundations of Speed and Scale

Computers are fast; software developers make them slow

Every Go program, no matter how simple, lives and dies by how it uses memory. Before we talk about data structures or clever algorithms, we need to understand where values are stored, how long they survive, and what that means for performance. By learning Go's memory model—the stack, the heap, and escape analysis—you'll gain the ability to design code that is not only correct but also efficient, predictable, and cost-aware.

Why Memory Layout Comes First

Memory is a scarce, expensive resource—and the way your program uses it directly impacts latency, throughput, and (in the cloud) your bill. A good developer doesn't treat memory as a black box. They know **which section** the data lives in, **how long** it lives, **who** is responsible for freeing it, and **what** the performance trade-offs are.

In this chapter, we'll look at Go's runtime memory architecture before we dive into types, so that when we later talk about "pointer vs. value," "slice vs. array," or "constant vs. variable," you'll already know what those choices *mean* at runtime.

S. Shahsavan, *Building Enterprise Projects with Go*, https://doi.org/10.1007/979-8-8688-2370-1_8

Escape Analysis: The Compiler's Decision

Escape analysis is Go's way of answering a simple but critical question:

Does this value outlive its function?

The Go compiler runs this analysis to decide where a variable should be stored. If it can prove that a value stays within the function where it was created, it keeps it on the stack. If not, it escapes to the heap.

Keeping data on the stack is always preferred. It's fast to allocate, fast to access, and doesn't burden the garbage collector. But if there's any chance the value might be used after the function returns, the compiler moves it to the heap to keep your program safe.

Let's look at how this works in practice.

```go
// Example: variable stays on the stack
func stackExample() int {
    x := 42          // local variable
    return x + 1     // value is copied, x does not escape
}

// Example: variable escapes to the heap
func heapExample() *int {
    x := 42
    return &x        // returning pointer forces escape
}
```

In the second example, x is returned by reference. That means the caller could access it later—after the function ends. Since stack memory disappears when the function returns, Go must copy x to the heap to keep it valid.

Figure 8-1 shows how certain values escape to the heap.

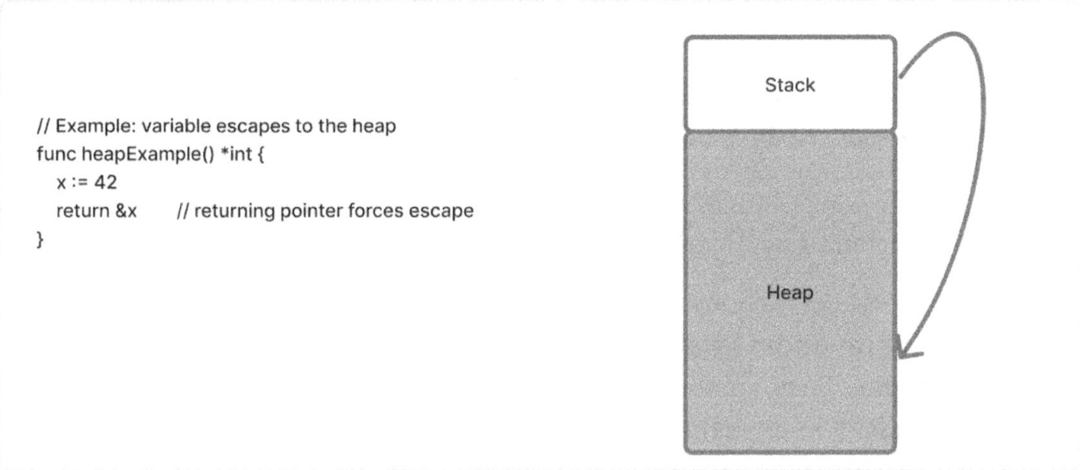

Figure 8-1. *How values escape from the stack to the heap*

What Causes a Variable Escape?

The Go compiler uses a set of safe, predictable rules when deciding if a variable should be stored on the stack or moved to the heap. It always prefers to keep values on the stack, but if there's any chance the value might still be needed after the function returns, the variable is marked as "escaping." Escaping means it will be stored in the heap.

Let's look at one of the most common escape cases:

1. **Returning a Pointer to a Local Variable**

   If you return the address of a local variable, the variable escapes. This is because the function ends, and the stack frame disappears—but the returned pointer must still work. So the compiler places the variable on the heap to keep it alive.

   ```
   func makePointer() *int {
       v := 10
       return &v // escape!
   }
   ```

   In this example, v is a local variable. If it stayed on the stack, the returned pointer would point to memory that no longer exists. Go avoids this bug by copying v to the heap.

Important This escape behavior is automatic. You cannot override it manually. But by understanding what causes a variable to escape, you can write code that avoids unnecessary heap allocations.

---

2. **Capturing a Local Variable in a Closure**

   Closures are functions defined inside other functions. When a closure captures a local variable, it may keep using that variable even after the outer function has returned. To make this possible, the compiler moves the captured variable to the heap.

```
func closureExample() func() int {
    v := 20
    return func() int { return v } // escape!
}
```

   In this code, the closure `func() int { return v }` needs access to v after `closureExample` finishes. Since v must stay alive beyond the stack frame, Go moves it to the heap.
   This escape is necessary for the program to work correctly, but it does come with a cost. Heap allocations are slower, and they add load to the garbage collector. Avoid capturing large or performance-sensitive variables in closures unless necessary.

3. **Sending a Pointer Through a Channel**

   Channels are used to send data between goroutines. When you send a pointer to a local variable through a channel, the receiving goroutine may access that value long after the sending function has returned. To keep the data alive, the compiler moves the variable to the heap.

```
func channelExample() {
    ch := make(chan *int, 1)
    v := 30
    ch <- &v // escape!
}
```

In this example, &v is a pointer to a local variable. Since v might still be in use when the function `channelExample` is done, Go moves it to the heap to avoid invalid memory access.

This type of escape is common in concurrent programs. When sharing pointers across goroutines, be aware that you are creating a long-lived reference—and increasing garbage collection workload.

4. **Storing a Pointer in a Heap-Allocated Structure**

   If you store the address of a local variable inside a data structure that already lives on the heap—such as a map, a slice, or a struct—Go must move that variable to the heap too. Otherwise, the structure could hold an invalid pointer after the function ends.

```
func storePointer() {
    m := make(map[string]*int) // map lives on the heap
    v := 50
    m["key"] = &v // escape!
}
```

   Here, the variable v is declared locally, but its address is stored in a map. Since the map may outlive the function, the compiler makes v escape to the heap to ensure safety.

   This rule also applies to slices, structs, or any container that is already heap-allocated. When you store local pointers in them, you're extending the lifetime of the local variable. Go adjusts memory placement to prevent memory errors—but at the cost of a heap allocation.

Seeing It Yourself

You can ask the Go compiler to show which variables escape using

```
./main.go:12:6: moved to heap: v
```

This outputs lines like

```
./main.go:12:6: moved to heap: v
```

This means the variable v escaped and was placed on the heap. The compiler gives this feedback during compilation, so you can catch memory issues early—before running your program or reaching production.

Understanding this output is essential for improving memory efficiency and reducing garbage collector load in performance-critical code.

Practical Insight

You cannot directly tell Go where to place a variable. But you can write code that encourages the compiler to keep values on the stack.

By limiting variable scope, avoiding unnecessary pointers, and keeping data local to the function, you reduce the chance of escape and improve memory performance.

To minimize heap allocation:

- Return values, not pointers, when a copy is sufficient.
- Pass small structs by value instead of using pointers.
- Avoid capturing local variables in closures or goroutines unless necessary.

Escape analysis is not a formal part of the language specification, and its details may vary between compiler versions. Still, its role is always the same: to keep your program efficient by avoiding unnecessary allocations and reducing GC pressure.

A Professional's Mindset

This knowledge is not just theory—it directly shapes how you design and structure your code. As you begin building a feature, consider the following:

- **Lifetime:** Will the variable be used only within its function, or must it survive beyond? If it lives longer, it will likely be heap-allocated. Can you restructure your logic to keep it local?
- **Size and Copy Cost:** Is the data small enough to pass by value without penalty? For large structs or frequently passed data, using pointers may be better to reduce copy overhead.

- **Escape Risk:** Are you returning a reference, capturing a variable in a closure, assigning it to a map or slice, or sending it through a channel? These operations increase the chance of heap allocation.

Thinking this way helps you write memory-efficient code by design, not by accident.

Go's Memory Architecture

Go uses a modern memory layout and garbage collector. Its improvements reduce allocation overhead and make GC more cache-friendly. But the fundamentals still matter. The decisions you make—about where and how values are stored—have a direct effect on performance and cost.

The following breakdown shows how Go organizes memory at runtime and when to think carefully about stack, heap, and the less visible parts in between.

Stack

Each goroutine in Go is assigned a private stack—a memory region used to store function call frames, parameters, and local variables. Stack memory is extremely fast to allocate and reclaim. Allocation is just a pointer movement, and memory is automatically reclaimed when a function returns. Unlike the heap, the stack does not involve garbage collection, which makes it ideal for short-lived data.

Stacks in Go are dynamic. Every new goroutine starts with a small stack (usually 2 KB), and the runtime expands it as needed. If a function call would exceed the current capacity, Go allocates a larger block, copies the existing data into it, and updates the stack pointer. This growth is transparent to the developer and does not require manual handling. Go uses a contiguous stack model for goroutines, replacing the earlier segmented approach. The new model is more efficient and easier for the runtime to manage, especially under heavy concurrency.

Each goroutine has its own user stack, isolated from others. In addition, each operating system thread has a small fixed-size system stack, used by the runtime to run internal operations like scheduling and garbage collection. Your application code never runs on the system stack.

The Go compiler uses escape analysis to decide whether a variable can safely stay on the stack. If the lifetime of a variable is clearly limited to the current function, it stays on the stack. If it might be accessed after the function returns—for example, if it is returned by pointer or captured by a closure—it is moved to the heap automatically. These decisions are made at compile time.

To inspect these decisions, you can use

```
go build -gcflags="-m"
```

This shows which variables are moved to the heap and why. Reviewing escape analysis output is a key step when optimizing memory usage in performance-critical code.

Stack-based memory reduces pressure on the garbage collector and improves CPU cache locality. While you don't control where a variable is stored directly, structuring your code to limit variable scope and avoid unnecessary pointer use helps the compiler keep more values on the stack, where access is faster and cleanup is automatic.

Heap

The heap is a shared memory region managed by Go's garbage collector. It is used for values whose lifetimes extend beyond the scope of a single function. You don't allocate memory to the heap directly. Instead, the compiler decides, based on escape analysis, whether a variable must be moved to the heap. This happens when a value is returned by reference, captured in a closure, or stored in a longer-lived structure.

Unlike the stack, heap memory does not follow a strict allocation and release pattern. It is dynamic and global across all goroutines. When a variable escapes to the heap, it becomes part of the garbage collector's responsibility. The GC periodically scans for values no longer in use and reclaims their memory.

Heap allocations are slower than stack allocations. They involve more metadata and bookkeeping, and they increase GC workload. In large systems or high-throughput services, unnecessary heap allocations can become a source of latency and memory pressure.

Go's heap is structured into arenas: large contiguous blocks of virtual memory reserved by the runtime. On 64-bit systems, each arena is 64 MB. The heap grows as needed by reserving more arenas. Memory is allocated from spans inside these arenas, which are grouped by size classes. Go tracks each allocation with metadata stored in off-heap structures such as `heapArena` and `mspan`.

Garbage collection in Go is concurrent and uses a tri-color mark-and-sweep algorithm. It runs alongside your application and tries to minimize pause times, but every heap allocation still adds work to the GC. Fewer allocations mean fewer pauses and better CPU cache locality.

Heap memory is not shared per goroutine. All goroutines share the same heap. That means synchronization and false sharing can occur if multiple goroutines write to the same memory locations.

To understand heap usage in your code, use the escape analysis output:

```
go build -gcflags="-m"
```

It will tell you why a variable escapes and whether it is placed on the heap. This helps you refactor or restructure code to keep values stack-bound when possible.

Reducing heap usage doesn't mean avoiding all pointers. It means understanding their cost, avoiding unnecessary sharing, and limiting the lifetime of data. For example, copying a small struct can be cheaper than passing a pointer to it, because the struct may stay on the stack.

Go 1.25 also supports an optional garbage collection tuning mode with:

```
GODEBUG=gc=greentea
```

This groups related allocations to improve cache locality, especially in memory-intensive programs. While still experimental, it shows how the runtime is evolving to reduce GC impact in real-world workloads.

BSS (Block Started by Symbol)

The **BSS segment** is a low-level part of Go's memory layout. It holds **global and package-level variables that are zero-initialized by default**—meaning you didn't explicitly assign a value at declaration time. In compiled Go programs, the BSS region is created by the linker and initialized by the operating system when the binary loads.

Unlike stack or heap memory, you do not allocate memory in the BSS segment manually. It is reserved for static data that has a predictable lifetime and a known zero value at startup. Because these variables do not consume space in the binary itself (only a size header is recorded), the BSS segment keeps binaries smaller while still ensuring memory is allocated at runtime.

For example:

```
var count int       // goes into BSS (zero-initialized)
var names []string // also goes into BSS (nil by default)
```

These variables are placed in the BSS section of the binary. The operating system zeros this region before the Go runtime starts, so there is no performance cost at runtime for initializing them.

Variables in the BSS segment persist for the lifetime of the program. They are not collected by the garbage collector, but any memory they point to—such as slices or maps initialized later—may be allocated on the heap and thus managed by the GC.

This segment is **distinct from the data segment**, which stores variables with non-zero initial values. In Go, both types of globals are declared similarly, but behind the scenes, the linker separates them to optimize binary size and startup performance.

Although you rarely need to think about BSS in day-to-day Go development (especially in enterprise projects), understanding its behavior helps in debugging, binary optimization, and reasoning about memory usage at scale.

Key Facts

- BSS holds **zero-initialized global or package-level variables**.
- Values are implicitly set to zero (`0`, `nil`, `false`, etc.).
- Memory is **not stored in the binary**, only reserved by the OS.
- Not garbage collected, but pointers it holds may point to the heap.
- Managed by the **linker and OS**, not the Go runtime.

Data

The **data segment** stores global and package-level variables that are explicitly initialized to a non-zero value at compile time. This includes scalar types, structs, arrays, and string values assigned directly in the declaration.

Example

```
var version = 3          // stored in data (initialized global)
var greeting = "hello"  // stored in data with pointer to rodata
```

These variables are placed in the `data` section of the final binary by the linker. Unlike the BSS segment, which only reserves space for zero-initialized variables, the data segment holds actual bytes representing the initialized values. These bytes become part of the executable image on disk and are loaded into memory by the operating system when the program starts.

The Go runtime does not manage the data segment directly. Allocation, initialization, and cleanup are handled by the OS loader. However, **if a variable in the data segment points to a heap object**, that memory is managed by Go's garbage collector. The variable itself is not garbage collected, but its references may be.

The data segment is **read/write**, which means variables stored here can be updated during execution. They persist for the entire life of the program and are shared across all goroutines.

Like BSS, the data segment belongs to the **static memory region**, but unlike BSS, its contents increase the binary size because they are fully materialized in the compiled output.

Key Characteristics

- Holds **non-zero initialized** global or package-level variables.
- Variables are **mutable** and **persist** for the lifetime of the program.
- **Memory is part of the binary**, increasing its size.
- Not garbage collected, but references may point to GC-managed heap.
- Managed by the **OS loader and linker**, not the Go runtime.

Understanding the data segment is useful when analyzing memory usage, tuning binary size, or debugging issues related to application state or configuration. When you declare global constants with an initial value, you are contributing to this part of your program's memory footprint—even if you don't realize it.

Text

The **text segment** contains the compiled machine code of your Go program. This includes all executable instructions from your code, the Go runtime, imported packages, and standard library symbols. Once compiled, this code becomes part of the program binary and is loaded into a protected, read-only region of memory at runtime.

This memory area is **not writable** and **not managed by the Go runtime**. It is controlled by the operating system. Any attempt to modify code in the text segment results in a runtime fault. This immutability is a deliberate design choice that improves both **security** (by preventing code injection) and **performance** (by allowing aggressive CPU caching and instruction pipelining).

Although you don't interact with the text segment directly in Go, understanding its behavior is important in some scenarios:

- **Profiling:** CPU profilers and sampling tools operate by analyzing instruction pointers (PCs) that reference locations in the text segment.
- **Tracing Panics:** When a panic occurs, the runtime prints a stack trace with function names and line numbers, resolved by mapping return addresses in the text segment.
- **Reflection:** Advanced features such as `runtime.FuncForPC` and symbol lookup work by querying the metadata associated with the text segment.
- **Binary Size Optimization:** Understanding how much of the binary is text (vs. data or debug info) helps when minimizing build artifacts or embedded deployments.

The Go compiler groups **function bodies**, **inlined code**, and **deferred call handlers** into this segment. Also included are internal runtime helpers used for goroutine scheduling, garbage collection, memory allocation, and synchronization.

Although Go gives you no control over the text segment, your design decisions affect it:

- **Inlining** short functions increases text size but reduces call overhead.
- **Generic instantiation** and heavy use of reflection can significantly grow the text region.
- **Build flags** (like `-ldflags="-s -w"`) can strip debug symbols to reduce binary size.

Text segment layout and symbol arrangement are handled by the Go linker. You can inspect it using tools like

```
go tool nm <binary>      # symbol listing
go tool objdump <binary> -s main.main
```

Key Characteristics

- Holds compiled instructions from your Go code and runtime
- Read-only and executable; not addressable or modifiable
- Shared among all threads and goroutines
- Not garbage collected
- Critical for profiling, stack tracing, and binary analysis

Understanding the text segment is essential when you're working close to the runtime, debugging performance bottlenecks, or analyzing crash reports. It is the core of what your CPU actually runs—and everything else in memory exists to support it.

In Figure 8-2, you can see the different memory sections—stack, text, BSS, data, and heap—along with their relative performance characteristics.

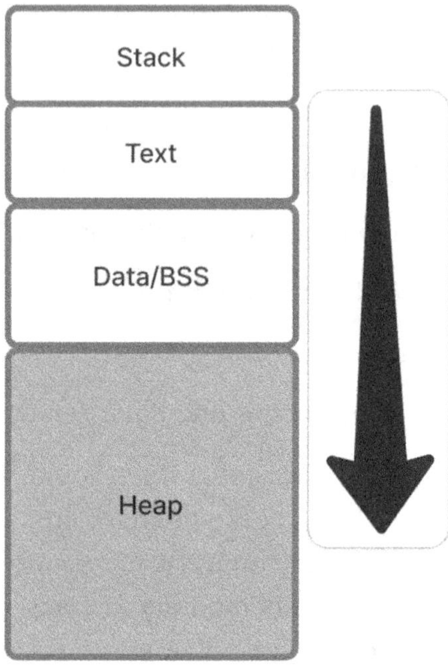

Figure 8-2. *Performance characteristics of Go's memory segments*

Pointers: A Map to Memory

A pointer is a variable that holds a memory address. It's like a signpost pointing to a specific location where a piece of data lives. On a 64-bit system, a pointer itself is a small, word-sized value (8 bytes), while the data it points to (the "pointee") can be of any size.

The pointer variable itself lives wherever it's allocated—on the stack, on the heap, or inside another object. The zero value for a pointer is nil, representing a signpost that points to nowhere. Figure 8-3 shows how a pointer is represented in memory.

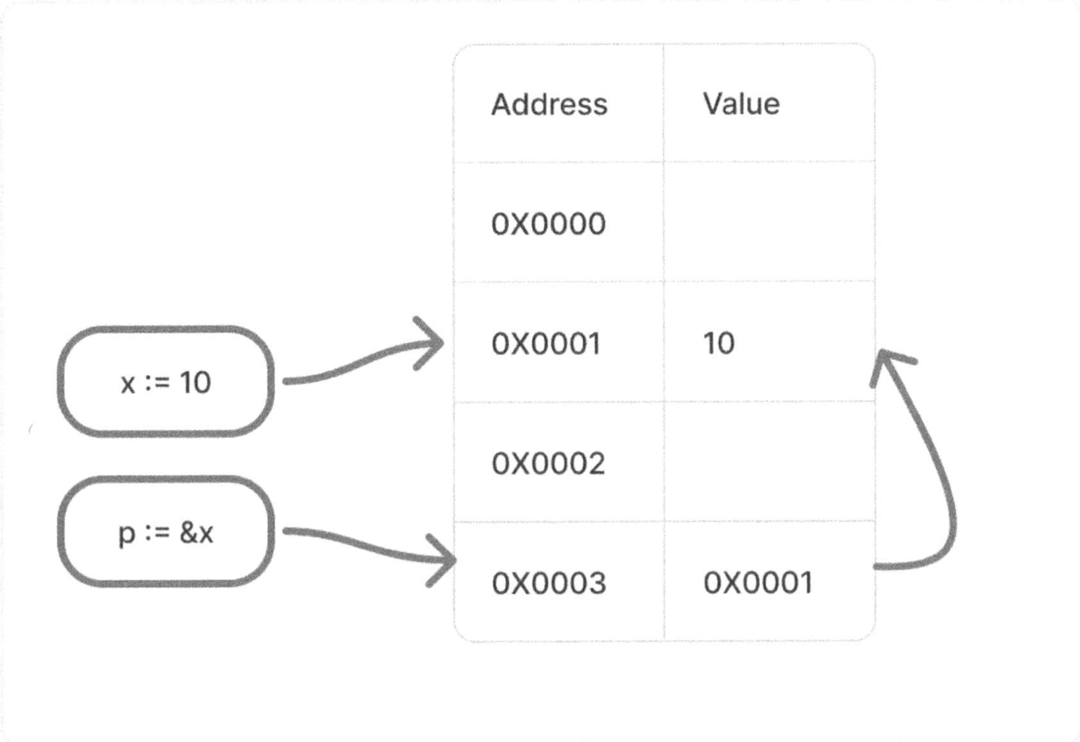

***Figure 8-3.** How a pointer references data in memory*

Why Pointers Matter for Performance

Using a pointer introduces a layer of indirection, which has significant performance implications. Every time you access a value through a pointer, the CPU has to perform an extra step: it must first load the pointer's address and then follow it to find the actual data.

This extra step can be a major performance concern, especially if the pointee is located in a different area of memory. If the data isn't in a CPU cache (a "cache miss"), the CPU has to fetch it from much slower main memory, which can stall the program for hundreds of CPU cycles. This is why contiguous data layouts, like slices of structs, are often much faster than pointer-rich structures like linked lists, which scatter data across the heap.

```
type Vehicle struct {
    ID   string
    Type string
}

// By value: copies the whole struct
func processByValue(v Vehicle) {
    fmt.Println(v.ID)
}

// By pointer: only an 8-byte address is copied
func processByPointer(v *Vehicle) {
    fmt.Println(v.ID)
}
```

There are a few key performance considerations to keep in mind:

- **Heap Promotion:** Taking the address of a variable or storing it in a data structure that lives on the heap (like a map or a slice) can force that variable to escape to the heap. As we've learned, more heap objects mean more work for the Garbage Collector and increased latency.
- **Memory Footprint and Padding:** A pointer itself consumes memory. Adding a pointer field to a struct can increase its overall size and may introduce padding—empty space inserted by the compiler to align fields correctly. This increases memory traffic and can hurt cache performance.

Choosing Between Values and Pointers

The decision to use a pointer or a value is a fundamental design choice. It's not about one being inherently "better," but about choosing the right tool for the job.

```
// Small, cheap type: pass by value
func distance(a, b int) int {
    return b - a
}
```

```
// Larger type: pass by pointer
type Assignment struct {
    ID        string
    VehicleID string
    RouteID   string
    Payload   [1024]byte // big field
}

func updateStatus(a *Assignment, status string) {
    a.VehicleID = status // modify in place
}
```

Use a value when

- The data type is small (typically one to three machine words).
- The value is short-lived and used within a local or performance-critical code path.
- The data doesn't need to be shared or mutated by multiple functions.

Copying small structs is often cheaper than using pointers, which add indirection and may hurt cache locality. Prefer values by default for lightweight types like coordinates, colors, or simple configurations.

Use a pointer when

- The object is large and would be expensive to copy on each use.
- The value must survive beyond the scope of a single function.
- Several parts of your program need to read and update the same data.
- You need to represent optional or nil values explicitly.

A good rule is to start with a value. Switch to a pointer only when there's a clear reason—such as reduced copying, shared mutation, or necessary escape. Let profiling and clarity guide your decision, not habit.

The Reality of Stack vs. Heap Performance

Understanding the trade-offs between stack and heap isn't about dramatic differences; it's about the very real cost of memory access latency.

- **The Stack's Advantage:** The stack gives you contiguity and reuse. Stack frames are small, dense blocks of memory. Accessing local variables repeatedly means you are likely hitting the same cache lines, leading to near-instantaneous access. On top of that, stack variables require no GC involvement, and copying small values is extremely fast, often handled by the CPU's registers.
- **The Heap's Trade-off:** The heap gives you longevity and sharing. When data needs to be shared across function calls or live for a long time, the heap is the only option. But this flexibility comes with a cost: indirection and potential cache misses.

```
// Fast: all values on stack
func stackLoop(n int) {
    for i := 0; i < n; i++ {
        x := i * 2
        _ = x
    }
}

// Slower: every value escapes to heap
func heapLoop(n int) []*int {
    results := make([]*int, 0, n)
    for i := 0; i < n; i++ {
        x := i * 2
        results = append(results, &x) // &x escapes
    }
    return results
}
```

The performance gap between a cache hit (sub-10 nanoseconds) and a cache miss (over 100 nanoseconds to get to main memory) is massive—roughly 10× to 200×. This is why pointer-heavy data structures can be significantly slower on a hot path.

Profiling Memory with pprof

So far, we have talked about memory in theory: stack vs. heap, escapes, and garbage collection work. At some point, you need to see numbers, not feelings. That is where Go's profiling tools come in, especially pprof.

What Is pprof?

`pprof` is Go's built-in profiling tool. It collects and visualizes runtime data such as CPU usage, memory allocations, heap size, and blocking behavior. Using `pprof`, you can see exactly where time and memory are being spent in your program, down to individual functions and call paths. It is the primary tool for turning performance assumptions into measurable facts.

Capturing a Heap Profile

For deeper analysis, you can ask go `test` to write a heap profile:

```
go test -run=^$ -bench . -memprofile=mem.out ./...
go tool pprof mem.out
```

Inside `pprof`, you can start with

```
(pprof)top
(pprof) web
```

- `top` shows which functions hold the most live heap. `top` interface looks like the Linux top command.
- `web` opens a graph view in your browser. Figure 8-4 shows how `pprof web` renders memory usage.

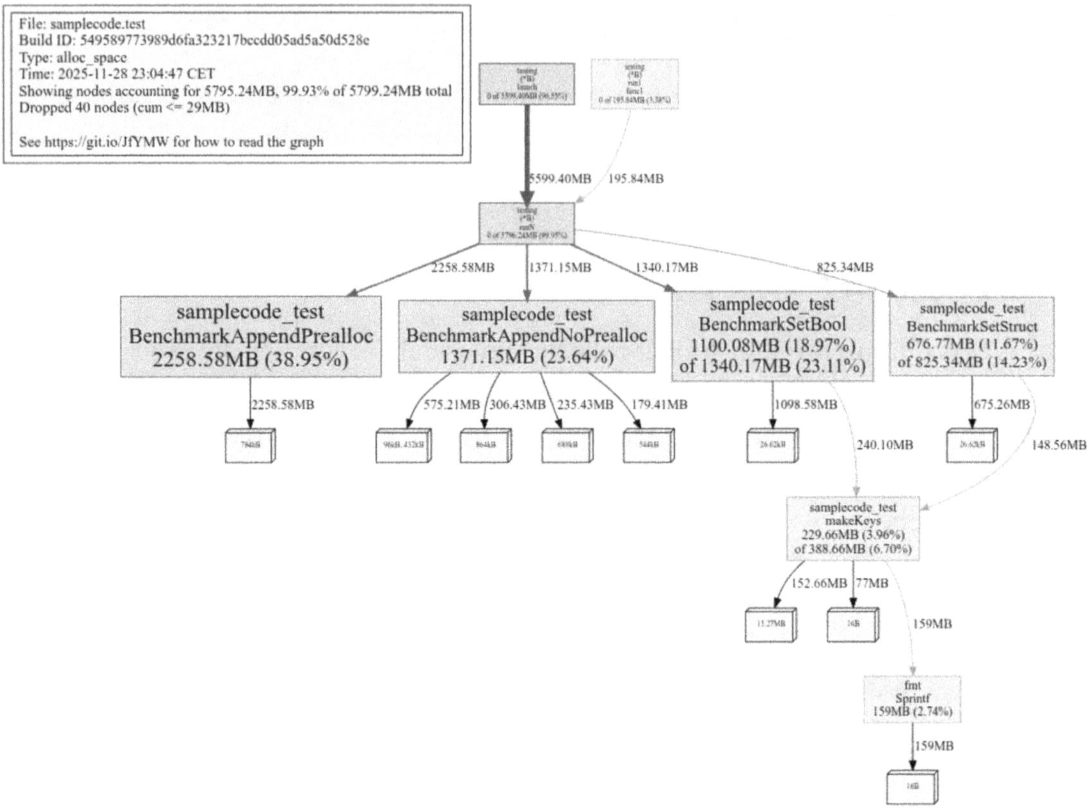

Figure 8-4. *Visualizing heap allocations with pprof's web interface*

This is where you can see, for example, that a small change in how you pass a struct (by value vs. pointer) doubles the number of allocations.

Profiling a Running Service

For long-running services (like HTTP APIs in our transport system), you can enable a profiling endpoint using `net/http/pprof`:

```
import (
    "log"
    "net/http"
    _ "net/http/pprof"
    "time"
)
```

```
func main() {
   go func() {
       log.Println(http.ListenAndServe("localhost:6060", nil))
   }()
   // start your real HTTP server or worker here
   time.Sleep(1 * time.Hour)
}
```

Now you can connect with pprof:

```
go tool pprof http://localhost:6060/debug/pprof/heap
```

From here, the same top and web commands work as before, but now they show heap usage of your live service under real traffic.

Summary

In this chapter, you explored how memory shapes the performance and structure of every Go program. You learned the difference between stack and heap allocation and how Go's escape analysis decides where values live. You studied the distinct roles of memory segments like BSS, data, and text and how they impact binary size, lifetime, and access speed. We examined pointers not just as technical tools, but as architectural choices that affect cache locality, GC load, and code clarity. Finally, you gained a working understanding of Go's garbage collector and how your allocation patterns influence its efficiency—knowledge that empowers you to write scalable, resource-aware software by design.

What's Next

Now that you understand how Go manages memory and why placement matters, you're ready to explore the second major design axis: concurrency. In the next chapter, you'll move from where data lives to how tasks flow. You'll learn how goroutines and channels shape scalable, responsive systems—and how to use them not just to run code faster, but to design it better.

CHAPTER 9

Concurrency by Design: Goroutines and Channels in Go

"Don't communicate by sharing memory; share memory by communicating."

—Rob Pike

Concurrency in Go is not only about speed. It is about **responsiveness**, **clarity**, and **control**. Go was shaped around this idea from day one: tiny goroutines for doing work, channels for passing data, and a simple mental model inspired by CSP (Communicating Sequential Processes). You do not fight the runtime; you collaborate with it.

In real systems, concurrency is not optional. A transport platform assigns vehicles to routes, ingests GPS updates, settles payments, and answers APIs at the same time. If we design this poorly, the system freezes under pressure. If we design it well, the system **breathes** under load.

For a mid-level developer, concurrency can look like "add go in front of a function." For a senior developer, it is about **predictability**: every goroutine has a lifecycle, every external call has a timeout, every pipeline has backpressure, and every piece of shared state has one clear owner.

This chapter will teach you to **design** with Go's concurrency model, not just to launch goroutines. We will cover the mechanics and the idioms that keep enterprise systems healthy for years: goroutines, channels, `select`, and **context** for cancellation. We also connect these ideas to modern Go 1.25 details that matter in production:

S. Shahsavan, *Building Enterprise Projects with Go*, https://doi.org/10.1007/979-8-8688-2370-1_9

- **Container-Aware Scheduling:** Go detects cgroup limits and sets GOMAXPROCS more accurately in containers, which helps throughput and latency.
- **Garbage Collector Improvements:** Smoother GC pacing reduces tail latency in services with many short-lived goroutines.
- **Better Testing for Concurrency:** `testing/synctest` lets you write deterministic tests for timeouts and retries without sleeping.

By the end, you will know how to choose between channels, mutexes, and atomics; how to prevent goroutine leaks; how to shape fan-out/fan-in and worker pools; and how to observe the runtime so you can act before an incident. The goal is simple: systems that scale, stay readable, and shut down cleanly when their work is done.

Foundations of Concurrency in Go

Before knowing how to implement concurrent programs, we need to know the fundamentals; Go, as a modern programming language, is a rich language.

Concurrency vs. Parallelism

Concurrency and parallelism are related, but they are not the same thing. Concurrency is about **design**, parallelism about **execution**.

- **Concurrency** means structuring a program so multiple tasks *can* make progress independently.
- **Parallelism** means those tasks actually run simultaneously on multiple CPU cores.

Think of a busy transport system. While one goroutine fetches vehicle information, another can retrieve the driver's details, and a third can load the route plan. Even if your machine has only one CPU core, these operations can still overlap by yielding control between tasks rather than waiting one after another.

```go
go func() { vehicle, _ = repo.GetVehicle(ctx, vehicleID) }()
go func() { driver, _ = repo.GetDriver(ctx, driverID) }()
go func() { route, _ = repo.GetRoute(ctx, routeID) }()
```

Each go statement tells the runtime to start a new unit of concurrent work. The Go scheduler multiplexes these goroutines across available OS threads. If your system has multiple cores, the runtime may execute several at once. If not, they still make progress cooperatively without blocking each other.

Goroutines vs. OS Threads

A **goroutine** is not the same as an **operating system thread**. It is much lighter and more flexible, managed by Go's runtime instead of the operating system.

- **Small, Dynamic Stacks:** A new goroutine starts with only a few kilobytes of stack memory, which grows and shrinks automatically as needed. In contrast, an OS thread usually reserves several megabytes up front.
- **M:N Scheduler:** Go maps many goroutines (the *M*) onto a smaller number of OS threads (the *N*). This allows millions of goroutines to run cooperatively, yielding execution when they block or sleep.
- **Fast Startup:** Creating a goroutine is almost as cheap as calling a normal function. The runtime only adds minimal scheduling work to register and manage it.

```go
go func() {
    trip := repo.LoadTrip(ctx, tripID)
    processTrip(trip)
}()
```

This design gives Go a unique advantage in enterprise systems. In a transport service, for example, you can safely start a goroutine for every incoming route calculation or GPS update without overloading the server. The runtime scheduler keeps CPU usage balanced and automatically parks goroutines that are waiting for I/O.

The Go Scheduler

The Go scheduler is the engine that decides which goroutine runs, when it runs, and on which CPU thread. You do not control it directly, but understanding its behavior is essential for writing concurrent code that remains predictable under load.

At its core, the scheduler follows an **M:N model**. Many goroutines are multiplexed onto a smaller number of operating system threads, which are then executed on available processor cores. This design enables high concurrency without creating one thread per task.

Each logical processor maintains its own queue of runnable goroutines. When a goroutine blocks on I/O, network operations, or channel communication, the scheduler parks it and immediately runs another goroutine from the same queue. This allows thousands of concurrent tasks to make progress efficiently without exhausting operating system resources.

Because workloads are rarely balanced, the scheduler uses **work stealing**. If one processor runs out of runnable goroutines while others remain busy, it can steal work from another processor's queue. This evens out CPU utilization, improves throughput, and reduces latency spikes under uneven or bursty workloads.

In Go 1.25, the scheduler became **container-aware**. It now respects cgroup CPU limits automatically when setting `GOMAXPROCS`, ensuring that applications running in Docker or Kubernetes use the correct number of CPU threads without manual tuning. The runtime can also adapt if container CPU limits change while the program is running.

In production, incorrect `GOMAXPROCS` values can degrade performance. Setting it higher than the available CPU quota increases contention and unstable latency, while setting it too low underutilizes CPU capacity and reduces throughput. Automatic cgroup awareness in Go 1.25 makes CPU usage more predictable in containerized environments.

You can still read or adjust the current setting manually:

```
current := runtime.GOMAXPROCS(0)
```

In this sample code, passing 0 to GOMAXPROCS means don't change anything and just return the current value.

Finally, Go uses **preemptive scheduling** to ensure fairness. If a goroutine runs for too long without yielding, the runtime can preempt it and allow another goroutine to execute. This prevents CPU-bound loops from blocking unrelated work and helps keep the system responsive.

Lifecycle of a Goroutine

A goroutine behaves like a small living process. It is created, it does its work, and it should eventually end. In a healthy system, every goroutine follows a clear lifecycle: **spawn, execute, and terminate**. When that lifecycle is unclear, goroutines can turn into "zombies" that never die, quietly consuming memory and scheduler time.

Created

A goroutine begins when you add the go keyword before a function call. The runtime registers it with the scheduler and runs it independently.

```
go func() {
    trip := repo.GetTrip(ctx, "T100")
    processTrip(trip)
}()
```

This example launches a background operation to load and process a trip while the main flow continues. Based on the Go source code, its first status is idle.

Runnable

At this stage, goroutine is on a run queue. But it is not currently running. The stack is not owned yet.

Running

Once running, a goroutine stays alive until it finishes naturally or until its **context** signals cancellation. Contexts are essential in enterprise systems because they define the lifetime of concurrent work. If the parent operation ends, all child goroutines must stop.

While executing, a goroutine uses its own stack. Go starts each goroutine with a small stack and grows it as needed. When the stack grows, the runtime allocates a larger stack and copies the existing data. This operation is usually inexpensive, but in memory-constrained environments or systems with very high goroutine churn, repeated stack growth can increase memory pressure and affect performance.

Termination

When the function returns or the context is canceled, the goroutine should exit cleanly. Always check for cancellation inside long-running loops or blocking calls.

Parked

Not all active goroutines are actively using the CPU. When a goroutine waits for a database query or a channel message, the Go scheduler "parks" it. This is Go's superpower: it moves the stalled goroutine aside and puts a productive one in its place. However, if the signal it's waiting for never arrives, a "Parked" goroutine becomes a **Leak**.

Leaks

A leak happens when a goroutine never finishes. Common causes include waiting forever on a channel that no one writes to, looping without checking `ctx.Done()`, or forgetting to close a channel that others depend on.

To avoid leaks, always design **explicit exit paths** and respect context deadlines:

```
ctx, cancel := context.WithTimeout(context.Background(), 500*time.
Millisecond)
defer cancel()

var wg sync.WaitGroup
wg.GO(func() {
    select {
    case <-ctx.Done():
        return
    case res := <-repo.QueryAssignments(ctx):
        process(res)
    }
})

wg.Wait()
```

In this pattern, the goroutine stops cleanly when the timeout expires or the work is done.

Enterprise Lesson A goroutine without a clear exit is a risk to production stability. In high-traffic systems, even a small leak can lead to thousands of stuck goroutines over time. Always tie your goroutines to a context, document their purpose, and decide when they should stop.

As shown in Figure 9-1, a goroutine doesn't just run from start to finish; Understanding these transitions is key to diagnosing performance bottlenecks and memory leaks.

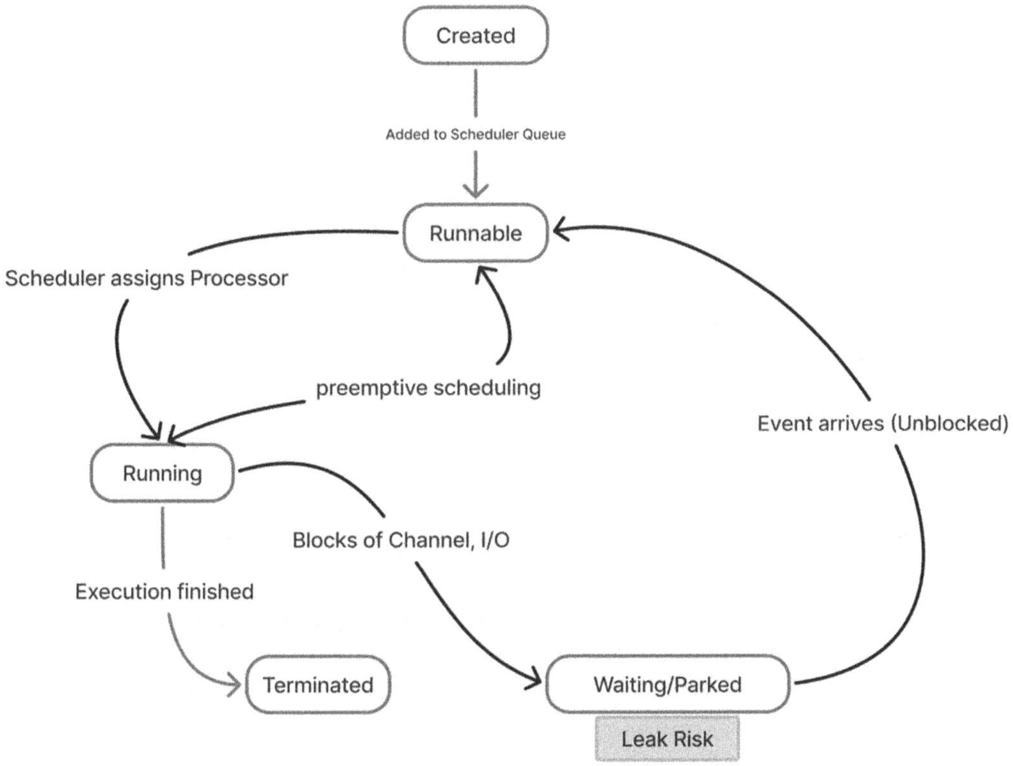

***Figure 9-1.** The internal state transitions of a Go goroutine*

The Life Behind go: What Actually Happens

When you write the word go, something remarkable happens beneath the surface. What looks like a simple function call actually starts a lightweight concurrent process, fully managed by the Go runtime. Understanding how this works is key to writing fast, reliable, and predictable enterprise systems.

What Happens When You Use go

When the compiler sees a statement such as

```
go processTrip(ctx, tripID)
```

It does not create an operating system thread. Instead, it creates a new **goroutine**, represented internally by a small data structure called **g** (read more in Go Runtime Code). This struct keeps track of the goroutine's current stack pointer, status, and related metadata.

Each goroutine begins with a tiny stack—usually about 2 KB—allocated from the heap. The stack automatically grows and shrinks as the function runs, so you never have to decide how much memory to reserve.

Once created, the new goroutine is placed into a **run queue**, a list of tasks waiting for CPU time. Each logical processor (P) managed by the runtime has its own queue. When one queue is empty, it can steal work from another, keeping all processors busy.

From this point, the Go **scheduler** handles the rest. It decides when each goroutine runs, pauses, or yields control, based on I/O events and runtime signals.

How Goroutines Yield During I/O and Channels

Unlike threads, goroutines don't rely on the operating system to manage waiting. When a goroutine performs an I/O operation, waits on a channel, or locks a mutex, the runtime automatically **parks** it. Parking means it is suspended and removed from the run queue until it becomes runnable again.

For example:

```
func fetchVehicle(ctx context.Context, id string) Vehicle {
    v := <-repo.LoadVehicle(ctx, id) // goroutine is parked until
                                        data arrives
    return v
}
```

While this goroutine waits for a channel's value, the scheduler immediately switches to another ready goroutine. This is why thousands of concurrent operations can run efficiently on a few OS threads—waiting costs almost nothing.

Go 1.25: Improved Preemption

Before Go 1.14, long-running loops could block the scheduler. A goroutine performing heavy CPU work without calling a blocking operation might monopolize a thread.

Go continues to refine the runtime's **preemptive scheduling**. Now, even CPU-bound loops are interrupted safely. This means you rarely need to call `runtime.Gosched()` manually to let others run.

However, in rare cases where a loop performs pure computation with no function calls, you can still yield voluntarily:

```
for i := 0; i < 1_000_000; i++ {
    updateCache(i)
    if i%10_000 == 0 {
        runtime.Gosched() // hint scheduler to run other goroutines
    }
}
```

It forces the thread to give up the CPU, and other threads can run. This keeps the system responsive even when a few goroutines are doing intensive work.

Example: When CPU Work Starves Others

Imagine a monitoring service that continuously computes performance statistics for every route:

```
func monitorRoutes() {
    for {
        calculateStats() // heavy CPU work, no I/O
    }
}
```

If you launch this with go `monitorRoutes()`, it may prevent other goroutines from running on the same thread.

The fix is to make the computation **cooperative** by yielding periodically or splitting the work:

```
func monitorRoutes() {
    for {
        for i := 0; i < 1000; i++ {
            calculatePartialStats(i)
        }
        runtime.Gosched() // allow other goroutines to run
    }
}
```

Enterprise Lesson The Go scheduler keeps latency predictable even under heavy CPU load. Still, when writing computational code, measure responsiveness with `pprof` or `go tool trace`. If goroutines appear blocked in "runnable" state for long periods, you may need to break up work or yield more often.

Channels: The Heart of Go Concurrency

Channels are Go's built-in communication pipes that let goroutines exchange data safely without sharing memory. They connect independent parts of a program, turning concurrency into cooperation. Each send and receive is synchronized, so you never need explicit locks for message passing. With buffering, channels can absorb bursts and smooth uneven workloads. In enterprise systems, well-designed channels make the flow of data clear, predictable, and free from race conditions.

Unbuffered vs. Buffered Channels

An **unbuffered channel** is a pure synchronization point. A send happens only when a matching receive is ready. Both sides meet in the middle—if one arrives early, it waits. This makes unbuffered channels perfect for strict sequencing or signaling between goroutines.

```
assignments := make(chan Assignment) // unbuffered

go func() {
    // blocks until another goroutine receives
    assignments <- repo.GetAssignment(ctx, "A123")
}()

a := <-assignments // resumes sender when value received
```

Here, the sender and receiver synchronize at the exact moment of exchange. If the receiver is not ready, the sender pauses. This coordination keeps tasks in order and ensures that every message is processed immediately.

A **buffered channel** introduces a small queue. The sender can place a few values without waiting, as long as the buffer has space. Once full, the next send blocks until a receiver reads. Buffered channels absorb short bursts and help systems stay responsive when producers are slightly faster than consumers.

```
assignments := make(chan Assignment, 5) // buffered channel with capacity 5
```

This setup allows up to five pending assignments to wait in the queue before producers block.

In a transport system, buffering is often the difference between stability and overload. If each route update takes 100 milliseconds to save, but GPS devices send bursts of updates, a small buffer keeps the pipeline smooth without dropping data.

Enterprise Lesson Use **unbuffered channels** for synchronization or request-reply patterns where timing matters. Use **buffered channels** to absorb short bursts and prevent upstream blocking. Size the buffer deliberately—guessing leads to either wasted memory or hidden latency.

Channel Ownership and Closing Rules

Every channel in Go should have a single clear owner. The **sender** is responsible for closing the channel when all values have been sent. A **receiver** should never close a channel it did not create. Following this rule prevents panics and data corruption in concurrent systems.

Single Producer

In a simple one-producer setup, the sender closes the channel after finishing its work.

```
ch := make(chan Assignment)

go func() {
    defer close(ch) // close when done sending
    for _, id := range ids {
        ch <- repo.loadById(id)
    }
}()

for a := range ch {
    process(a)
}
```

Here, the receiver reads until the channel is closed. The `range` loop ends gracefully when all assignments are processed.

Multiple Producers

When several goroutines send to the same channel, no single one should close it. Instead, use a `sync.WaitGroup` to wait until all senders finish, then close the channel once, safely, from a separate goroutine.

```
ch := make(chan Assignment)
var wg sync.WaitGroup

for _, id := range ids {
    wg.Add(1)
    go func(id string) {
        defer wg.Done()
        for a := range repo.LoadById(id) {
            select {
            case <-ctx.Done():
                return // respect cancellation
```

```
                case ch <- a:
                }
            }
        }(id)
}

// Close the channel only after all senders complete
go func() {
    wg.Wait()
    close(ch)
}()

for a := range ch {
    process(a)
}
```

This pattern is simple, safe, and fully deterministic. The final consumer exits automatically when the channel is closed.

Directional Channels Encode Intent

Channels in Go+ can be declared with **direction** to express exactly how they should be used. A send-only channel (`chan<- T`) can only send values, while a receive-only channel (`<-chan T`) can only receive values. This small detail adds clarity and safety by letting the compiler prevent common mistakes such as writing to an input channel or closing a channel you do not own.

```
func processChannel(chIn <-chan Assignment, chOut chan<- Result) {
    for a := range chIn {
        result := process(a)
        select {
        case chOut <- r:
        case <-ctx.Done():
            return // exit gracefully if canceled
        }
    }
}
```

Here, chIn is a read-only channel that supplies assignments, and chOut is a write-only channel for results. The worker can only receive from chIn and send to chOut, which clearly defines its role and avoids misuse.

Using directional channels is especially valuable in enterprise systems where many goroutines interact through shared pipelines. It documents ownership and makes your APIs self-explanatory.

Deadlocks and Livelocks

A **deadlock** happens when all goroutines are waiting, but none can continue. Go detects this at runtime and reports it with a panic, because the program has reached a state where progress is impossible. The most common cause is an unbuffered channel with a send operation that has no receiver.

```
ch := make(chan string)
ch <- "vehicle" // deadlock: no receiver is ready
```

To fix this, either add a receiver or use a buffered channel if temporary queuing makes sense.

```
ch := make(chan string, 1) // buffered channel
ch <- "vehicle"            // succeeds immediately
fmt.Println(<-ch)
```

Be careful, though—adding buffers blindly can hide design problems. The right fix is usually to review your channel topology and verify that every send has a corresponding receive under all conditions.

A **livelock** is subtler. The program is running, but goroutines are busy doing work that never finishes. For example, two workers might endlessly exchange messages, each waiting for the other to release something.

```
a := make(chan struct{}, 1)
b := make(chan struct{}, 1)

a <- struct{}{}
for {
    select {
    case <-a:
```

```
        b <- pa(a)
    case <-b:
        a <- pb(b)
    }
}
```

This code loops forever, passing tokens back and forth without ever reaching a useful result. The solution is to introduce **ownership, backoff, or timeouts** so that one side eventually stops waiting or yields control.

```
ctx, cancel := context.WithTimeout(context.Background(), 1986*time.
Millisecond)
defer cancel()

for {
    select {
    case <-a:
        b <- pa(a)
    case <-b:
        a <- pb(b)
    case <-ctx.Done():
        return // graceful exit
    }
}
```

Timeouts and cancellation signals keep your system responsive even if parts of it become slow or unresponsive.

Enterprise Lesson Deadlocks and livelocks are not just bugs—they are **production outages**. A blocked goroutine can hold locks, memory, or channels that stop other services from progressing. Always design your channel graph with clear ownership, backpressure, and cancellation paths. Use tools like `pprof` and goroutine dumps to detect blocked or looping goroutines before they impact users.

Understanding Select

The select statement in Go is a control structure that listens to multiple communication channels at the same time and reacts to whichever becomes ready first. It is like a traffic controller for concurrent operations, letting your program stay responsive without blocking on any single channel. At its core, select waits until one of its case branches can proceed. Each case represents a send or receive operation on a channel. When one becomes ready, Go executes that branch and ignores the others. If multiple cases are ready at once, one is chosen randomly to keep execution fair.

```
select {
case ev := <-events:
    processEvent(ev)
case err := <-errors:
    return err
case <-ctx.Done():
    fmt.Println("context canceled")
}
```

In this example, select waits for either an event, an error, or a cancellation signal. No busy waiting, no locks, no manual synchronization—just simple event-driven flow.

A select with a default case runs immediately if none of the channels are ready. This allows for non-blocking behavior:

```
select {
case ev := <-event:
    processEvent(ev)
default:
    fmt.Println(" I'm bored! ")
}
```

Adding a default can be useful for quick checks, but overusing it may cause CPU-heavy loops. It is usually better to block briefly on meaningful events or use timers for controlled waiting.

Patterns with Select

We will explore some patterns using select in this section.

Basic Multiplexing

select is most often used for **multiplexing**, which means listening to several channels at once and reacting to whichever one becomes ready first. It lets your program handle multiple asynchronous events without blocking or locking.

```
select {
case a := <-assignments:
    processAssignment(a)
case e := <-errors:
    log.Println("error:", e)
}
```

In a transport management system, this approach allows you to wait for either a successful route assignment or an error message from the repository. The first channel that becomes ready decides the next action. This way, your service remains responsive even when one of the operations takes longer than expected.

The Go runtime ensures fairness between cases. If multiple channels are ready, one is chosen randomly, preventing starvation. This fairness was further improved in **Go**, making select-based coordination more predictable under heavy concurrency.

You can also add more branches to handle timeouts or cancellation using ctx.Done() to ensure that no goroutine waits forever.

```
select {
case a := <-assignments:
    processAssignment(a)
case e := <-errors:
    log.Println("error:", e)
case <-ctx.Done():
    return ctx.Err()
}
```

This pattern is common in enterprise systems that need to merge signals from different components like databases, message queues, or telemetry feeds while respecting request lifetimes.

Enterprise Lesson Use `select` when handling multiple asynchronous events. It keeps your service responsive even under mixed loads. Avoid deeply nested `select` statements—compose smaller, focused functions instead.

Timeout Handling with time.After

Every enterprise system needs a way to avoid hanging forever while waiting for a slow back end, such as a database or API. Go provides a simple built-in tool for this: **`time.After`**. It returns a channel that delivers a signal after a given duration, allowing you to enforce deadlines directly inside a `select` statement.

```
select {
case res := <-repo.QueryAssignments(ctx):
    return res
case <-time.After(200 * time.Millisecond):
    return errors.New("timed out")
}
```

This structure guarantees that even if the repository call stalls, your service remains responsive. Once the timeout expires, the `time.After` channel fires, and the program can safely move on or return an error.

Better Practice with Reusable Timers

Inside loops or recurring operations, creating a new `time.After` for each iteration is inefficient. Each call allocates a new timer that cannot be reused or canceled, which can lead to small but steady memory growth over time. Instead, create a reusable timer with **`time.NewTimer`** and reset it as needed.

```
timer := time.NewTimer(200 * time.Millisecond)
defer timer.Stop()

select {
case res := <-repo.QueryAssignments(ctx):
    return res
```

```
case <-timer.C:
    return errors.New("timed out")
}
```

If you use this pattern in a loop, remember to **stop** and **drain** the timer's channel before resetting it.

```
if !timer.Stop() {
    <-timer.C // drain if timer already fired
}
timer.Reset(200 * time.Millisecond)
```

This ensures the timer behaves predictably and avoids subtle race conditions or goroutine leaks.

Enterprise Lesson Timeouts are not optional—they are your first defense against cascading failures. Always set explicit deadlines for external calls such as databases, APIs, and message queues. Combine `time.After` or `time.NewTimer` with `ctx.Done()` for full control over request lifetime.

Fan-In and Fan-Out with Select

The **fan-out/fan-in** pattern is one of the most practical concurrency designs in Go. It allows you to distribute work across multiple goroutines (fan-out) and then merge their results into a single channel (fan-in). This pattern fits naturally in enterprise systems such as transport platforms, where multiple vehicle status checks, route computations, or payment validations can run at the same time.

```
out := make(chan Result)

for _, v := range vehicles {
    go func(id string) {
        result := repo.CheckAvailability(ctx, id)
        select {
        case out <- result:
```

```
        case <-ctx.Done():
            return // stop early if canceled
        }
    }(v)
}

for range vehicles {
    select {
    case r := <-out:
        fmt.Println("availability:", r)
    case <-ctx.Done():
        return // stop collecting if context canceled
    }
}
```

Each goroutine works independently and sends its result to the shared out channel. The main loop merges results as they arrive, keeping the system responsive. If the request is canceled, all goroutines exit gracefully through ctx.Done(), preventing leaks or wasted work.

You can also bound the number of concurrent workers using a **semaphore channel** to avoid overloading the database or CPU.

```
sem := make(chan struct{}, 8) // limit to 8 cpu cores
out := make(chan Vehicle)

for _, v := range vehicles {
    sem <- struct{}{}
    go func(id string) {
        defer func() { <-sem }()
        vhcl := repo.CheckAvailability(ctx, id)
        select {
        case out <- vhcl:
        case <-ctx.Done():
            return
        }
    }(v)
}
```

This small adjustment gives you precise control over concurrency while keeping throughput high. It's important to keep the number of goroutines limited. You can find more patterns in **Chapter 20**.

Enterprise Lesson Fan-out/fan-in is ideal for balancing workloads and improving response time in I/O-heavy systems. Use context cancellation to ensure proper cleanup and avoid orphaned goroutines. When scaling horizontally, limit concurrency with a buffered semaphore so your system remains stable under load.

Synchronization and Alternatives

Goroutines and channels are at the heart of Go's concurrency model, but they are not the only coordination tools you need. When your goal is **data protection** rather than **communication**, the `sync` package offers lightweight and efficient primitives that complement channels. A good Go developer knows when to send a message and when to take a lock.

Mutexes, RWMutex, and Cond

Channels are perfect when data flows between goroutines or when ownership changes hands, but when you simply need to **protect shared memory**, locks are the better choice. The `sync` package provides simple, low-overhead primitives that make critical sections safe without introducing extra communication.

- **`sync.Mutex`** allows exactly one goroutine to access a section of code at a time.
- **`sync.RWMutex`** permits multiple readers or a single writer, making it ideal for read-heavy workloads.
- **`sync.Cond`** provides coordination between goroutines that must wait for a condition to change, such as a queue becoming non-empty or a resource becoming available.

Protecting Shared Data

Consider a transport management system that stores trip distance in memory. Multiple components may access distances concurrently, while only a few update them.

```
var mu sync.RWMutex
var distances = make(map[string]int)

func GetDistance(route string) int {
    mu.RLock()
    defer mu.RUnlock()
    return distances[route]
}

func SetDistance(route string, distance int) {
    mu.Lock()
    defer mu.Unlock()
    distances[route] = distance
}
```

Here, `RWMutex` enables high read concurrency, since many readers can access data at once without blocking each other. Writers, however, must wait until all reads finish to ensure consistent updates.

If you need goroutines to wait for an event—such as the next trip being available—you can use `sync.Cond`.

Understanding sync.Cond: Coordinating Goroutines with Shared Conditions

While `Mutex` and `RWMutex` protect shared data from concurrent access, sometimes goroutines must **wait for a specific condition to become true**—for example, when a queue is empty or a resource is not ready yet. In these cases, busy waiting (constantly checking a variable in a loop) wastes CPU time.

`sync.Cond` solves this problem. It allows goroutines to **wait efficiently** until another goroutine signals that the condition has changed. It combines a lock (`sync.Mutex` or `sync.RWMutex`) with a condition variable that supports three main methods:

- **`Wait()`:** Atomically releases the lock, suspends the goroutine, and waits for a signal

- **Signal():** Wakes one waiting goroutine (if any)
- **Broadcast():** Wakes all waiting goroutines

When Wait() returns, the goroutine automatically reacquires the lock before resuming, so you can safely recheck the condition.

Enterprise Lesson I highly recommend you check Go documents for these important methods; you can also find them online https://go.dev/src/sync/cond.go and know more details.

Imagine a transport dispatch service where new trips arrive at unpredictable times and drivers must wait until a trip is available. Instead of polling the queue repeatedly, we can use a sync.Cond to efficiently block until new data arrives.

```
var mu sync.Mutex
var cond = sync.NewCond(&mu)
var trips []Trip

func addTrip(trip Trip) {
    mu.Lock()
    trips = append(trips, trip)
    cond.Signal() // wake one waiting driver
    mu.Unlock()
}

func waitForAvailableTrip() Trip {
    mu.Lock()

    for len(trips) == 0 {
        cond.Wait() // release lock and sleep until signaled
    }
    t := trips[0]
    trips = trips[1:]
    mu.Unlock()
    return t
}
```

This pattern is simple and memory-safe. Each waiting goroutine releases the lock when sleeping and reacquires it automatically when awakened.

How It Works

1. A driver goroutine calls `waitForAvailableTrip()`. Since there are no trips, it enters the `for` loop and calls `cond.Wait()`.
2. `Wait()` releases `mu` and suspends the goroutine. It will sleep without consuming CPU.
3. When `addTrip()` is called, it locks `mu`, adds a new trip, and calls `cond.Signal()`.
4. The waiting goroutine wakes up, automatically reacquires `mu`, and checks the condition again. It then retrieves the trip and proceeds.

Using `Signal()` wakes only one waiting goroutine—ideal when each event (like a new trip) should wake a single consumer. If multiple goroutines should react to the same event, use `cond.Broadcast()` instead.

`sync.Cond` is the right tool when you have **state-dependent coordination** between goroutines that share memory and must wait for a change in that shared state.

When to Prefer Locks over Channels

While channels are powerful tools for communication and task coordination, they are not always the best choice for protecting shared memory. When multiple goroutines need quick access to shared data structures, such as maps, caches, or counters, **locks** are often simpler, faster, and easier to reason about.

Locks work best when

- **The data is shared but not streamed.** You are protecting access, not passing ownership.
- **Operations are short and frequent.** Reads and writes take microseconds, so you want minimal overhead.

Using channels to serialize access to shared memory can introduce unnecessary scheduler work and increase latency.

Atomics and sync/atomic

When you only need to update a simple value like a counter, flag, or pointer, **atomic operations** are the fastest and simplest way to achieve safe concurrency. The `sync/atomic` package provides low-level primitives that modify data in a single, indivisible CPU instruction. Unlike locks, atomics never block; they let multiple goroutines update shared values without waiting for each other.

Example: Counting Active Database Queries

In a transport platform, you might want to track how many database queries are active at any moment.

```
var active int64

func StartQuery() {
    atomic.AddInt64(&active, 1)
}

func EndQuery() {
    atomic.AddInt64(&active, -1)
}

func ActiveQueries() int64 {
    return atomic.LoadInt64(&active)
}
```

Here, each query increments `active` when it starts and decrements it when it finishes. Because these operations are atomic, no lock or channel is needed. The counter always stays consistent, even if thousands of goroutines run simultaneously.

Atomics are **ideal for lightweight metrics**, hot-path counters, or signal flags like "ready," "closed," or "shutdown." However, they do not protect **multiple related values**. If several updates must happen together (e.g., adjusting both a balance and a transaction count), use a `sync.Mutex` instead.

Enterprise Lesson Atomics are powerful but low-level. Use them **only for independent values** such as counters, timestamps, or readiness flags. Once your logic involves multiple variables that must change together, switch to a **mutex** for safety and clarity. Complex atomic sequences are hard to reason about and often lead to hidden bugs that are difficult to reproduce in production.

Goroutine Overhead: What "Lightweight" Really Means

By now, you already know how to use goroutines correctly. The more important question for large systems is this:

What does a goroutine actually cost, and when does that cost matter?

Goroutines are often described as cheap. This is true, but it doesn't mean they are free. A goroutine is cheaper than an operating system thread, but it is still a runtime-managed object. It consumes memory, it participates in scheduling, and it has a lifecycle that the Go runtime must manage.

At a small scale, these costs are negligible. At enterprise scale, they directly affect throughput, latency, and stability. Creating a goroutine involves multiple runtime steps:

- Allocating or reusing a goroutine
- Allocating an initial stack
- Registering the goroutine with the scheduler
- Reclaiming memory when the goroutine finishes

Although the cost is tiny, repeated thousands or millions of times, it becomes visible.

"Drop by drop, it gathers—eventually it becomes a sea."

—Mohsen Fayz Kashani

Stack and Scheduler Effects

Each goroutine starts with a small stack, only a few kilobytes. Stacks grow and shrink automatically, allowing Go to support very large numbers of goroutines. Tens of thousands of goroutines consume significant memory. At that point, cache behavior and garbage collection become important. The scheduler cost appears when too many runnable goroutines compete for limited CPU cores. A system with eight cores and tens of thousands of runnable goroutines is not more parallel. It is so expensive to schedule.

Garbage Collection Pressure

Every goroutine allocates memory. Short-lived goroutines are especially expensive because they allocate stacks and captured variables, then quickly become garbage. This increases garbage collection work even when pause times remain small. CPU time is spent managing memory instead of executing business logic.

Enterprise Lesson Goroutines are cheap enough to encourage clear designs, but expensive enough to punish careless ones. At scale, concurrency design is resource management.

What Is the Solution?

Engineers find a way, or they will build a way. Every problem has possible solutions. Especially in modern programming languages like Go. For the challenges discussed in this section, Go offers design patterns that help systems remain predictable, efficient, and performant, even under heavy load. One of the most important patterns is the **Worker Pool**. This pattern limits concurrency, reuses goroutines, and introduces natural backpressure, making system behavior easier to reason about in production.

We discuss the worker pool pattern in detail in **Chapter 20**, where we explore common **design patterns in Go** and explain how to apply them effectively in enterprise systems.

One-Time Initialization with sync.Once

sync.Once guarantees that a specific function runs only once, no matter how many goroutines call it. It is the safest way to handle shared initialization logic like setting up a database connection, loading configuration, or starting a background worker.

```
var once sync.Once

func InitDB() {
    once.Do(func() {
        initContainers()
    })
}
```

The first goroutine that calls once.Do() executes the provided function, while all others wait until it finishes. After that, subsequent calls do nothing. This pattern prevents race conditions that might occur if multiple goroutines tried to initialize the same resource at the same time.

If the function inside once.Do panics, it is **not** retried. In that case, you should handle recovery or reinitialization explicitly.

Error Handling in Concurrent Programs

Error handling in concurrent systems is one of the easiest areas to get wrong. A single missed error can leave your system in an inconsistent or half-finished state. In Go, every goroutine that can fail should have a clear and reliable way to report its failure. If you launch goroutines without collecting their results, you may never know that one of them failed—until production data starts behaving strangely.

Collecting Errors from Multiple Goroutines

When multiple goroutines run together, each one may succeed or fail independently. If you ignore their errors, you risk partial success—some work may be completed, while other parts silently fail.

```
errs := make(chan error, 3)
go func() { _, err := repo.GetDriver(ctx, driverID); errs <- err }()
go func() { _, err := repo.GetVehicle(ctx, vehicleID); errs <- err }()
go func() { _, err := repo.GetRoute(ctx, routeID); errs <- err }()
for i := 0; i < 3; i++ {
      if err := <-errs; err != nil {
            return err // return on first failure
      }
}
```

This example launches three independent lookups. Each goroutine reports its result on the `errs` channel. Using a buffered channel ensures no goroutine blocks when sending.

However, this pattern scales poorly if you forget to drain all channels or need cancellation after the first error. That's where structured concurrency comes in.

Structured Concurrency with errgroup

The `x/sync/errgroup` package helps you manage multiple goroutines as **a single, coordinated unit**. It provides a simple structure that automatically handles error collection, context propagation, and cancellation. Instead of manually tracking goroutines with channels or counters, `errgroup` lets you write concurrent code that is both safe and clean.

```
g, ctx := errgroup.WithContext(ctx)

g.Go(func() error {
    _, err := repo.GetDriver(ctx, driverID)
    return err
})

g.Go(func() error {
    _, err := repo.GetVehicle(ctx, vehicleID)
    return err
})
```

```
g.Go(func() error {
    _, err := repo.GetRoute(ctx, routeID)
    return err
})

if err := g.Wait(); err != nil {
    return err // first error cancels the rest
}
```

Here, three goroutines fetch data concurrently. If any one of them returns an error, errgroup automatically **cancels the shared context**, stopping the other goroutines as soon as possible. When all have finished or been canceled, g.Wait() returns the first error that occurred.

Why errgroup is Safer and Cleaner

1. **Automatic Cancellation:** If one goroutine fails, all others sharing the same context are canceled immediately.
2. **Consistent Context Propagation:** The same ctx travels through all goroutines, so timeouts and cancellations behave uniformly.
3. **Built-in Error Collection:** You no longer need custom error channels or manual aggregation.

You can also combine errgroup with errors.Join() (introduced in Go 1.20) to collect **all** non-nil errors instead of just the first one:

```
var allErrs []error
g, ctx := errgroup.WithContext(ctx)

g.Go(func() error {
    _, err := repo.GetDriver(ctx, driverID)
    if err != nil { allErrs = append(allErrs, err) }
    return err
})
g.Go(func() error {
    _, err := repo.GetVehicle(ctx, vehicleID)
    if err != nil { allErrs = append(allErrs, err) }
    return err
})
```

```
g.Go(func() error {
    _, err := repo.GetRoute(ctx, routeID)
    if err != nil { allErrs = append(allErrs, err) }
    return err
})

_ = g.Wait()
if len(allErrs) > 0 {
    return errors.Join(allErrs...)
}
```

This approach gives you complete visibility into what went wrong, which is especially useful for batch processing or diagnostic APIs.

Enterprise Lesson `errgroup` uses lightweight synchronization internally and scales easily across thousands of concurrent tasks. It has almost no scheduling overhead compared to manual channel management.

Enterprise Tip In high-throughput systems, you can combine `errgroup` with a concurrency limit to avoid spawning too many goroutines at once. This allows you to keep structured cancellation and error handling while still bounding concurrency.

Deterministic Concurrency Tests with testing/synctest (Go 1.25)

Testing concurrent code has always been one of the hardest parts of Go development. Using `time.Sleep` to "wait for something to finish" often leads to flaky and slow tests. The `testing/synctest` package, introduced in Go 1.25, solves this problem by running tests inside an isolated simulation environment with a **virtual clock**.

Inside this controlled environment—called a *bubble*—time does not move forward automatically. Instead, it advances only when all goroutines in the bubble are **durably blocked**, meaning they are waiting on a timer, channel, or synchronization primitive.

This design lets you write tests that behave deterministically: if a timer is supposed to fire after five seconds, the fake clock will jump straight to that moment instantly, with no real waiting.

For example, inside a bubble, `time.Now` always starts from midnight UTC on January 1, 2000. Any timers, tickers, channels, `sync.WaitGroup`, or `sync.Cond` created in the bubble are automatically tracked. When no progress can be made, `synctest.Wait()` advances time to the next scheduled event. If there is a true deadlock (no goroutine can proceed), `synctest.Test` will panic to reveal it immediately.

```
func QueryWithTimeout(ctx context.Context, loadFunc func() error, d
time.Duration) error {
    timer := time.NewTimer(d)
    defer timer.Stop()

    done := make(chan error, 1)
    go func() {
        done <- loadFunc() // simulate query
    }()

    select {
    case err := <-done:
        return err
    case <-timer.C:
        return errors.New("timed out")
    case <-ctx.Done():
        return ctx.Err()
    }
}

func TestQueryWithTimeout(t *testing.T) {
    synctest.Test(t, func(t *testing.T) {
        ctx := t.Context()
        // Load never responds
        loadFunc := func() error {
            select {} // block
            return nil
        }
```

```
        err := QueryWithTimeout(ctx, loadFunc, 1986 * time.Millisecond)

        synctest.Wait() // advance time to the timeout event
        if err == nil {
            t.Fatalf("expected error, got nil")
        }
        if err.Error() != "timed out" {
            t.Fatalf("expected timeout error, got %v", err)
        }
    })
}
```

In this example, the test verifies that a query correctly times out after 500 milliseconds. There is **no real waiting**; the `synctest` framework advances time to when the timer would fire. The behavior is fully deterministic and completes instantly, regardless of CPU speed or system load.

`synctest` also fails a test if any goroutine in the bubble remains runnable or blocked when the test finishes. If you simulate a stuck worker, make sure your test **cancels** it or **unblocks** it before the bubble ends; otherwise, `synctest` will panic with a deadlock trace on purpose. In the example above, the panic occurs because the goroutine running `loadFunc()` never exits. To make the test pass, let the worker return or watch the test's context (e.g., `<-ctx.Done()`) so it stops when the main function finishes.

Change to Make It Work

In the test, replace the repo function's infinite select {} with a line that waits for the context to be canceled, for example:

```
loadFunc := func() error {
    <-ctx.Done() // exit when the test context finishes
    return ctx.Err()
}
```

This lets the worker goroutine exit cleanly when the main test ends, so `synctest` no longer reports a deadlock.

How It Works

When you wrap your test with `synctest.Test(t, func(t *testing.T){ ... })`, Go runs the entire body inside a **virtual time bubble**. Everything that happens inside this function—goroutines, channels, timers, tickers, and synchronization primitives—operates under a controlled, fake clock.

Inside this bubble:

- **Virtual time replaces real time.** Functions like `time.Now`, `time.After`, `time.NewTimer`, and `time.NewTicker` are driven by the bubble's clock, not the system clock. No real milliseconds pass; time advances only as needed.
- **`synctest.Wait()`** is your main synchronization point. It pauses the test until all other goroutines are durably blocked (e.g., waiting on a channel, timer, or condition). Once they are, `synctest` advances the virtual clock to the next unblocking event.
- **Automatic Time Jumps:** When the next event (like a timer firing or a message arriving) becomes ready, the bubble "jumps forward" to that moment, unblocking the waiting goroutine instantly.
- **Deadlock Detection:** If no goroutine can proceed and there are no future events, `synctest` panics with a detailed stack trace that helps you find deadlocks or missing signals.

This design lets you test code that relies on time or coordination deterministically. No more guessing sleep durations, waiting for random delays, or chasing race conditions that only happen sometimes. Every test run behaves exactly the same, making concurrent systems far easier to verify and maintain.

Enterprise Lesson Tests using `synctest` complete almost instantly because no real time passes. The virtual clock moves directly to the next event, even across thousands of goroutines. In Go 1.25, this package is optimized to track timers, tickers, and synchronization primitives efficiently, giving you precise, high-speed testing for concurrent behavior.

Monitoring Goroutines in Production

Concurrency problems rarely appear first as system failures. In most cases, they appear earlier as a slow increase in the number of goroutines, higher memory usage, or unstable response times. For this reason, production systems should continuously monitor goroutines, not only during debugging or incident analysis. Go provides two practical tools for this purpose: `runtime.NumGoroutine()` and `pprof`.

Tracking Goroutine Count with runtime.NumGoroutine

The simplest signal of goroutine health is the total number of active goroutines. You can simply get it using the following function:

```
runtime.NumGoroutine()
```

This function returns the number of goroutines currently alive in the process. In production systems, this value is not used as a strict limit. Instead, engineers observe **how it changes over time**.

- A healthy system usually shows a stable number.
- A slow but continuous increase often indicates a goroutine leak.
- Sudden spikes typically indicate unbounded concurrency.

This function is inexpensive to call and safe for production use. It is commonly exposed through a health endpoint or exported as a metric.

Enabling pprof in a Go Service

To inspect goroutines in more detail, Go provides `pprof`. It can be enabled with a single import:

```
import _ "net/http/pprof"
```

Once enabled, the application exposes profiling endpoints under the `"/debug/pprof/"` path prefix.

These endpoints include CPU, memory, and goroutine profiles and are available in Go without additional configuration.

Inspecting Goroutines with pprof

To inspect goroutines, open the goroutine profile:

```
http://localhost:8080/debug/pprof/goroutine
```

For interactive analysis and a watch graph, start the pprof web interface:

```
go tool pprof -http=:6060 http://localhost:8080/debug/pprof/goroutine
```

It is important to understand that pprof does not display individual goroutines. Instead, it groups goroutines that share the same call stack. This behavior is intentional and allows patterns to become visible at scale. Figure 9-2 shows a goroutine call graph captured using pprof while the system is under load.

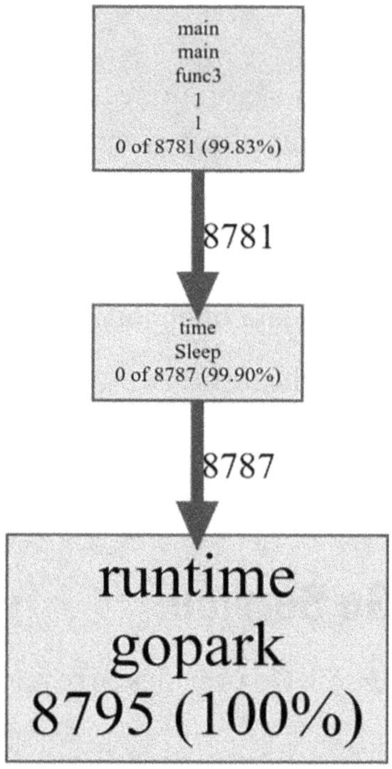

Figure 9-2. *Goroutine call graph illustrating unbounded goroutine creation and blocking*

The graph represents an aggregated view of goroutines that share the same call stack. This tells us

- How many goroutines are running
- Where goroutines were created
- What is their status
- Where they are blocked
- Why they are not completing

A single thick path dominating the graph is a strong signal of unbounded goroutine creation.

Reading the Raw Goroutine Dump

For a more detailed view, you can open:
`http://localhost:8080/debug/pprof/goroutine?debug=2`.

This endpoint prints stack traces of all goroutines, grouped by state.

Example 1

```
goroutine 1 [IO wait]:
net/http.(*Server).Serve(...)
```

This shows the main goroutine waiting for incoming HTTP connections.

Example 2

```
goroutine 10 [chan receive]:
main.main.func1(...)
created by main.main
```

This shows a worker goroutine blocked on a channel receive, which is typically healthy.

Example 3

```
goroutine 8795 [sleep]:
time.Sleep
runtime.gopark
```

This shows many goroutines blocked in the same location. If this number grows continuously, it often indicates a goroutine leak.

Full Example of Goroutine Monitoring in Go

Below is a complete, runnable example that demonstrates how to monitor goroutines in a Go program. This example is intentionally small, but it mirrors patterns you can safely apply in real production systems. The goal is not to build a full service, but to make goroutine behavior visible and measurable.

```go
package main

import (
    "fmt"
    "log"
    "net/http"
    _ "net/http/pprof" // registers /debug/pprof handlers
    "runtime"
    "time"
)

func main() {
    // A small worker pool (bounded concurrency).
    jobs := make(chan int, 1000)

    for i := 0; i < 8; i++ { // fixed number of workers
        go func(workerID int) {
            for job := range jobs {
                _ = job
                time.Sleep(5 * time.Millisecond) // simulate work
            }
        }(i)
    }

    // Generates work continuously.
    go func() {
        i := 0
        t := time.NewTicker(1 * time.Millisecond)
        defer t.Stop()

        for range t.C {
            i++

            // Normal mode: send to workers (stable goroutine count).
            select {
            case jobs <- i:
```

```
        default:
            // Queue full: backpressure; drop or block in real systems.
        }
    }
}()

// Optional: create goroutine buildup intentionally (to observe
in pprof).
// Visit: /start?leak=1
http.HandleFunc("/start", func(w http.ResponseWriter, r *http.Request) {
    if r.URL.Query().Get("leak") == "1" {
        go func() {
            for {
                // This pattern is intentionally bad: one goroutine
                per task,
                // and the tasks block for a while.
                go func() {
                    time.Sleep(30 * time.Second)
                }()
                time.Sleep(1 * time.Millisecond)
            }
        }()
        fmt.Fprintln(w, "started leak mode (intentional goroutine
        buildup)")
        return
    }
    fmt.Fprintln(w, "running normally (worker pool mode)")
})

// Simple health signal: goroutine count.
http.HandleFunc("/health/goroutines", func(w http.ResponseWriter,
r *http.Request) {
    fmt.Fprintf(w, "goroutines=%d\n", runtime.NumGoroutine())
})
```

```
    // A tiny index page.
    http.HandleFunc("/", func(w http.ResponseWriter, r *http.Request) {
        fmt.Fprintln(w, "Try:")
        fmt.Fprintln(w, "  /health/goroutines")
        fmt.Fprintln(w, "  /debug/pprof/")
        fmt.Fprintln(w, "  /debug/pprof/goroutine?debug=1")
        fmt.Fprintln(w, "  /start            (normal mode)")
        fmt.Fprintln(w, "  /start?leak=1     (intentional goroutine
        buildup)")
    })

    addr := ":8080"
    log.Printf("listening on %s", addr)
    log.Printf("pprof at http://localhost%s/debug/pprof/", addr)
    log.Fatal(http.ListenAndServe(addr, nil))
}
```

How to Use This Example

Run the program and observe its behavior through the following endpoints:

- `/health/goroutines`

  Shows the current number of active goroutines. Watch this value over time.

- `/debug/pprof/*`

  Exposes profiling endpoints, including goroutine profiles.

- `/start`

  Runs the system in normal, bounded mode.

- `/start?leak=1`

  Intentionally starts unbounded goroutine creation so you can observe growth in `runtime.NumGoroutine()` and inspect it using `pprof`.

In normal mode, the goroutine count should remain mostly stable. In leak mode, the count should grow continuously, making the problem visible both in metrics and in profiling output.

Summary

In this chapter, you learned how to design concurrency, not only how to start goroutines. We compared goroutines with OS threads and explained the scheduler, including Go 1.25 behavior that sets GOMAXPROCS correctly in containers. You saw how stacks grow, how goroutines yield on I/O, and why clear lifecycles with context and graceful shutdown prevent leaks. We treated channels as the main communication tool and covered unbuffered and buffered use, ownership and closing rules, nil and closed channels, directional typing, and how to avoid deadlocks and livelocks. You practiced selecting for multiplexing, timeouts with reusable timers, cancellation, fan-in and fan-out, and how to avoid busy default loops. We bounded concurrency with semaphore channels, worker pools, and sized buffers. You learned when locks, RWMutex, Cond, atomics, Once, and WaitGroup are better than channels. Finally, we handled errors with errgroup and errors.Join and added observability and testing with the race detector and testing/synctest to keep services reliable under real load.

What's Next

Now that you understand Go's concurrency model in depth, it's time to connect these concepts to a real project. In the next chapter, we step from isolated examples into system design—defining the project you will build throughout the rest of the book. You will see how concurrency, structure, and data persistence fit together in an enterprise context, preparing you to apply everything you've learned in a cohesive, real-world application.

PART II

Building the Enterprise: From Blueprint to Mastery

CHAPTER 10

The Blueprint of Vision: Defining the Project Road Map

> *"Good business leaders create a vision, articulate the vision, passionately own the vision, and relentlessly drive it to completion."*
>
> —Jack Welch

Projects reveal what no theory alone can teach: how ideas behave when they meet the limits of time, scale, and people. In this book, our project becomes a controlled experiment in turning design into reality. We will build a complete enterprise-grade system step by step, using Go as our programming language.

You will see how Go's clarity, concurrency, and database integration perform under real-world pressures such as persistence, validation, and scalability. Each chapter expands the system by a minimum of steps, helping you connect language features to real-world usage. By the end, this project will show how to implement a Go project and a map of how professional Go systems are designed, tested, and evolved—preparing you to approach enterprise development with structure, confidence, and craftsmanship. You can find the source code in the `https://github.com/shahsavan/building-enterprise-projects-with-go` GitHub repository.

S. Shahsavan, *Building Enterprise Projects with Go*, https://doi.org/10.1007/979-8-8688-2370-1_10

Project Overview

We will build a real, working application that grows with each chapter. The project is not an abstract example; it is a small but complete enterprise system designed to help you apply Go programming concepts in real situations. The application will simulate a simplified **transport management system**, where vehicles are registered, assigned to routes, and tracked through various services. This scenario is realistic, yet small enough to understand and extend.

The back end of the system will be written entirely in Go, using its modern standard library and features such as improved `encoding/json/v2`, native context handling in `net/http`, and the optimized database connection pooling in `database/sql`. For data persistence, we will use **MySQL**, one of the most reliable and widely used open source relational databases in enterprise environments. Working with MySQL allows us to practice writing safe and efficient SQL queries, managing transactions, and designing normalized database schemas that can scale as data grows.

You will begin with a minimal, functional setup and add features gradually. Each new chapter introduces a real improvement—user input validation, concurrency handling, business logic, or database schema enhancement. By the end, the application will serve multiple users, perform concurrent requests safely, and expose a clean HTTP interface for interacting with the system.

This step-by-step approach allows you to learn in layers. Every concept—whether it is about concurrency, error handling, or database design—is immediately applied in code. This way, your understanding grows with each practical step, helping you develop the mindset and discipline required for professional Go development in enterprise-scale projects.

Technologies Used

- **Go Programming Language:** The core application logic will be written in Go. We leverage Go's strengths—simplicity, concurrency support, and a strong standard library—to build the project. Go's built-in libraries will be used to avoid external dependencies and keep the project straightforward.

- **MySQL Database:** MySQL will serve as the project's database management system. All persistent data is stored in a MySQL database, and we interact with it using SQL queries. We chose MySQL MySQL 8.0.44 for its reliability and widespread use in web applications. Working with MySQL in this project will familiarize you with using a relational database in Go, including writing SQL statements, and using drivers to connect Go with MySQL.
- **HTTP and RESTful API:** The project utilizes the HTTP protocol for client–server communication. Whether we build web pages or a pure RESTful API, the Go application will define endpoints (URLs) that clients can call to perform actions (like `/assignments` for creating a new assignment). We will adhere to RESTful principles in designing these endpoints (using appropriate methods GET, POST, PUT, DELETE for different actions) to make our web service intuitive and well-structured. Tools like curl or Postman can be used to test these HTTP endpoints.
- **Apache Pulsar for Event-Driven Communication:** Our project also uses **Apache Pulsar** for asynchronous, event-driven communication between services. The examples in this book are based on version 4.0.8. Pulsar provides high throughput, low latency, and easy horizontal scalability, making it ideal for decoupling components in enterprise systems. When a new assignment is created, for example, an event is published to Pulsar and consumed by other services without blocking the main flow. Using Pulsar helps us design a system that is **scalable, fault-tolerant, and responsive**—concepts that will be explored in depth later in the book.
- **gRPC for Internal Service Communication:** Our system also uses **gRPC** for fast and efficient communication between internal microservices. Built on **HTTP/2** and using **Protocol Buffers**, gRPC offers strong typing, low latency, and compact data exchange. While REST handles external APIs, gRPC is ideal for service-to-service calls where speed and reliability matter most. In our project, some services use gRPC to interact with other services, demonstrating how enterprise systems achieve **high performance and clear contracts** across distributed components.

Modules and Their Responsibilities

Our project is split into small services. Each one has a clear purpose and its own interface. The code uses hexagonal ideas: ports in the core and adapters.

1) **Ride Service**

   This is the entry point for creating and reading assignments. It exposes a REST API generated from OpenAPI and runs with **Gin**. The service validates input (e.g., vehicle ID must exist), stores assignments, and returns results.

2) **Vehicle Service**

   This service provides vehicle data over **gRPC**. The service implements RPCs that will be implemented at the end.

3) **Notification Service**

   This module is planned as a lightweight event consumer that reacts to events.

Why This Structure?

- **Simplicity for Readers:** The main flow is easy to grasp: register a vehicle, create an assignment, and emit a notification. Each step has a clear owner and a clear API. This lets you focus on one concern at a time and see how concepts connect in a real system.
- **Breadth of Technical Coverage:** You will touch the tools that matter in enterprise Go: REST with `net/http`, internal gRPC calls, events for decoupling, MySQL with `database/sql`, configuration via env or YAML, structured logging, metrics, and tests at different levels. Where helpful, we point out Go 1.25 updates like container-aware GOMAXPROCS and `encoding/json/v2`.
- **Modularity:** Each service has its own `go.mod` and owns its data and API. Communication happens only through HTTP, gRPC, or events. Inside each service, we keep the domain in the core and place HTTP, gRPC, and MySQL in adapters. This makes refactors safer and tests faster.

- **Extensibility:** The design leaves space for new capabilities such as driver management or route planning, but you do not need them to learn. You can add new adapters or use cases without rewriting existing code, which mirrors how real teams grow systems.

Why "Edge API" Modules Are a Trap

When designing a microservices architecture, it may feel intuitive to put a separate module or team in front of your business services—a so-called "edge API module" whose sole job is to publish HTTP/gRPC endpoints and transform data, while the "real" business logic hides behind it. This approach *seems* clean: one team owns the exposure layer; another owns the logic. But in practice, this creates serious structural issues. Let's walk through why.

Coupling to Transport Rather Than Domain

When the module closest to the client handles request/response logic, it starts shaping business decisions. Routes, controllers, JSON tags, DTOs, middleware, and protocol concerns drift into the heart of the logic. The domain language becomes blurred: instead of "Assign a vehicle to a route," you find "HTTP POST /v1/assignments returns JSON inside wrapperStatus." Over time, the design is governed by network concerns rather than business concerns. In my experience, the team will end up in a situation where they have to implement each task into multiple microservices just because the API and logic are separated. Because the business logic is hidden behind an API surface, making a change in transport becomes expensive. The "edge" has absorbed so much logic that you cannot swap the transport layer without rewriting core behavior.

Hand-Off Tax and Slower Delivery

In the edge-module pattern, one team owns the "exposure" layer (controllers, endpoints, DTOs) and another team owns the "behavior" (domain logic). Every change now crosses a team border and likely crosses repository boundaries. A small change in the API design triggers a pull request to the edge team, which then asks for changes in the logic team, which then refers back, and so on. The result: coordination overhead trumping engineering time.

Versioning Pain and Duplication

When the edge API module handles data structures (DTOs) separate from the domain model, you often end up with duplicated models: one in the edge module, one in the core service. A tiny change (say, renaming a field) ripples across modules and teams. Coordination becomes necessary, and breaking changes become scary.

This duplication also means you maintain version logic twice (in the edge API and in the domain). When API v1 remains for external clients, the logic may live behind newer versions—but the edge layer still has to translate or support both. That leads to extra complexity, module sprawl, and eventual technical debt.

Testing Becomes Brittle

Because domain logic lives behind the edge API, verifying that logic often means testing the edge layer (controllers + DTOs) rather than the domain. Developers write end-to-end tests that hit HTTP endpoints, mock services externally, or simulate full workflows. This is brittle and slow. Unit tests for domain logic disappear or become hard to isolate. When the edge API handles many wrappers, transformations, or adaptors, observers note that test code grows in size and complexity faster than production code. In addition, when the edge module is thin in behavior but thick in translation and routing, observability becomes weak: logs and metrics often record HTTP status codes but rarely the domain state transitions or invariants that tell *why* a business process failed.

Observability Blind Spots

Another consequence of separating the API module from domain logic is the decoupling of telemetry from the business flow. Because the edge layer handles most inbound/outbound data, it becomes the "visible" piece in monitoring dashboards—while the real business logic deeper in the stack remains opaque. When a failure happens, you may see "HTTP 500 in EdgeAPI" but not "Vehicle already in maintenance state rejected assignment." You lose context. The monitoring tools may report HTTP latency, but they cannot easily correlate that with domain invariants like "assignments per vehicle," "maintenance window status," or "assignment load per driver." This lack of domain-aware observability makes SLIs (Service Level Indicators) less useful and increases mean time to resolution.

The Alternative: Ports, Adapters, and Domain Ownership

When an edge API module begins to slow teams down, the solution is not to remove APIs but to **place them where they belong**—inside the service that owns the behavior. In a well-designed system, each service owns its **API, domain, and runtime**. This keeps boundaries clear, avoids duplication, and gives teams both speed and accountability.

This idea is not new. It builds on classic architecture principles—most clearly captured in **Hexagonal Architecture (Ports and Adapters)** and **Clean Architecture**. The essence is simple: keep the **domain model** at the center, and make every technology or protocol an adapter around it.

One Team, One Runtime

A healthy microservice has one owning team that builds, runs, and monitors it. The same team writes the code, deploys it, and watches its logs and metrics. This "you build it, you run it" approach removes the hand-off tax that plagues edge API systems. Ownership stays unified, and observability becomes meaningful. When a service fails, the same team that understands the business logic investigates the issue, not an external "edge" team with no domain context.

Gateway As Configuration, Not Code

Many organizations still need centralized policies: authentication, rate limiting, routing, and TLS termination. These belong at the **gateway level**, but they should be managed as **infrastructure configuration**, not code duplication.

Modern API gateways such as **Envoy**, **Kong**, or **NGINX** can handle these cross-cutting concerns declaratively. The gateway forwards requests to the appropriate service, applies policies, and leaves business behavior untouched.

This separation of responsibility mirrors DevOps principles:

- **Platform/DevOps teams** manage shared infrastructure and policies.
- **Service teams** manage domain logic and APIs.

As a result, platform changes (e.g., a new routing rule) do not require redeploying application code, and service changes do not risk breaking global infrastructure.

Observability and Metrics Where They Matter

When APIs and domain logic live together, observability can reflect the real state of the business, not just the health of infrastructure. Instead of only counting HTTP requests or response times, we can expose domain-centric signals that describe how the system is behaving. For example:

- Assignments created per minute
- Vehicles currently available
- Average assignment time per route

In *Building Microservices (2nd ed.)*, Sam Newman distinguishes **monitoring** from **observability**. Monitoring is an activity—we look at dashboards and react to alerts. Observability, on the other hand, is a **property of the system**. Metrics and logs that we expose. He also cautions against reducing observability to a checklist of tools; the goal is to make the system understandable, and logs, metrics, and traces are just possible means to that outcome.

Go's standard library and ecosystem provide excellent support for metrics and tracing. The /metrics endpoint can expose Prometheus-compatible data, while context-aware logging helps correlate API calls with domain events. This gives you visibility into the why, not just the what, allowing faster root-cause analysis and more accurate performance tuning. In practice, we use a few simple patterns to keep that outcome achievable in a distributed system: **domain-centric metrics** (what the business cares about), **structured, context-aware logging**, but we don't go through so much details as in each project there are different tools and approaches. You will be familiar with this topic in the next chapters.

Learning Outcomes

By completing this project, you will gain practical experience in building a production-grade Go application composed of multiple services. Each part of the project reflects real enterprise practices—structuring code for clarity, managing persistence, handling concurrency, and building for reliability.

By the end of this project, readers of the book will have gained practical experience in developing a Go application. Specifically, you will learn to

- **Design and Structure a Multi-service Go Application**

  You will learn how to organize a professional Go project that consists of several independent services: Ride, Vehicle, and Notification. Each service follows an internal structure. You will practice using Go modules to isolate dependencies and understand how clear package boundaries improve readability and testability. Configuration management is done through YAML or environment variables, giving you experience in parameterizing services for different environments.

- **Implement REST, gRPC, and Event-Driven Logic**

  You will learn the importance of OpenAPI and implement a RESTful API for the Ride Service. You will also implement a gRPC API for the Vehicle Service, and event-driven communication using Apache Pulsar for notifications. This combination demonstrates how Go can support different communication patterns efficiently. You will define OpenAPI and `.proto` contracts alongside code, generate handlers and stubs, and see how to keep APIs versioned and type-safe. By working with these technologies, you will understand how services communicate while remaining loosely coupled.

- **Integrate Go with a MySQL Database**

  You will connect Go services to a MySQL database using the standard `database/sql` package and the official MySQL driver. You will learn how to open connections safely, execute queries, and handle transactions using connection pooling (enabled by default in Go). Each service will store and query data independently, which mirrors how enterprise systems maintain bounded contexts. The examples will show how to write prepared statements, use query parameters safely, and scan results into structs that match domain models.

- **Implement CRUD Functionality and Business Logic**

  Gain experience implementing the core functionality of a typical web app—namely, creating, reading, updating, and deleting data. You'll write the business logic that sits between the incoming HTTP requests and the database. For example, when a user creates a new vehicle, you will validate the input, then construct an SQL `INSERT` statement (or use an ORM call) to save it to MySQL, and finally return a success response. This teaches how to translate real-world requirements into code.

- **Test and Debug Go Applications**

  Each module is built to be testable. You will write unit tests for business logic and integration tests for database operations and APIs. The book uses Go's built-in `testing` package and shows how to use test. You will learn to run tests with coverage, use benchmarks for performance checks, and debug live services using logs. By the end, testing will feel like a natural part of development, not an afterthought.

Through this journey, you will not only learn to build functional services but also to **think like a Go architect**—designing systems that are modular, efficient, and easy to evolve. Each concept you apply in the transport system will help you approach real enterprise projects with confidence and precision.

Summary

This chapter defined the project we will build: a small transport system in Go that grows step by step, using clear module boundaries and a hexagonal design. You saw the core technologies and why we use them—Go with `net/http`, gRPC for internal calls, MySQL for persistence, and Pulsar for events—so the system stays simple, reliable, and ready to scale. By the end of the road map, you will know how the services fit together and what skills you will gain next: designing APIs, writing safe database code, and testing like a professional.

What's Next

Now that the vision and road map of our transport system are clear, it's time to turn that vision into a structure. In the next chapter, we will lay the foundation of the project by setting up a clean multi-module layout using Go workspaces. You'll learn how Go organizes multiple services under one repository, when to use separate modules, and how good structure makes everything that follows—coding, testing, and scaling—simpler and stronger.

CHAPTER 11

Building a Multi-module Project: Foundations of Maintainability

"For every minute spent in organizing, an hour is earned."

—Benjamin Franklin

Before we write a single line of Go, we must first decide **where that line will live**. Structure is not decoration; it is direction. The way we shape our project determines how easily we can change it later—how confidently teams collaborate, how safely we refactor, and how clearly our ideas scale.

In Go, structure carries intent. A well-designed layout tells you what belongs together, what evolves separately, and what boundaries must never blur. The same principles that govern distributed systems—cohesion, coupling, and contracts—apply just as powerfully within a repository.

In this chapter, we will design the **skeleton of our Transport System** project. We will see how Go's **multi-module workspaces** translate architectural principles into practical form and how **Git repository strategies**—whether mono-repo or multi-repo—shape collaboration and maintainability. Step by step, we will build a working foundation: a clean, modular workspace where each service can stand on its own yet remain part of a larger whole.

By the end, you will not only understand how to organize a Go project—you will understand how structure itself becomes architecture.

S. Shahsavan, *Building Enterprise Projects with Go*, https://doi.org/10.1007/979-8-8688-2370-1_11

Repository Strategies: One Tree or a Forest?

Every system hides an architectural truth inside its version control. Before you decide how to divide your Go modules, you must decide how your teams will grow. The repository layout is not just a technical preference. It is a map of your organization's trust, coordination, and rhythm of change.

In Go, we often start with a single workspace. It feels simple, cohesive, and convenient. But as systems mature and teams multiply, the question arises: *Should every service still live under one roof?*

The decision of repository architecture is one of the most important decisions in each enterprise project. Let's examine both sides of that decision through the lens of maintainability, scalability, and enterprise life.

The Single Repository: Unity and Velocity

A **monorepo** keeps every service, module, and shared library inside one repository. It gives developers a complete view of the system: how services connect, how data flows, and how shared code evolves. With one repository, you can run tests across modules, refactor safely, and release changes in a single atomic commit.

This structure works especially well when

- The team is **small or medium-sized**, or there is one main delivery group.
- Services have **tight integration** or evolve quickly together.
- **Cross-module refactoring** happens often and needs to be simple.

A single repository helps the team move fast. Everyone sees the same picture and can work with the same tools, the same Go version, and the same build rules. It also takes full advantage of the **Go workspace feature (`go.work`)**, which lets multiple modules build and test together without using complicated `replace` directives. Local dependencies resolve automatically, so you can update shared code and test everything in one pass.

As the project grows, however, a monorepo begins to reveal structural limits. The repository becomes heavier, CI pipelines slow down as more unrelated components are tested together, and access control turns into a real challenge. In large organizations, not every team should be able to modify every service: core domain logic, security-sensitive components, or regulated modules often require stricter ownership and review rules. In practice, companies enforce these boundaries through fine-grained directory permissions, mandatory code owners, and path-based build and deployment pipelines. Some organizations go even further by limiting visibility or write access to sensitive folders or by triggering isolated CI pipelines only for the affected service, reducing both security risk and blast radius. While these mechanisms can keep a large monorepo safe, they add operational complexity and coordination overhead. As teams scale, developers may end up waiting on unrelated merges, shared pipelines, or cross-team approvals. What once acted as a single source of truth can gradually become a single point of friction.

Enterprise Lesson Shared repositories speed up learning but slow down autonomy. When collaboration begins to feel like coordination overhead, it may be time to move toward smaller, more independent repositories.

Multiple Repositories: Autonomy and Isolation

A **multi-repository** strategy gives each service its own home: a separate repository with its own code base, issues, version tags, and release pipeline. This structure fits microservices well. Each team owns its service from design to deployment, with minimal coupling to others.

This approach works best when

- Several teams work in parallel on different services.
- Each service has its own release cycle or specific compliance rules.
- You need fine-grained access control or strict security boundaries.

Multi-repo makes every service a true unit of independence. Teams choose their release timing, set branch protection rules, and manage dependencies without blocking others.

There are always trade-offs. Refactoring that affects several services takes more time, because each change must be coordinated and versioned separately. When services depend on shared logic or common libraries, those libraries must have a well-defined release and versioning process. Without it, copies start to appear in different places, and differences slowly turn into hidden bugs. A reliable process—semantic versioning, clear ownership, and regular updates—keeps shared code healthy and predictable.

Documentation also becomes more important in a multi-repo system. New developers need to understand not only how one service works but also how all services connect and communicate. Maintaining diagrams, API documentation, and a central developer guide helps everyone see the full picture, even when code lives in many repositories.

Enterprise Lesson Independence grows with isolation, and so does responsibility. A multi-repo structure gives freedom to teams that maintain shared conventions, stable versions, and consistent documentation.

When used well, this approach enables real autonomy, stronger security boundaries, and smooth scaling across teams. When used carelessly, it increases friction, duplicates effort, and hides complexity between repositories. The key is balance: give each team ownership of its code and lifecycle, but preserve harmony through shared standards and communication.

Choosing the Right Strategy

There is no single perfect structure. The right choice depends on your team's size, how fast your system changes, and how easily you can coordinate that change. In practice, the structure you choose should match how your project is expected to evolve, not just how it looks today.

Table 11-1 summarizes which repository structure works best under different project contexts and team dynamics.

Table 11-1. Choosing a repository structure based on project context

Project Context	Recommended Structure	Reasoning
Single team, tight integration, frequent refactors	**Monorepo**	Keeps everything visible and aligned. Easier to test, refactor, and release together.
Growing teams, stable service boundaries, separate lifecycles	**Multi-repo**	Gives each team control of its release schedule and dependencies. Reduces coordination effort.
Early-stage startup or proof-of-concept	**Start with one repository**	Focus on development speed and learning. Split into multiple repos only when the project grows.
Enterprise platform with strict security or compliance rules	**Multi-repo**	Protects trust domains, controls access per service, and isolates regulated components.

Choosing structure is less about technical preference and more about how your teams work together. If a team needs to change shared interfaces every week, a single repository avoids overhead. If teams own stable, long-lived services, separate repositories protect independence and security. Each choice should reduce friction, not increase it.

In this book, our **Transport System** project uses a **single repository with multiple Go modules.** This approach keeps the learning process simple while still following real-world design principles. Each service is implemented as a separate module inside the same repository.

By keeping all modules in one repository, you can easily follow relationships between services without managing multiple code bases. At the same time, this design reflects how modern Go projects are built: small, focused modules that communicate through clear interfaces.

Go's improved **workspace support (`go.work`)** makes it natural to develop and test several modules together, keeping development fast and configuration clean.

If this project later evolves into a large enterprise environment with separate teams, each module could move to its own repository without rewriting the code. The boundaries are already clear, the modules already versioned, and the dependencies already explicit. That is the sign of a maintainable foundation—simple at the beginning, scalable in the future.

Our Project Layout

When Go first introduced modules, working with multiple modules in a single repository was not simple. Developers had to use several `replace` directives in each `go.mod` file, linking one module to another by local paths. This worked, but it was difficult to maintain and easy to break.

Starting with **Go 1.18**, the Go team introduced **workspaces**. A workspace lets you develop and test several modules together without touching their individual `go.mod` files. The configuration lives in a single `go.work` file at the root of your project. This file tells the Go toolchain to use the local modules instead of downloading them from a remote repository. It keeps development fast, consistent, and dependency-safe.

With this feature, Go automatically recognizes modules that belong to the same workspace. You can now build, test, and run code across modules without adding `replace` statements or manually switching dependencies. This is now the recommended way to organize multiple related modules during development.

Creating the Modules

Once you have decided on the project layout, the next step is to create the **Go modules** for each service. In our transport system, every service—**Ride**, **Vehicle**, and **Notification**—is an independent module. Each module has its own `go.mod` file, which defines its dependencies, Go version, and module path. This separation allows every service to evolve at its own pace while still being part of the same workspace.

Open a terminal in the root directory of the project (`transport/`) and run the following commands.

```
# From the repo root: transport/
mkdir -p ride vehicle notification
```

These directories represent the three main services of our system. Next, initialize each directory as a Go module. Run these commands one by one, or use a grouped version as shown below.

```
# Initialize each service as its own Go module (run inside each dir)
( cd ride         && go mod init github.com/yourname/transport/ride )
( cd vehicle      && go mod init github.com/yourname/transport/vehicle )
( cd notification && go mod init github.com/yourname/transport/notification )
```

Each `go mod init` command creates a new `go.mod` file and sets the module path. The module path should follow the same structure as your repository's remote URL, for example, `github.com/yourname/transport/ride`. If you are working locally, you can use a placeholder path and update it later when you publish your repository.

Once the modules are created, you can connect them inside a shared workspace using the **Go**.

From the root of the repository, run

```
# Create a workspace at the repo root that "uses" all local modules
go work init ./ride ./vehicle ./notification
# (equivalently)
# go work init
# go work use ./ride ./vehicle ./notification
```

This command generates a `go.work` file in the root directory and lists the three module paths inside it. The workspace tells Go to use these local modules directly when building or testing, instead of downloading them from a module proxy. This makes local development faster and ensures that code changes in one service are instantly visible to the others.

You can check the workspace configuration with

```
go work edit -json   # shows listed modules as json

go list -m   # shows listed modules as list of names
```

If everything is configured correctly, Go will display all three modules in the list. At this point, each service has its own `go.mod`, but they are all connected through a single `go.work` file. Imports between modules will now resolve automatically, and you can build or test the whole system with one command from the root.

This structure makes development simple and predictable. Each service stays independent, yet the workspace keeps them synchronized during active development. When you later push the project to a remote repository, the workspace ensures that every module works exactly the same way on any machine.

Project Structure

After creating the modules and initializing the workspace, your repository should now look like this:

```
transport/
├── go.work
├── ride/           # Ride Service (REST API)
│   └── go.mod
├── vehicle/        # Vehicle Service (gRPC API)
│   └── go.mod
└── notification/   # Notification Service (Event Consumer)
    └── go.mod
```

Each folder represents a Go module, and the `go.work` file at the root connects them into one workspace. This design allows you to develop several services side by side while keeping their dependencies, versions, and builds separate. You can run `go build` or `go test` inside any module, and Go automatically knows how the others fit together.

Your `go.work` file might look like this:

```
go 1.25.1

use ./ride
use ./vehicle
use ./notification
```

This file tells Go that these modules belong to the same local workspace. Whenever one module imports another, Go will use the local folder instead of fetching the dependency from a remote repository.

You can inspect the workspace configuration using the following command:

```
go work edit -json
```

A typical output looks like this:

```
{
    "Go": "1.25.1",
    "Use": [
        {
```

```
            "DiskPath": "./notification"
        },
        {
            "DiskPath": "./ride"
        },
        {
            "DiskPath": "./vehicle"
        }
    ],
    "Replace": null
}
```

This confirms that Go recognizes all three modules as part of your workspace. The `"Go": "1.25.1"` line shows the Go version used by the workspace, and each `"DiskPath"` entry points to one of your local modules.

To verify that Go can see every module, run:

```
go list -m
```

You should see output similar to this:

```
github.com/yourname/transport/notification
github.com/yourname/transport/ride
github.com/yourname/transport/vehicle
```

Each line represents a registered module in your workspace.

If you add or remove modules in the future, you can update the workspace easily with:

```
go work use ./newmodule
go work sync
```

Understanding What You Have Built

At this point, your workspace acts as a small ecosystem of services. Each module has its own `go.mod` file with independent dependencies, but all modules live under a shared `go.work` umbrella. This lets you

- Develop and test multiple services together.
- Import one service into another without remote publishing.
- Keep version control simple and project layout clean.

In production environments, teams often keep this pattern for internal microservices that evolve together. In Go 1.25, workspaces are fully mature and optimized, making them the default choice for multi-module projects. They provide the simplicity of a single repository with the flexibility of independent services—a structure that scales gracefully as the system grows.

Shared Dependencies and Version Resolution

When a project moves from a single module to a multi-module structure, dependency management becomes more visible. Modules such as `ride`, `vehicle`, and `notification` are developed independently, but they are still built together as one system. This raises an important question: **How does Go decide which dependency versions are actually used during a build?**

For enterprise systems, this behavior must be predictable. Teams need to understand not only what version they requested in their own module but also what version is finally selected when all modules are combined. Go perfectly solved this issue.

Minimal Version Selection (MVS)

Go uses an algorithm called **Minimal Version Selection**, usually referred to as **MVS**, to resolve dependency versions. This algorithm has been part of Go Modules since their introduction.

Instead of locking dependencies globally or resolving them separately for each module, MVS looks at the entire module dependency graph. For every dependency, Go selects the highest version that is required by any module in the build, as long as that version satisfies all requirements. A direct consequence of this model is that a module may be compiled against a newer dependency version than the one it explicitly declared. This can happen when another module in the same workspace requires a higher version of that dependency. This behavior is intentional and central to Go's approach to dependency management.

A Simple Dependency Conflict Example

Consider our workspace with the following dependencies:

- `ride` depends on `libA v1.2`.
- `vehicle` depends on `libA v1.4`.
- `notification` depends on an unrelated library.

Figure 11-1 illustrates how a shared dependency is resolved across multiple modules in a workspace.

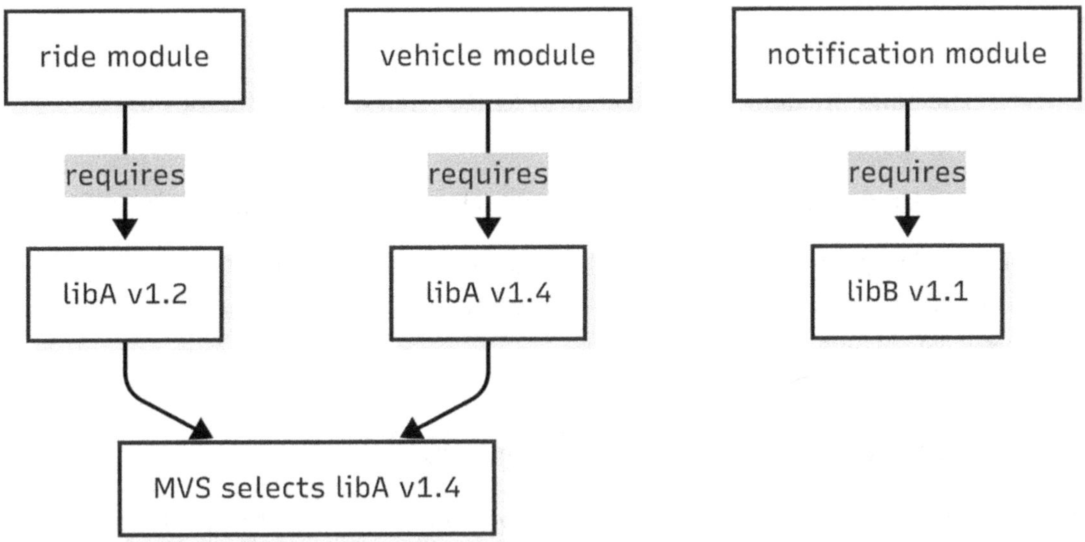

Figure 11-1. *Multi-module dependency graph with MVS*

When these modules are built together, Go does not report a conflict. Instead, MVS selects the higher required version of `libA`. As a result, all modules in the workspace are compiled using **`libA v1.4`**. This avoids version fragmentation and ensures that every module sees a consistent dependency set.

From an enterprise point of view, this has a practical implication: a module's effective dependencies are influenced by other modules in the workspace. Because of this, dependency upgrades should be planned deliberately, and shared libraries should be updated with awareness of their impact across the system.

Build Automation As an Executable Contract: Makefile and Dockerfile

In professional Go projects, build automation is not a secondary concern. It is part of the system's architecture. Two files usually carry this responsibility: the **Makefile** and the **Dockerfile**. Together, they define an **executable contract** that describes how the system is built, tested, packaged, and prepared for deployment.

This contract must work in all environments: on a developer's laptop, inside a CI pipeline, and in production build systems. If the process changes depending on where it runs, the system becomes fragile.

The responsibilities are intentionally separated:

- The **Makefile** defines which actions exist and in which order they are executed.
- The **Dockerfile** defines *the environment* in which those actions run.

When used together, they remove build logic from CI scripts and infrastructure configuration. The result is a system that is easier to understand, easier to reproduce, and more easily evolved.

The Role of the Makefile in Go Projects

Go already provides a strong and opinionated toolchain. However, real projects still need coordination: formatting, testing, dependency management, building binaries, and preparing artifacts for deployment. The Makefile provides a **thin orchestration layer** on top of Go tools. Its purpose is not to replace the Go toolchain. Its purpose is to **standardize how the toolchain is used**. In enterprise projects, the Makefile is rarely used only by developers. Its primary consumers are often

- CI pipelines
- Docker build stages
- Release automation scripts

A Makefile Designed for Docker and CI/CD

The following Makefile is intentionally simple and production-oriented. It is designed to be executed locally and from inside a Docker build without modification.

```
.PHONY: fmt test tidy build run clean

BIN_DIR ?= ../bin
BIN_NAME ?= ride

fmt:
	go fmt ./...

test:
	go test ./...

integration_test:
	go test ./... -timeout 90s -tags=integration_test

tidy:
	go mod tidy

build:
	mkdir -p $(BIN_DIR)
	go build -o $(BIN_DIR)/$(BIN_NAME) ./cmd

run:
	go run ./cmd

clean:
	rm -rf $(BIN_DIR)/$(BIN_NAME)
```

Each target expresses **intent**, not implementation detail:

- `fmt` enforces consistent formatting across the code base.
- `test` validates correctness using Go's testing framework.
- `integration_test` runs tests using test containers.
- `tidy` keeps module dependencies accurate and minimal.
- `build` produces a deterministic binary.

A typical CI pipeline simply executes

```
make tidy
make test
make build
```

The CI system does not need to understand the project. It only needs to call `make`.

The Dockerfile

The Dockerfile defines **where and how** the application is built and executed. It does not describe business logic, and it does not replace the Makefile. Instead, it provides a **controlled and reproducible environment** in which the Makefile can run. In this project, the Dockerfile delegates all build responsibility to the Makefile. During the build stage, the container simply executes `make build`. This ensures that the same build rules are used:

- By developers on their machines
- By CI pipelines
- By Docker-based deployments

Because the Dockerfile does not duplicate build commands, there is a single source of truth for how the application is compiled. The runtime stage contains only the compiled binary and a minimal operating system. This keeps the final image small, secure, and fast to start, which is especially important for web services that expose HTTP endpoints.

Here is an example:

```
# ---------- Build stage ----------
   FROM golang:1.25-alpine AS builder

   # Set working directory inside the container
   WORKDIR /app

  # Install build tools required by Makefile
   RUN apk add --no-cache make

  # Copy the rest of the source code
   COPY . .
```

```
# Build the application using the Makefile, placing the binary in /out
RUN BIN_DIR=/out make build

# ---------- Runtime stage ----------
FROM gcr.io/distroless/base-debian12

# Set working directory for the runtime container
WORKDIR /app

# Copy the compiled binary from the builder stage
COPY --from=builder /out/ride /app/ride

# Expose the HTTP port used by the web application
EXPOSE 8080

# Run the application
ENTRYPOINT ["/app/ride"]
```

This approach significantly simplifies continuous integration and deployment:

- CI pipelines do not need to know how the project is built.
- They only need to run `docker build`.
- All build logic lives inside the repository, not in CI configuration files.

As a result, changes to the build process are versioned, reviewed, and tested like any other code change. This reduces pipeline fragility and makes deployments more predictable.

Enterprise Lesson A Dockerfile should execute a build contract, not redefine it. By letting the Makefile define *what* to build and Docker define *where* it runs, you create a system that is easier to automate, easier to maintain, and easier to trust in production.

Branching Strategies: Order in the Flow of Change

In every growing project, version control becomes more than a storage of code—it becomes the nervous system of the team. How branches are organized determines how safely changes move from development to production. Ignore this structure, and every release turns into stress, coordination meetings, and last-minute fixes.

Many teams start with a single `main` branch. At first, it feels simple: everyone merges, tests, and deploys from the same line. But as the system grows, that simplicity turns into chaos. During release time, developers must stop merging. CI pipelines freeze. Nobody is sure which commit is actually deployed. I have seen a team where deployment took days, not because of code quality, but because their **branching strategy was chaos by design**. They called it "freeze time," when everyone had to wait until the test was done and the branch was ready to deploy in production. It made life difficult for everyone.

The Reality of Change

A healthy repository needs **isolation for testing** and **stability for deployment**. Without these boundaries, development and operations constantly block each other. The solution is not more process—it is a clear structure.

A good branching strategy gives each stage of work its own safe place:

- **`main` (or `dev`)** is where day-to-day work happens. Developers can merge their pull requests freely without worrying about production deployment.
- **`staging` (or `preprod`)** represents what is tested and ready for release. This branch should always be stable and deployable to a staging environment for final validation.
- **`prod`** mirrors what is currently running in production. Nothing merges here directly except controlled releases or hotfixes. This branch is your source of truth—if you deploy it, you know exactly what is live.

When a release is ready, the tested code from `staging` is merged into `prod` and tagged with a version, for example, `v1.3.0`. If an urgent issue appears in production, create a small **hotfix branch** from `prod`, apply the patch, test it, tag it, deploy, and then cherry-pick the fix back into `staging` and `main`. This flow keeps history clean and avoids blocking developers who continue their normal work.

Enterprise Lesson A calm production comes from clear branches, not lucky merges. Keep development, testing, and deployment separate but connected, so that each part of the system can move at its own speed.

Branching As Architecture

Think of your branches as **layers of stability** within the system. Each one serves a different purpose, just like layers in a well-designed software architecture.

- The **development layer (`main`)** is fast-moving and flexible. This is where developers integrate their work, test new ideas, and merge pull requests freely. The focus here is speed and collaboration.
- The **testing layer (`staging`)** is stable and controlled. Code that reaches this branch has passed automated checks and peer review. It is ready for integration testing, performance checks, and user validation.
- The **production layer (`prod`)** is the final line of trust. Nothing changes here unless it has been tested and approved. This branch always reflects the exact code deployed in production.

Each branch defines a **clear boundary** for change. When code flows through these layers—first into development, then to testing, and finally to production—it follows a safe, predictable path. This separation prevents the common pain of release freezes, where teams must stop all work just to test and deploy. Instead, you can move code confidently from one stage to the next, knowing exactly what is being tested, approved, and released.

A healthy branching model behaves like a layered system:

- **Fast on the surface**, where new features are developed
- **Stable in the middle**, where testing happens
- **Solid at the base**, where production code lives

This structure brings calm to the release process. Developers keep their creative freedom, testers work with reliable builds, and operators know exactly what is in production. When branches are treated like architectural layers, the flow of change becomes organized, safe, and repeatable.

Enterprise Lesson Good architecture is not only in code—it is also in process. Treat branches as boundaries of stability, and your delivery process will mirror the clarity of your code.

Summary

In this chapter, we built the foundation of our Transport System project by designing a clear and maintainable structure. We learned how project layout shapes collaboration, testing, and long-term stability. We compared monorepo and multi-repo strategies, understanding that each fits a different scale and team structure. Our project uses a single repository with multiple Go modules connected through a Go workspace, combining simplicity with modular independence. We also explored branching as part of architecture, where development, testing, and production flow safely through `main`, `staging`, and `prod`. A strong structure in both code and process turns deployment from a stressful event into a confident routine.

What's Next

Now that we have a solid project structure and clear branching strategy, it's time to bring our services to life with a real configuration. In the next chapter, we will explore how Go applications load settings safely across environments—from local YAML files to production secrets. You'll learn how to design flexible loaders, override values with environment variables, and protect sensitive data, building the habits that make configuration a foundation of security and maintainability.

CHAPTER 12

Loading Configuration: Building Environment-Aware Go Systems

"It is not the strongest of the species that survive, nor the most intelligent, but the one most responsive to change."

—Charles Darwin

Before a Go service can run, it must first understand *where* it is. Configuration is how software reads the world around it—the ports it should open, the timeouts it should respect, the database it should trust. Unlike code, configuration is fluid: it shifts between development, staging, and production like a traveler adapting to each new climate.

In enterprise systems, adaptability is survival. Managing configuration safely and flexibly means our applications can evolve without recompilation, embrace new environments without fear, and keep secrets where they belong. In this chapter, we'll explore how Go turns simple files and environment variables into the foundation of environment-aware systems—reliable, secure, and ready for change.

Different Approaches to Configuration

During the past two decades, the ways developers and DevOps teams manage configuration have evolved with technology itself. Each approach represents a balance between simplicity, flexibility, and security. Understanding these methods helps

S. Shahsavan, *Building Enterprise Projects with Go*, https://doi.org/10.1007/979-8-8688-2370-1_12

you choose the right strategy for your project instead of relying on defaults or habits. Table 12-1 summarizes the most common configuration approaches used in modern enterprise projects, along with their trade-offs and typical enterprise use cases.

Table 12-1. *Common configuration approaches in enterprise projects*

Approach	Advantages	Disadvantages	Typical Use Case
JSON file	Native support in Go's standard library using `encoding/json`. Simple and widely understood format.	No comments allowed, and long configurations become hard to read.	Lightweight APIs, internal tools, or when configuration must be shared with JavaScript.
YAML file	Easy for humans to read and write. Supports comments and nesting. The most common choice for cloud-native environments and Kubernetes.	Not part of Go's standard library; requires a package such as `gopkg.in/yaml.v3`. Incorrect indentation can cause parsing errors.	Most enterprise or containerized applications.
TOML file	Clean, structured, supports comments, and is easier to parse than YAML.	Less common in Go projects, fewer community examples.	Configuration for CLI tools or cross-language projects that already use TOML.
Environment variables only	No files needed, ideal for container deployments. Simple to override values without rebuilding.	Flat structure, no nesting, not suitable for large configuration sets.	Injecting secrets or a few dynamic values like API tokens.
Secret managers (Vault, Sealed Secrets)	Best practice for production security. Supports automatic secret rotation and encryption at rest.	Requires external infrastructure and DevOps setup; not something developers manage directly.	Enterprises with regulated environments or cloud-based deployments.

In modern Go applications, YAML is usually the most practical balance between readability and structure, while environment variables handle sensitive or environment-specific overrides.

Enterprise Lesson In enterprise environments, developers rarely access production secrets directly. These are managed by DevOps platforms such as **HashiCorp Vault**, **AWS Secrets Manager**, or **Kubernetes Sealed Secrets**. As an application developer, your responsibility is not to fetch these secrets manually but to design your configuration loader so it can receive them—typically through environment variables or mounted files at runtime. This separation of duties keeps systems secure, auditable, and easier to manage.

Our Choice

In this book, we follow the same philosophy that Go itself follows: keep things simple, but never simplistic. Enterprise software should be practical, testable, and safe to deploy. For that reason, our configuration approach focuses on clarity and flexibility rather than using heavy external frameworks.

We will use **a YAML file** as the main configuration source. YAML is easy to read, supports comments, and can express structured data without becoming hard to maintain. The file will contain the stable, non-sensitive defaults that developers can version in Git, such as server timeouts or connection pool limits.

To handle secrets and environment-specific details, we let **environment variables override selected values** from the YAML file. This makes the same binary run safely in different environments: local development, staging, or production. Sensitive values such as database passwords or API tokens are never written into configuration files. Instead, they are provided at runtime through the environment, which allows integration with secret managers and CI/CD pipelines.

We only add one external dependency, **`gopkg.in/yaml.v3`**, to parse YAML files. It is a stable and widely used library in the Go ecosystem.

Designing the Config

Every service in a real enterprise system has its own settings that describe how it should behave in its environment. For our service, we will design a configuration that includes two main parts:

1. **HTTP Server Configuration:** Controls how the REST API behaves, including the port to listen on and timeout settings
2. **Database Configuration:** Defines how the service connects to its MySQL database for storing ride assignments

Here is an example configuration file in the ride module that will live inside the configs directory. You can find it in `ride/configs/config.yaml`:

```
server:
  port: 8080
  read_timeout_sec: 30
  write_timeout_sec: 30

database:
  host: "mysql.internal"
  port: 3306
  user: "ride_user"
  password: ""        # left blank, provided via DB_PASSWORD env var
  name: "transportdb"
  max_open_conns: 20
  max_idle_conns: 5
```

This file represents the default values used during development. Notice that the password is intentionally empty. In production, the real password will be injected safely through an environment variable such as `DB_PASSWORD`. This practice keeps sensitive data out of version control and makes the same binary safe to deploy in multiple environments without modification.

The configuration also defines **connection pool settings** for the database. Parameters like `max_open_conns` and `max_idle_conns` are critical for performance tuning in enterprise systems. They allow the database driver to reuse existing connections instead of creating new ones for each request. We will discuss connection pooling and tuning further when we reach the database chapter.

Where to Place Configuration Files

A clean and predictable project layout helps every team member find configuration files quickly. In most Go projects, configuration files are placed under a dedicated directory inside each service, for example:

```
transport/
└── ride/
    ├── configs/
    │   └── config.yaml
    └── ...
```

Keeping the configuration inside the service directory avoids clutter at the root of the repository and makes it clear which settings belong to which service.

For **local development**, you can check in a `configs/config.yaml` file that contains safe defaults or mock values. During **deployment**, DevOps systems such as Kubernetes or Docker Compose mount or inject the real configuration values into the container. Developers usually never edit these files manually in production.

Your job as a developer is to make the service capable of reading these files, validating their structure, and applying environment variable overrides when needed. Understanding this separation of responsibilities between developers and DevOps engineers is one of the key skills that turns good code into a reliable production system.

Representing Config in Go

To make our configuration usable inside the application, we must map the YAML file into Go structs. Using structured types gives us strong typing, autocompletion, and compile-time safety. It also prevents common mistakes such as misspelled field names or unexpected value types.

Each service should contain its own configuration definition and loader function. Keeping configuration code **next to the service** (e.g., inside `ride/configs/`) makes the module easier to test and keeps dependencies isolated. Avoid placing configuration types at the root of the repository unless they are truly shared by all services.

A typical directory layout looks like this:

```
transport/
└── ride/
    ├── configs/
    │   └── config.yaml
    │   └── config.go
    └── . . .
```

This structure keeps configuration files and their related Go code close together. Anyone joining the project can easily find where the configuration is defined and loaded.

Below is a simple implementation that defines the configuration types for the **Ride** service.

```go
package configs // if file is ride/configs/config.go
// package ride   // if you keep it as ride/config.go at the service root

import (
	"fmt"
	"os"
	"strconv"

	"gopkg.in/yaml.v3"
)

type ServerConfig struct {
	Port            int `yaml:"port"`
	ReadTimeoutSec  int `yaml:"read_timeout_sec"`
	WriteTimeoutSec int `yaml:"write_timeout_sec"`
}

type DatabaseConfig struct {
	Host     string `yaml:"host"`
	Port     int    `yaml:"port"`
	User     string `yaml:"user"`
	Password string `yaml:"password"`
	Name     string `yaml:"name"`
```

```
    MaxOpenConns int     `yaml:"max_open_conns"`
    MaxIdleConns int     `yaml:"max_idle_conns"`
}

type Config struct {
    Server   ServerConfig   `yaml:"server"`
    Database DatabaseConfig `yaml:"database"`
}
```

Loading Config from File

Once the configuration structure is defined, the next step is to load real data from a YAML file into our Go structs. This allows the application to start with settings that can be easily modified without recompiling the program.

Adding the YAML Dependency

The Go standard library does not include a YAML parser, so we need to add one small, stable dependency. The most common choice in the Go ecosystem is **gopkg.in/yaml.v3**, which is maintained by the Go community and works well with Go 1.25. It supports streaming, strict decoding, and proper error handling for invalid or unknown fields.

To install the dependency for the **Ride** module, run the following command in your terminal:

```
cd transport/ride
go get gopkg.in/yaml.v3
```

This command updates the `go.mod` and `go.sum` files of the service. These files record which version of the dependency is used, ensuring reproducible builds across environments.

After adding the dependency, import it in your configuration file:

```
import "gopkg.in/yaml.v3"
```

At this point, your project is ready to read configuration files written in YAML format. In the next section, we will write a simple `LoadConfig` function that reads a file from disk, parses it, and returns a fully populated `Config` struct.

Implementing the Load Function

After defining the Config struct, the next step is to create a helper function that reads and parses the configuration file from disk. This function turns a simple YAML file into a fully initialized Go structure that our service can use at startup.

It is a good practice to keep this function in the same file as the configuration types (e.g., configs/config.go). Keeping related logic together improves readability and makes the code easier to test and maintain.

Here is a clean and idiomatic implementation:

```go
// LoadConfig reads and parses the configuration file from the given path.
// It returns a Config struct or an error if loading fails.
func LoadConfig(path string) (*Config, error) {
	if path == "" {
		return nil, fmt.Errorf("config path cannot be empty")
	}

	data, err := os.ReadFile(path)
	if err != nil {
		return nil, fmt.Errorf("cannot read config file: %w", err)
	}

	var cfg Config
	if err := yaml.Unmarshal(data, &cfg); err != nil {
		return nil, fmt.Errorf("cannot parse config: %w", err)
	}

	return &cfg, nil
}
```

Understanding the Implementation

1. **Fail Early and Clearly**

   The function immediately checks for an empty file path and returns an error. Failing early helps developers catch mistakes such as missing configuration paths or incorrect file references before the application starts.

2. **Error Wrapping with `%w`**

   When returning an error, the `%w` verb wraps the underlying cause, which allows callers to inspect or unwrap it later using `errors.Is` or `errors.As`. This feature, introduced in Go 1.13, is still a best practice in Go 1.25 for maintaining error context throughout the call chain.

3. **Parsing YAML**

   The `yaml.Unmarshal` function maps the content of the file directly into the `Config` struct using the `yaml` tags we defined earlier. If the file structure or field names do not match, the function immediately reports an error, making configuration issues visible at startup instead of at runtime.

4. **Returning Instead of Logging**

   The function only returns errors; it does not print or log anything. Logging inside a library or helper function can make testing harder and lead to duplicated log entries. Instead, the caller (usually `main.go`) decides how to handle or display the error. This design keeps the function flexible and reusable in different contexts, such as integration tests or CLI tools.

Overriding with Environment Variables

In real-world deployments, configuration values often need to change without editing config files. For example, production may use a different database password or port than your local environment. To handle this, we can let **environment variables override values** from the YAML file.

Environment variables are a universal mechanism for passing configuration to applications. They are easy to manage in containerized or cloud environments, where tools like Docker, Kubernetes, or CI/CD pipelines inject values automatically at runtime. This makes your Go service flexible and secure without adding unnecessary complexity.

Here is how we can apply environment-based overrides in Go:

```go
if pw := os.Getenv("DB_PASSWORD"); pw != "" {
    cfg.Database.Password = pw
}
```

```
if portStr := os.Getenv("SERVER_PORT"); portStr != "" {
    if p, err := strconv.Atoi(portStr); err == nil {
        cfg.Server.Port = p
    }
}
```

In this snippet, the program checks for two optional environment variables:

- **DB_PASSWORD** replaces the password field from the configuration file, allowing secure secret injection.
- **SERVER_PORT** replaces the default port defined in the YAML file, which is useful for running the same binary on different ports in various environments.

If an environment variable is set, its value takes precedence over the value in the configuration file. This creates a clear order of priority. For this reason, it is important to test configuration loading explicitly, ensuring that environment variable overrides and failure cases behave as expected.

Environment variables can also be read through the new `os.Environ()` iterator for more advanced setups, such as automatically applying overrides for all variables with a specific prefix. Usually, in production systems, developers add the service name as a prefix of their configurations (e.g., `RIDE`). However, for most enterprise services, explicit overrides like those shown above are safer and easier to maintain. This pattern keeps your configuration system clean and controlled: values in files define the defaults, and environment variables provide the flexibility needed in real deployment environments.

Validate Configuration Before Returning

Before using the configuration, it's important to validate it and make sure we have valid configs. If these configuration values are wrong, the application may still compile and start, but it will fail later—often under load. In production, this is difficult to diagnose.

For this reason, configuration validation should be explicit, intentional, and executed as early as possible. The natural place is at the end of `LoadConfig`, after all sources of configuration have been applied—file-based defaults, environment variable overrides, and any platform-provided values.

```
func LoadConfig(path string) (*Config, error) {
      //......... after load values

      // Validate after all sources (file + env) have been applied.
      if err := cfg.Validate(); err != nil {
            return nil, fmt.Errorf("invalid configuration: %w", err)
      }
      return &cfg, nil
}
```

By validating before returning the configuration, you enforce a fail-fast startup model: the application either starts with a known-good configuration, or it does not start at all. This approach dramatically reduces the operational blast radius of configuration mistakes and provides immediate, actionable feedback during local development, CI pipelines, and production rollouts.

Once this principle is clear, the question becomes how to structure validation so it remains readable and scalable.

Splitting validation logic into focused private methods—such as `validateServer` and `validateDatabase`—keeps each rule close to its domain and prevents the validation logic from collapsing into a single, monolithic function. A public `Validate` method then acts as the single contract for correctness, coordinating these internal checks and presenting a clear outcome to the rest of the application. This mirrors how we design production systems in Go: small, explicit units composed behind a simple, stable API.

Here is an example:

```
func (c Config) Validate() error {
      var errs []error

      if err := c.validateServer(); err != nil {
            errs = append(errs, fmt.Errorf("server: %w", err))
      }
      if err := c.validateDatabase(); err != nil {
            errs = append(errs, fmt.Errorf("database: %w", err))
      }

      // If you prefer fail-fast, just return the first error instead of
      joining.
      return errors.Join(errs...)
}
```

```
func (c Config) validateServer() error {
// implementaion
}
func (c Config) validateDatabase() error {
// implementaion
}
```

As you can see, the Validate method calls internal validate methods and at the end joins all errors to return all incorrect configurations and make maintenance easy.

Using the Loader in `main.go`

Now that we have our configuration loader, it is time to connect it to the main entry point of the service. In every Go application, `main.go` serves as the starting point where the program wires together its dependencies and prepares to run.

At this stage, we are not yet running an HTTP server or connecting to the database. Our goal is to confirm that the configuration file can be successfully read, parsed, and displayed in a safe way.

Here is a simple example of how to use the loader inside the **Ride** service:

// ride/cmd/main.go

```
package main

import (
   "log"

   "github.com/yourname/transport/ride/configs"
)

func main() {
   cfg, err := configs.LoadConfig("configs/config.yaml")
   if err != nil {
       log.Fatalf("failed to load config: %v", err)
   }
   // Mask secrets before logging
   safe := *cfg
```

```
    safe.Database.Password = "<redacted>"
    log.Printf("Loaded config: %+v", safe)
}
```

Key Points to Notice

1. **Centralized Initialization**
   The `main` function is clean and focused. It calls `LoadConfig` to get all necessary settings, keeping configuration logic outside of the application startup. This separation improves readability and makes it easier to extend later.

2. **Fail Fast, Fail Early**
   If the configuration cannot be loaded, the application immediately exits with `log.Fatalf`. Failing at startup is the correct approach in production-grade systems because it prevents running with missing or invalid settings.

3. **Redacting Sensitive Information**
   Before printing the configuration, we create a shallow copy and replace the database password with `<redacted>`. Logging sensitive information such as credentials or tokens is one of the most common mistakes in real-world systems. By redacting them, you protect both developers and logs from security leaks.

Exercises

1. Extend `ServerConfig` with a new field `IdleTimeout` of type `time.Duration`. Update the YAML file to include it and verify that the new value is loaded.

2. Run the program with `SERVER_PORT=9090` set. Confirm in the log output that the service uses port 9090 instead of the YAML value.

3. Leave the password empty in `config.yaml`. Set `DB_PASSWORD=topsecret` in your terminal and run the program. Confirm that the loaded configuration shows `<redacted>` instead of the real password.

Summary

Configuration is what allows a Go application to adapt to its environment without changing a single line of code. In this chapter, we learned how to design a configuration system that balances simplicity and flexibility while keeping security and clarity in focus. YAML files provide human-readable defaults, while environment variables make the same binary safe to run in development, staging, and production.

We explored how to define configuration types in Go using structs, load data from files using the `gopkg.in/yaml.v3` package, and apply environment variable overrides for secrets or deployment-specific values. We also saw why startup validation and safe logging are essential practices in enterprise systems.

A well-designed configuration loader does more than read files—it creates a clear contract between code and operations. It enables automation, improves reliability, and helps teams separate responsibilities between developers and DevOps. As you build larger systems, this foundation will let your services evolve safely as the environment around them changes.

What's Next

With the configuration in place, your service is ready to face the real world. In the next chapter, you'll use this foundation to run an HTTP server the right way—configurable, reliable, and ready for production. You'll learn how timeouts, routes, and health checks turn a simple server into a resilient system.

CHAPTER 13

Serving the Web: Running HTTP Servers the Right Way

"Everybody can be great...because anybody can serve."

—Martin Luther King Jr.

Running an HTTP server is one of the first things every Go developer learns, yet doing it correctly is what separates a simple tutorial from a real production system. In this chapter, we will learn how to build a professional HTTP server that is configurable, secure, and ready for real-world traffic. You will see how small details—like timeout values, routing choices, and health endpoints—determine the difference between a system that just "runs" and one that runs reliably under pressure.

We will start by configuring the server through environment-aware settings, instead of hard-coding values like ports and timeouts. Then we will design meaningful routes, including health and readiness endpoints, which form the backbone of every resilient service. Finally, you will learn to start and manage the server using Go's `http.Server` type, understanding how to control its lifecycle and behavior in production environments.

By the end of this chapter, you will be able to run your own Go HTTP server with confidence, knowing it is prepared to serve users, handle failures gracefully, and integrate smoothly with cloud platforms such as Kubernetes or Docker-based deployments.

S. Shahsavan, *Building Enterprise Projects with Go*, https://doi.org/10.1007/979-8-8688-2370-1_13

Configuring the Server Properly

A reliable system never hides its behavior inside the code. Hard-coding values such as ports or timeouts might seem harmless at first, but it quickly becomes a trap. Imagine your operations team asking to change the service port from 8080 to 9090, and you need to edit several files, rebuild, and redeploy the service just for that. It is like rebuilding every bus station in a city just because the schedule has changed.

In a professional Go project, configuration belongs outside the code. The application should **read its settings at startup**, not depend on developers to recompile it for every environment. Earlier in this book, we introduced a `configs.Config` structure that loads data from files or environment variables. This structure is the perfect place to keep your server settings.

For an HTTP server, a few values are essential. Each one controls how your service behaves under real traffic, and knowing why they matter will help you build faster and safer systems.

Port

The port is the entry point through which clients reach your service. When an HTTP server starts, it listens on a specific TCP port such as 8080 or 9090. This number is like the station gate where requests arrive. If two programs on the same host try to listen on the same port, the second one will fail to start. That is why port management becomes critical when several services run on one machine or inside the same container network.

In professional systems, the port should never be fixed inside the code. Each environment—development, testing, or production—usually needs its own port configuration. The correct approach is to define the port in an external configuration file or through an environment variable, so operators can change it without modifying or recompiling the program.

For example:

```
type ServerConfig struct {
    Port int `yaml:"port"`
}
```

This value is then injected into the server when it starts:

```
server := &http.Server{
    Addr: fmt.Sprintf(":%d", cfg.Server.Port),
    Handler: mux,
}
```

This approach follows modern DevOps and cloud-native practices. It keeps your service portable and prevents conflicts when several containers share the same host. Using external configuration for ports fits naturally with this adaptive design, helping your service scale and run safely in any environment.

Timeouts

Timeouts are the invisible safety system of every HTTP server. They decide how long the server should wait at different stages of communication before giving up on a connection. Without proper timeouts, even a few slow or broken clients can occupy all your resources and make a healthy system appear overloaded.

Go's `http.Server` offers three timeout controls: `ReadTimeout`, `WriteTimeout`, and `IdleTimeout`. Each one protects a different part of the request lifecycle. Understanding how to use them correctly is one of the most important steps in building a reliable and secure web service.

The **read timeout** limits how long the server waits to receive a complete request, including headers and body. Imagine a client sending data one byte every few seconds and never finishing. Without a timeout, your server keeps the connection open forever, holding a file descriptor and memory that could be used by someone else. This is how the *Slowloris* attack works: it slowly opens many connections until the server can no longer accept new ones. Setting a short read timeout prevents this and keeps your system responsive. For public APIs, five to ten seconds is a good range; internal systems can safely use even less.

The **write timeout** defines how long the server will spend delivering a response. Your handler might complete its work in milliseconds, but a client on a poor connection could take much longer to receive the data. If no limit is set, the server keeps the goroutine alive until all bytes are sent, which reduces throughput and wastes memory. Setting a write timeout, typically 10 to 15 seconds, ensures that slow clients do not block the server. Larger files or streaming responses may need higher values, but the principle is the same: every connection must have a clear deadline.

The **idle timeout** controls how long an open connection is kept alive when no requests are in progress. Keep-alive connections improve performance by avoiding the cost of repeated TCP handshakes, but they should not stay open forever. Setting the idle timeout to around one or two minutes is usually enough to balance efficiency and safety.

Here is an example configuration:

```
server := &http.Server{
    Addr:         fmt.Sprintf(":%d", cfg.Server.Port),
    Handler:      mux,
    ReadTimeout:  time.Duration(cfg.Server.ReadTimeoutSec) * time.Second,
    WriteTimeout: time.Duration(cfg.Server.WriteTimeoutSec) * time.Second,
    IdleTimeout:  time.Duration(cfg.Server.IdleTimeoutSec) * time.Second,
}
```

When any of these limits are reached, the server automatically closes the connection and releases its resources. This prevents memory leaks, keeps goroutines under control, and ensures that your service remains stable under heavy traffic.

Professional Go developers always set these values explicitly. The shortcut `http.ListenAndServe` does not configure timeouts and should never be used in production. Instead, create an `http.Server` instance and define the limits through configuration so that they can be changed later without code modification.

Once configured, these timeouts can be tuned through environment variables or YAML settings, without rebuilding or redeploying the service. This simple discipline turns a basic HTTP listener into a robust, enterprise-ready component that serves confidently under any conditions.

Enterprise Lesson In enterprise systems, timeouts are often configured in DevOps tools such as Nginx, Envoy, or cloud load balancers. While these outer layers provide a first line of defense, relying only on them is risky. Each service must still enforce its own timeouts to manage internal resources and avoid hanging connections. Always configure timeouts both in the proxy layer and inside your Go application. This layered protection keeps your system stable even when one layer fails to respond correctly.

Define Routes

A transport hub without signs leaves passengers lost, and an HTTP server without routes leaves clients just as confused. Routes are the signposts of your service. They connect a client's request path to the correct piece of code that should handle it. Good routing gives your API structure, clarity, and predictability.

Go's standard library includes a built-in router called `http.ServeMux`. The name stands for *server multiplexer*, which means it decides which handler should receive each incoming request. When you create a new multiplexer using `http.NewServeMux()`, you can register handlers for specific paths like this:

```
mux := http.NewServeMux()
mux.HandleFunc("/hello", handler)
```

Whenever a request arrives at `/hello`, the function assigned to that path is called. If you want to truly master the code you use in Go, Chapter 20 explains the design patterns in Go; find the "**Gin Middleware Example**" section to understand the philosophy behind middleware chaining in detail.

This built-in router is intentionally minimal. It is very fast, uses no extra dependencies, and is perfect for small or internal services. Many enterprise projects choose routers like **Chi** or **Gorilla Mux** because they offer useful features such as URL parameters (`/vehicles/{id}`), middleware chaining, or route grouping. Those are valuable tools for complex APIs, but it is always best to start by understanding the standard library. Once you master `ServeMux`, using third-party routers becomes a matter of convenience, not necessity.

In REST services, placing resource identifiers directly in the URL, such as `/vehicles/{id}`, is very common. Even with ServeMux, you can extract such identifiers using standard path matching.

```
mux.HandleFunc("GET /vehicles/{id}", func(w http.ResponseWriter, r *http.
Request) {
    id := r.PathValue("id")
    fmt.Fprintln(w, "vehicle id:", id)
})
```

Alternatively, identifiers can also be passed as query parameters. In Chapter 15, where we focus on API-first design, we explore RESTful service design and these patterns in more detail.

```
mux.HandleFunc("/vehicles", func(w http.ResponseWriter, r *http.Request) {
    id := r.URL.Query().Get("id")
    fmt.Fprintln(w, "vehicle id:", id)
})
```

Endpoint Definitions

Every reliable service begins with a few essential routes. These form the operational backbone of your application:

- /: The root endpoint, often returning a simple greeting to confirm that the service is reachable
- /healthz: The **liveness probe**, used by orchestration tools like Kubernetes to check whether the process is running
- /readyz: The **readiness probe**, which reports whether the service is ready to accept traffic. Kubernetes uses this to add or remove pods from load balancers without interrupting others.
- /startupz: The **startup probe**, useful for applications that need time to initialize, such as loading large caches or waiting for database connections.

In this stage, we only need the first two routes: / and /healthz. The others will become useful later when we introduce dependencies such as databases and external services.

Here is a simple example using ServeMux:

```
mux := http.NewServeMux()

// Root endpoint: a friendly hello.
mux.HandleFunc("/", func(w http.ResponseWriter, r *http.Request) {
    fmt.Fprintln(w, "Hello from the ride service!")
})

// Liveness probe: reports the process is alive.
mux.HandleFunc("/healthz", func(w http.ResponseWriter, r *http.Request) {
    w.WriteHeader(http.StatusOK)
    fmt.Fprintln(w, "Ok")
})
```

The root handler returns a friendly message, confirming that the service is responding. Later, it will be replaced by real endpoints such as vehicle or route APIs. The liveness handler always responds with `HTTP 200`. If this endpoint ever fails, it signals to your orchestration system that the process is unhealthy and needs to be restarted.

Clear routes make an API predictable, testable, and easy to monitor. In the same way that a transport hub needs clear signs, a reliable service needs well-defined endpoints that guide both people and systems.

HTTP Headers and Observability Keys

In distributed systems, a single user action often involves multiple services. One HTTP request may travel through several processes, each running on different hosts. Without a way to track this journey, understanding failures or performance issues becomes guesswork.

To solve this, services share metadata through HTTP headers. These headers act like travel stamps on a request. Each one helps you follow its journey from start to finish.

Here are the most common headers used in modern systems:

- **`X-Request-ID`**

  This ID identifies *one specific HTTP request*. It changes with each retry or new call, even if the input is the same. It helps you trace the exact moment something happened, like a unique receipt for one visit.

- **`X-Correlation-ID`**

  This ID connects *multiple related requests* that happen as part of the same workflow. It stays the same across services. Think of it as the ticket number for the whole ride, not just one stop.

- **`Idempotency-Key`**

  This key is a logical key based on the unique identifier of each request. It prevents a request from being applied more than once. In event-sourced systems, where every action creates a new event, retries must not record duplicate events. The idempotency key tells the service, "I've seen this request before—ignore it if already processed." It ensures consistency even under network retries or duplicate submissions.

- **RequestID (Go Context)**

  Go's `http.Request` has no built-in ID, but you can add one using middleware. Frameworks like Gin or Chi often inject this for you. In the standard library, you'll do it manually and pass the ID through `context.Context`.

Extracting Headers

Let's write a middleware using Go's standard library. It will extract headers from the incoming request, generate them if missing, and store them in the context.

```
func withMetadata(next http.Handler) http.Handler {
    return http.HandlerFunc(func(w http.ResponseWriter, r *http.Request) {
        reqID := r.Header.Get("X-Request-ID")
        if reqID == "" {
            reqID = generateUUID() // replace with your own UUID generator
        }

        corrID := r.Header.Get("X-Correlation-ID")
        if corrID == "" {
            corrID = reqID // fallback: use request ID as correlation ID
        }

        idemKey := r.Header.Get("Idempotency-Key")

        // Add metadata to context
        ctx := context.WithValue(r.Context(), "requestID", reqID)
        ctx = context.WithValue(ctx, "correlationID", corrID)
        ctx = context.WithValue(ctx, "idempotencyKey", idemKey)

        // Add request ID to response for easier debugging
        w.Header().Set("X-Request-ID", reqID)

        log.Printf("Received request %s with correlation ID %s",
        reqID, corrID)

        next.ServeHTTP(w, r.WithContext(ctx))
    })
}
```

This middleware gives each request a fingerprint. If the client didn't provide an ID, we generate one. This ID is added to logs and also returned in the response header. Public APIs often do this to help clients track failures.

Passing Headers to Downstream Services

When your service calls another one, pass along the same IDs to continue the trace. Here's a basic example:

```
// injectRequestMetadata copies known observability headers from context
into the request.
func injectRequestMetadata(ctx context.Context, req *http.Request) {
    if req == nil {
        return
    }

    if reqID, ok := ctx.Value("requestID").(string); ok && reqID != "" {
        req.Header.Set("X-Request-ID", reqID)
    }

    if corrID, ok := ctx.Value("correlationID").(string); ok &&
    corrID != "" {
        req.Header.Set("X-Correlation-ID", corrID)
    }

    if idemKey, ok := ctx.Value("idempotencyKey").(string); ok &&
    idemKey != "" {
        req.Header.Set("Idempotency-Key", idemKey)
    }
}
```

This simple pattern ensures that the next service in the chain receives the full context. When each service logs the same correlation ID, tools like OpenTelemetry, Jaeger, or even plain log aggregators can reconstruct the full request path.

Add the Server Engine

Now that our configuration and routes are ready, it is time to assemble the heart of the service: the `http.Server`. This structure is the engine that keeps everything running. It brings together the network address, the handler, and all the control options we defined earlier, such as timeouts.

Some tutorials use the shortcut function `http.ListenAndServe()`, but that approach is too limited for professional systems. The convenience is not worth the risk. It hides important settings and does not give you control over timeouts, graceful shutdowns, or TLS configuration. A well-structured Go service should always create and manage its own `http.Server` instance.

Here is the typical setup:

```
server := &http.Server{
        Addr:         fmt.Sprintf(":%d", cfg.Server.Port),
        Handler:      mux,
        ReadTimeout:  time.Duration(cfg.Server.ReadTimeoutSec) *
        time.Second,
        WriteTimeout: time.Duration(cfg.Server.WriteTimeoutSec) *
        time.Second,
    }
```

Once created, we start the server using `ListenAndServe()`. This method blocks the current goroutine and keeps the process alive, waiting for requests:

```
// The ListenAndServe call is blocking. It will only return on an
   // unrecoverable error. We return that error to the caller (main).
   if err := server.ListenAndServe(); err != nil && err != http.
   ErrServerClosed {
       return fmt.Errorf("could not listen on %s: %w", server.Addr, err)
   }
```

The second condition checks for `http.ErrServerClosed`. This value is returned when the server stops intentionally, for example, during a graceful shutdown. It is not a real failure, so we ignore it. Only unexpected errors should be reported or logged.

From this point on, your Go application is officially serving traffic. The `ListenAndServe()` call starts a listener on the configured port and runs the handler logic in separate goroutines for each connection. Go's runtime scheduler efficiently multiplexes these goroutines across all available CPUs, and since version 1.25, the runtime automatically detects container limits for CPU and memory. This means your server adapts better when running inside Kubernetes or Docker, without needing manual tuning of `GOMAXPROCS`.

This is the moment when your service becomes "alive." It starts listening, responding, and managing its own connections. In enterprise systems, even this simple operation must be done with precision. By using the full `http.Server` type instead of shortcuts, you gain the fine-grained control needed for reliability, observability, and graceful lifecycle management.

Run with Graceful Shutdown

A professional service is not only defined by how it starts, but also by how it stops. In production, servers are restarted frequently—for deployments, scaling, maintenance, or security updates. If a shutdown happens abruptly, in-flight requests are dropped, open connections may leak, and data can remain half-written. A **graceful shutdown** ensures that your service finishes its current work, cleans up its resources, and exits safely, even under pressure.

In our `RunGraceful` function, we extend the basic server setup with the ability to listen for termination signals and stop in a controlled way.

Listening for Shutdown Signals

The first step toward a graceful shutdown is to teach the server how to listen. When a Go service runs in production—whether inside Docker, Kubernetes, or on a physical machine—it eventually receives a signal from the operating system telling it to stop. These signals are usually **SIGINT**, which happens when the process is interrupted manually (e.g., with *Ctrl + C*), or **SIGTERM**, which is the standard termination request sent by orchestrators during deployments or scaling events.

Before Go 1.16, developers had to build a custom signal channel and manage cleanup manually. Since then, the standard library has made this easier, and now, the preferred and most reliable method is to use `signal.NotifyContext`. This function connects operating system signals to a **context** that automatically cancels when a signal arrives.

Here's how we create it in our server:

```
sigCtx, stop := signal.NotifyContext(context.Background(), os.Interrupt,
syscall.SIGTERM)
defer stop()
```

This small piece of code is more powerful than it looks. The `sigCtx` variable becomes a shared cancellation context for the entire application. When the operating system sends a termination signal, this context is cancelled, and any goroutine, request handler, or background job that uses it will be notified instantly.

You can pass this context to other parts of the system, such as database calls, message consumers, or workers. When it is cancelled, they know they must stop safely instead of being cut off abruptly. This approach keeps your service predictable: one clean signal from the operating system reaches every running component through a single, unified context.

By reacting to shutdown signals in this controlled way, your Go service stops behaving like a passive process and starts acting like a cooperative system component—aware of its environment, ready to finish its work responsibly, and safe to restart at any time.

Running the Server in the Background

Once the server is configured and ready, we need a way to keep it running while also listening for shutdown signals. By default, the call to `server.ListenAndServe()` blocks the main goroutine—it takes full control and never returns until the process stops. In simple examples, that is fine, but in a real system, we need the main routine to stay awake, monitoring termination signals or startup errors.

The solution is to start the HTTP server inside a **separate goroutine**. This allows the server to handle incoming requests in the background, while the main goroutine remains free to coordinate the application's lifecycle.

Here is the pattern used in our code:

```
errCh := make(chan error, 1)
go func() {
    if err := server.ListenAndServe(); err != nil && err != http.
    ErrServerClosed {
        errCh <- fmt.Errorf("listen failure on %s: %w", server.Addr, err)
```

```
        return
    }
    errCh <- nil
}()
```

In this small function, the HTTP server starts running in its own goroutine. If it encounters an unexpected error, that error is sent through the `errCh` channel to the main routine, where it can be handled or logged.

The check against `http.ErrServerClosed` is especially important. When we later call `server.Shutdown()`, Go's HTTP server returns this specific error to indicate that it is closing **gracefully**—not because something went wrong. Treating it as a failure would lead to false alarms in logs and monitoring systems.

By structuring the code this way, we achieve two important goals:

1. The server can continue serving live traffic in the background.
2. The main goroutine remains available to react to system events, such as a signal to stop or a critical startup error.

This design reflects a core principle of Go: **keep the main goroutine in control and let workers do their job independently.** It also prevents race conditions during shutdown because the signal listener and the HTTP server operate in clear, separate contexts.

By running the server in the background, we gain both flexibility and safety. The system can keep responding to requests while still being fully aware of its surroundings—a true sign of maturity in enterprise-grade Go services.

Waiting for the Right Moment

Once the server is running in the background, the main goroutine must stay alert. It acts as the **controller** of the entire process, waiting for the right moment to begin a clean shutdown. This is done using a `select` block that listens to two channels at the same time: one for operating system signals and one for server errors.

Here is the core logic:

```
select {
case <-sigCtx.Done():
    log.Println("shutdown signal received")
```

```
case err := <-errCh:
    if err != nil {
        return err
    }
    log.Println("server exited")
    return nil
}
```

This pattern might look simple, but it gives your service a clear and predictable lifecycle. The main goroutine waits quietly until one of two things happens:

1. **A Termination Signal Arrives:** When Kubernetes, Docker, or a human operator asks the process to stop.
2. **The Server Reports an Error:** For example, the port is already in use, or the listener failed to start.

If a signal arrives first, the program logs that a shutdown has been requested and moves into the graceful termination phase. If an error is received, it means something went wrong at startup or during runtime, and the function returns immediately so the system can report or restart the service.

This design is safer than constantly checking conditions in a loop. The `select` statement allows Go to sleep efficiently until one of the channels receives a message, consuming no unnecessary CPU time.

In a production environment, this small coordination mechanism plays a big role. It ensures that your application responds to system events instantly, without delay or missed signals. It also avoids common pitfalls like race conditions or partial shutdowns that leave background goroutines running.

When a signal triggers the context's cancellation, all dependent goroutines that share the same context are notified almost immediately. This means your service can begin shutdown procedures in milliseconds, keeping deployments and restarts smooth and predictable.

By waiting for the right moment before shutting down, you give your service time to exit in an orderly way—neither too early nor too late. This is how mature systems behave: alert, responsive, and always in control of their own lifecycle.

Giving Ongoing Requests Time to Finish

The true purpose of a graceful shutdown is not just to stop the server—it is to stop **politely**. When a shutdown signal arrives, a responsible service must reject new requests but still allow active ones to finish safely. This prevents users from seeing partial responses or failed operations during deployment or scaling.

Go's `http.Server` makes this process simple through the `Shutdown` method. When called, it stops accepting new connections and waits for all active handlers to complete, up to a defined timeout. If all handlers finish before the timeout, the server closes cleanly. If not, it forces the remaining connections to close to prevent the process from hanging forever.

Here is the key part of the code:

```
ctx, cancel := context.WithTimeout(context.Background(), 3*time.Second)
defer cancel()

if err := server.Shutdown(ctx); err != nil {
    log.Printf("graceful shutdown timed out, forcing close: %v", err)
    _ = server.Close()
}
```

The context created with `context.WithTimeout` defines the **maximum grace period** for the shutdown. In this example, the server gives active requests three seconds to finish. You can adjust this duration through configuration, depending on how long typical requests take in your system. For example, an API returning large files or performing database writes might need a longer timeout.

This small block of code changes everything. It turns the server from a simple reactive component into a **responsible participant** in a distributed environment. It makes sure that no in-progress request is cut off and that sockets, files, and goroutines are all released cleanly.

Go also provides a useful hook for final cleanup work: `RegisterOnShutdown`. This method lets you define custom actions that run just before the server closes. It is the perfect place to flush metrics, save logs, close message queues, or stop background workers.

```
server.RegisterOnShutdown(func() {
    log.Println("server is shutting down, cleanup started")
    // close queues, flush metrics, release resources
})
```

By using `RegisterOnShutdown`, you ensure that important cleanup operations happen in an orderly way, every time. It gives you a final chance to leave the system in a healthy state before the process exits.

Graceful shutdowns are not just a feature—they are a sign of engineering maturity. They show that your service respects its users, its resources, and the environment it runs in. By letting requests finish and cleaning up properly, you give your system a professional rhythm: start well, run well, and stop well.

Why Graceful Shutdown Matters

During development, stopping a service is easy. You press *Ctrl + C*, the process ends, and you run it again a few seconds later. In production, things are different. Modern systems run inside orchestrators like **Kubernetes**, **Nomad**, or **Docker Swarm**, where containers are started and stopped automatically during deployments, scaling events, or node maintenance. When an orchestrator sends a termination signal, it expects the service to react correctly: finish what it is doing, stop accepting new requests, and exit cleanly.

If a service ignores this signal and terminates immediately, clients and users experience sudden failures. Requests in progress are cut off mid-response, leading to errors such as *connection reset* or *502 Bad Gateway* during rollout. Even a few milliseconds of dropped traffic can affect monitoring systems, trigger false alerts, or corrupt business workflows.

A **graceful shutdown** prevents this chaos. The server stops listening for new connections, lets ongoing requests finish, and notifies the orchestrator when it is safe to remove the instance from the load balancer. From the user's point of view, the transition is invisible; the system continues to respond normally even as new versions are deployed behind the scenes.

By practicing graceful shutdown, you teach your service to cooperate with its environment. It becomes predictable under change, safe to deploy automatically, and resilient against resource leaks. In large distributed systems, this reliability is what separates code that merely runs from code that can be trusted in production.

Running the Server

With the code complete, starting the service is simple. From the module's root directory, run:

```
go run ./cmd/httpserver/main.go
```

This command builds and runs your main package. The terminal should show a log message confirming that the server has started and is listening on the configured port.

To verify that everything works, you can send a few test requests from another terminal:

```
curl http://localhost:8080/
# Hello from the ride service!

curl http://localhost:8080/healthz
# Ok
```

If both commands return the expected responses, your service is up and healthy. The first endpoint proves that the server can handle basic requests, while the `/healthz` endpoint confirms that the process is alive and ready to serve traffic.

Behind the scenes, Go's `http.Server` creates a listener on the configured TCP port and starts a lightweight goroutine for every new connection. The Go runtime manages these goroutines efficiently across all available CPU cores. At this point, your application is more than just a piece of code—it is a running system component. It listens, responds, and can be observed through logs, metrics, and health checks.

Congratulations, your depot gates are open, and your first passengers—the incoming requests—are arriving safely.

Exercises

1. Add a new endpoint `/hello?name=Alice` that responds with a JSON message such as

   ```
   {"message": "Hello, Alice!"}
   ```

   Try handling both the case where the `name` query parameter is provided and when it is missing. This exercise teaches you how to read query parameters, format responses as JSON, and write proper content headers with `w.Header().Set("Content-Type", "application/json")`.

2. Set the server's `ReadTimeout` to `1s`. Then, simulate a slow client using the command

   ```
   curl --limit-rate 10 http://localhost:8080/
   ```

Watch how the server closes the connection after the timeout. This demonstrates how timeouts protect your system from slow clients or network abuse, keeping resources available for real users.

3. Add a new `/readyz` endpoint that returns **503 (Service Unavailable)** until a `ready` flag is set to `true`. You can simulate readiness by flipping this flag in memory after a short delay. Think about how an orchestration tool like Kubernetes would interpret this probe and how it prevents traffic from reaching an uninitialized service.

4. Start a request that takes a few seconds to complete, then stop the process manually in the middle of that request. Observe what happens with and without the graceful shutdown code. Compare how the server behaves—Are connections closed cleanly, or does the client see errors?

   This exercise helps you understand the importance of graceful shutdown in keeping user experience and system stability consistent.

Summary

In this chapter, we turned a simple HTTP listener into a dependable service. We externalized configuration so ports and limits can change without code edits, then set `ReadTimeout` and `WriteTimeout` to protect the server at every stage of a request. We defined clear routes for operation, starting with / and `/healthz`, and we used `http.Server` instead of shortcuts to gain control over behavior, observability, and lifecycle. We also taught the service to stop politely with a graceful shutdown: it stops taking new traffic, lets active work finish, runs cleanup hooks, and exits cleanly. Finally, we noted that proxy timeouts help at the edge, but each service must still enforce its own limits.

What's Next

You now have a server that runs responsibly; next, we will make sure the **business** stays clean as the system grows. In the Hexagonal Architecture chapter, we'll put the domain at the center and keep HTTP, databases, and messaging at the edges. You will learn how ports and adapters let us swap MySQL for Postgres or REST for gRPC without touching core rules and how this structure keeps our transport system testable, flexible, and ready for change.

CHAPTER 14

Hexagonal Architecture in Go: Keeping Business Clean

> *"If there's one thing we've learned about coupling over the last fifty years, it's that nothing is better at slowing you down."*
>
> —Robert C. Martin

In enterprise software, code often ages faster than the business it supports. The cause is simple: we mix things that should stay stable—like business rules—with things that change often, such as databases, frameworks, and protocols.

I've seen systems where business logic was buried deep inside Oracle PL/SQL and proprietary APIs. When the team later wanted to switch to PostgreSQL, they faced an impossible choice: rewrite everything or stay locked in. They chose to stay locked in. That wasn't architecture—it was a trap.

Hexagonal Architecture (invented by Alistair Cockburn) helps us avoid this kind of lock-in. It protects the domain—the core reason the software exists—from the constant churn of tools and technologies. It gives us a clear boundary between logic and implementation, so the system stays focused on what it truly needs to do.

As Maulana Jalaluddin Balkhi (Rumi) once said:

> *"Tear off your chains and live in freedom, my son.*
>
> *How long will you let silver and gold enslave your soul?"*

Of course, he didn't mean you should work for free. (I'm definitely getting paid for this book.)

S. Shahsavan, *Building Enterprise Projects with Go*, https://doi.org/10.1007/979-8-8688-2370-1_14

But in the software world, I've seen teams chained to tools. Their code was built so tightly around a database, a framework, or a protocol that change became painful—or even impossible. Hexagonal Architecture helps us break those chains. It lets us enjoy the benefits of tools without letting them control the structure of our software. That is real freedom: to choose, to switch, to grow—without rewriting everything.

The Core Idea

Hexagonal Architecture starts with a clear principle: **separate what your system does from how it connects to the outside world**.

This approach gives us a clear method to organize software that stays flexible as tools evolve. It separates the stable business logic from the unstable technical details, so our systems stay clean and adaptable—even as frameworks, databases, or protocols change around them.

In enterprise systems, I recommend splitting the core into four internal layers: **models**, **service**, **ports**, and **adapters**. This structure helps us reason about responsibilities, test logic in isolation, and scale the code base without breaking the business.

Models

The `models` package defines the shape of your data. It includes entities, value objects, and identifiers. These types describe what exists in your domain—such as `Vehicle`, `Route`, or `Assignment`—but they contain no business rules or coordination logic.

For example, the `Vehicle` struct may hold fields like ID, status, or current assignment. It may include simple methods that work directly with its data, but it does not decide whether or how to assign itself. That responsibility belongs to the service layer.

This package has no dependencies. It uses only the Go standard library and remains free from adapters, protocols, or frameworks. Because of that, it is safe to reuse across other layers and even across services.

Ports

Ports are Go interfaces that describe what the core expects from the outside world. They represent dependencies such as repositories, clocks, or message buses.

For example, `VehicleRepository` defines methods to load or store vehicle data. Ports describe behavior, not implementation. This means the direction of dependency always points inward: from adapters to the core.

Each port defines a clear contract. In some cases, a single port supports many use cases. In others, each use case might have its own port. The structure is flexible as long as responsibilities remain clear.

Service

The `service` package holds the business logic of the application. This is where workflows are defined and decisions are made. It coordinates data from the `models` package, uses ports to interact with external systems, and enforces domain rules.

A service might take a vehicle ID and a route ID, load both using repositories, check that the vehicle can serve the route, and then assign it. All business rules—including constraints, validation, and orchestration—belong here.

This layer does not talk to HTTP, SQL, Kafka, or file systems directly. It only uses interfaces defined in the ports layer. Because of that, it is easy to test with fake or in-memory adapters.

In this structure, the service layer is where the meaning of the system comes to life.

Adapters

Adapters are technical components that implement the ports. They know how to talk to real tools: PostgreSQL, gRPC, Kafka, JSON, or HTTP servers.

For example, a `PostgresVehicleRepo` uses SQL to fetch and store vehicle records. Sometimes they are complex. They may include circuit breakers, caching, or retry logic to handle instability, latency, or temporary failures. These concerns are technical, not business-related, and they belong to the adapter layer. The key rule is isolation. Services must not know whether data came from a cache or a database, whether a call was retried, or whether a circuit is open. From the service perspective, an adapter simply returns data or an error. In mature systems, this complexity is handled through adapter composition. Adapters wrap other adapters while keeping the port interface unchanged. This allows infrastructure strategies to evolve without affecting the core.

Adapters may know about formats, protocols, and I/O, but they do not contain business logic. They are replaceable and testable in isolation.

You can build multiple adapters for the same port: one for production, one for testing, and another for CLI tools or background jobs.

Enterprise Lesson Separating models, services, ports, and adapters gives your system clarity, testability, and long-term stability. When business logic depends only on behavior—not on databases, protocols, or frameworks—you gain freedom to evolve. Tools can change. The core should not. This principle—**technical details depend on business logic, never the reverse**—is what keeps enterprise systems clean, safe, and ready for the future.

Structure in Go

Hexagonal Architecture is not just about ideas—it shows up clearly in how we organize the project. Clean structure makes responsibilities visible, reduces bugs caused by hidden dependencies, and helps new developers get started faster.

Here is a typical single-module Go project using this pattern:

```
transport-system/
├── cmd/                    # entry points (runners)
│   ├── http-server/        # Gin HTTP server
│   ├── grpc-server/        # gRPC server
│   └── consumer/           # Kafka consumer
├── configs/                # configuration files (YAML, JSON)
├── proto/                  # gRPC .proto + generated code
├── schema/                 # Avro schemas for Kafka
├── internal/
│   ├── models/             # entities (Vehicle, Route, Assignment)
│   ├── service/            # use-cases (AssignVehicleToRoute)
│   ├── ports/              # interfaces (repositories, message bus, clock)
│   ├── adapters/           # technology edges
│   │   ├── http/           # Gin handlers, routes, middleware
│   │   ├── grpc/           # gRPC services
```

```
│   │   ├── db/         # Postgres/MySQL repositories
│   │   ├── kafka/      # producers/consumers, Avro serdes
│   │   ├── metrics/    # Prometheus/OpenMetrics collectors
│   │   └── events/     # (future) event-sourcing store
│   └── util/           # cross-cutting helpers (logging, tracing, uuid)
└── go.mod
```

How This Layout Works

- **cmd/** contains one folder per executable. Each runner sets up the configuration, wiring, and startup. For example, `cmd/http-server/main.go` builds the dependency graph and starts the HTTP server. It is the only place where the full application is assembled.
- **internal/models/** holds the domain entities and value objects. These are plain Go types with no external dependencies. This layer defines the structure of the business but does not implement behavior.
- **internal/service/** contains your use cases. Each service coordinates multiple models, applies rules, and interacts through ports. It is the heart of the application's business logic.
- **internal/ports/** defines the interfaces the core logic relies on. These include repositories, rest, and event buses. By depending only on interfaces, the service layer stays clean and swappable.
- **internal/adapters/** connects the system to the outside world. Each subfolder serves one external technology. Adapters implement ports using real tools like PostgreSQL, Kafka, or Gin.

Rules to Keep Your Architecture Clean

- **Data Transfer Objects (DTOs)** like HTTP JSON payloads, gRPC messages, or Avro records belong to the `adapters` layer, not the core. They should be translated to and from core types using simple mappers.

- **Each `cmd/*` runner must wire its own dependencies**. There should be no global shared main. This keeps responsibilities isolated and supports multi-process systems. When you wire these graphs, constructors are the common starting point, but they are not your only tool. We cover additional wiring and creation techniques in **Chapter 20**; it is worth reviewing that chapter to build cleaner, more scalable composition roots.
- **Utilities must stay generic**. Avoid pulling in frameworks or external dependencies into helpers that might be used in core code. If a logger requires a third-party dependency, keep it confined to the adapter layer.

This structure helps you scale your project while staying safe. The deeper logic remains clean and testable. The outer layers handle integration, but they never leak complexity inward.

A Transport Example

Let's walk through a real-world example using the transport system. This shows how ports, services, and adapters fit together in code. You'll see that the core logic is clean and testable, while the infrastructure stays replaceable.

Port

```
// internal/ports/assignment_repository.go
type AssignmentRepository interface {
   Save(ctx context.Context, a models.Assignment) (models.
   Assignment, error)
   FindByID(ctx context.Context, id string) (models.Assignment, error)
   FindAll(ctx context.Context, status *string) ([]models.
   Assignment, error)
}
```

This interface defines what the service needs: a way to fetch and save `Assignment` records. The service does not know how this will be done. It could be PostgreSQL, in-memory for testing, or even Kafka in a reactive flow.

Service (Business Logic)

```
// internal/service/ride_service_impl.go

func (s *AssignmentService) AssignVehicleToRoute(ctx context.Context, vid
domain.VehicleID, rid domain.RouteID) error {
    v, err := s.Vehicles.FindByID(ctx, vid); if err != nil { return err }
    r, err := s.Routes.FindByID(ctx, rid);   if err != nil { return err }
    if err := v.CanServe(r, s.Clock.Now()); err != nil { return err }
    v.Assign(r.ID)
    return s.Vehicles.Save(ctx, v)
}
```

This service coordinates a complete business use case. It loads the required data, applies domain rules, and persists the result. Notice that it only uses interfaces and simple models. It has no idea about databases, HTTP, or JSON.

You can test this service using a fake repository without any setup cost.

Adapter (Repository Implementation)

```
// internal/ports/assignment_repository.go

type sqlAssignmentRepository struct {
    db *sql.DB
}

func (r *sqlAssignmentRepository) FindByID(ctx context.Context, id string)
(models.Assignment, error) {
    row := r.db.QueryRowContext(ctx, `
        SELECT id, vehicle_id, route_id, starts_at, status
        FROM assignments WHERE id = ?`, id,
    )

    var a models.Assignment
    err := row.Scan(&a.ID, &a.VehicleID, &a.RouteID, &a.StartsAt,
    &a.Status)
```

```
    if err != nil {
        if err == sql.ErrNoRows {
            return models.Assignment{}, nil // caller decides how to handle
                                               "not found"
        }
        return models.Assignment{}, err
    }

    return a, nil
}
```

This adapter is a concrete implementation of a repository that uses a relational database—such as PostgreSQL—to load assignment data. It implements a `FindByID` method that fulfills the needs of the core through a port interface like `AssignmentRepository`.

It uses the standard `database/sql` package and executes a parameterized SQL query to fetch a record by its ID. The fields are scanned into a `models.Assignment` value. If the record does not exist, it returns an empty struct. The caller is responsible for deciding how to handle the "not found" case.

This adapter stays focused. It handles database access and nothing more. It does not contain any business rules, and it does not care how the result will be used. This makes it easy to replace, test in isolation, or evolve without touching the core application logic.

You can register this adapter in your `main.go` file during startup. If one day you want to switch to another database or even a distributed store, you only need to create a new adapter. The service layer and the models remain the same.

Architecture As Leverage: Two Lessons from the Field

Design is not about buzzwords. In enterprise projects, architecture becomes real when it either opens a door or closes one. The following two stories show both outcomes: one shaped by foresight and structure, the other limited by short-term speed.

Solr to Elasticsearch: Change Without Pain

In one of my past projects, we started with Apache Solr as the search engine. Over time, we found that Elasticsearch was a better fit for our scaling and analytics needs. Fortunately, we had planned for this.

Instead of wiring Solr directly into our code base, we defined an interface that captured what the search layer was supposed to do. The adapter for Solr was just one implementation. When the time came to switch, we built an Elasticsearch adapter in parallel and used **Branch by Abstraction** along with a **Feature Toggle** to control which engine was active.

It worked exactly as we hoped. The switch was smooth, gradual, and reversible. If something failed in production, we could toggle back to Solr immediately without redeploying. But it never did. We made the switch completely, with no need to rewrite the core.

This is the reward of decoupling: you are free to move.

The Trap of Query-Centered Design

In another project, I saw a team using a database as their main data store. At first, it looked flexible, but they made one subtle decision that changed everything: they let queries leak into every layer.

Instead of isolating database calls behind ports and repositories, they spread queries across projection builders, service layers, and even inside domain logic. Some business rules were implemented inside queries themselves.

I am no longer in contact with that project. But if I had to guess, I would say they are still tied to that specific version database. Changing the database now would mean rewriting large parts of the system—possibly the whole thing.

That is not architecture. That is dependency spread in disguise.

Testing Strategies Across Hexagonal Layers

One of the strongest advantages of Hexagonal Architecture is not flexibility alone. It is the ability to **test each part of the system**. Every layer requires a different testing approach.

Testing the Models

The model layer contains only defined models; Most of the time, there is no business logic. These models must be tested **in isolation**, without mocks, infrastructure, or external dependencies. At this level, you can use fast unit tests that are easy to design and implement.

Testing the Service Layer

The service layer holds the main business logic of the system. It connects domain logic with ports. This makes it the **most critical layer to test in Hexagonal Architecture**.

Service tests should

- Inject mock adapters that implement the expected fake behavior.
- Verify business flows, decision logic, and error handling.
- Assert system behavior when dependencies fail.

Service tests must not start real databases or message brokers. Their goal is to validate orchestration logic, not infrastructure correctness. Personally, I put most effort into service tests; I believe that by implementing service tests, they can cover most of the models as well, because service works with models, and we don't mock models.

Testing Ports

Ports are just interfaces in the Go implementation. We don't implement tests for them. But as services use ports, we mock ports for service tests. By mocking them for service, the system will automatically cover their contract.

Testing Adapters

Adapters connect your system to external technologies. For unit tests, you always use mocks to mock them, but how do you test a query string that is supposed to return expected values from the database? To make sure how adapters work, they should be tested with **integration tests**, not with mocking. We discuss integration tests in ***Chapter 17***.

These tests are fewer, slower, and more expensive to run. That is acceptable. Their value lies in catching configuration errors, schema mismatches, and real integration problems that unit tests cannot detect.

Exercise

1. Define a `VehicleRepository` port in `internal/ports`.
2. Implement two adapters: `InMemory` (for tests) and `MySQL`.
3. Write a service that saves a `Vehicle`.
4. Swap between the two implementations at runtime—Does the service change?

Summary

Hexagonal Architecture helps us keep business logic clean, stable, and independent from fast-changing tools. By separating a Go project into models, ports, services, and adapters, we protect the core while staying open to new technologies. This structure improves testability, eases migration, and supports parallel team development. You saw how to model this in Go using idiomatic layout and interfaces. Through real-world examples, we explored both the freedom that comes from clean boundaries and the risk of letting tools dictate design. Architecture is not about what we use—it's about what we're free to change.

What's Next

In the next chapter, we move from internal structure to external contract. You'll learn how to design robust, stable REST APIs that speak clearly to the outside world—even as your code evolves behind the scenes. We'll cover JSON struct tags, model boundaries, API first topic, and how to keep your API a promise you can keep.

CHAPTER 15

API First: Building Robust REST APIs

"APIs should be designed to be easy to use and hard to misuse."

—Joshua Bloch

In an enterprise system, an API is more than a technical detail. It is the public contract of your service and also the first clear plan of what the application will do. When you publish this contract, every team that depends on your service commits to it. Front-end developers, mobile apps, automation scripts, and partner systems all build their work around the shapes and rules you define. They may never see your code, but they trust your API to stay stable for a long time. This makes the API one of the most important documents in the entire project.

Because changing a published API is difficult and often risky, mature teams follow an API-First approach. The OpenAPI specification is created before any business logic implementation, and it is reviewed by all stakeholders. This file becomes the shared plan for the application and a working document that stays valid for the whole lifetime of the service. It is stored in version control, updated through code review, and treated with the same care as production code. With a stable contract in place, front-end teams can generate clients and begin testing, while back-end teams implement domain logic. Both sides move in parallel with full alignment.

API-First design also protects the long-term health of your system. As long as the external contract stays the same, you can refactor code, optimize performance, or even switch from MySQL to Postgres without affecting any clients. Stability on the outside gives you freedom on the inside.

S. Shahsavan, *Building Enterprise Projects with Go*, https://doi.org/10.1007/979-8-8688-2370-1_15

REST provides a set of principles that help keep this contract simple and predictable. Resources should use clear nouns such as Assignment, Vehicle, or Route. Actions are expressed through HTTP methods like GET, POST, PUT, and DELETE. Each request must carry all required data so the server remains stateless and easy to scale. Proper caching headers reduce unnecessary load and improve performance. Clients should not need to care whether they communicate directly with your service or through a gateway.

When you follow REST principles and work with an API-First mindset, the API becomes a stable promise and a clear plan for your application. It gives consumers confidence, and at the same time, it gives your internal code base the freedom to grow and adapt without fear of breaking external users.

OpenAPI As Executable Contracts

OpenAPI, previously known as Swagger, is a way to describe your REST API in a machine-readable YAML or JSON file. This file is not only a piece of documentation. It is a working contract that both humans and tools can understand. When written correctly, a single OpenAPI file becomes

- Documentation that developers can read and follow
- A source for generating clients and server stubs
- A way to create mock servers for early testing
- A contract for CI pipelines to check backward compatibility

An OpenAPI file captures the full shape of your service. It contains descriptions, examples, request and response schemas, headers, status codes, and error structures. Because everything is written in one place, the API becomes clear, predictable, and easy to test. Teams can explore the contract without running the service or reading the implementation. This is why OpenAPI is often called an "executable contract." Tools can use it to generate models, validate requests, or detect breaking changes long before code reaches production.

In a hexagonal architecture, the OpenAPI specification is part of the HTTP adapter layer. It describes how the outside world communicates with the service. The core domain does not know anything about HTTP, JSON, query parameters, or status codes. This separation keeps your core logic clean and independent. It also ensures that future changes in frameworks or transport protocols do not affect your business rules.

Ride Service API Definition

The following OpenAPI specification describes the first version of the Ride service. It defines how clients create and retrieve assignments. This contract is the shared language between the service and any team or application that depends on it. The specification also demonstrates composition through `$ref` and shows how to reuse common error responses across endpoints.

```
openapi: 3.0.3
info:
 title: Ride Assignment API
 version: 1.0.0
 description: >
   API for creating and retrieving ride assignments.
  Once published, fields and semantics must remain stable.

servers:
 - url: https://api.city-transport.com/v1

paths:
 /assignments:
   post:
     summary: Create a new assignment
     operationId: createAssignment
     requestBody:
       required: true
       content:
         application/json:
           schema:
             $ref: '#/components/schemas/NewAssignment'
     responses:
       '201':
         description: Assignment created
         headers:
           Location:
             description: URL of the created assignment
             schema: { type: string, format: uri }
```

```
          content:
            application/json:
              schema: { $ref: '#/components/schemas/Assignment' }
        '400': { $ref: '#/components/responses/BadRequest' }
        '404': { $ref: '#/components/responses/NotFound' }

    get:
      summary: List all assignments
      operationId: listAssignments
      parameters:
        - name: status
          in: query
          schema:
            type: string
            enum: [pending, active, completed]
      responses:
        '200':
          description: List of assignments
          content:
            application/json:
              schema:
                type: array
                items:
                  $ref: '#/components/schemas/Assignment'

  /assignments/{id}:
    get:
      summary: Get a single assignment
      operationId: getAssignment
      parameters:
        - name: id
          in: path
          required: true
          schema: { type: string }
      responses:
        '200':
```

```
          description: Assignment found
          content:
            application/json:
              schema: { $ref: '#/components/schemas/Assignment' }
        '404': { $ref: '#/components/responses/NotFound' }

components:
  schemas:
    EntityMetadata:
      type: object
      properties:
        id: { type: string }
        createdAt: { type: string, format: date-time }
        updatedAt: { type: string, format: date-time }

    NewAssignment:
      type: object
      required: [vehicleId, routeId, startsAt]
      properties:
        vehicleId: { type: string }
        routeId: { type: string }
        startsAt: { type: string, format: date-time }

    Assignment:
      type: object
      required: [vehicleId, routeId, startsAt, status]
      properties:
        vehicleId: { type: string }
        routeId: { type: string }
        startsAt: { type: string, format: date-time }
        status:
          type: string
          enum: [pending, active, completed]
        metadata: { $ref: '#/components/schemas/EntityMetadata' }

  responses:
    BadRequest:
```

```
      description: Invalid request
      content:
        application/json:
          schema:
            type: object
            properties:
              error: { type: string }
              details: { type: string }
    NotFound:
      description: Resource not found
      content:
        application/json:
          schema:
            type: object
            properties:
              error: { type: string }
```

The `Assignment` schema includes `EntityMetadata` inside a `metadata` field. This is a simple form of **composition** that keeps the structure clear and avoids complicated inheritance-style hierarchies. By placing shared information in a separate object, you can reuse metadata across multiple resources while keeping each schema focused on its main purpose. Later in this chapter, you will see how Go structs use the same idea, allowing you to build clean, flexible models that remain easy to maintain as the system grows.

Implementing REST in Go (Hexagonal Style)

Now that we've defined our API in OpenAPI, it's time to let tools do some heavy lifting. Instead of hand-writing every request struct and route binding, we'll use a generator to produce HTTP boilerplate and type-safe models directly from our OpenAPI file. This makes our API both **consistent** and **future-proof** while still fitting cleanly into our hexagonal design.

Preparing Dependencies

We'll use oapi-codegen, a Go code generator for OpenAPI 3. With it, we can generate

- **Models** → Go structs for request/response bodies
- **Server interfaces** → Go interfaces we must implement, with routes pre-wired for Gin

  First, install the needed modules:

  ```
  go get github.com/gin-gonic/gin
  go get github.com/oapi-codegen/runtime
  go get github.com/oapi-codegen/oapi-codegen/v2/pkg/codegen
  ```

- gin → Our chosen HTTP framework
- runtime → Helpers used by generated code (e.g., for query param parsing)
- codegen → Required internally by the generator

Folder Structure (Hexagonal Placement)

To keep generated code separate from business logic, we follow the hexagonal principle: **adapters depend on core, but core never depends on adapters.**

```
ride/
├── api/                        # API contract + generator
│   ├── openapi.yaml            # OpenAPI spec
│   ├── oapi-types.cfg.yaml     # Generator config for models
│   ├── oapi-server.cfg.yaml    # Generator config for Gin server
│   └── generator.go            # go:generate commands
├── internal/
│   └── adapters/
│       └── http/
│           ├── api/            # Generated OpenAPI code (DO NOT EDIT)
│           │   ├── types.gen.go
│           │   └── server.gen.go
│           └── converter/      # Manual converters between API and domain
│
```

```
│                   └── rest_converter.go
└── internal/
    ├── models/                 # Pure business entities
    │   └── ride.go
    └── ports/                  # Interfaces (ports)
        └── ride_service.go
```

Why this matters:

- `/api` holds the contract and generator.
- `/internal/adapters/http/api` is where generated DTOs and handlers live.
- `/internal/adapters/http/converter` contains mapping code between generated API structs and domain entities.
- `/internal/models` remains pure and free from JSON tags or HTTP imports.

This layout makes the boundaries crystal clear, even for junior developers.

Generator Configs

To keep our generated code organized, we use two separate configuration files in the `/api` folder. One is responsible for generating only the data models, and the other is responsible for generating the Gin server interfaces and routing glue.

`/api/oapi-types.cfg.yaml` → generate only models

```
package: api
generate:
  models: true
output: ../internal/adapters/http/api/types.gen.go
```

This file tells `oapi-codegen` to place all generated models into the `API` package and write them into `types.gen.go` under the HTTP adapter.

The second config generates the server interface and the registration helpers for Gin:

/api/oapi-server.cfg.yaml → generate server stubs

```
package: api
generate:
  gin-server: true
  embedded-spec: true
output: ../internal/adapters/http/api/server.gen.go
```

Here, we ask `oapi-codegen` to create a Gin server implementation that exposes a `ServerInterface` based on our OpenAPI file. The `embedded-spec` option adds the OpenAPI document into the generated code, which makes it easy to serve or validate against the exact same specification at runtime.

By keeping model generation and server generation in separate config files, we can regenerate them independently. For example, you can regenerate only models when schemas change or only server stubs when routes are added, without touching the rest of your code.

Generator File

To keep the generation process simple and reproducible, we place a small helper file (/`api/generator.go`). This file is not part of the application at runtime. It exists only to support the `go generate` command.

```
//go:build generate

// This file is not built into the app. It is only used with `go
generate ./api`.

package main

//go:generate go run github.com/oapi-codegen/oapi-codegen/v2/cmd/oapi-
codegen --config=oapi-types.cfg.yaml openapi.yaml
//go:generate go run github.com/oapi-codegen/oapi-codegen/v2/cmd/oapi-
codegen --config=oapi-server.cfg.yaml openapi.yaml

import (
    _ "github.com/oapi-codegen/oapi-codegen/v2/pkg/codegen"
    _ "gopkg.in/yaml.v2"
)
```

Using package main keeps this file isolated and prevents any accidental imports from leaking into your real code base. The build tag at the top (//go:build generate) ensures that the file is ignored during normal application builds.

Running the following command regenerates all models and server stubs in one step:

```
go generate ./api
```

This helps keep the generated code consistent with your OpenAPI specification and reduces manual work as the API evolves.

Converters

Generated DTOs live in internal/adapters/http/api, but we keep the **domain pure**. The bridge is a converter in /internal/adapters/http/converter/rest_converter.go:

```
package converter

import (
   "github.com/yourname/transport/ride/internal/adapters/http/api"
   "github.com/yourname/transport/ride/internal/models"
)

// API -> Domain
func AssignmentToDomain(r api.Assignment) models.Assignment {
   return models.Assignment{
        ID:        *r.Metadata.Id,
        VehicleID: r.VehicleId,
        RouteID:   r.RouteId,
        StartsAt:  r.StartsAt,
        Status:    string(r.Status),
   }
}

// Domain -> API
func AssignmentFromDomain(r models.Assignment) api.Assignment {
   return api.Assignment{
        Metadata: &api.EntityMetadata{
```

```
            Id: &r.ID,
        },
        VehicleId: r.VehicleID,
        RouteId:   r.RouteID,
        StartsAt:  r.StartsAt,
        Status:    api.AssignmentStatus(r.Status),
    }
}
```

Now the core never sees JSON tags, and adapters never sneak into domain logic.

Summary

- **Generated Code ≠ Domain Code:** Keep them apart to avoid coupling your business model to today's API.
- **Spec and Generator Live Together:** When the contract changes, regeneration is one command away.
- **Keep it obvious for newcomers** where the generator is located and where the generated and business code are.
- **Invest in Converters:** They seem like boilerplate, but they are the firewall that keeps your architecture clean.

The HTTP Layer (Adapter) Implements the OpenAPI Contract

The generated `api.ServerInterface` defines the HTTP contract that our service must implement. To connect this contract to the domain layer, we create an `AssignmentHandler` inside the HTTP adapter. The handler receives requests in Gin's format, converts them when needed, and then calls the core `AssignmentService` through the port interface. Even without a database, we can already start the server and test the routes end-to-end.

```go
// internal/adapters/http/handler/assignment_handler.go

package handler

import (
	"net/http"

	"github.com/gin-gonic/gin"
	"github.com/yourname/transport/ride/internal/adapters/http/api"
	"github.com/yourname/transport/ride/internal/ports"
)

// AssignmentHandler is the HTTP adapter. It implements api.ServerInterface
// and delegates to the core AssignmentService (a hexagonal port).
type AssignmentHandler struct {
	service ports.AssignmentService
}

// NewAssignmentHandler constructs an AssignmentHandler with the given
service.
func NewAssignmentHandler(service ports.AssignmentService)
*AssignmentHandler {
	return &AssignmentHandler{service: service}
}

func (h *AssignmentHandler) ListAssignments(c *gin.Context, params api.
ListAssignmentsParams) {
	notImplemented(c)
}
func (h *AssignmentHandler) CreateAssignment(c *gin.Context) {
	notImplemented(c)
}
func (h *AssignmentHandler) GetAssignment(c *gin.Context, id string) {
	notImplemented(c)
}

func notImplemented(c *gin.Context) {
	c.JSON(http.StatusNotImplemented, gin.H{
		"error":   "not implemented",
```

```
        "message": "ListAssignments endpoint is not implemented yet",
    })
}

// Ensure we implement the generated interface
var _ api.ServerInterface = (*AssignmentHandler)(nil)
```

- This small stub gives the project an early working shape.
- The contract is already connected to Gin, all routes are registered, and the server can run without errors.

Later chapters will replace the placeholder responses with real logic, without changing the public API or the handler signatures.

Wiring the Server

The final step is to connect the generated handlers to a running HTTP server. We use Gin as the router for this chapter. The liveness endpoint `/healthz` remains outside the OpenAPI contract because it is only used for monitoring. The function `api.RegisterHandlers` then attaches all OpenAPI-defined routes to the router.

```
// internal/httpserver/httpserver.go
func Run(cfg configs.Config) error {
      log.Printf("Starting server on port %d", cfg.Server.Port)

      router := gin.Default()
      // Add health endpoint
      router.GET("/healthz", func(c *gin.Context) {
            c.String(http.StatusOK, "Ok")
      })
      var repo ports.AssignmentRepository //No need to initialize, as we
                                            don't have a DB yet
      assignmentService := service.NewAssignmentService(repo)
      // Initialize your handler that implements api.ServerInterface,
      injecting any services needed
      hndlr := handler.NewAssignmentHandler(assignmentService)
      // Register OpenAPI routes (e.g. /assignments)
```

```
    api.RegisterHandlers(router, hndlr)

    server := &http.Server{
        Addr:         fmt.Sprintf(":%d", cfg.Server.Port),
        Handler:      router,
        ReadTimeout:  time.Duration(cfg.Server.ReadTimeoutSec) *
                      time.Second,
        WriteTimeout: time.Duration(cfg.Server.WriteTimeoutSec) *
                      time.Second,
    }

    log.Println("Starting server on port", cfg.Server.Port)
    // The ListenAndServe call is blocking. It will only return on an
    // unrecoverable error. We return that error to the caller (main).
    if err := server.ListenAndServe(); err != nil && err != http.
    ErrServerClosed {
        return fmt.Errorf("could not listen on %s: %w", server.
        Addr, err)
    }

    log.Println("Server exited gracefully.")
    return nil
}
```

With this wiring in place, the service can start and respond to requests.

Even before we add a database or real business logic, the API contract is already live, and every endpoint is reachable. This allows front-end teams, QA, and other services to integrate early using a working HTTP surface, which is one of the main advantages of the API-First approach.

As you can see in this code, we ignored graceful shutdown to keep it simple.

Struct Tags and JSON

After running the OpenAPI generator, you will see code like this in the API package:

```
// Assignment defines model for Assignment.
type Assignment struct {
   Metadata  *EntityMetadata  `json:"metadata,omitempty"`
```

```
    RouteId   string            `json:"routeId"`
    StartsAt  time.Time         `json:"startsAt"`
    Status    AssignmentStatus `json:"status"`
    VehicleId string            `json:"vehicleId"`
}
```

Each field has a back-quoted part such as `` `json:"metadata,omitempty"` ``. These are **struct tags**. They tell the JSON encoder and decoder exactly how to map Go fields to JSON and back.

Why We Need Tags

When your service exposes an API, it must send data in a format that clients in any language can understand. Go values cannot travel over the network directly, so we encode them into a wire format. In most systems that build REST APIs, this format is JSON because it is simple, human-readable, and supported almost everywhere. Other formats like Protobuf, Avro, or CBOR are also common in more specialized setups.

Go's `encoding/json` package performs the conversion between Go structs and JSON. Struct tags are small pieces of metadata attached to fields that control this conversion. They decide

- What JSON key name is used for a field
- Whether a field should be omitted when it is empty
- How numbers, booleans, or timestamps should be represented

These decisions directly shape the public API and how clients interpret your data. A small tag change can affect mobile apps, front ends, batch jobs, or other microservices. That is why tags must be treated as part of your API contract.

What Struct Tags Control

The `encoding/json` package uses tags to adjust several important behaviors.

Field Names

If you do not specify this tag, the JSON key matches the Go field name, including the capital letter. Tags let you choose a consistent and stable naming style, for example:

```
Plate string `json:"plate"`
```

This makes sure that the JSON key is "plate", even if the Go field is later renamed to LicensePlate.

Omitting Empty Values

The omitempty option removes a field from JSON output when its value is empty (zero) in Go. This helps reduce noise in responses:

```
EpochMs int64 `json:"epoch_ms,omitempty"` // omitted when 0
```

Encoding Numbers and Booleans As Strings

Some clients cannot safely handle large integers or precise numeric types. The ,string option tells the encoder to send the value as a quoted string and to parse it back correctly:

```
Capacity int16 `json:",string"`
```

This is useful when you integrate with JavaScript or legacy systems.

A Basic Example

After generating the models from your OpenAPI file, you will see struct tags used throughout the code. The Assignment type is a good example:

```
// Assignment defines model for Assignment.
type Assignment struct {
    Metadata  *EntityMetadata  `json:"metadata,omitempty"`
    RouteId   string           `json:"routeId"`
    StartsAt  time.Time        `json:"startsAt"`
    Status    AssignmentStatus `json:"status"`
    VehicleId string           `json:"vehicleId"`
}
```

Each field has a tag such as `json:"routeId"` or `json:"metadata,omitempty"`. These tags tell the JSON encoder how each field should appear in API responses. Some fields have simple names, and others use omitempty which removes the field when the value is empty.

Here is another generated type:

```
// EntityMetadata defines model for EntityMetadata.
type EntityMetadata struct {
```

```
    CreatedAt *time.Time `json:"createdAt,omitempty"`
    Id        *string    `json:"id,omitempty"`
    UpdatedAt *time.Time `json:"updatedAt,omitempty"`
}
```

Notice how all the fields are pointers. If a value is not present, the field is omitted from JSON because of the `omitempty` tag. This matches the API contract in the OpenAPI file and keeps the JSON output clean and predictable.

Important Rules Illustrated by the Generated Code

Exported Fields Only

Only capitalized fields (`Metadata`, `RouteId`, `Id`) are included in encoding and decoding. Lowercase fields would be ignored completely.

Tag Name Defines JSON Name

A field like `RouteId` becomes `"routeId"` in JSON because of its tag:

```
RouteId string `json:"routeId"`
```

Without this tag, the output would be `"RouteId"` which does not match the API contract.

`omitempty` Hides Empty Values

Fields such as `Metadata` and `CreatedAt` will not appear in the JSON output when they are `nil`:

```
Metadata *EntityMetadata `json:"metadata,omitempty"`
```

This is very useful for optional data or partial responses.

Pointer Fields Show Intent

In models such as `EntityMetadata` and `ListAssignmentsParams`, pointers help the decoder tell the difference between “field missing” and “field provided with zero value”. This becomes important in filtering, patching, and optional parameters.

No Accidental Exposure

Generated code does not include fields without tags. When you write your own types, using `` `json:"-"` `` ensures the field is never sent over the wire.

Why This Matters

These examples show how struct tags make the models match the API specification exactly. The generator follows the OpenAPI file, but as you write your own data types inside the service, you will use the same patterns. Tags are small details, but they control the shape of your public API. Changing one without care is a breaking change, so treat them with the same discipline as any other part of the contract.

Common Tag Patterns You Will Use Often

To use struct tags, like anything else in the software industry, you need to understand usages, pitfalls, and patterns. Let's take a look at some of them.

Rename a Key

Use this when the JSON field name must differ from your Go field name or when you want to protect against future field renames:

```
Plate string `json:"plate"`
```

This keeps the JSON key `"plate"` stable even if the Go code evolves.

Omit Zero Values

The `omitempty` option skips fields that are empty (zero, nil, or ""). It's ideal for optional or rarely used fields:

```
EpochMs int64 `json:"epoch_ms,omitempty"`
```

Exclude a Field Entirely

Use this when a field should never appear in JSON, such as secrets or transient data.

```
Secret string `json:"-"`
```

This is a strong signal that the value belongs only in memory, not in logs or API payloads.

Marshal Numbers or Booleans As Strings

Forces numeric or boolean values to be encoded as quoted strings and automatically decodes them back.

```
Capacity int16 `json:",string"`
```

This is particularly useful when integrating with **legacy systems** or **JavaScript clients** that mishandle large integers.

Optional vs. Present-But-Empty

In many APIs, especially those supporting **partial updates (PATCH)**, you need to tell the difference between a field that's *missing* and one that's *intentionally set to zero or false*. Go's zero values blur this distinction—an empty string, a zero integer, or `false` could mean either "not provided" or "explicitly cleared". The idiomatic way to represent **optional fields** is to use **pointers** in your Data Transfer Objects (DTOs):

```
type VehiclePatch struct {
	Plate    *string `json:"plate,omitempty"`
	Capacity *int16  `json:"capacity,omitempty"`
	Active   *bool   `json:"active,omitempty"`
}
```

- `nil` → Absent (no change).
- non-`nil` → Apply value (even if zero/false).

This pattern mirrors how nullable fields work in databases and aligns naturally with JSON's distinction between *missing* and *null*.

Enterprise Lesson For PATCH and other partial-update APIs, pointer fields are safer and more scalable than magic sentinel values (like `-1` or `""`). They make intent explicit, interoperate cleanly with JSON, and avoid ambiguity when updates are merged across microservices.

Time on the Wire (Default vs. Custom)

When Go structs cross service boundaries, time values must serialize consistently. By default, `encoding/json` encodes `time.Time` values in **RFC 3339** format (e.g., `"2025-10-16T09:30:00Z"`). That's human-readable and interoperable.

Sometimes your API contracts require custom encoding, like **numeric epochs**—seconds since Unix time—for compactness or legacy compatibility. To standardize this across your code base, wrap `time.Time` in a small custom type that defines its own JSON behavior:

```
type EpochSeconds time.Time

func (e EpochSeconds) MarshalJSON() ([]byte, error) {
	return json.Marshal(time.Time(e).Unix())
}
func (e *EpochSeconds) UnmarshalJSON(b []byte) error {
	var sec int64
	if err := json.Unmarshal(b, &sec); err != nil { return err }
	*e = EpochSeconds(time.Unix(sec, 0).UTC())
	return nil
}
```

Now you can use it naturally in your DTOs:

```
type Telemetry struct {
	Received EpochSeconds `json:"received"`
}
```

Trade-off: Custom codecs add code but standardize formats across services.

Defensive Decoding (And Streaming)

In real-world APIs, decoding JSON safely is more than a technical detail—it's a line of defense. Malicious or simply careless clients can send extra fields, wrong types, or huge payloads. If your decoder silently ignores them, bugs and over-posting vulnerabilities can slip through unnoticed.

A simple guard is to **reject unknown fields** during decoding:

```
// Reject unknown fields to catch client typos/over-posting.
func decodeStrict(dec *json.Decoder, v any) error {
	dec.DisallowUnknownFields()
	return dec.Decode(v)
}
```

This small line of defense prevents dangerous surprises—for example, a client sending `{"role":"admin"}` to an endpoint that never intended to accept it. In production systems, these silent mismatches can become data integrity or security issues.

Pitfalls to Avoid

Even experienced Go developers fall into subtle traps when working with struct tags and JSON.

These issues often go unnoticed until production data silently disappears or APIs drift out of sync. Here are the key pitfalls—and how to avoid them:

Unexported Fields with Tags

JSON ignores unexported (lowercase) fields, even if they have tags.

```
type Vehicle struct {
    id string `json:"id"` // ignored: unexported
}
```

To include a field in JSON, it must be **exported** (capitalized), or you must implement custom `MarshalJSON` and `UnmarshalJSON` methods. Hidden fields remain invisible to the encoder—by design.

omitempty Surprises

The `omitempty` option removes fields whose values are "empty":

`false`, `0`, `""`, `nil`, or empty slices/maps.

```
Active bool `json:"active,omitempty"`
```

This can lead to missing data in updates or logs if `false` and "not present" mean different things. Use **pointer fields** when you must distinguish between "absent" and "explicitly false."

Tag Typos

Struct tags are plain strings—the compiler won't catch misspellings or mismatched key names.

```
Plate string `json:"plaet"` // typo silently changes JSON key
```

Always include **tests** or **schema assertions** that verify serialized JSON field names. A single typo can silently break clients downstream.

Avoid Overcommitting in Your API Contract

At the beginning of this chapter, we described an API definition as a contract. Once published, you are expected to support it, often for many years. The most common mistake teams make is overcommitting: exposing fields or endpoints that no client actually needs. These extra details increase coupling and make future changes more difficult, because removing them becomes a breaking change.

In practice, it is much safer to expose only what is required. If a field or an endpoint is not needed yet, do not include it in the contract. This is a natural application of the YAGNI principle: "You are not going to need it." Adding unnecessary fields creates long-term obligations, even when nobody uses them.

A careful and minimal API definition gives you more freedom inside the service, keeps your external surface stable, and avoids carrying commitments that bring no value to your clients.

API Design Strategies

API design is a published language; it's not a holy book, during the time this published language and its features can be changed. Once clients depend on a published API, every modification becomes a design decision with real operational consequences. Adding new endpoints or introducing new optional fields allows the system to grow without disrupting existing consumers. In contrast, renaming fields, removing endpoints, or changing data types forces clients to update their code and should be avoided whenever possible. API versions should represent changes to the external contract, not internal refactoring. Rewriting a service, switching databases, or migrating to a new programming language does not justify a new API version as long as observable behavior remains unchanged.

A well-designed API assumes a certain level of tolerance on the client side. Clients are expected to ignore fields they do not recognize and handle optional data safely. When these assumptions hold, versioning becomes an exception rather than the default response to change.

Forward Compatibility and Backward Compatibility

API evolution usually follows one of two design approaches: **forward compatibility** or **backward compatibility**. The right choice depends on how well the domain is understood, the number of consumers, and how much control the team has over client behavior.

Forward-Compatible Design

A forward-compatible API is designed with a clear long-term shape in mind, even if the full implementation does not yet exist. The contract is published early so that teams can integrate against it, while the underlying functionality is delivered gradually.

This approach is common in large organizations where multiple teams work in parallel and early agreement on the API shape is more important than immediate completeness. The API defines what *will* exist, not only what exists today. Imagine you need to implement a search engine. You can imagine what type of searches we have in the system, what parameters we pass, and so on, but the team doesn't have enough time to implement all features, and at the moment, they just implement a simple search for a single type of entity. In this example, consumers don't have to wait for implementation, and they can work in parallel.

In a forward-compatible system, it is acceptable for parts of the API to be temporarily unavailable. If a client calls a feature that is defined in the contract but not yet implemented, the server should respond explicitly with a `501 Not Implemented` status code. This response communicates that the request is valid, the capability is planned, and the absence is intentional rather than an error.

Forward compatibility also affects response design. Some fields may be present but not fully populated in early stages. This is acceptable only when it is clearly documented. Clients must know which fields are optional, provisional, or not yet supported. When communication is clear, forward compatibility enables rapid development without destabilizing integrations.

Backward-Compatible Design

Backward-compatible design treats the API as a long-lived public contract. Once a version is published, existing clients must continue to work without any code changes. This approach is essential for public APIs, partner integrations, and systems with many independent consumers.

In a backward-compatible API, change is strictly constrained. Existing fields must not change. Optional fields must not become required. Data types must remain stable, and default behavior must not change in ways that clients can observe. Only additive changes are allowed, such as introducing new endpoints or adding new optional fields.

This discipline reduces the need for frequent versioning, but it requires careful design and strong review processes. Every change must be evaluated from the client's perspective. A change that looks harmless on the server side may still break a client in production.

Versioning Strategies

APIs can expose versions in several different ways. Each strategy has trade-offs, and none of them are universally correct. The right choice depends on factors such as cache behavior, operational complexity, security, and, of course, management reasons.

URI Path Versioning

With path-based versioning, the version is embedded directly in the URL, for example, `/v1/assignments` or `/v2/assignments`. This approach is explicit and easy to understand. Routing is simple, testing is straightforward, and caches naturally treat different versions as separate resources.

The downside is that resource identity changes with the version. Once the URL structure is published, it becomes difficult to evolve, and supporting multiple versions often leads to parallel endpoints or even parallel deployments. Despite these limitations, path versioning is widely used and works well when long-term URL stability is not a strict requirement. To be honest, this is always my first choice!

Query Parameter Versioning

In this approach, the version is passed as a query parameter, such as `/assignments?api-version=2`. The main advantage is that base URLs remain stable, and default versions can be introduced easily.

Query parameters are not so transparent, often interacting poorly with caches and intermediaries, which may ignore them by default. Over time, this strategy also encourages mixing multiple versions behind the same endpoint, making behavior harder to reason about. For these reasons, query-based versioning is not usually the best option for long-lived public APIs.

Header-Based Versioning

Header-based versioning moves version information into HTTP headers, for example, `X-API-Version: 2`. URLs remain clean and stable, and resource identity is preserved across versions. This approach works particularly well in controlled environments, such as internal platforms or B2B systems.

Versions are no longer obvious from the URL, which makes debugging and manual testing difficult. Caches must be configured carefully, and clients must consistently send the correct headers.

Media-Type Versioning

Media-type versioning encodes the version into the `Accept` header, such as `application/assignment.v2+json`.

In practice, this strategy is complex. Clients must construct precise headers, debugging is difficult, and tooling support is often limited. Without strong API governance and disciplined consumers, this approach quickly becomes operationally heavy.

Error Handling in REST APIs

In enterprise systems, errors are part of the public contract. They influence how clients retry, how load propagates through the system, and how quickly teams can diagnose production incidents. A mature API is not defined by how often it succeeds, but also by how clearly and consistently it fails. When failures are predictable, systems remain stable even under pressure.

Errors As First-Class API Responses

Enterprise systems must be explicit about responsibility. HTTP status codes provide high-level information, like is it a system problem? Is the request valid? Common HTTP status codes like 4xx and 5xx give a big picture to API clients and monitoring systems. Blurring this boundary causes operational problems. Returning 500 for invalid input encourages retries that will never succeed. Returning 400 for a temporary database outage prevents legitimate retry logic. Some status codes are especially important, for example:

- 409 Conflict

  The request is valid, but it conflicts with the current system state.

- 422 Unprocessable Entity

  The request is valid, but the content is not processable.

Considering these codes enables clients to implement correct recovery or user feedback strategies. Using a status code, you can differentiate between error categories, but in enterprise APIs, an error response must answer questions like

1. What went wrong?
2. Why did it happen?
3. What action is appropriate next?

Plain text error messages are insufficient for this purpose. They are hard to parse, difficult to evolve, and impossible to reason about automatically. This naturally leads to structured error responses. Modern REST APIs increasingly adopt the *Problem Details* pattern, defined in RFC 7807 and refined in RFC 9457. Instead of inventing a custom error schema per service, the API returns a standardized error document together with the HTTP status code.

The architectural idea is simple and powerful:

- The HTTP status code represents a high-level outcome.
- The error body represents the detailed problem.

This separation allows gateways, proxies, and monitoring tools to rely on HTTP semantics, while clients use the structured payload for decision-making.

A well-designed error typically includes

- A stable error type identifier, often expressed as a URI

- A short, human-readable summary that stays constant for the error type
- A detailed explanation describing this specific failure
- A correlation or trace identifier

The error type itself becomes part of your public API. Clients should be able to branch logic on it in the same way they branch on HTTP status codes.

Partial Failure and Bulk Operations

In bulk operation APIs, failure is often partial rather than absolute.

A mature pattern is to

- Return 207 Multi-Status with per-item result objects.
- Report success and failure independently for each item.

Exercises

1. Suggest two more REST endpoints for the Ride service that align with business nouns.
2. Imagine you need to add a `driverId` field to `Assignment`. How would you do it without breaking consumers?
3. Extend the OpenAPI definition with a `422 Unprocessable Content` for validation failures.

Summary

In this chapter, we treated the API as both a long-lived contract and a clear plan for what the service will do. We saw how an API-First approach, built around an OpenAPI specification, lets teams agree on behavior before any code is written and then move in parallel with confidence. OpenAPI acted as an executable contract: one file that tools can use to generate models, server stubs, clients, documentation, and even CI checks for backward compatibility. We placed this specification in the HTTP adapter of a hexagonal architecture and used oapi-codegen to create type-safe handlers that stay in sync with the contract while keeping the domain model clean and independent.

We then looked closely at how struct tags in the generated code control JSON. Finally, we discussed why you should avoid overcommitting in your API: expose only what clients actually need, apply YAGNI (explained on Martin Fowler's website) to your contracts, and remember that every extra field becomes a long-term promise you must keep.

What's Next

In the next chapter, we will move from API contracts to persistence and see how data lives in a database without turning that database into the center of the universe. You will learn how to model repositories as ports, implement a concrete SQL adapter, and keep business rules in Go while MySQL (or any other store) becomes a replaceable detail. By the end, you will know how to wire repositories in main.go and how to manage schema changes with proper migration tools.

CHAPTER 16

Building Persistence: Databases As Servants, Not Architects

> *"Show me your flowcharts and conceal your tables, and I shall continue to be mystified. Show me your tables, and I won't usually need your flowcharts; they'll be obvious."*
>
> *—Frederick P. Brooks, Jr.*

Most enterprise systems exist to manage data. They receive requests from citizens, issue driving licenses, store bank customer profiles, track vehicle assignments, and much more. Because of this, it is impossible to become a senior enterprise developer without understanding how to work with data and databases.

Many teams fall into one of two extremes. Some let the database drive every decision. They design tables first, use every special feature of their chosen engine, and then spread those database choices across the whole code base. Other teams design only at the code level and ignore how the data will live in a real database. The model looks clean in diagrams, but queries are slow, migrations are painful, and reporting becomes almost impossible. Both extremes fail in the long run.

In this chapter, we will take a balanced path. You will see how to treat the database as an important dependency while still keeping the domain at the center of the design. We will look at how to choose suitable database types for different kinds of data in our transport system and how to avoid tight coupling to a specific database engine so that your Go code can evolve even if the persistence technology changes.

Step by step, we will build a persistence layer where the database is a powerful servant and not the hidden architect of your system.

S. Shahsavan, *Building Enterprise Projects with Go*, https://doi.org/10.1007/979-8-8688-2370-1_16

Databases in the Hexagon

In a typical enterprise project, the database often pulls everything toward itself. When teams start with schema design, database features slowly influence naming, structure, and sometimes even business rules. After a few months, the whole system feels shaped by tables rather than by real domain needs.

Hexagonal architecture offers a healthier approach. The domain sits at the center of the system, and the database becomes one of many adapters around it. This mindset gives us freedom: the freedom to keep business logic clean, the freedom to test without a real database, and the freedom to replace a storage engine when requirements change.

In this style of architecture, the domain defines **ports**—interfaces that describe what the system needs from persistence. These ports do not mention SQL, transactions, or specific database engines. The domain only speaks its own language: assignments, vehicles, and routes. Where the data actually lives—MySQL, Postgres, MongoDB, or Redis—is a decision outside the domain.

Here is a simple domain model:

```
// models/assignment.go
type Assignment struct {
   ID        string
   VehicleID string
   RouteID   string
   StartsAt  time.Time
   Status    string
}
```

And here is the port that the domain depends on:

```
// ride/internal/ports/assignment_repository.go

type AssignmentRepository
 {   Save(ctx context.Context, a models.Assignment) (
, error)   FindByID(ctx context.Context, id string) (
, error)   FindAll(ctx context.Context, status *string) ([]models
, error)
}
```

This interface is the contract between the domain and the persistence layer. It describes what the domain needs: saving an assignment, loading one by ID, and listing assignments by status. It does not include any SQL details or database concepts. This helps the domain stay focused on business rules, not storage concerns.

A concrete adapter then implements this contract using a real database. Here is the beginning of a MySQL-based repository:

```
package repository

import (
        "context"
        "database/sql"

        "github.com/yourname/transport/ride/internal/models"
        "github.com/yourname/transport/ride/internal/ports"
)

type sqlAssignmentRepository struct {
        db *sql.DB
}

func NewSQLAssignmentRepository(db *sql.DB) ports.AssignmentRepository {
        return &sqlAssignmentRepository{db: db}
}
```

The repository translates between SQL rows and domain structures. It contains no business logic. Its job is to execute queries, scan results, and return domain-friendly values.

The Save method below uses an SQL pattern that inserts a row when the ID is new or updates the row when the ID already exists.

```
func (r *sqlAssignmentRepository) Save(ctx context.Context, a models.
Assignment) (bool, error) {
   res, err := r.db.ExecContext(ctx, `
       INSERT INTO assignments (id, vehicle_id, route_id, starts_
       at, status)
       VALUES (?, ?, ?, ?, ?)
       ON DUPLICATE KEY UPDATE
```

```
            vehicle_id = VALUES(vehicle_id),
            route_id   = VALUES(route_id),
            starts_at  = VALUES(starts_at),
            status     = VALUES(status)`,
        a.ID, a.VehicleID, a.RouteID, a.StartsAt, a.Status,
    )
    if err != nil {
        return false, err
    }

    rows, _ := res.RowsAffected()
    isNew := rows == 1 // MySQL returns 1 for insert, 2 for update

    return isNew, nil
}
```

This method returns a boolean value. The value is true when the operation created a new row and false when it updated an existing one. The caller can use this information to decide which HTTP status code to return or to apply other business logic. The domain does not see any SQL details and does not need to understand how the `ON DUPLICATE KEY` clause works. It only knows that a record was saved successfully.

The key idea is separation. The core domain depends only on the `AssignmentRepository` interface. It does not import the SQL adapter. It does not know which database engine is used. It does not know how many columns exist in the table or how the SQL query is written. This makes the system free to evolve. If the team decides to replace MySQL with PostgreSQL or move from SQL to a document store, only the repository implementation will change. The domain code stays untouched.

A Note on Transactions

A transaction is necessary when a method performs multiple data-changing SQL statements that must succeed or fail together. For example, creating an assignment and updating a vehicle record in the same operation should happen inside one transaction so the system does not end up with half-applied changes.

In the Save method above, there is only one DML operation. The method runs a single `INSERT ... ON DUPLICATE KEY UPDATE` statement. Because there is only one write operation, a transaction is not required here. The database will treat the statement as an atomic action. If later this method needs to perform multiple updates, deletes, or inserts, wrapping them in a transaction will be important to protect the integrity of the data.

This design keeps your adapter small, clear, and consistent with the principles of hexagonal architecture.

How to Use Transactions in This Repository

The current Save method runs a single `INSERT ... ON DUPLICATE KEY UPDATE` statement. A single DML operation is already atomic inside the database, so a transaction is not required. If you ever extend the method to include more write operations, you must wrap the entire set inside a transaction.

A typical transaction in this repository has four steps:

1. Start the transaction.
2. Run all SQL statements using the transaction.
3. Commit if everything is successful.
4. Rollback if any operation fails.

Here is how you would add a transaction to this method if future changes require it:

```
func (r *sqlAssignmentRepository) Save(ctx context.Context, a models.
Assignment) (bool, error) {
   tx,err:=r.db.BeginTx(ctx,nil)
   if err!=nil{
       return false,err
   }
   defer tx.Rollback()

   res, err := tx.ExecContext(ctx, `
       INSERT INTO assignments (id, vehicle_id, route_id, starts_at,
       status)
       VALUES (?, ?, ?, ?, ?)
       ON DUPLICATE KEY UPDATE
           vehicle_id = VALUES(vehicle_id),
           route_id   = VALUES(route_id),
           starts_at  = VALUES(starts_at),
```

```
            status      = VALUES(status)`,
        a.ID, a.VehicleID, a.RouteID, a.StartsAt, a.Status,
    )
    if err != nil {
        return false, err
    }

    rows, _ := res.RowsAffected()
    isNew := rows == 1 // MySQL returns 1 for insert, 2 for update
    if err := tx.Commit(); err != nil {
        return false, err
    }

    return isNew, nil
}
```

Why `defer tx.Rollback()` Is Important

The rollback call acts as a safety net. It makes sure that the transaction is cancelled if

- An error happens before the commit.
- The function returns early.
- A panic happens inside the method.

If the commit succeeds, the rollback has no effect. This pattern is recommended by the Go `database/sql` package and works well in production systems.

A Tour of Database Types

Choosing a database is one of the most important decisions in an enterprise project. Every database has strengths and weaknesses, and each one fits a specific pattern of data. There is no perfect choice for all cases. Your goal as an engineer is to understand the options well enough to match the database to the real shape of your data, not to an abstract ideal.

In our transport system, we work with structured assignments, flexible telemetry events, and GPS positions that change many times per minute. These different types of information naturally point us toward different database families.

Relational Databases (SQL)

Examples: MySQL, PostgreSQL

Structure: Tables, rows, and a stable schema

Relational databases work best when your data has clear relationships. They offer ACID transactions, foreign keys, and expressive queries. These features make them a strong choice for core business records such as vehicles, routes, and assignments. When the system needs reliable updates or when records must stay consistent across several tables, SQL databases handle the work with confidence.

The main challenge in relational systems is schema evolution. Adding or removing columns requires careful migrations, and growing beyond a single server can be harder than in other models.

Transport example: storing assignments that connect vehicles, routes, and schedules.

Document Databases

Examples: MongoDB, CouchDB

Structure: Documents stored in JSON-like formats

Document databases are a good fit when your data does not follow a strict shape or changes often. Instead of columns, each record can contain whatever fields it needs. This flexibility is valuable for data that evolves quickly, such as telemetry or analytics events.

These systems also scale horizontally with less effort, but they do not support complex joins. Because of this, it is often better to keep related data inside the same document, which can influence the design of your model.

Transport example: storing telemetry logs for each vehicle, where sensors may send new fields over time as hardware changes.

Key/Value Stores

Examples: Redis, Memcached

Structure: Simple keys mapped to values, usually held in memory

Key/value stores focus on speed. They deliver very fast reads and writes, making them ideal for temporary or fast-changing data. They do not support complex queries or joins, so they are often used as caches or as storage for short-lived values.

Transport example: storing the current GPS position of each vehicle by ID, updated several times per second.

Graph Databases

Examples: Neo4j, ArangoDB, Amazon Neptune

Structure: Nodes and edges that represent entities and the connections between them

Graph databases work best when the relationships between your data are more important than the individual records. Instead of using joins, they store connections directly as edges. This makes it fast to move from one entity to another, even across many layers of relationships. They are especially useful when your queries involve paths, networks, or patterns such as "find all vehicles that share drivers within three hops."

The challenge with graph systems is that they are less suited for large aggregations or heavy transactional workloads. They shine in traversal-based queries but may be more complex to operate when your data is mostly tabular or needs strong ACID guarantees.

Transport example: finding the best path between two stations, detecting overlapping schedules across several drivers, or analyzing how vehicles, routes, and assignments connect over time.

Choosing the Right Database

Big data is like teenage sex: everyone talks about it, nobody really knows how to do it, everyone thinks everyone else is doing it, so everyone claims they are doing it...

—Dan Ariely

Many teams follow trends or copy other companies without understanding their own data. A practical guide can help you start with confidence:

- Use a relational database when your data has a clear structure, strong relationships, or requires strict consistency.

- Use a document database when your data is flexible, high-volume, or changes shape often.
- Use a key/value store when you need extremely fast access to frequently updated values.
- Use a graph database when relationships and connections are the main focus of your queries.

In most enterprise projects, a relational database is still the safest and most reliable first choice. SQL systems are mature, easy to operate, and suitable for the majority of business data. But modern architectures allow you to use more than one database in the same project. It is common to store the same record in multiple places, each for a different purpose. For example, you may keep the assignment in MySQL as the source of truth but index it in Elasticsearch to support search features.

The important lesson is to avoid the golden hammer. Do not use the same database for every problem only because you know it well. Instead, choose the database that fits the real shape of your data and the real needs of your system. A careful choice today saves you from performance issues, slow migrations, and expensive redesigns later in the project.

Where Should Business Logic Live?

One of the oldest questions in software architecture is deciding where business rules should run. Should they live inside the database using stored procedures and triggers or inside the application using Go code? Both options have benefits, but they also create very different long-term consequences.

Database-side logic such as stored procedures or triggers can be fast because they run close to the data. They are also a central place to enforce rules. But database logic is harder to test, harder to version, and harder to evolve. It also ties your system to the dialect of one database engine, which increases the risk of vendor lock-in.

Application logic written in Go is easier to test and much easier to review. It follows the ideas of domain-driven design, where business rules belong to the domain, not to the infrastructure. The main drawback is the extra network round-trip between the application and the database, which can add a small cost for some operations. On modern hardware and with proper indexing, this cost is usually not a problem.

A simple guideline helps most teams: keep business rules in the application, and use the database only for invariants. Invariants include things like unique constraints, foreign keys, and indexes that protect the integrity of your data. You can also use the database for tasks like audit logging or batch operations that process many rows at once.

For example, the rule that limits a vehicle to three assignments per day is a true business rule. It belongs in your Go code, close to the domain, where it can be tested, versioned, and evolved with confidence.

This separation keeps your system flexible. If you later move from MySQL to PostgreSQL or introduce a caching layer, your core logic stays clean and unchanged.

Adding the Persistence in Code

Implementing persistence starts with adding the database to the application. But how we add this dependency matters. A clean setup keeps the domain free of infrastructure details and prepares the system for long-term growth.

Adding the Database Dependency in Go

Go includes the `database/sql` package in the standard library. This package gives you a common interface for connection pooling, running queries, and managing transactions. To use a real database, you also need a driver that knows how to talk to the specific engine.

For MySQL, the most widely used driver in production systems is

```
go get github.com/go-sql-driver/mysql
```

Once the driver is added to your module, `database/sql` can create a connection pool and execute SQL queries.

Instantiate the Repository in main.go: The Composition Root

In a well-designed system, there should be one place where all the dependencies are created and connected. This place is called the **composition root**. In a Go application, this role naturally belongs to `main.go`.

This keeps wiring in one place and keeps the rest of the code clean.

Originally, the server looked like this:

```
func Run(cfg configs.Config) {
    // server started, but config carried secrets
    // and HTTP layer had to know about DB setup
}
```

This approach mixed concerns. The HTTP layer had to understand how to build the database connection, which tied it to infrastructure details.

Here is the improved version:

```
func main() {
   cfg, err := configs.LoadConfig("configs/config.yaml")
   if err != nil {
       log.Fatalf("failed to load config: %v", err)
   }
   safe := *cfg
   safe.Database.Password = "<redacted>"
   log.Printf("Loaded config: %+v", safe)
   dsn := fmt.Sprintf("%s:%s@tcp(%s:%d)/%s?parseTime=true",
       cfg.Database.User,
       cfg.Database.Password,
       cfg.Database.Host,
       cfg.Database.Port,
       cfg.Database.Name,
   )
   db, err := sql.Open("mysql", dsn)
   if err != nil {
       log.Fatalf("failed to open database: %v", err)
   }
   defer db.Close()

   assignmentRepo := repository.NewSQLAssignmentRepository(db)

   httpserver.Run(cfg.Server, assignmentRepo)
}
```

And the server now receives only what it needs:

```
func Run(cfg configs.ServerConfig, repo ports.AssignmentRepository) error {
    // Server wires its routes using the repository,
    // without knowing about DB credentials or driver setup
}
```

This structure has several advantages:

Separation of Concerns

`main.go` handles wiring. The repository handles persistence. The server handles HTTP. Each layer focuses on its own job.

Hexagonal Purity

The HTTP layer talks to a port, not directly to the database. If you replace MySQL with PostgreSQL, MongoDB, or even a mock repository for testing, the HTTP layer does not change.

Testability

You can pass a fake repository into the server during tests. This removes the need for a real database and speeds up test execution.

Flexibility

New infrastructure components can be added without changing domain logic or adapters. Only the wiring in `main.go` needs adjustment.

Security

Only `main.go` sees the database credentials. The rest of the system receives ready-to-use interfaces, which reduces the chance of leaking secrets.

Enterprise Lesson In enterprise systems, every request may touch the database, and without a controlled pool, your service can overload the database or create too many active sessions. Always set clear limits for open, idle, and lifetime connections. A predictable pool keeps the system stable under real traffic.

Connection Pooling

What we implemented works as a tutorial, but in production systems, database performance problems are rarely caused by slow queries alone. More often, they emerge from unmanaged concurrency: too many goroutines opening connections at the same time, overwhelming the database long before CPU or I/O limits are reached. This is why **connection pooling is not an optimization**. It is a **correctness and stability requirement** in any serious production system.

This responsibility is handled by the standard library itself. `sql.DB` is **not a single database connection**. It is a **concurrency-safe handle that manages a pool of connections internally**. Every call to `Query`, `Exec`, or `Begin` borrows a connection from that pool, uses it, and then returns it. This design allows Go programs to scale database access safely across thousands of goroutines—*but only if the pool is configured deliberately*. A connection pool acts as a **backpressure**. It protects the database by limiting concurrency and protects the service by making overload visible and controllable.

Connection Pool with sql.DB

A crucial design principle in this chapter is that **persistence is an infrastructure concern**. Pool configuration belongs in the composition root—where the database is wired—not inside repositories or domain logic.

In Go, all pool configuration is applied directly to `*sql.DB`:

```
db, err := sql.Open("mysql", dsn)
    if err != nil {
        log.Fatalf("failed to open database: %v", err)
    }
    defer db.Close()

    // Pool configuration (database/sql pool lives inside *sql.DB)
    db.SetMaxOpenConns(cfg.Database.MaxOpenConns)
    db.SetMaxIdleConns(cfg.Database.MaxIdleConns)
    db.SetConnMaxLifetime(time.Duration(cfg.Database.ConnMaxLifetime) *
    time.Second)
    db.SetConnMaxIdleTime(time.Duration(cfg.Database.ConnMaxIdleTime) *
    time.Second)
```

Maximum Open Connections

`SetMaxOpenConns` limits how many connections can exist at the same time.

This setting is your primary safety valve. Once the limit is reached, new database operations block until a connection becomes available. This behavior is intentional: it turns database access into a controlled, bounded resource.

However, this also means:

- Too low → Goroutines queue up and latency increases.
- Too high → The database becomes the bottleneck and may fail.

In production, this value must be aligned with

- Database connection limits
- Expected request concurrency
- Query duration under load

Maximum Idle Connections

`SetMaxIdleConns` controls how many idle connections are kept alive.

Keeping idle connections avoids the cost of reconnecting during bursts of traffic. This is especially important in systems with spiky workloads. The default is conservative; production systems with real concurrency almost always benefit from raising it. Idle connections are not free, but reconnecting repeatedly is worse.

Maximum Idle Time

`SetConnMaxIdleTime` ensures idle connections do not live forever.

This is essential in cloud and containerized environments where

- Load balancers silently drop idle connections.
- Firewalls enforce inactivity timeouts.

By proactively closing idle connections, your service avoids reusing broken ones.

Maximum Connection Lifetime

`SetConnMaxLifetime` forces connections to be recycled periodically.

This setting is critical when

- Databases sit behind proxies or load balancers.

- Long-lived connections accumulate server-side state.
- Credentials or routing rules change dynamically.

Recycling connections prevents subtle, long-lived failure modes that only appear after days or weeks in production.

ORMs in Go: Blessing or Burden?

When working with relational databases in Go, you normally choose one of two approaches:

- Write SQL directly with the `database/sql` package.
- Use an ORM (Object-Relational Mapper) such as GORM, Ent, or SQLBoiler.

Both approaches can build a real system, but they lead to different trade-offs in performance, control, and long-term maintainability.

How ORMs Work in Go

An ORM tries to map tables and columns in your database to normal Go structs. Instead of writing SQL, you work with structs, methods, and high-level APIs. For example, with GORM, you can define a struct like this:

```
type AssignmentORM struct {
    ID         string    `gorm:"primaryKey"`
    VehicleID  string
    RouteID    string
    StartsAt   time.Time
    Status     string
}
```

And you can insert it with a simple call:

```
db.Create(&AssignmentORM{
    ID: "a1", VehicleID: "v42", RouteID: "r77",
    StartsAt: time.Now(), Status: "PENDING",
})
```

Behind the scenes, the ORM builds the SQL statement, prepares parameters, and executes the insert. Most ORMs also provide tools for migrations, schema generation, relationship management, and event hooks.

This makes the first steps very fast. You can create working code with fewer lines, and the API feels familiar to developers who have used ORMs in other languages.

But using an ORM also means that it becomes part of your architecture. Its choices, its assumptions, and its rules start to shape your code. This is why understanding the trade-offs matters before deciding which path to take.

Why Two Structs with an ORM?

When you use an ORM in a hexagonal architecture, the domain model must stay clean and free from technical details. The domain speaks the language of the business. The ORM speaks the language of the database. Mixing both responsibilities inside one struct creates long-term problems.

Keep the Domain Pure

Your domain struct, such as `Assignment`, should not contain ORM tags, JSON tags, or anything that belongs to the storage layer. These tags describe how the record is saved in a database, not what the entity means in the business. Once you add tags from GORM or any other library, the domain becomes tied to a specific technology. This breaks the separation that hexagonal architecture tries to protect.

Keep the Adapter Independent

Your ORM struct, such as `AssignmentORM`, is part of the infrastructure layer. It may include tags for primary keys, indexing, table names, or other details needed by the ORM. When you keep these structs in the adapter layer, you can update or replace the database technology later without touching the domain.

If you ever decide to stop using an ORM and move to `database/sql`, only the adapter code needs to change. The domain stays intact. If ORM tags were mixed into domain structs, you would be forced to clean the entire core every time a storage decision changes.

Different Lifecycles

The domain and the ORM evolve at different speeds:

- The domain changes when the business rules change.
- The ORM model changes when the schema or the database requirements change.

Separating the two prevents one from influencing the other. This keeps the core stable, testable, and easy to reason about.

Why Developers Like ORMs

Many Go developers choose an ORM because it helps them move quickly, especially at the beginning of a project. An ORM hides most of the SQL details and gives you a higher-level API for working with the database.

Faster Development

With an ORM, you do not need to write `INSERT`, `UPDATE`, or `SELECT` statements for each operation. You work with Go structs, and the ORM turns your changes into SQL automatically. This can speed up early development or proof-of-concept work.

Built-in Schema Support

Some ORMs can generate tables or update them based on Go structs. This reduces the amount of manual migration work during the early stages of a project. It can also help teams who are less familiar with SQL.

Query Builders

Instead of writing SQL as strings, ORMs often provide query builders. You can express queries with Go functions and types. This removes some common mistakes in hand-written SQL and can make the code easier to search and refactor.

Strong Community

Popular ORMs such as GORM have active communities. This means many examples, tutorials, and ready-made solutions. For teams who want quick answers or guidance, this support can be valuable.

The Hidden Costs

Using an ORM can feel smooth at the beginning, but it introduces several risks that become visible only when the project grows. Understanding these costs early helps you choose the right tool for each part of the system.

Abstraction Leaks into the Domain

If you place GORM tags or ORM-specific fields directly on your domain structs, you mix business rules with database technology. The domain becomes tied to the ORM, and changing the persistence layer later becomes painful. This breaks the separation that hexagonal architecture tries to protect.

Performance Surprises

ORMs often generate SQL that looks correct but performs poorly. Examples include N+1 queries, unnecessary joins, or missing indexes. These problems rarely appear in small tests but become serious in enterprise systems with large datasets and heavy traffic. When performance drops, you still need to debug the SQL yourself. I remember in a project using Hibernate, it was a big problem for us in production with millions of users.

Harder Debugging

When issues appear in production, the ORM is no longer a comfortable abstraction. You need to understand the generated SQL, the transaction patterns, and the query plan of the database engine. This reduces the benefit of hiding SQL in the first place.

Technology Lock-In

An ORM API becomes part of your code base. If you decide later to replace the ORM with `database/sql` or move to a different database, a large amount of code must be rewritten. In contrast, when you work with small, well-defined ports and simple SQL, replacing the persistence layer is much easier.

My Recommendation for Enterprise Go

There is no universal rule that fits every team or every system. Choosing between an ORM and `database/sql` depends on the skills of the team, the shape of the data, and the complexity of the project. What follows is based on experience from real enterprise systems, where performance, scale, and long-term maintainability matter.

Use an ORM when the data model is simple, development speed is important, and the team is not yet confident with SQL. ORMs work well for CRUD operations and basic relationships. In these situations, writing SQL manually often adds more cost than value.

Choose a direct SQL approach when the data model is complex or the team has at least some database experience. In high-traffic systems or systems with advanced reporting and filtering needs, having full control over the SQL becomes a real advantage. In my own work, large production systems with millions of users exposed the limits of generated queries. Optimizing ORM-generated SQL was harder than writing the queries directly.

There is also a middle path. In an ERP project early in my career, the team used Hibernate as the main ORM, but I wrote custom SQL for heavy financial reports. This gave us the speed of the ORM for common features and the accuracy of hand-written queries where performance mattered. The only risk with this approach is keeping both worlds in sync. If a table or column name changes, you must update the ORM models and the SQL queries together.

There is no single correct decision. The right choice is the one that fits your team, your data, and your future plans for the system. The best developers are flexible and choose the tool that brings clarity and safety to the project.

Database Migration

A database schema is not static. Even a well-planned design must grow as business rules change. New features introduce new fields, indexes, and tables. Without a controlled migration process, different environments quickly fall out of sync, and debugging becomes harder than it should be.

Why Migrations Matter

Applications evolve, so the schema must evolve with them. When you add a new property to a struct in your project, the database needs the same change. Doing this with ad hoc SQL is risky. A manual `ALTER TABLE` might work on one machine but fail in staging or production.

A reliable system updates its schema the same way it updates its code. This is why schema migrations must be part of your CI/CD pipeline. Every deployment should apply the exact same migration scripts in the exact same order.

How Tools Like Liquibase Help

Version-Controlled Schema

Each change lives in a separate file, such as `V001__create_assignments.sql` or `V002__add_status.sql`. These scripts are stored in Git, reviewed like any other code, and stay in project history forever.

Consistency Across All Environments

The migration tool applies the same script in development, staging, and production. This prevents silent schema drift and keeps behavior predictable.

Rollback Options

Most tools support rollback scripts. If a migration causes problems in production, you can safely revert it.

Audit and Compliance

Liquibase and Flyway track which scripts ran, when they ran, and who triggered them. In regulated industries, this history is essential for audits and operational safety.

A Hard Lesson from Experience

I learned the importance of reliable migrations the hard way. Many years ago, I worked on an enterprise payment system that handled the daily transactions of an entire organization. One release included a new column in a critical table. We deployed the new version, expecting Hibernate to update the schema automatically. It did not.

The result was immediate failure. The service could not start, payments stopped, and rollback was far more difficult than it should have been. Because this module powered all other systems, the impact spread quickly. For several days, thousands of people were affected. In a moment of pressure and stress, even simple decisions became hard, and the lack of a structured migration process made everything worse.

The same project taught us another lesson. Performance was extremely important, and sometimes we needed special types of indexes that Hibernate could not generate. We had to create them manually, and keeping those changes in sync across environments was an ongoing challenge.

If I were to build that system today, I would never rely on automatic schema changes. A proper migration tool would have prevented the outage, kept environments aligned, and reduced the operational risk. Experience shows that controlled migrations are not optional in enterprise systems.

Example in Our Project

To see how migrations work in practice, let's look at the `assignments` table from our transport system. The first migration creates the table with the fields we need at the start of the project:

```
-- V001__create_assignments.sql
CREATE TABLE assignments (
    id          VARCHAR(36) PRIMARY KEY,
    vehicle_id  VARCHAR(36) NOT NULL,
    route_id    VARCHAR(36) NOT NULL,
    starts_at   TIMESTAMP   NOT NULL,
    status      VARCHAR(20) NOT NULL DEFAULT 'PENDING'
);
```

Later, the business introduces a new requirement. We now need to track when an assignment is completed. Instead of editing the first script, we add a new migration:

```
-- V002__add_completed_at.sql
ALTER TABLE assignments ADD COLUMN completed_at TIMESTAMP NULL;
```

These files live in version control together with the code. Any developer can pull the latest changes and run a single command such as `liquibase update` or `flyway migrate`. The tool applies the scripts in order, and the local database becomes consistent with the current version of the application.

This process keeps every environment aligned and makes schema evolution predictable and safe.

Best Practices in Enterprise Projects

Managing database changes in a safe and predictable way is essential for any enterprise system. The following practices help teams keep their schema clean, stable, and easy to evolve.

Use a Migration Tool for All Schema Changes

Production databases should never be updated with ad hoc SQL. Every change must go through a structured migration file.

Treat Migration Scripts Like Application Code

Store them in version control, review them in pull requests, and add rollback steps when possible. This keeps the history clear and supports safe releases.

Automate Migrations in Your CI/CD Pipeline

Deployments should apply migrations automatically. Manual steps increase the risk of mistakes and cause environments to fall out of sync.

Use Clear and Predictable Naming

Version numbers such as `V001__...`, `V002__...` keep the execution order consistent. This removes ambiguity and avoids accidental reordering.

Keep Old Migrations Untouched

Never modify an existing migration file. If you need a change, add a new script. Immutable migrations preserve history and simplify debugging.

Database Performance Tips

Since you can use database migrations to apply your custom DDL and design your schema deliberately, this is a good place to share some practical experience that can save your project significant time and effort in production.

1. Always **divide and conquer** performance problems before trying to optimize anything. The first and most important step is to identify *which part of the system is actually slow*. I have seen cases where the real bottleneck was the network, but a lot of time was wasted optimizing SQL queries instead. Without clear evidence, optimization efforts often target the wrong layer.

2. In practice, nearly **80% of performance issues are rooted in design**, not in individual SQL queries. Before focusing on query tuning, revisit your data model. We all learn normalization rules and indexing strategies from books and university courses, but in real systems, we sometimes forget to re-evaluate them in context.

   In one project, for example, we stored a very large number of records across two normalized tables and frequently queried them using joins. From a textbook perspective, the design was correct: normalized tables with proper indexes. In reality, the queries became almost unusable under load. The lesson was simple but important: **in some cases, denormalization is the correct design choice**. This does not invalidate normalization as a principle, but it highlights that usage patterns and access paths matter more than theoretical purity. There are also many cases where normalization works perfectly well. It is impossible to list all scenarios, but the key takeaway is this: **before spending a lot of time optimizing queries, question the data model itself**.

3. Indexes are another area where trade-offs are often overlooked. In general, indexes improve read performance but reduce write performance. If your workload is write-heavy, this cost can be significant. Create indexes when they are needed, but always consider their impact on inserts and updates.

4. Do not assume that an index is always used. Query optimizers can ignore indexes for many reasons—for example, when `OR` conditions are present or when the column has low cardinality. You do not need to be a database administrator to validate this; simply check the query execution plan and confirm whether the index is being applied.

5. When you are confident that a column contains unique values, **unique indexes** can provide excellent read performance. However, they come with an additional write cost, so the same trade-off applies.

6. Bitmap indexes are another powerful but dangerous tool. In most systems, they significantly slow down write operations and must be used with care. When applied in the right scenarios, their performance benefits can be substantial.

7. If you have queries that consistently apply multiple filters in the `WHERE` clause using `AND`, consider a **multi-column index**. Place the column with the highest cardinality first. When done correctly, the performance improvement can be dramatic—sometimes surprisingly so.

Exercises

1. Add a new method to the `AssignmentRepository` interface: `FindByStatus(ctx context.Context, status string) ([]Assignment, error)`
   Implement this method in `sqlAssignmentRepository`. Create a unit test using an in-memory fake repository to verify the behavior.

2. Your transport system must store millions of GPS points per day for each vehicle. Decide whether SQL, a document store, or a key/value store is the best choice.
   Explain your decision based on consistency needs, query patterns, and scalability.

3. The system has a rule: a vehicle must not have overlapping assignments.

   - Describe how you would enforce the rule inside your Go code.
   - Describe how you would enforce it at the SQL level.
   - Choose the approach you prefer and explain why.

4. Write a new Liquibase or Flyway script called `V003__add_priority_column.sql` that adds a `priority INT` column to the `assignments` table. Write a matching rollback script.

Summary

In this chapter, we learned how to treat the database as a servant of the domain, not the hidden architect of the system. We used a hexagonal architecture to keep business logic talking to clean ports such as `AssignmentRepository`, while concrete repositories handled SQL details in the adapter layer. We saw how to design a simple Save method, when to use transactions, and why the composition root in `main.go` is the right place to wire database connections and repositories. We explored different database families—relational, document, key/value, and graph—and matched each of them to real needs in our transport system, instead of following trends or golden hammers.

We discussed the trade-offs between using `database/sql` directly and using ORMs, and we kept the domain free from ORM tags by separating domain structs from persistence structs. From real production experience, we saw how ORM-generated queries and automatic schema updates can become dangerous at scale and how a careful mix of ORM and hand-written SQL can sometimes be a practical compromise. Finally, we treated schema migration as a first-class concern: using tools like Liquibase or Flyway, versioning migration scripts, automating them in CI/CD, and never touching production with ad hoc SQL. Together, these practices give you a persistence layer that is testable, replaceable, and ready for real enterprise load.

What's Next

Now that your persistence layer is stable, realistic, and ready for real traffic, it's time to test how it behaves in the real world. In the next chapter, we move beyond unit tests and use Testcontainers to run MySQL, Redis, or Kafka inside real Docker environments. You'll learn how to verify your SQL repository against an actual database and run integration tests that expose problems long before they reach production.

CHAPTER 17

Testing the Real World: Integration Tests with Testcontainers in Go

> *A system tested only with mocks is a fortress built on fog: impressive from afar, gone in the first real storm.*

Unit tests give us speed and confidence for isolated logic, but enterprise systems never run in isolation. They talk to databases, cache servers, and message brokers. Integration tests are our way of asking: *Does everything still work when the pieces are assembled?*

In this chapter, we'll learn how to write integration tests in Go using **Testcontainers**, a library that spins up real dependencies (like MySQL or Kafka) in Docker containers. We'll see how to set up containers only once, reuse them across tests, and run them separately from fast unit tests. Along the way, we'll test our `sqlAssignmentRepository` against a live MySQL instance.

Why Integration Tests Matter

Unit tests help us check each screw and bolt of a vehicle. Integration tests are the road test, where the engine, wheels, steering, and brakes must move the vehicle forward together. A real system succeeds only when all of its parts cooperate under real conditions. Table 17-1 summarizes the practical differences between unit tests and integration tests, highlighting how each contributes to confidence, speed, and realism in enterprise systems.

S. Shahsavan, *Building Enterprise Projects with Go*, https://doi.org/10.1007/979-8-8688-2370-1_17

Table 17-1. Unit tests vs. integration tests in enterprise systems

Aspect	Unit Tests (Mocked)	Integration Tests (Real)
Speed	Milliseconds	Seconds (containers boot)
Scope	One function or package	Multiple components
Dependencies	None (mocked)	Real services (DB, broker)
Confidence	Logic works in theory	System works in practice

Integration tests matter because real systems fail for real reasons like a changed SQL column name or a missing index. These problems never appear in mocked environments.

Enterprise Lesson Relying only on mocks is like flying a plane tested only in a simulator. Integration tests reveal schema mismatches, SQL errors, and network issues before your users do.

Tools for Containerized Tests in Go

When we write integration tests, we need real services such as MySQL, PostgreSQL, Redis, or Kafka. Managing these services manually slows down development. Container-based tools solve this problem by starting and stopping dependencies automatically during tests.

testcontainers-go

`testcontainers-go` is the main tool used in modern Go projects, especially enterprise systems. It's similar to testcontainers in Java projects, which makes your life easy if you come from Java. It gives you

- Ready-to-use modules for common services like MySQL, PostgreSQL, Redis, Kafka, and RabbitMQ
- Built-in wait strategies that pause tests until the service is ready

- Automatic cleanup through the Testcontainers reaper process
- Snapshot support for fast database resets, useful when several tests need a clean state

The library works smoothly with Go 1.25, and most teams choose it because it is actively maintained and follows the official Testcontainers design.

dockertest

`ory/dockertest` is a smaller and simpler option. It creates containers using the Docker API and is easy to understand.

However:

- Cleanup must be done manually (e.g., using `pool.Purge`).
- It does not have the richer modules and wait strategies that Testcontainers provides.

Tip For enterprise projects, start with `testcontainers-go`. It's feature-rich and actively maintained.

Choosing the Right Tool

For enterprise projects, `testcontainers-go` is usually the better choice. It saves time, avoids manual Docker setup, and gives consistent results on both local machines and CI pipelines.

Pattern: One Container, Many Tests

Starting a new container for every test is slow and unnecessary. A MySQL container may take several seconds to start, and repeating this work for every test wastes time and system resources. Instead, we follow a simple and effective pattern.

1. **Create the Container Setup in a Separate File**

   For example: `test_containers/mysql_test_container.go`. This keeps container logic away from your test code and makes it easier to reuse.

2. **Start the Container Only Once**

   Use `sync.Once` to make sure the container is created a single time during the test run. All tests then reuse the same container and the same connection details.

3. **Guard These Files with a Build Tag**

   Usually, developers run tests using `go test ./...` command. This command will run all tests in your module. Adding integration tests will slow down your tests, but you don't always need to run them. What you can do is to add `//go:build integration_test` at the top of the file. This will tell go that it should ignore compile and run these files, except if the go command contains the same tag. So these tests run only when you ask for them, such as

   ```
   go test -tags=integration_test ./...
   ```

With this pattern, you get a good balance:

- **Fast feedback** during development because unit tests run quickly
- **Realistic behavior** when you need it, because integration tests use a real MySQL instance started once for all tests

This approach helps the team keep the test suite clean, predictable, and efficient, especially as the number of integration tests grows.

Example: Testing `sqlAssignmentRepository` with MySQL

Add Dependencies

Before we write the test, we need to add the required dependencies. These packages give us access to Docker, Testcontainers, and the MySQL driver. Each one plays a small but important role in running container-based tests.

```
# Docker core API (includes api/types/container)
go get github.com/docker/docker@latest

# Docker helpers for networking (includes nat)
go get github.com/docker/go-connections@latest

# Testcontainers for Go
go get github.com/testcontainers/testcontainers-go@latest

# MySQL driver for database/sql
go get github.com/go-sql-driver/mysql@latest

# MySQL test container
go get github.com/testcontainers/testcontainers-go/modules/mysql
```

These dependencies give us everything we need to start a real MySQL container during tests, connect to it with `database/sql`, and verify that our repository behaves correctly under real conditions.

Test Container util functions

In most enterprise projects, MySQL is not the only service that needs a container. You may also add Redis, Kafka, or PostgreSQL. To avoid repeating the same setup logic, it is better to keep common container code in one place.

We use a small helper type, `testContainerRunner`, inside `test_container_util.go`. Each specific container (MySQL, Redis, and so on) can build a `testContainerRunner` with its own settings and then call the `Run` method.

This keeps the code

- **Reusable**: The same logic works for many services.
- **Easy to Change**: If you change how containers are started, you can do so in a single file.
- **Clear**: Tests focus on behavior, not Docker details.

```
//go:build integration_test

package test_containers

import (
   "context"
   "fmt"
   "time"

   "github.com/docker/docker/api/types/container"
   "github.com/docker/go-connections/nat"
   "github.com/testcontainers/testcontainers-go"
   "github.com/testcontainers/testcontainers-go/wait"
)

type testContainerRunner struct {
   servicePort         int
   name                string
   image               string
   exposedPorts        []string
   env                 map[string]string
   cmd                 []string
   hostConfigModifier func(*container.HostConfig)
}

func (o testContainerRunner) Run(ctx context.Context)
(testcontainers.Container, error) {
   // Give containers more time to start; network can take
   a while.
   timeout := 3 * time.Minute
   req := testcontainers.ContainerRequest{
```

```
        Name:               o.name,
        Image:              o.image,
        ExposedPorts:       o.exposedPorts,
        Env:                o.env,
        Cmd:                o.cmd,
        WaitingFor:         wait.ForListeningPort(nat.Port(fmt.
        Sprintf("%d", o.servicePort))).WithStartupTimeout(timeout),
        HostConfigModifier: o.hostConfigModifier,
    }
    container, err := testcontainers.GenericContainer(ctx,
    testcontainers.GenericContainerRequest{
        ContainerRequest: req,
        Started:          true,
    })
    if err != nil {
        return nil, err
    }
    return container, nil
}
```

This utility type is the foundation for all of our container-based tests. Each concrete helper, such as `GetMySqlContainer`, will only be responsible for MySQL-specific details and will delegate the actual startup to `testContainerRunner`.

MySQL Container Setup

To keep our tests fast and reliable, we start the MySQL container only once and reuse it across all integration tests. This setup lives in its own file, `test_containers/mysql_test_container.go`, where we describe how the container should be created and how other tests can access it.

The function `GetMySQLContainer` hides all Docker and Testcontainers details. It returns the host and port of the running MySQL instance, and the rest of the test code can focus on behavior, not infrastructure.

```
//go:build integration_test

package test_containers
```

```go
import (
    "context"
    "fmt"
    "sync"

    "github.com/docker/docker/api/types/container"
    "github.com/docker/go-connections/nat"
    "github.com/rs/zerolog/log"
)

var (
    mysqlOnce sync.Once
    mysqlHost string
    mysqlPort string
)

func GetMySqlContainer(ctx context.Context, db, user, pass string, port
*int) (string, string) {
    mysqlOnce.Do(func() {
        c, err := testContainerRunner{
            servicePort:  3306,
            name:         "mysql",
            image:        "mysql:8.0.44", // pin to a stable version
            exposedPorts: []string{"3306/tcp"},
            env: map[string]string{
                "MYSQL_ROOT_PASSWORD": pass, // root password
                "MYSQL_DATABASE":      db,   // database name
                "MYSQL_USER":          user, // user
                "MYSQL_PASSWORD":      pass, // user password
            },
            hostConfigModifier: mysqlHostConfigModifier(port),
        }.Run(ctx)

        if err != nil {
            log.Fatal().Err(err).Msg("Failed to run Test Container")
        }
        mp, err := c.MappedPort(ctx, "3306")
```

```
        if err != nil {
            log.Fatal().Err(err).Msg("Failed to get port")
        }
        h, err := c.Host(ctx)
        if err != nil {
            log.Fatal().Err(err).Msg("Failed to get host")
        }
        mysqlHost = h
        mysqlPort = mp.Port()
    })
    return mysqlHost, mysqlPort
}

func mysqlHostConfigModifier(port *int) func(hostConfig *container.
HostConfig) {
    return func(hostConfig *container.HostConfig) {
        hostConfig.AutoRemove = true
        if port != nil {
            hostConfig.PortBindings = nat.PortMap{"3306/tcp": []nat.
            PortBinding{
                {
                    HostIP:   "0.0.0.0",
                    HostPort: fmt.Sprintf("%d", *port),
                },
            }}
        }
    }
}
```

This setup gives us a clean structure:

- `mysqlOnce` ensures the container starts only once.
- `testContainerRunner` handles all common container logic.
- Tests only call `GetMySQLContainer` and receive a ready-to-use database.

This makes integration tests simple, stable, and fast enough to run regularly without slowing down development.

Integration Test

With the container utilities in place, we can now write a real integration test for the sqlAssignmentRepository.

This test runs next to the repository code and uses a live MySQL instance started by Testcontainers. The goal is simple: confirm that the repository can save and load an assignment exactly as the system expects.

```
//go:build integration_test

package repository_test

import (
    "context"
    "database/sql"
    "fmt"
    "testing"
    "time"

    _ "github.com/go-sql-driver/mysql"
    "github.com/yourname/transport/ride/internal/adapters/repository"
    "github.com/yourname/transport/ride/internal/models"
    "github.com/yourname/transport/ride/test_containers"
)

func TestSQLAssignmentRepository_SaveAndFind(t *testing.T) {
    ctx, cancel := context.WithTimeout(context.Background(), 3*time.Minute)
    defer cancel()
    host, port := test_containers.GetMySqlContainer(ctx, "testdb",
    "testuser", "testpass", nil)

    dsn := fmt.Sprintf("testuser:testpass@tcp(%s:%s)/testdb?parseTime=true",
    host, port)
    db, err := sql.Open("mysql", dsn)
    if err != nil {
```

```
    t.Fatalf("failed to connect: %v", err)
}

t.Cleanup(func() {
    _ = db.Close()
})

// Schema setup
_, err = db.ExecContext(ctx, `CREATE TABLE IF NOT EXISTS assignments (
    id VARCHAR(50) PRIMARY KEY,
    vehicle_id VARCHAR(50),
    route_id VARCHAR(50),
    starts_at DATETIME,
    status VARCHAR(20)
);`)

if err != nil {
    t.Fatalf("failed to create table: %v", err)
}

repo := repository.NewSQLAssignmentRepository(db)


assignment := models.Assignment{
    ID:        "A1",
    VehicleID: "V1",
    RouteID:   "R1",
    StartsAt:  time.Now(),
    Status:    "pending",
}

_, err = repo.Save(context.Background(), assignment)
if err != nil {
    t.Fatalf("Save failed: %v", err)
}

got, err := repo.FindByID(context.Background(), "A1")
if err != nil {
    t.Fatalf("FindByID failed: %v", err)
```

```
    }

    if got.ID != assignment.ID {
        t.Errorf("expected ID %s, got %s", assignment.ID, got.ID)
    }
}
```

Enterprise Hint `Fatalf` is equivalent to `Logf` followed by `FailNow`. `Errorf` is equivalent to `Logf` followed by `Fail`. Use `Fatalf` when an error prevents the test from proceeding safely—like a failed container setup or missing dependency. It stops execution immediately. Use `Errorf` when the test can still continue to check other conditions. Failing fast on infrastructure setup errors avoids misleading results and saves debugging time.

Run the test with

```
go test -timeout 90s -tags=integration_test ./...
```

A normal `go test ./...` will skip this test because it is behind the `integration_test` build tag. This separation keeps your fast unit tests clean and your integration tests available when you want full-system validation.

Beyond MySQL: Other Services

Testcontainers supports many other services. You can use the same pattern for them. For each service:

1. Create a small setup file in `test_containers/`.
2. Wrap the container start in `sync.Once`.
3. Call it from your tests just like the MySQL example.

This approach keeps your integration testing tools organized, reusable, and ready for future services as your system grows.

Run Parallel Integration Tests

Running integration tests with Testcontainers often takes several seconds per container, especially for services like MySQL or Pulsar. When each test uses its own container, and there's no shared state, you can dramatically speed up test execution by running them in parallel.

Go makes this easy:

- Inside each test, call `t.Parallel()` in the beginning to mark it as parallel-safe:

```
func TestSQLAssignmentRepository_SaveAndFind(t *testing.T) {
    t.Parallel()
    // ... rest of the test
}
```

- Invoke the test suite with the `-p` flag to run tests in different packages in parallel and control the level of parallelism:

```
go test ./... -timeout 90s -tags=integration_test -p 4
```

This tells Go to run tests from up to four packages at once, using multiple OS threads—ideal when tests are isolated and containers don't conflict. For independent container-based tests, parallel execution reduces CI runtime and developer wait time—without adding complexity. Just make sure tests don't fight over ports or file resources. On multi-core CI runners, setting `-p` to match available cores unlocks full parallelism, significantly reducing feedback latency.

CI Integration and Performance

Running integration tests locally is important, but running them inside a Continuous Integration (CI) pipeline is essential for software quality. CI is the place where your code is built and tested automatically after every change. If integration tests do not run in the pipeline, you lose the main benefit of having them: catching real failures before they reach production.

Container-based tests add extra requirements to the pipeline. The CI runner must be able to start Docker containers, pull images, and wait for services such as MySQL or Redis to become ready. When this setup is missing, integration tests may fail for reasons unrelated to your code.

Because of this, it is important to dedicate a step in the pipeline to integration tests. This step should be prepared to run containers reliably, use stable image versions, and avoid unnecessary delays. A good pipeline creates confidence: developers trust the results, and the team sees real issues early, not after deployment.

Key Practices for CI

1. **Make Sure the Pipeline Can Start Containers**

   Testcontainers needs access to Docker or a compatible container runtime. Without it, no integration test will run.

2. **Use Fixed Image Versions**

   Avoid image tags like `latest`. Always choose a clear version such as `mysql:8.0.44`. This keeps results stable and prevents sudden failures when an image is updated.

3. **Keep Image Pulls Fast**

   If the pipeline downloads large images every time, tests slow down. Many CI systems support caching Docker layers or reusing images between runs. This keeps feedback fast.

4. **Reset Database State Efficiently**

   Most projects need a clean database for each test. Testcontainers supports snapshots, which allow instant resets without restarting the container.

5. **Control Parallelism**

   Parallel tests are fast, but they can cause conflicts when several tests use the same database. You can solve this by separating schemas, restoring snapshots, or starting dedicated containers for critical cases.

6. **Wait for Real Readiness**

   Services start at different speeds in CI. Always use proper wait strategies instead of fixed sleep times. This avoids flaky tests that pass sometimes and fail randomly.

7. **Run Integration Tests in a Separate Stage**

   Integration tests are slower and more expensive than unit tests, so it is often better to run them in a separate stage of the CI pipeline. If unit tests fail, there is no benefit in running integration tests afterwards. Some teams even place integration tests in their own workflow or run them only in test or staging environments. This separation keeps pipelines efficient while still protecting overall software quality.

When these practices are in place, integration tests become a reliable part of the pipeline. They validate that the service works with real dependencies, and they help the team deliver stable software with confidence.

Exercises

1. Extend the test to check `FindAll` by seeding multiple rows with different statuses.
2. Use an init SQL script (`WithScripts`) to bootstrap the schema automatically.
3. Add a Redis container and test caching + DB consistency.

Summary

Integration tests give us a clear view of how our system behaves when real components work together. In this chapter, we learned how to bring Testcontainers into our Go projects and use it to start real services such as MySQL directly in our tests. By keeping container setup in one place, starting each service only once, and separating integration tests behind a build tag, we gained a structure that is both fast and realistic. We saw how `sync.Once`, context timeouts, and small helper functions build a clean foundation for container-based testing in Go 1.25.

We also explored how Testcontainers fits into continuous integration. A reliable pipeline needs stable image versions, efficient container startup, and a dedicated stage for integration tests. When these pieces are in place, the pipeline becomes a safety net that protects the whole team. With these practices, your project stays fast in daily development while still proving itself against real databases, real brokers, and real conditions—the environment that truly matters.

If integration tests are the rehearsal with reality, these tools and patterns give you the stage, the lights, and the clarity needed to perform with confidence.

What's Next

In the next chapter, we move from testing single services to wiring them together with events, treating our transport system as a living stream of facts. You will see how events become the nervous system of the project, decoupling services and turning state into a replayable history.

We will explore how you can design event-driven Go systems that stay scalable, resilient, and ready for the future.

CHAPTER 18

Events As the Nervous System: Building Stream-Driven Systems in Go

> *"A business is a series of events and the reactions to those events."*
>
> *—Jay Kreps*

In enterprise systems, synchronous APIs are like phone calls: direct, immediate, but blocking. Events are like group chats: everyone can listen, no one is forced to respond right away, and the conversation lives on.

In a transport system, when a **new Assignment** (bus → route) is created, it might trigger

- Notifying drivers
- Updating schedules
- Recalculating passenger capacity
- Alerting monitoring dashboards

With synchronous calls, the Assignment service must talk to every other service—creating **tight coupling**. With events, the Assignment service just **announces** what happened. Whoever cares subscribes.

Events reduce coupling, unlock scalability, and create systems that are resilient to failure.

S. Shahsavan, *Building Enterprise Projects with Go*, https://doi.org/10.1007/979-8-8688-2370-1_18

Synchronous vs. Asynchronous Thinking

When two services communicate synchronously—such as through REST or gRPC—it works like a phone call. One service dials the other, waits for a response, and cannot continue until the call is complete:

- The caller must know exactly who to contact.
- The callee must be available and responsive.
- Both remain blocked until the exchange finishes.

This approach can work in small systems with a few services and stable, low-latency networks. But in large-scale environments, synchronous dependencies introduce fragility:

- If the Assignment Service calls the Driver Service, Route Planner, and Monitoring Dashboard directly, a single failure can block the entire flow.
- Latency stacks up. If each call takes 100 milliseconds, three calls may take over 300 milliseconds in total—and even longer under load.
- Scaling becomes complex. Each dependency must scale together, or the slowest one limits the system.

Asynchronous communication offers a better model for enterprise systems. Instead of calling each service, the Assignment Service publishes an event—like "AssignmentCreated"—and continues without waiting.

This is more like sending a message in a group chat:

- Any service can subscribe and react when ready.
- The sender doesn't need to know who receives it.
- The message remains available, even if some services are temporarily offline.

This decoupling is not just an optimization. In enterprise systems, it is essential for resilience, scalability, and long-term maintainability.

Transport Example: Assignment Creation

Let's return to the transport system. When a new assignment is created—such as assigning bus V42 to route R9—several actions must follow:

- The driver must be notified.
- The schedule must be updated so passengers see the correct arrival times.
- Passenger capacity must be recalculated for analytics and planning.
- Monitoring dashboards must reflect the updated route information.
- Notifications must be delivered to users or operators when needed.

If the system uses synchronous APIs, the Assignment service would need to call each of these downstream services directly:

- Assignment → Driver Service
- Assignment → Schedule Service
- Assignment → Capacity Service
- Assignment → Monitoring Service
- Assignment → Notification Service

This creates five separate calls, each one adding latency and introducing a potential point of failure. More importantly, the Assignment service becomes tightly coupled to the APIs of every other team. It cannot change easily without understanding all its dependencies.

With event-driven design, the Assignment service simply publishes one or more events:

- `AssignmentCreated` with fields like assignment ID, vehicle ID, route ID, and timestamp
- `NotificationIssued` for downstream subscribers that handle alerts

Each service that needs the information subscribes independently:

- The Notification Service sends out SMS or other alerts.
- The Schedule Service adjusts future arrival times.

- The Capacity Service recalculates available seating.
- The Monitoring Service updates the live dashboard.

The Assignment service does not know, and does not need to know, who will process the events. It publishes facts. Other services react.

This separation makes the system more flexible, scalable, and easier to evolve.

Why Enterprises Choose Events

Large systems must be built for change, scale, and failure. Events help achieve this not by adding complexity, but by separating responsibilities across services. In enterprise environments, this separation is not optional—it is the only way to keep systems maintainable as they grow. In the sections below, you'll see the key reasons why events are essential for enterprise architecture.

Cross-System Coordination

In enterprise projects, systems often span departments and responsibilities. What happens in one domain must be reflected in others.

For example, if a driver retires or takes a vacation, that change happens in the HR system. But the transport system must respond—removing the driver from active assignments and updating schedules. These systems are not part of the same code base, and they should not depend on each other's APIs. Events allow them to stay in sync without direct coupling.

This is a key difference between enterprise systems and isolated applications: teams must design for cross-domain reactions from the beginning.

Loose Coupling

In an event-driven system, services do not call each other directly. Instead, they publish events and react to the ones they care about. This design lets each service focus on its own logic without depending on the internal structure or behavior of others.

This model helps reduce several types of coupling described in *Building Microservices* by Sam Newman:

- **Pass-Through Coupling:** When one service simply forwards requests to another. With events, no service acts as a pass-through—each reacts to events in its own way.

- **Common Coupling:** When services rely on shared data stores or formats. Events encourage services to exchange only what they need, through well-defined schemas.
- **Content Coupling:** When a service depends on the internal structure of another. In event-driven systems, only the event contract matters—not how the sender processes it.

  Keep in mind: you need to minimize the number of fields that you are exposing; every single field is like a commitment in your published language.
- **Domain Coupling:** When a service cannot complete its work without relying on another service's behavior or logic. In event-driven systems, this kind of dependency is reduced. Instead of calling another service directly, a service can emit an event and let others act if needed.

For example, you can introduce a new consumer, like a Traffic Optimizer, without changing the service that emits the `RouteChanged` or `AssignmentCreated` event. The publisher just announced what happened. Consumers decide how to act.

This flexibility makes it easier to scale teams, introduce new services, and adapt to change without risk of breakage.

If you want to dive deeper into these concepts, *Building Microservices* by Sam Newman offers excellent explanations of coupling types and how to reduce them in distributed systems.

Scalability

In event-driven systems, each consumer scales on its own. If one service is slow, it does not block or delay others.

Events are stored in an event-streaming platform, such as a Pulsar or Kafka. Each consumer reads and processes messages at their own speed. Fast consumers stay close to real time, while slower ones catch up later—without affecting the system as a whole.

This design makes it easy to scale based on demand. During peak seasons like Christmas, you can simply add more pods or instances to handle higher traffic for specific topics. There's no need to scale unrelated services.

By isolating workload and traffic per consumer, you gain both performance and cost control.

Resilience

In event-driven systems, a temporary failure in one service does not result in lost data.

Event brokers like Kafka and Pulsar store messages on disk with strong durability guarantees. If a consumer crashes or is temporarily offline, the events remain safe in the log.

When the service comes back, it can resume from where it left off. It can replay past events, reprocess them, and rebuild its state without needing help from other services.

This ability to recover from failure without data loss is critical in production environments, especially when uptime and correctness are non-negotiable.

Auditability and Time Travel

Every event-driven system leaves behind a history. Events are stored in order, forming a reliable record of what actually happened over time.

This history is useful for many reasons. You can inspect past events to debug issues, run audits for compliance, or generate reports for analysis.

For example, you can answer questions like

> "Show all assignments created last week."

This kind of visibility is almost impossible with purely synchronous systems, where state changes are often hidden inside service internals or overwritten in databases. Events make business behavior observable.

Messaging Concepts: Publish, Send, Subscribe, and Receive

Every event-driven system must handle communication between services. But not all communication is the same. Depending on the use case, the system may need to deliver a message to one service, to many, or allow consumers to fetch messages when they are ready.

Before choosing how to use a messaging system, it is important to understand core concepts. These concepts might seem simple at first, but each messaging tool (like Kafka,

Pulsar, NATS, or RabbitMQ) implements them differently. The choice affects how tightly your services are coupled, how much throughput you can achieve, how fast messages are delivered, and how your system handles failure.

Broker

A **broker** is the core component that connects producers and consumers in a messaging system. It is responsible for receiving messages, storing them safely, and delivering them to the right consumers.

Think of the broker like a post office. Services (producers) send messages to it, and other services (consumers) come to pick up the ones they care about. The broker handles message routing, storage, and delivery.

In systems like **Kafka** and **Pulsar**, brokers manage **topics** and **partitions**, which help organize and distribute messages efficiently. When a message is sent, it is stored in a partition. Each broker may hold one or more partitions, depending on how the system is configured.

Brokers support **durability** by writing messages to disk and **resilience** through replication. For example, in Kafka, each partition has one broker as a leader and others as followers. If the leader fails, one follower takes over to avoid data loss.

Brokers also allow **scalability**. You can add more brokers to a cluster when traffic grows and remove them when it decreases. This makes it easy to handle busy periods like holidays by just spinning up more broker nodes or pods.

In modern versions of Kafka, brokers also manage their own metadata and coordination using **KRaft**, removing the need for external tools like ZooKeeper.

When you run a broker locally, understanding how it handles topics, partitions, and replication helps you tune performance and reliability. In cloud-managed systems (like Confluent Cloud), this is often abstracted away, but the concept is still essential to understanding how your events move through the system.

Topic and Partition

A **topic** in a message broker is a logical channel where messages are published and grouped by category. It acts like a named stream of related events, such as `notifications`. Each message usually includes a key, a value, and a timestamp. Once written, the message is immutable, allowing systems to preserve a full history of what happened. To handle high traffic and enable scaling, topics are divided into one or more **partitions**. A partition is a storage unit that holds a subset of messages in a strict order. Message brokers use partitions to enable parallel writing and reading: producers can write to different partitions, and consumers can process them independently. This design increases throughput while keeping message order within each partition.

Publish/Subscribe Model

The publish/subscribe model (pub/sub) is a messaging pattern where a producer sends events to a shared channel called **topic**. The producer does not know who will receive the event. Any service that wants to react can **subscribe** to the topic and receive new messages automatically.

This pattern separates the sender from the receiver. The producer just emits the event and moves on. It does not wait for a response and does not care if one or many services are listening. Each consumer handles the message in its own way and at its own speed.

In message brokers like Kafka or Pulsar, topics are stored safely and split into **partitions** to handle large volumes of data. Multiple producers can write at the same time. Multiple consumers can read in parallel, without interfering with each other. Each partition keeps the order of events, and consumers can replay old data if needed.

Pub/sub is powerful in enterprise systems where many services must react to the same change. For example, if the HR system publishes a `DriverRetired` event, the Transport Service and Schedule Planner can both act on it—without talking directly to HR. This reduces system complexity, improves reliability, and allows new features to grow without changing the core logic. Figure 18-1 explains the pub/sub model.

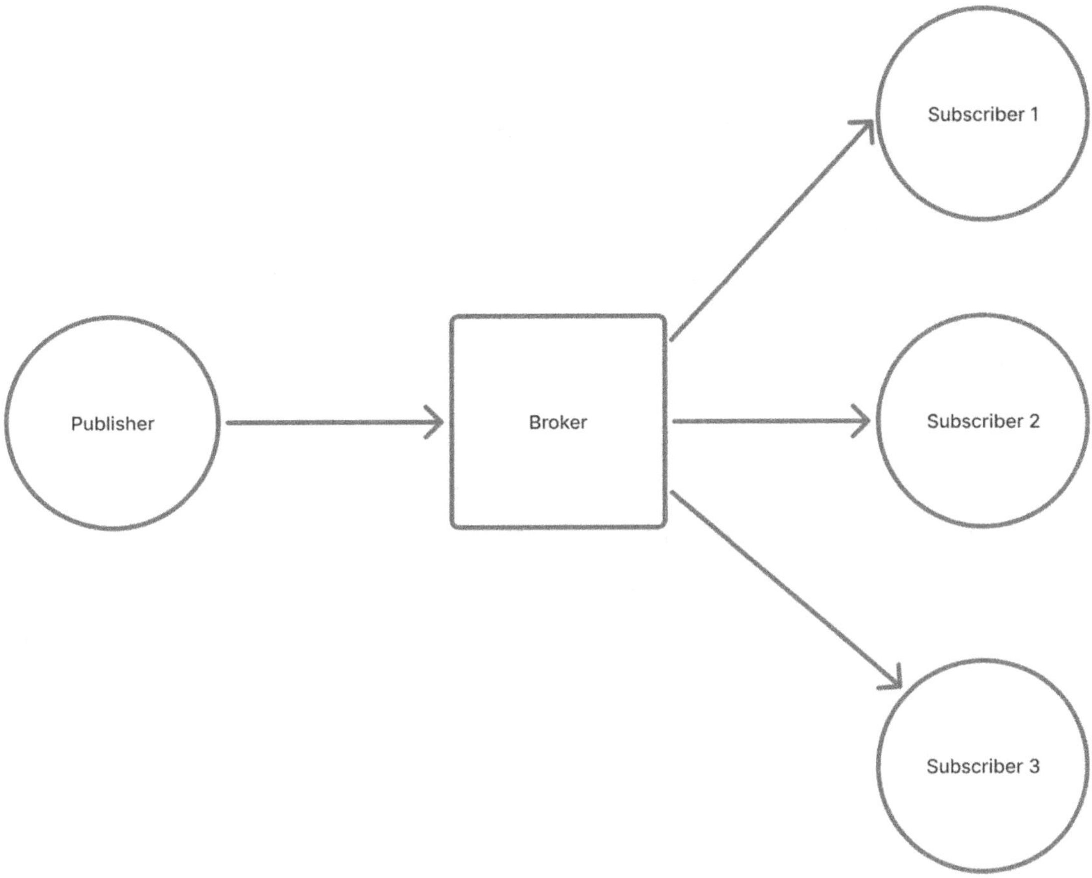

Figure 18-1. *Publish/subscribe model*

Avro Schema

When services exchange messages, it's not safe to send raw or unstructured data. You need a clear, validated format that defines exactly what should be included in each message. This format is known as a **published language**, and in many messaging systems, that language is defined using an **Avro schema**.

Avro is a compact, efficient, and widely adopted format for **serializing** and **deserializing** structured data. It's supported by major message brokers like **Apache Pulsar** and **Apache Kafka** and has tooling in many programming languages, making it ideal for microservice environments.

In Go, for example, you can use the Hamba Avro code generator to create Go structs directly from an Avro schema:

```
go install github.com/hamba/avro/v2/cmd/avrogen@latest
```

Once you define and publish an Avro schema for an event, it becomes your **contract** with other services. This contract explains what data is required, what types it has, and how to interpret it. Other teams will implement their code that depend on this schema, so **changing it later is difficult** and potentially dangerous.

Keep these best practices in mind:

- Only include **required fields** that truly need to be shared.
- Avoid exposing internal implementation details.
- Choose stable, clear names for each field.

You should think of your schema like a public API. Once published, you are **committed** to supporting it. Removing or renaming a field later can break consumers in production. Even optional fields, if added carelessly, may get adopted by other services and become hard to remove.

Avro Schema Versioning

In Apache Pulsar, the **broker is the authority** for schema enforcement. The Go client is a **participant**. It presents a schema when you create a producer or subscribe to a consumer, and the broker accepts or rejects it based on the compatibility strategy configured for that topic or namespace. This has a very practical implication: if the broker rejects your schema, your Go call fails immediately. You will see an error from `CreateProducer` or `Subscribe`. That is exactly what we want in production.

From the Go application's point of view, you control two things:

- Which schema version each producer or consumer uses
- The rollout order of producers and consumers during deployment

Everything else, including compatibility checks, schema versioning, and schema storage, is managed by Pulsar. Let's take a look at an example.

Schema V1 (Initial Contract)

Below, you can see the initial version of the schema:

```
{
  "type": "record",
  "name": "NotificationIssued",
  "namespace": "transport.notifications",
  "fields": [
    { "name": "recipientId", "type": "string" },
    { "name": "channel", "type": { "type": "enum", "name": "Channel",
    "symbols": ["SMS", "EMAIL", "PUSH"] } },
    { "name": "message", "type": "string" },
    { "name": "eventType", "type": "string" },
    { "name": "timestamp", "type": "string" }
  ]
}
```

Once V1 is registered on a topic, Pulsar assigns it a **schema version**. Each produced message is tagged with that version. On the consumer side, Pulsar clients use the version tag to fetch the correct schema and deserialize safely.

Schema V2 (Compatible Evolution)

The safest evolution is adding a field with a default.

```
{
  "type": "record",
  "name": "NotificationIssued",
  "namespace": "transport.notifications",
  "fields": [
    { "name": "recipientId", "type": "string" },
    { "name": "channel", "type": { "type": "enum", "name": "Channel",
    "symbols": ["SMS", "EMAIL", "PUSH"] } },
    { "name": "message", "type": "string" },
    { "name": "eventType", "type": "string" },
```

```
    { "name": "timestamp", "type": "string" },
   { "name": "priority", "type": "string", "default": "NORMAL" }
  ]
}
```

That `default` is not cosmetic. It is the key mechanism that makes V2 interoperable during rollouts. Without it, a V2 reader would not know how to populate `priority` when reading a V1 message.

Backward-Compatible Rollout

In backward compatibility, consumers using the newest schema can read data written by producers using the previous schema. For both `BACKWARD` and `BACKWARD_TRANSITIVE`, the upgrade order is consumers first. When the consumer reads a V1 message, Avro fills `priority` with `"NORMAL"`.

By deploying a producer, if the broker rejects the schema (incompatible evolution under the configured strategy), this call fails immediately; fail fast is exactly what you want.

Forward-Compatible Rollout

In forward compatibility, consumers using the previous schema can read data written by producers using the new schema. For both `FORWARD` and `FORWARD_TRANSITIVE`, the upgrade order is producers first. As there is no guarantee for old consumers that they can read data from the old schema, upgrade all producers first to ensure that the data that has already been produced using the old schema is not available to consumers.

Technical Details That Matter in Production

For Avro, Pulsar's default compatibility strategy is often **FULL**. Under `FULL` (or `FULL_TRANSITIVE`), producers and consumers can typically be upgraded in any order. If you want to enforce a strict rollout order (consumer-first or producer-first), your platform team must explicitly set the strategy to `BACKWARD` or `FORWARD` at the namespace/topic level using broker administration tools.

Transport Case Study

Imagine the Assignment Service publishes an `AssignmentCreated` event when a new vehicle is assigned to a route. Several other services react in different ways:

- **Driver Service:** Uses a job queue to deliver the right assignment to each driver
- **Schedule Service:** Subscribes to the event and updates timetables in real time
- **Monitoring Dashboard:** Listens and pushes updates to operator dashboards
- **Analytics Service:** Periodically scans the event stream to compute key performance indicators (KPIs)

These services interact with the same event, but each uses a different messaging pattern. That flexibility is the power of messaging.

Notification Service

The Notification Service subscribes to notification events from across the system. Instead of every service calling it directly, they just publish a `NotificationIssued` event to a shared topic. This decouples all services from notification logic and allows the notification flow to evolve independently. Here is an example of a notification schema definition:

```
{
  "type": "record",
  "name": "NotificationIssued",
  "namespace": "transport.notifications",
  "fields": [
    { "name": "recipientId", "type": "string" },
    { "name": "channel", "type": { "type": "enum", "name": "Channel",
    "symbols": ["SMS", "EMAIL", "PUSH"] } },
    { "name": "message", "type": "string" },
    { "name": "eventType", "type": "string" },
    { "name": "timestamp", "type": "string" }
  ]
}
```

The **event schema** is now your contract. Once published, that schema becomes a shared language. If it changes, all consumers must understand the new format.

Design your schemas with care and stability in mind—changing them later can ripple across the system. Once you've defined your Avro schema, you can generate Go code directly from it. This lets your services use strongly typed, pre-validated data structures instead of working with raw JSON or byte arrays.

Using a code generator removes manual effort and reduces bugs. It ensures the Go structs match the schema exactly and remain consistent across services.

Here's an example using the Hamba Avro code generator to generate Go types from .avsc files:

```
~/go/bin/avrogen -pkg ports -o internal/ports/generated_messages.go avro_
schemas/*.avsc
```

This command does the following:

- `-pkg ports`: Sets the target package name to `ports`
- `-o internal/ports/generated_messages.go`: Writes the generated code to that file
- `avro_schemas/*.avsc`: Processes all schema files in the `avro_schemas` directory

You can run this as part of your CI or makefile to regenerate types whenever schemas change. This keeps your application aligned with the published language, reducing integration friction across teams and services.

You can see the generated code below:

```go
// Code generated by avro/gen. DO NOT EDIT.
package ports

// NotificationIssued is a generated struct.
type NotificationIssued struct {
   RecipientID string `avro:"recipientId"`
   Channel     string `avro:"channel"`
   Message     string `avro:"message"`
   EventType   string `avro:"eventType"`
   Timestamp   string `avro:"timestamp"`
}
```

Pulsar Producers and Consumers: One Generic to Rule Them All

In many event-driven Go systems, developers end up rewriting nearly identical producer and consumer code for each new topic. The only things that usually change are the event type, topic name, and a few configurations. Everything else—the logic for sending and receiving messages—stays the same.

This repetition is not only wasteful; it's also risky. It invites small inconsistencies and bugs. More importantly, it hides what could be a reusable pattern.

With Go's generics, introduced in Go 1.18 and improved further in later versions, you can abstract that common logic once and apply it across the system. Instead of duplicating producer and consumer code for each message type, you define a generic component that works for any type and schema.

This lets you enforce consistent behavior across your system, reduce boilerplate, and focus on what matters: the actual events that drive your business logic.

Ports and Adapters (Hexagonal): What Sits Where?

In the Ports and Adapters (also called Hexagonal) architecture, your code is separated into two layers: what the application needs (ports) and how those needs are fulfilled (adapters). This helps your system stay testable, modular, and open to future changes.

- **Ports** are interfaces. They define how your application talks to the outside world. For messaging, ports describe what messages your app sends or receives and how message handlers are triggered. Keep them small and generic. Put them in `internal/ports`.
- **Adapters** are concrete implementations of those interfaces. They wire your app to external systems like Pulsar, Kafka, or NATS. These contain all the code for producing or consuming events. Place them in folders like `internal/adapters/pulsarproducer` or `internal/adapters/pulsarconsumer`.
- **Domain code** should not know anything about Pulsar or any message broker. It only relies on the ports you defined. This isolation makes it easier to write tests, change infrastructure later, or even switch to a different broker.

This structure keeps your code clean and focused. Your domain logic stays independent, while adapters handle the external integration details.

Generics

In Go, generics allow you to write reusable functions and types that work with any data type. Instead of repeating the same logic for each struct, you can define a single generic implementation.

Here's a simple example:

```
func Box[T any](v T) T { return v }
```

This function takes a value `v` of any type `T` and returns it. The `[T any]` part declares that `T` is a type parameter that can be anything.

In our event-driven system, we'll use `T` to represent the type of message we are sending or receiving—for example, `ports.AssignmentCreated`. A generic **producer** will serialize a `T` into bytes. A generic **consumer** will take those bytes, deserialize them back into `T`, and hand them to your application logic. This keeps the messaging code reusable and type-safe across your entire service.

Messaging Ports (Generic, Reusable)

This section defines the messaging interfaces your domain code depends on. These are called **ports**, and they describe *what* your application expects from a messaging system—not *how* it works behind the scenes.

```
package ports

import "context"

// Encoder/Decoder isolate schema mechanics (Avro via hamba, etc.).
type Encoder[T any] func(T) ([]byte, error)
type Decoder[T any] func([]byte) (T, error)

// Message carries decoded payload + minimal metadata.
type Message[T any] struct {
   Key      string
   Value    T
```

```
    Attempt  int // redelivery count (if available)
    Metadata map[string]string
    Ack      func() error // ack on success
    Nack     func() error // request redelivery
}

// Outbound port for publishing events (incl. DLQ).
type EventProducer[T any] interface {
    Send(ctx context.Context, value T) (string, error)
}

// Business logic hook. Your app implements this per event.
type Processor[T any] interface {
    Process(ctx context.Context, msg Message[T]) error
}

// Inbound port: the consumer owns receive/ack/nack plumbing and delegates
to Processor.
type EventConsumer[T any] interface {
    // Start registers the Processor and begins consuming until ctx is done
    or a fatal error occurs.
    Start(ctx context.Context, processor Processor[T]) error
    Stop(ctx context.Context) error
}
```

Enterprise Tip Notice that the Message struct includes Ack and Nack functions. This gives your business logic full control over acknowledgment. You don't need to deal with broker-level retries or redelivery tracking manually—it's abstracted here.

The EventConsumer interface accepts a Processor at startup. In fact, the processor is where you implement your business logic. This design allows you to reuse the same consumer infrastructure across multiple event types simply by implementing a new processor.

If you ever need to run multiple jobs on the same message—for example, logging, metrics, and business logic—you have two options:

1. Extend the `Start` method to accept a list of processors.
2. Wrap multiple jobs inside a single `Processor` implementation.

To keep this example simple, we are not doing that here. But the flexibility is already built into the design.

Adding the Pulsar Go Client to Your Project

To start using Apache Pulsar in your Go project, first add the official Pulsar Go client to your module:

```
go get github.com/apache/pulsar-client-go/pulsar
```

This command downloads the Pulsar client library, which includes everything you need to produce and consume messages.

After running it, your `go.mod` file will include a line similar to

```
require (
    github.com/apache/pulsar-client-go v0.17.0 // example version
)
```

You're now ready to interact with Pulsar in your code. This library gives you access to features like schema support, shared subscriptions, and message acknowledgment out of the box.

Connecting to Pulsar

Once you've added the Pulsar Go client to your project, the next step is to connect your application to a Pulsar broker. The client is your entry point for creating producers and consumers.

Here's a basic example of how to connect to a local Pulsar instance:

```
client, err := pulsar.NewClient(pulsar.ClientOptions{
    URL: "pulsar://localhost:6650",
})
if err != nil {
    log.Fatal().Err(err).Msg("Failed to connect to Pulsar")
}
```

This code tries to open a connection to the broker at `localhost:6650`. If the connection fails, the application exits immediately with a clear error message. This is important for system reliability—if your service can't connect to the broker, it should not continue running in a broken state.

In Go applications, wiring dependencies like this is usually done in the `main` function. That means the `main` function is responsible for creating the Pulsar client and passing it into the rest of your application.

In production environments, the broker URL comes from configuration. Use a config struct or environment variable instead of hard-coding it.

This simple setup ensures your service is ready to publish or consume messages through Pulsar reliably.

Reusable Generic Producer

In most Go projects that use messaging, developers end up writing the same producer logic again and again—only the topic, schema, or event type changes. This duplication grows fast in enterprise systems with many events. Go generics give us a better solution: one reusable producer for all event types. Let's walk through how to build this.

We define a generic `Producer[T]` type that wraps Pulsar's native producer:

```
type Producer[T any] struct {
   topic    string
   encoder  ports.Encoder[T]
   producer pulsar.Producer
}
```

The type parameter T allows this producer to work with any event type, like AssignmentCreated, NotificationIssued, or any other schema-defined struct.

To create a producer, we call NewProducer, which receives a ProducerConfig[T] with the client, topic, schema, and optional encoder:

```
func NewProducer[T any](cfg ProducerConfig[T]) (*Producer[T], error)
```

Inside this function, the key part is

```
opts := pulsar.ProducerOptions{Topic: cfg.Topic}
if cfg.Schema != nil {
```

```
    opts.Schema = cfg.Schema
}
prod, err := cfg.Client.CreateProducer(opts)
```

We prepare the producer with the topic name and schema (like Avro), and then call Pulsar's CreateProducer. The returned producer is wrapped in our generic Producer[T], which knows how to encode and send your message.

Now comes the Send method, which handles serialization and delivery:

```
func (p *Producer[T]) Send(ctx context.Context, payload T) (string, error)
```

Here's the important logic: We send the message and return the message ID:

```
msgID, err := p.producer.Send(ctx, &msg)
```

This makes the Send method flexible: it supports messages based on the schema, and you don't need to copy this logic for each message type.

The producer also includes a `Close` method to release resources when the application shuts down gracefully:

```
func (p *Producer[T]) Close() {
    p.producer.Close()
}
```

This ensures all pending messages are flushed, and the connection is properly cleaned up.

Once this generic producer is in place, creating a concrete one becomes a short and consistent task. For example, to create a producer for `AssignmentCreated` events:

```
schema := pulsar.NewAvroSchema(string(avroschemas.Assignment), nil)
prod, err := NewProducer(ProducerConfig[ports.AssignmentCreated]{
    Client: client,
    Topic:  "assignments",
    Schema: schema,
})
```

Now, you have a strongly typed producer that can send `AssignmentCreated` messages without writing any new boilerplate.

This pattern reduces code duplication, improves safety, and helps teams stay consistent. In enterprise systems where events grow quickly, a single generic producer like this can save hundreds of lines of code and many bugs.

Reusable Generic Consumer

In most enterprise systems, every message consumer follows the same flow: receive a message, decode it, run business logic, and ack or nack the result. Only the message type and the processing logic change. That's why you can build one reusable, type-safe consumer using Go generics and use it for any topic.

The heart of this consumer is the generic `Consumer[T]`:

```go
type Consumer[T any] struct {
   consumer pulsar.Consumer
   decoder  ports.Decoder[T]
}
```

Here, `T` represents the event type (like `NotificationIssued`). We also support an optional custom decoder—for example, if you use Avro.

To configure a consumer, we use `ConsumerConfig[T]`. It contains the required configs to create a Pulsar consumer, like

- `Topic`: The Pulsar topic name
- `Subscription`: The consumer group name
- `Schema` or `Decoder`: How to convert bytes into a typed value

To create the consumer:

```go
opts := pulsar.ConsumerOptions{
    Topic:            cfg.Topic,
    SubscriptionName: cfg.Subscription,
    Type:             cfg.SubscriptionType,
}
if cfg.Schema != nil {
    opts.Schema = cfg.Schema
}
consumer, err := cfg.Client.Subscribe(opts)
```

This prepares the Pulsar subscription. Our default is shared subscriptions, so you can scale consumers horizontally.

The main logic lives in the `Start` method. It runs a loop that

1. Waits for the next message using `consumer.Receive`
2. Decodes the payload using your decoder or schema
3. Wraps the result into a `Message[T]`, which contains the value and ack/nack handlers
4. Calls your `Processor[T]` implementation to handle the message

The most important part looks like this:

```
wrapped := ports.Message[T]{
    Value:   value,
    Ack:     func() error { return c.consumer.Ack(msg) },
    Nack:    func() { c.consumer.Nack(msg) },
    // other fields like metadata or redelivery count...
}
```

This gives your business logic full control over how and when to acknowledge the message. To consume a message, you just implement a processor. For example:

```
func (p captureProcessor) Process(ctx context.Context, msg ports.
Message[ports.NotificationIssued]) error {
    select {
    case p.ch <- msg.Value:
        return nil
    case <-ctx.Done():
        return ctx.Err()
    }
}
```

This decouples consumer wiring from message handling. You can now reuse the same consumer for any message type—just pass a different processor.

To wire it all together:

```
schema := pulsar.NewAvroSchema(string(avroschemas.Notification), nil)

consumer, err := NewConsumer(ConsumerConfig[ports.NotificationIssued]{
    Client:       client,
    Topic:        "notifications",
```

```
    Subscription: subscriptionName,
    Schema:       schema,
})
```

This reusable structure becomes especially powerful when your project handles dozens of topics. You avoid duplicated code and keep your messaging logic consistent.

Handling Failures with a DLQ

Not all messages can be processed successfully—some might be malformed or trigger business errors. To avoid losing them or retrying forever, enterprise systems use a **Dead Letter Queue (DLQ)**. The easiest way to handle DLQ is DLQ configuration in ConsumerOptions, but if you need to do extra actions or you need to create a different message, manual implementation can be helpful.

Not all messages can be processed successfully—some might be malformed or trigger business errors. To avoid losing them or retrying forever, enterprise systems use a **Dead Letter Queue (DLQ)**.

You don't need a new producer for DLQ. Just reuse the existing `Producer[T]` and call its `Send` method when processing fails. You can extend the consumer to accept a DLQ producer and send failed messages there for later inspection or recovery.

This pattern keeps your event pipeline safe, recoverable, and production-ready. Remember: DLQ producer and other producers have the same job: produce a message. You can easily reuse the same generic implementation.

Performance Tuning Guide by Design Goal

Every distributed system has different design goals (latency, throughput, fault tolerance, etc.). It's almost impossible to have all of them at the same time as a first priority. This guide groups Pulsar Go client settings (producer, consumer, client) by system priorities: **low latency**, **high throughput**, **fault tolerance**, and **resource efficiency**. For each goal, we explain what it means and list relevant configuration options, noting defaults and tuning trade-offs. Throughout, we assume the latest Pulsar Go client (v0.18.0) and Go environment, as of late 2026. But similar configs can apply to other message brokers.

Low Latency

Low latency means minimizing the time from producing a message to the topic, being received by the consumer. To optimize latency, we generally **turn off buffering and batching** and use smaller timeouts. In the Pulsar client:

- **Producer.DisableBatching** (default `false`)**:** Batching on (default) collects multiple messages before sending, which **improves throughput but adds delay**. For lowest latency, set `DisableBatching=true` so each message is sent immediately. Disabling batching sacrifices throughput and uses more network calls. You can also tune batching buffers (`BatchingMaxPublishDelay`, `BatchingMaxMessages`, `BatchingMaxSize`) to send sooner.
- **Producer.SendTimeout** (default 30s)**:** Time to wait for a broker ACK. Lowering this (or even disabling by setting `-1`) causes failed sends to error out faster, which keeps the client responsive (at the risk of more send errors if the network is slow). For strict low-latency use cases, shorten this timeout; if reliability is more important, keep it longer.
- **Producer.DisableBlockIfQueueFull** (default `false`)**:** When the producer's internal queue is full, the client can either block or return an error. With default `false`, calls to `Send`/`SendAsync` will block (and accumulate wait time). Setting `DisableBlockIfQueueFull=true` makes the call fail immediately on a full queue, avoiding long blocks (good for latency) but dropping messages if the application isn't keeping up.
- **Producer.MaxPendingMessages** (default 1000)**:** Size of the producer's outbound queue. A large queue can buffer many messages but also add queuing delay. For lowest latency, you might reduce this so the client errors out or slows when overloaded, rather than piling up messages.
- **Consumer.ReceiverQueueSize** (default 1000)**:** How many messages to prefetch to the consumer before the app calls `Receive()`. A high value boosts throughput but uses memory. For low consumer-side latency, you could use a smaller queue (or enable zero-queue mode)

so each message is delivered on-demand, avoiding extra buffering delay. Pulsar even supports **EnableZeroQueueConsumer** (`false` by default) to turn off prefetch entirely (queue size = 0). That minimizes memory but means the consumer will explicitly fetch each message (which can reduce throughput).

- **Consumer.NackRedeliveryDelay** (default 1 minute)**:** Delay before re-delivering a negatively-acked message. The default one minute means failed messages are retried much later, which is bad for the end-to-end latency of recovery. For faster retry (lower *latency to redelivery*), set this to a shorter interval (e.g., a few seconds). For scenarios where retries can wait, you may keep it longer.
- **Consumer.AckGroupingOptions** (default group up to 1000 acks or 100ms)**:** By default, the Go client batches ACKs up to 1000 or 100ms. This saves network calls but can delay the consumer's acks. To minimize latency (getting ACKs to the broker immediately), disable grouping by setting `AckGroupingOptions` to a smaller maxTime.
- **Client.ConnectionTimeout** (default 5s) and **OperationTimeout** (default 30s)**:** These affect how long the client waits to connect or perform operations. For very low latency (and willing to fail fast), you might shorten them so the client doesn't hang on a slow broker. If set too short, operations may fail unnecessarily.
- **Client.MaxConnectionsPerBroker** (default 1)**:** Number of TCP connections the client keeps to each broker. More connections can allow more concurrent in-flight requests, potentially lowering queuing delay under load. Raising this may improve both throughput and latency (at the cost of more sockets/threads).

In practice, Pulsar's producer enforces a trade-off: **either low latency or high throughput** (not both). Disabling batching and using small buffers achieves low latency but limits throughput, whereas enabling large batches yields high throughput with higher tail latency.

High Throughput

High throughput means maximizing messages (or bytes) processed per second. To boost throughput, we typically **enable buffering, batching, and parallelism**, at the expense of higher latency or memory. Relevant options:

- **Producer.DisableBatching:** Keep this `false` (batching enabled). Batching coalesces multiple messages into one request, dramatically improving throughput.
- **Producer.BatchingMaxPublishDelay** (default 10ms)**:** This is how long the client waits to fill a batch. You can increase it (e.g., to 50ms or higher) to allow more messages per batch. This increases throughput but adds up to that delay for each batch.
- **Producer.BatchingMaxMessages** (default 1000) and **BatchingMaxSize** (128KB)**:** Increase these thresholds to allow larger batches (more messages or larger total size). Larger batches improve throughput but use more memory and add processing delay before the batch is sent.
- **Producer.MaxPendingMessages:** Increase this above the default 1000 to let more messages queue up for sending under heavy load. A larger queue keeps the pipeline full. Ensure `DisableBlockIfQueueFull=false` so that the producer waits (instead of dropping) when the queue is full.
- **Producer.CompressionType** (default `NoCompression`)**:** Enable compression (e.g., LZ4 or ZSTD) to reduce data sent over the network, which can raise throughput, especially for large payloads. (Be mindful that compression uses CPU. If CPU is the bottleneck, you might skip it.)
- **Producer.EnableChunking** (default `false`)**:** For very large messages, chunking breaks them into smaller pieces. Chunking disables batching, but it allows handling large payloads. Use it if the message size exceeds broker limits, although chunking can slightly reduce throughput due to overhead.

- **Consumer.ReceiverQueueSize:** Increase beyond 1000 (the default) to prefetch more messages. A larger queue (e.g., 5000+) lets the consumer receive messages in advance, boosting throughput in bursty or high-rate scenarios. This uses more memory, however.
- **Consumer.EnableAutoScaledReceiverQueueSize** (default `false`)**:** If enabled, Pulsar will grow the receive queue up to a max (based on throughput). This can yield higher throughput when needed, then shrink back to save memory.
- **Consumer.SubscriptionType:** Use a parallel subscription mode. The default **Exclusive** (one consumer) limits scale. Switching to **Shared** (multiple consumers on the same subscription) or **Key_Shared** (parallel consumers by key) allows multiple consumers to work in parallel, greatly increasing end-to-end throughput. (Failover mode also allows one standby.) By default, Pulsar uses `Exclusive`, so choose `Shared` or `Key_Shared` if you want multiple clients consuming concurrently.
- **Consumer.EnableBatchIndexAcknowledgment** (default `false`)**:** If brokers send messages in batches, enabling batch-index ack lets the consumer ack individual messages within a batch. This can improve throughput in some cases (fewer round-trips), but requires to be enabled on the broker as well.
- **Consumer.AckGroupingOptions:** The default grouping (up to 100ms or 1000 acks) is generally fine for throughput, reducing ACK overhead. You can keep or even increase grouping.
- **Client.MaxConnectionsPerBroker:** More connections (e.g., >1) allow the client to pipeline requests in parallel to the broker. This can increase aggregate throughput if one connection was the limit.
- **Client.ConnectionMaxIdleTime:** The default is 180s. For sustained throughput, you can leave it high (or `-1` to disable idle-close) so connections remain open. Lowering it causes idle connections to close, which may slightly reduce steady throughput.

To **measure throughput**, monitor metrics like the producer's **msgRateIn** and **msgThroughputIn** and the consumer's **msgRateOut**. Pulsar's admin stats or Prometheus metrics expose these metrics.

Failover and Resilience

Failover/resilience means the system keeps working despite failures (broker or client crashes, network blips). We tune retries, subscription modes, and fault handling:

- **SubscriptionType:** For consumer-side failover, choose `Failover` or `Shared` instead of `Exclusive`. In **Failover** mode, one consumer is active and others standby (triggering a *BecameActive/BecameInactive* event on failover). In **Shared** mode, multiple consumers share the workload–if one dies, the others continue consuming. Exclusive mode has no backup. By default, it is `Exclusive`.
- **Consumer.EventListener** (ConsumerEventListener)**:** You can supply an event listener to react when this consumer becomes active/ inactive.
- **Consumer.Dead-Letter Queue (DLQ):** Configure a **Consumer. DLQPolicy** to handle messages that consistently fail processing. This sends any message to the `DLQ topic` after specified failed acks. (By default, `DLQ=nil`, so no dead-lettering.) Use DLQ to prevent stuck re-delivery loops.
- **Consumer.RetryEnable** (default `false`)**:** When `true`, Pulsar will automatically retry failed messages by re-queuing them (to the subscription or a DLQ) according to the configured DLQ policy. Enable it if you want automatic retry logic.
- **MaxReconnectToBroker** (Producer and Consumer)**:** Both producer and consumer have a `MaxReconnectToBroker` option. By default, it is "ultimate" (no limit). This controls how many times the client will retry connecting to a broker after a disconnect. Keeping it unlimited (the default) means the client will keep trying indefinitely, which is usually best for resilience. If you prefer to fail quickly, you could set a finite number (e.g., five retries).
- **BackOffPolicyFunc** (Producer and Consumer)**:** You can plug in a custom backoff policy (min/max delay, jitter) for reconnections. The default backoff is exponential. Use this to tune how fast the client retries connections.

- **Producer.SendTimeout:** A too-short send timeout can cause spurious failures under load or transient issues. You may increase it (or disable) so that messages have more time to be acknowledged, improving reliability at the cost of possible longer hangs.
- **Producer.DisableBlockIfQueueFull:** For resilience, you often want the producer to block (default) rather than error, ensuring every message eventually gets sent. Keep this `false` so the client queues even when busy. (If you set it to `true`, you must handle the dropped-message errors.)
- **Client.ConnectionTimeout/OperationTimeout:** The defaults (5s and 30s) are usually fine. For flaky networks, you might increase `ConnectionTimeout` so the client waits longer for a broker, and increase `OperationTimeout` to allow more time for creating producers/consumers on busy brokers.
- **Client.KeepAliveInterval:** The default 30s is good for detecting dead peers. You can lower it if you need faster failure detection at the TCP level.
- **Client.MaxConnectionsPerBroker:** Multiple connections can improve availability: if one connection is interrupted, others still stand by. However, the Pulsar client usually uses one connection per logical producer/consumer. Only increase this if you have many logical producers to the same broker and want separate TCP paths.
- **Client.ConnectionMaxIdleTime** (default 180s)**:** Lowering this (toward 60s) will close idle connections faster, freeing resources if clients are idle. For resilience, you might leave it high or disable (`-1`), so connections are kept ready for use.

In short, resilience settings favor **longer timeouts, more retries, and parallel consumers**. Pulsar's client automatically handles reconnect and failover internally. You can monitor metrics to ensure the client is reconnecting as expected.

Memory and Resource Efficiency

Resource efficiency means using as little memory/CPU as possible while meeting requirements. Tuning for efficiency often **limits buffers and CPU work**, at the cost of throughput or latency:

- **Producer.MaxPendingMessages:** Lower this from 1000 to reduce the producer's internal buffer. A smaller queue means less memory, but the producer will start blocking (or erroring if `DisableBlockIfQueueFull=true`) sooner under load.
- **Producer.BatchingMaxMessages/BatchingMaxSize:** Reducing these limits means smaller batches, which use less memory. However, smaller batches reduce the throughput benefit of batching.
- **Producer.DisableBatching:** Batching requires memory to hold pending messages; disabling batching avoids that buffer. If memory is very tight, you could disable batching (and also chunking) so messages go directly out. This saves memory but dramatically increases per-message overhead.
- **Producer.CompressionType** (default none)**:** Compression uses CPU (and some extra memory). If you are CPU-constrained or run on very lightweight clients, you might keep compression off (as it is by default) to save CPU.
- **Consumer.ReceiverQueueSize:** Reduce from 1000 to a smaller number to lower memory usage. E.g., 100 or 10 on low-memory devices. This will hurt throughput. As an extreme, setting **EnableZeroQueueConsumer=true** makes the consumer never prefetch, using minimal memory (one message at a time).
- **Consumer.EnableAutoScaledReceiverQueueSize:** If enabled, the client will shrink the queue when idle, saving memory during lulls.
- **Consumer.NackPrecisionBit** (default 8)**:** This trims internal clocks for NACK redelivery timing. A lower precision (e.g., 4 bits) uses less memory per pending message. Use it if you are extremely memory-limited, at the cost of coarser redelivery timing.

- **Client.MaxConnectionsPerBroker:** Keep this at 1 unless you truly need parallel connections. Each additional connection uses file handles and buffers.
- **Client.ConnectionMaxIdleTime:** Lowering the idle time (down to 60s min) closes unused connections sooner, freeing memory.
- **Client.MemoryLimitBytes** (default 64 MiB)**:** This caps the total heap memory the Pulsar client will use for buffering (e.g., pending messages, batches). By default, it is 64 MB ("to guarantee high throughput"). You can lower this to save memory, but be aware that it caps throughput. Setting it to a smaller value means the producer will start blocking or backpressuring when that memory is exhausted.
- **Others:** Fine-tune TLS and logging. For example, fewer TLS cipher suites or no SSL reduces CPU overhead (at security cost). Use a simple logger (default) to avoid extra CPU in logging.

In short, **smaller queues and buffers save memory** but throttle throughput. For example, a large `ReceiverQueueSize` greatly boosts throughput, whereas a very small queue keeps memory low at the cost of speed. The Pulsar docs note for `ReceiverQueueSize`: "Using a higher value could potentially increase the consumer throughput at the expense of bigger memory utilization." Similarly, batching and buffer limits in the producer use heap memory and CPU. Use this guide to match your Pulsar client settings to your system's goals. For low-latency paths, disable buffering and use short timeouts. For high throughput, enable large batches, prefetch, and parallel consumers. For fault tolerance, allow retries and multiple consumers. For tight resources, shrink buffers and disable extra features. Each setting has trade-offs, so choose based on your application's needs and measure with Pulsar's metrics.

Event-Driven Systems Quality Control

After developing the system, you need to make sure about its quality and maintainability. Tests help to make sure about quality before you deploy, but after deployment, you need to make sure what is happening in the deployed system.

Testing Event-Driven Systems

Testing event-driven systems requires more than unit tests. Messages cross process boundaries, schemas evolve, and timing plays an important role. A complete testing strategy must include multiple layers.

Unit Tests

Some parts of the eventing systems don't rely on message brokers, especially if you follow hexagonal architecture. For these parts like message processors, you can cover their business with unit tests. We already covered the test topic in Chapter 7.

Integration Testing with a Real Broker

Some behaviors cannot be tested without a real Pulsar broker. Schema registration, compatibility enforcement, redelivery timing, and dead-letter routing all require integration tests.

For these cases, use test containers; performance is not the goal here. Correctness and confidence are. We already covered integration tests in Chapter 17.

Monitoring and Observability

In an event-driven architecture, failures are rarely simple. Messages may arrive late, be retried many times, process slowly, or fail only under specific conditions. Without proper observability, these problems stay hidden until users report them. Good observability allows you to detect problems early, understand their impact, and react before the system becomes unstable.

At a minimum, a production-ready system should track the following metrics:

Message Lag

This shows how far consumers are behind producers. A growing lag usually means that consumers are too slow, under-provisioned, or blocked by downstream systems. It helps you to decide on the number of pods. If you have a lot of messages that are not processed, you can just increase the number of pods. When you are fine, turn them off to save money. It can be automatic in DevOps.

Processing Time

This measures how long it takes to process a single message. Sudden increases often point to slow databases, external APIs, or resource exhaustion. It helps the team to find bottlenecks before customers start to complain.

Error and Retry Rates

This includes how often messages are nacked, retried, or sent to a Dead Letter Queue. High values usually indicate poison messages, schema issues, or bugs in business logic.

Throughput

This shows how many messages are produced and consumed per second. Throughput metrics are essential for capacity planning and scaling decisions.

Using Pulsar's Built-in Metrics

Apache Pulsar exposes many broker-side metrics by default. These include topic throughput, backlog size, subscription lag, and redelivery counts. In most setups, these metrics are already available through Prometheus endpoints. Broker metrics are necessary, but they are not sufficient. They show what happens inside Pulsar, not what happens inside your application code.

Always assign explicit names to producers and consumers. Named producers and consumers make broker metrics understandable. Without names, dashboards show anonymous connections, which makes debugging and analysis difficult. In production systems, naming is not a cosmetic detail. It is part of operational discipline.

Client-Side Metrics Are Mandatory

Pulsar clients expose limited internal metrics, but they do not understand your business logic. Only your code knows whether a message was processed successfully or why it failed. You should always instrument producers and consumers in your own code.

Common application-level metrics include

- Message processing duration
- Number of successful acknowledgments

- Number of nacks and retries
- Dead Letter Queue routing count

These metrics should be exposed through an HTTP endpoint, for example, `/metrics`, and scraped by Prometheus. This allows you to correlate broker-level behavior with application-level behavior.

A strong production practice is to deploy **producers and consumers as separate pods**, not embedded inside a larger application. Each pod should expose its own metrics endpoint. This gives you clean dashboards, clear ownership, and independent scaling.

Logging Events

In event-driven systems, metrics are not always enough. Metrics can tell you that something is wrong, but they usually cannot tell you **which event failed** or **where the failure happened**. When you need to answer these questions, logs become your primary investigation tool.

The most important principle for logging in event-driven systems is **traceability**. At a minimum, every producer and consumer should log the message ID (or event ID). This ID is critical. It allows you to follow a single event as it moves through producers, consumers, retries, and Dead Letter Queues. Without a stable identifier, log entries become disconnected messages with no clear story.

Logs should be structured, not free text. Use key/value fields such as `message_id`, `topic`, `subscription`, and `status`. This makes logs searchable and allows log aggregation systems to group related events automatically. When an incident happens, the ability to filter logs by message ID is often the difference between minutes and hours of debugging.

Avoid logging full message payloads or large data structures in production. This causes several serious problems:

- Logs become noisy and difficult to search.
- Sensitive or private data may be exposed.
- Storage and processing costs grow very fast.

In large systems, excessive logging increases operational costs and hides important signals in noise.

Exercises

1. Change ride service to send messages to the notification topic.
2. Why don't we use assignment messages in the notification topic?
3. Implement a consumer for assignment in vehicle service.

Summary

In this chapter, we explored how event-driven systems improve scalability, flexibility, and resilience in enterprise Go applications. We compared synchronous vs. asynchronous communication and showed how events reduce service coupling. We introduced messaging concepts like brokers, topics, partitions, and the publish/subscribe model. You learned how to define Avro schemas as stable published languages and how to generate Go types from them. Finally, we built generic producers and consumers using Go generics to simplify code reuse and discussed how to handle failures using a Dead Letter Queue (DLQ).

What's Next

You've seen how events help services communicate loosely and scale independently. But some interactions need speed, structure, and direct responses. In the next chapter, we'll explore gRPC: a high-performance communication protocol built on HTTP/2 and Protobuf. You'll learn how to define service contracts using `.proto` files, generate Go code, and implement fast, type-safe RPCs. We'll also cover streaming, deadlines, and how to keep your domain clean using adapters.

CHAPTER 19

gRPC on the Fast Lane: High-Performance Go Services

In real systems, not all communication can be asynchronous. Some workflows depend on a guaranteed, timely response. For these synchronous operations, two protocols are commonly used: REST and gRPC.

REST is widely known, supported by nearly every platform, and simple to test. Its openness makes it ideal for external clients and loosely coupled services. But as systems grow more connected and performance-sensitive, REST can become a bottleneck. Verbose payloads, text encoding, and repeated TCP handshakes start to cost time and resources.

gRPC approaches the same problem from a different angle. It uses Protocol Buffers to define messages and HTTP/2 as its transport. That combination enables compact binary data, persistent connections, and native streaming support. The result is a protocol designed for speed, efficiency, and long-term maintainability—especially in internal service-to-service communication.

Choosing between REST and gRPC is not just about syntax or trend. It's about understanding your system's needs, constraints, and communication patterns. A mature engineer doesn't default to one tool for every job. Instead, they learn both and apply them with intention.

In this chapter, we will take gRPC from theory to practice. You will learn what gRPC is, where it came from, and how it solves problems REST does not. We will walk through schema design with Protobuf, code generation using Go 1.25 tools, service implementation, and integration patterns that hold up under real-world traffic.

S. Shahsavan, *Building Enterprise Projects with Go*, https://doi.org/10.1007/979-8-8688-2370-1_19

Our goal is not to cover every detail, but to equip you to use gRPC well—and make good decisions when designing synchronous APIs in enterprise systems.

What Is gRPC

gRPC is a high-performance communication framework for distributed systems. It allows one service to call another using function-like requests, even if they run on different machines. With gRPC, services talk through clearly defined APIs and structured messages. It was introduced by Google in 2015 to improve how internal services exchange data, and today it is widely adopted in microservices.

Instead of relying on hand-written HTTP endpoints with text-based JSON objects, gRPC uses a combination of two modern tools:

- **Protocol Buffers (Protobuf):** A binary format for encoding messages. It is fast, compact, and strongly typed.
- **HTTP/2:** A network protocol that supports multiplexing, persistent connections, and streaming in both directions.

When combined, these features make gRPC well-suited for high-throughput, low-latency communication between services.

gRPC services are defined using `.proto` files. These files describe the RPC methods and the message formats. The `protoc` tool then generates code that provides typed clients and server interfaces. This workflow brings consistency, reduces boilerplate, and helps teams share contracts across services.

From Resources to Procedures

RESTful APIs are based on resources. You expose data through URLs and use verbs like GET or POST to act on them. For example, to retrieve a vehicle, you might call `GET /vehicles/123`.

gRPC uses procedures instead. You define a method such as `GetVehicleInfo` and specify its request and response types. It feels more like calling a local function—but behind the scenes, gRPC handles the transport and encoding. This model is more expressive when working with business actions and service-to-service calls.

This shift matches Go's focus on explicit behavior. By keeping method signatures clear and consistent, gRPC helps you write code that is both predictable and testable.

Multi-language, Strongly Typed

One of gRPC's key strengths is that it works across many programming languages. You define your API once in Protobuf, and gRPC generates native clients and servers in Go, Java, Python, C#, Kotlin, and more.

This is especially helpful in enterprise environments where not every team uses the same language. For example, a Go-based Ride Service can safely call a machine learning model written in Python without needing to manually map fields or serialize data. The Protobuf schema keeps all sides in sync.

Understanding Protocol Buffers

Protocol Buffers, or Protobuf, is a cross-language system for defining structured data and turning it into fast, compact binary messages. Developed at Google, it powers gRPC as both the message format and the schema definition language.

In a distributed system, services need a shared understanding of the data they send and receive. Protobuf solves this by using a `.proto` file—a simple text file that describes your data models and the remote procedures that operate on them. Each field in a Protobuf message has a name, a type, and a unique numeric tag. These tags are used for encoding, not the field names, which keeps the binary output small and consistent.

Here's a real-world example from our transport system:

```
message InfoResponse {
  string vehicleId = 1;
  string type = 2;   // bus, tram, taxi
  string status = 3;
}
```

This definition becomes the contract (published language). You compile it with the `protoc` tool and the Go plug-in, which generates a strongly typed Go struct and helper functions. This eliminates manual marshalling logic, reduces bugs, and gives you compile-time checks across services.

Protobuf also supports service definitions. For example, our VehicleService declares an RPC method like this:

```
service VehicleService {
  rpc GetVehicleInfo(InfoRequest) returns (InfoResponse);
}
```

From this, gRPC generates both the server interface and the client stub. In Go, calling a remote method like `GetVehicleInfo` feels almost like calling a local function. Behind the scenes, gRPC handles encoding, transport, connection reuse, and error wrapping.

But Protobuf is more than just a format or toolchain. Its design helps services evolve safely over time. You can add new fields without breaking old clients. You can reserve field numbers to avoid accidental collisions. You can clearly document each part of your API (like OpenAPI). These features matter in long-lived systems where contracts must be reliable and changes must not cause production failures.

Why Protobuf Improves Performance

Because Protobuf messages are binary and schema-aware, they are much smaller than JSON or XML. In typical service calls, switching from JSON to Protobuf can reduce payload size. This reduces bandwidth use and lowers memory pressure on clients and servers.

Protobuf messages are also fast to encode and decode. The generated Go code uses tight memory layouts and avoids reflection, which improves performance under load. This becomes especially important in services that handle large volumes of traffic or communicate frequently between internal components.

In cloud-based enterprise systems designed to run for decades, even small performance gains can translate into major savings in cost and infrastructure over time. Protobuf brings performance, safety, and clarity—all essential traits in modern enterprise systems. It helps teams avoid versioning pain, reduce runtime costs, and move faster with confidence.

Built for Real-Time Interactions

gRPC supports more than just simple request/response. Because it runs on HTTP/2, it can stream data in both directions. This enables four styles of communication:

- **Unary:** One request, one response.
- **Server Streaming:** One request, many streamed responses.
- **Client Streaming:** Many streamed requests, one response.
- **Bidirectional Streaming:** Both sides send and receive streams.

This is useful when working with real-time systems. For instance, the Ride Service can stream assignment updates to the Vehicle Service rather than polling every few seconds. Streaming also helps when handling large results, telemetry feeds, or long-lived connections.

Production Features That Matter

gRPC is not just fast. It is designed to support the needs of real systems:

- Every call accepts a `context.Context`, so you can enforce timeouts, propagate request metadata, and handle cancellations.
- You can define interceptors to add cross-cutting concerns such as logging, tracing, or access control.
- TLS encryption is built in, making it easy to secure internal traffic.
- Deadlines and retries are part of the client API, helping prevent slow or stuck services from dragging down others.

Where gRPC Fits in Enterprise Architectures

As systems grow in size and complexity, communication becomes a design choice with long-term consequences. Choosing the right protocol is not just a matter of syntax or serialization format. It affects team boundaries, evolution speed, testing, monitoring, and system resilience.

While gRPC is powerful, it is not always the right tool for every interface. In most enterprise systems, a good rule of thumb is this: **use REST for external communication and gRPC for internal service-to-service calls**.

Let's break that down.

REST for the Outside World

Public APIs must be stable, loosely coupled, and well-documented. They're often consumed by external systems, mobile apps, browser clients, or even third parties. In these situations, REST remains the better choice.

REST works over plain HTTP/1.1, is easy to debug with tools like `curl`, and doesn't require the client to generate code or understand your Protobuf schema. JSON is verbose, but it's human-readable and compatible with almost every platform by default.

This loose coupling is critical. Clients evolve independently and may lag behind your internal deployments by months or years. REST's flexibility makes it easier to deprecate slowly, version routes, and keep the boundary between systems soft enough to survive organizational change.

In fact, Go's `net/http` standard library still forms the backbone of many production-grade REST APIs today.

gRPC for Internal Communication

Inside your system, the trade-offs change. Between services that you control, speed, structure, and strong typing matter more than human readability. You want compact payloads, efficient serialization, and formal contracts that both sides agree on. gRPC gives you exactly that.

It replaces brittle HTTP endpoints and ad hoc payloads with strongly typed RPCs. You define the schema once in a `.proto` file, generate idiomatic Go interfaces, and let the framework take care of transport, deadlines, and retries.

Because gRPC uses HTTP/2, connections are persistent and multiplexed. That means fewer open sockets, less connection churn, and better resource usage under load. For systems with high internal call volume—such as scheduling engines, fleet dispatchers, or assignment trackers—these savings scale quickly.

With gRPC, service boundaries are enforced by the compiler. This helps avoid accidental misuse, reduces duplication, and builds trust between teams that maintain separate services but share a code contract.

gRPC in Web Browsers

gRPC works very well between back-end services, but browsers operate under stricter constraints. JavaScript APIs such as Fetch and XMLHttpRequest intentionally hide low-level HTTP/2 details, including frame control and response trailers. Because native gRPC depends on full control over HTTP/2 for framing and status propagation, browsers cannot speak the real gRPC wire protocol directly. Any use of gRPC in the browser must adapt to the web platform rather than use native gRPC end-to-end.

To bridge this gap, the gRPC-Web was introduced. gRPC-Web is not native gRPC; it is a compatibility layer that maps gRPC-style calls onto standard HTTP POST requests that browsers can send. Protobuf messages are placed in the HTTP request and response bodies, and information that would normally be carried in HTTP/2 trailers is encoded into the message stream. This makes gRPC-style APIs accessible from browsers, but with clear limitations. Browsers cannot stream request bodies, so gRPC-Web does not support client-side or true bi-directional streaming; only unary calls work reliably, with limited support for server-side streaming. In some deployments, messages are Base64-encoded (`grpcwebtext`) to pass through older proxies, which increases size and CPU cost. In addition, requests usually pass through a proxy such as Envoy, which translates gRPC-Web HTTP traffic back into native gRPC over HTTP/2, meaning the browser never talks gRPC directly.

gRPC-Web makes it possible for web applications to call gRPC-based systems, but it does so by wrapping gRPC messages inside normal HTTP requests. This works well for simple request/response interactions, but it reduces available gRPC features and follows the same security and transport rules as any browser API.

Understanding these limits helps explain why many systems use gRPC internally while exposing REST APIs to web clients.

The BFF Pattern: A Real-World Use Case

One common enterprise pattern is the **Backend for Frontend** (BFF). The BFF acts as a gateway tailored to a specific client type—for example, a mobile app or dashboard UI. It exposes a RESTful API to the outside, shaped for that client's needs. But behind the scenes, it orchestrates data from multiple internal services. Figure 19-1 shows an example of Backend for Frontend.

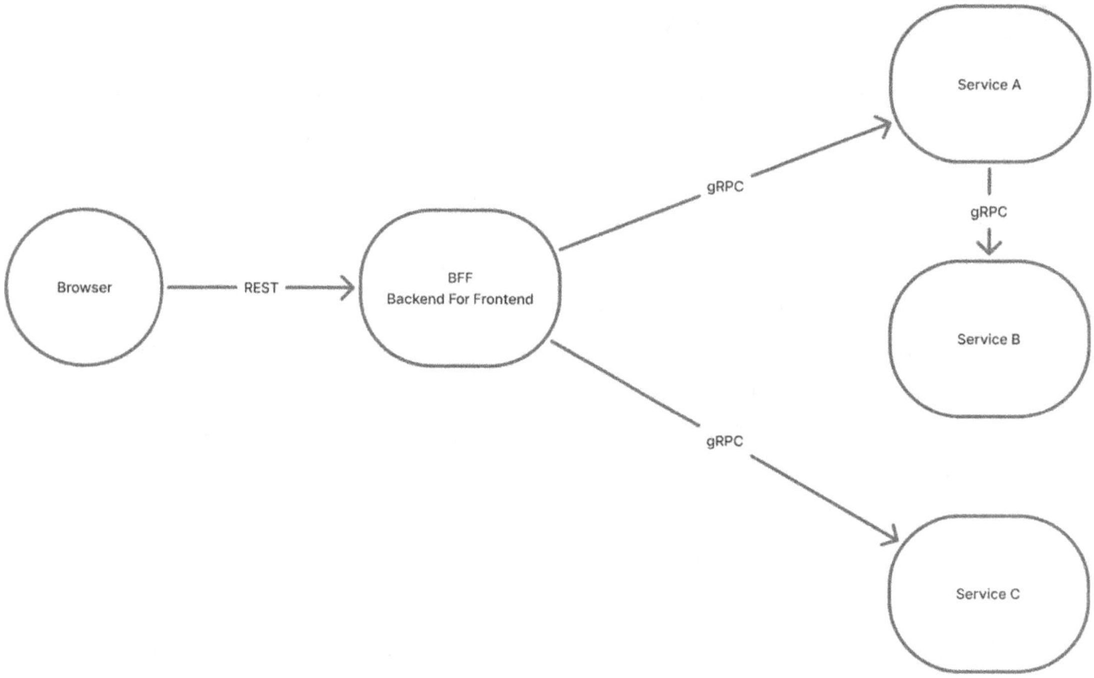

***Figure 19-1.** Backend for Frontend pattern using gRPC for internal service calls*

Inside the BFF, we can call services like `RideService`, `VehicleService`, and `RoutePlanner` using gRPC. These services might return compact Protobuf messages, stream updates, or enforce deadlines that REST can't express cleanly. The BFF handles translation: it converts RESTful client requests into gRPC calls, aggregates the results, and shapes them into a response the front end understands.

This approach keeps the client boundary flexible while letting internal systems optimize for performance and clarity.

Defining Protobuf Contracts

Every gRPC service starts with a `.proto` file. This file defines both the structure of your data and the shape of your service interface. It is the contract that connects producers and consumers—and from it, Protobuf generates client and server code across multiple languages, including Go.

In this section, you'll learn how to define Protobuf files using idiomatic syntax. We'll walk through how to set up a `.proto` file, declare messages, describe services, and use comments for clarity—all using real examples from our Vehicle module.

Starting a .proto File

A valid Protobuf file begins with two standard lines:

```
syntax = "proto3";
package vehiclepb;
```

- `syntax = "proto3"` sets the language version. Always use `proto3` unless you are working with legacy systems.
- `package vehiclepb` groups your definitions under a namespace. This helps prevent conflicts across modules or teams.

For Go projects, you also need to define the Go import path for generated code:

```
option go_package = "github.com/yourname/transport/vehicle/internal/
vehiclepb;vehiclepb";
```

This line controls how the generated code maps to your Go module. Without it, import paths may break or conflict during builds. The last part (`;vehiclepb`) sets the Go package name.

Defining Messages

A Protobuf message is like a Go struct. It holds typed fields, each with a unique tag number that determines its binary position in the encoded payload.

Here's an example request message:

```
message InfoRequest {
  string vehicleId = 1;
}
```

Each field has

- A name (`vehicleId`)
- A type (`string`)
- A tag number (`1`)

Tag numbers must be unique within a message. Once published, never reuse or reassign them. If a field is removed, mark its number as reserved to avoid accidental reuse.

Messages can carry more data. For example:

```
message InfoResponse {
  string vehicleId = 1;
  string type = 2;   // bus, tram, taxi
  string status = 3;
}
```

Protobuf supports standard types like `string`, `int32`, `bool`, `float`, and `double`. Use them precisely:

- Use `string` for identifiers, names, and categories.
- Use `bool` for binary flags, like `accepted` in `AssignmentAck`.
- Avoid overly generic types like `bytes` or `map` unless absolutely required.

Keep your messages simple and flat. Nested structures and untyped fields can make contracts harder to maintain and test.

Defining Services

Once your data types are in place, you define the gRPC service using a `service` block. Here's an example from our vehicle module:

```
service VehicleService {
  rpc GetVehicleInfo(InfoRequest) returns (InfoResponse);
}
```

Each `rpc` line defines a method signature, including

- A method name (`GetVehicleInfo`)
- A request message type (`InfoRequest`)
- A response message type (`InfoResponse`)

Use action-based names for your methods. gRPC defines behaviors, not resources. Stick with clear verbs like `Find`, `Get`, or `Stream` to communicate intent.

To define a streaming RPC, use the `stream` keyword:

```
rpc StreamAssignments(stream AssignmentRequest) returns (stream
AssignmentAck);
```

This creates a bidirectional stream. Both client and server can send messages over the same open connection. It's especially useful for scenarios like continuous assignment updates, live telemetry, or negotiations.

Comments and Field Conventions

Protobuf supports inline comments using `//`. Use them generously to document expected values, field formats, or business rules:

```
string status = 2; // available, maintenance, assigned
```

These comments carry over generated code across most languages and help clarify intent—especially for developers working on other teams or languages.

You can also group related fields, annotate optional fields, or mark deprecated ones using standard conventions. Keep your `.proto` files readable—they are the shared language between your services and teams.

Generating Go Code from Protobuf

Once your `.proto` file defines the messages and RPC services you need, it's time to turn that schema into actual Go code. This step generates

- Strongly typed structs for your messages
- gRPC service interfaces
- Client stubs to call other services

To generate this code, you need the Protobuf compiler (`protoc`) and Go-specific plug-ins that integrate Protobuf and gRPC with the Go toolchain.

Install the Required Tools

Start by installing the Go plug-ins using go install:

```
# Go plugin for generating Protobuf message types
go install google.golang.org/protobuf/cmd/protoc-gen-go@latest

# Go plugin for generating gRPC service code
go install google.golang.org/grpc/cmd/protoc-gen-go-grpc@latest
```

These plug-ins will be installed under your Go binary path (typically `$GOPATH/bin` or `$HOME/go/bin`). Make sure the directory is included in your system PATH, so that `protoc` can access the tools.

> **Tip** If you haven't installed `protoc` yet, follow the official guide:
>
> `https://grpc.io/docs/protoc-installation/`

You'll only need to set this up once. After that, any `.proto` file in your project can be compiled to Go using the same command.

Generate Code with protoc

Assuming your schema file is located at `proto/vehicle.proto`, and you want the generated Go code to be placed inside the `internal/grpc/` directory of your module, run the following:

```
protoc \
  --proto_path=proto \
  --go_out=internal/grpc \
  --go_opt=paths=source_relative \
  --go-grpc_out=internal/grpc \
  --go-grpc_opt=paths=source_relative \
  proto/vehicle.proto
```

Let's unpack what this command does:

- `--proto_path=proto`: Tells `protoc` where to look for `.proto` files

- `--go_out=internal/grpc`: Writes the generated message types (structs) into the `internal/grpc/` directory
- `--go-grpc_out=internal/grpc`: Writes the gRPC service interface and client code into the same location
- `paths=source_relative`: Ensures generated files stay in the same relative path as their source file (useful for clean imports)

This convention helps your project remain Go module-friendly and ensures consistency across different environments.

What You'll See

After running the command, you should have two new files in your `internal/grpc/` folder:

- vehicle.pb.go: Contains all message types, like FindRequest, InfoResponse, and AssignmentAck
- vehicle_grpc.pb.go: Contains the service interface, which looks like this:

```go
type VehicleServiceServer interface {
	FindAvailableVehicle(context.Context, *FindRequest)
	(*FindResponse, error)
	GetVehicleInfo(context.Context, *InfoRequest)
	(*InfoResponse, error)
	StreamAssignments(grpc.BidiStreamingServer[Assignment
	Request, AssignmentAck]) error
	mustEmbedUnimplementedVehicleServiceServer()
}
```

This interface defines the contract your server must implement. You'll write an adapter that handles each RPC, translating Protobuf messages into your domain models and back again.

Enterprise Tip Never edit the generated files. They're regenerated every time you change your `.proto` file. Always treat them as read-only build artifacts.

With this setup in place, you're ready to connect your service logic and build a working gRPC server.

Implementing a gRPC Server in Go

Once you've defined your `.proto` file and generated the corresponding Go code, it's time to build the actual server. The gRPC toolchain has already created an interface like `VehicleServiceServer`. Your job now is to implement that interface and connect it to your domain logic.

This section explains how to build that adapter, handle streaming RPCs, register your service with the gRPC runtime, and organize your code for clarity and testability.

Build the Adapter

The generated interface is only a contract. You still need to write a concrete type that implements each method.

For example, if your `.proto` file includes these RPCs:

- `FindAvailableVehicle`: Unary RPC for quick lookups
- `GetVehicleInfo`: Unary RPC with structured output
- `StreamAssignments`: Bidirectional streaming RPC for live updates

Then the Go plug-in creates an interface like this:

```
type VehicleServiceServer interface {
	FindAvailableVehicle(context.Context, *FindRequest)
	(*FindResponse, error)
	GetVehicleInfo(context.Context, *InfoRequest) (*InfoResponse, error)
	StreamAssignments(grpc.BidiStreamingServer[AssignmentRequest,
	AssignmentAck]) error
	mustEmbedUnimplementedVehicleServiceServer()
}
```

Your implementation might look like this:

```
type Service struct {
    vehiclepb.UnimplementedVehicleServiceServer
```

```
    repo VehicleRepository
}

func (s *Service) FindAvailableVehicle(ctx context.Context, req *vehiclepb.
FindRequest) (*vehiclepb.FindResponse, error) {
    // Convert request to domain input
    // Call your domain service
    // Return a response
}
```

This adapter pattern lets your core business logic stay clean. The gRPC layer stays focused on input/output translation and network interaction.

Enterprise Lesson Always isolate domain logic from transport details. Treat the gRPC handler as an adapter, not a home for business rules. This helps you test logic separately and adapt to future changes without breaking contracts.

Use the Unimplemented Base

Your service struct should embed `UnimplementedVehicleServiceServer`. This is a safety net. If the `.proto` definition changes and adds new RPCs, your code still compiles—but returns an "unimplemented" error until you handle them.

```
type Service struct {
    vehiclepb.UnimplementedVehicleServiceServer
}
```

This is especially useful in large systems where service evolution happens gradually.

Implement Streaming RPCs

Streaming RPCs, like `StreamAssignments`, give you full control over a two-way connection. You can receive multiple messages from the client and respond to each one—without closing the connection.

Inside the method:

- Use `stream.Recv()` to read client messages.
- Use `stream.Send()` to reply.
- Handle `io.EOF` to detect when the client closes the stream.
- Use context deadlines to avoid hanging connections.

This model is ideal for high-frequency updates, such as live vehicle status changes or negotiation loops.

Register the Server

gRPC server must remain stable under load, observable during failures, and secure by default. To make your service respond to incoming RPCs, you must register it with the gRPC server runtime. Server options are the primary control surface for achieving goals:

```
opts := []grpc.ServerOption{
        grpc.UnaryInterceptor(LoggingUnaryInterceptor),
        grpc.StreamInterceptor(LoggingStreamInterceptor),
        grpc.ConnectionTimeout(time.Duration(cfg.ConnectionTimeoutSec) *
        time.Second),
   }
```

Interceptors allow you to inject cross-cutting behavior such as structured logging, metrics collection, authentication, and tracing without polluting business logic. Connection and keepalive timeouts protect the server from slow or misbehaving clients, preventing resource exhaustion. In production deployments, these options are often combined with TLS or mutual TLS (mTLS) credentials to enforce service-to-service identity and with monitoring hooks that expose latency, error rates, and request volumes to systems like Prometheus. The key design principle is to treat the gRPC server as an operational boundary: all resilience, observability, and security concerns should be configured at this boundary, leaving service implementations focused purely on domain behavior. You can see opts usage in the following code:

```
grpcServer := grpc.NewServer(opts...)
vehiclepb.RegisterVehicleServiceServer(grpcServer, myService)
```

Enterprise Tip Always configure timeouts and limits. This protects your server from slow clients or dropped connections. For internal RPCs, a timeout between three and ten seconds is typical.

Running the gRPC Server

Running a gRPC server in production is not a single blocking call—it is a controlled lifecycle. A well-designed server must coordinate **network binding**, **serving**, **error propagation**, and **graceful shutdown** in a predictable manner. This section explains how to run a gRPC server as a long-lived process that integrates cleanly with operating systems and orchestration platforms.

Binding to the Network

Before serving requests, the server must bind to a network interface. This is a critical failure point: port conflicts, missing permissions, or misconfigured containers should fail fast and clearly.

A typical pattern is to create a TCP listener explicitly and surface errors immediately:

```
lis, err := net.Listen("tcp", fmt.Sprintf(":%d", port))
if err != nil {
    return fmt.Errorf("failed to listen: %w", err)
}
```

In production systems, **retrying a failed bind is usually a mistake**. If the port is unavailable, the process should exit and let the supervisor (such as systemd or Kubernetes) decide what to do next.

Serving Without Blocking Control Flow

Calling `Serve` directly blocks the current goroutine. That makes it impossible to respond to shutdown signals or runtime failures. Instead, production servers typically run the serving loop in a separate goroutine and keep the main control flow free to coordinate lifecycle events.

A common pattern looks like this:

```
errCh := make(chan error, 1)

go func() {
    if err := grpcServer.Serve(lis); err != nil {
        errCh <- err
    }
}()
```

This design gives you two important capabilities:

- You can react to fatal server errors.
- You can listen for shutdown signals concurrently.

This separation is essential for controlled shutdown and observability.

Handling OS Signals for Shutdown

Production services must respond to operating system signals such as `SIGINT` and `SIGTERM`. These signals are how deployment platforms communicate intent: stop this process, but do it cleanly. The standard approach is similar to HTTP server graceful shutdown, as we discussed before in Chapter 13: register a signal channel, and wait for either a shutdown request or a server error:

```
sigCh := make(chan os.Signal, 1)
signal.Notify(sigCh, os.Interrupt, syscall.SIGTERM)
```

At this point, your server is waiting on **two events**:

- An external shutdown signal
- An internal failure while serving

This dual-channel design makes shutdown behavior explicit and testable.

Graceful Shutdown Semantics

When a shutdown signal is received, the gRPC server should **stop accepting new connections** while allowing in-flight RPCs to complete. Abrupt termination risks partial writes, duplicated retries, or inconsistent downstream state.

gRPC provides built-in support for this through graceful stopping:

```
grpcServer.GracefulStop()
```

A graceful stop

- Closes the listener
- Rejects new RPCs
- Waits for active handlers to finish

This behavior is especially important for

- Long-running unary calls
- Streaming RPCs
- State-modifying operations

In contrast, an immediate stop (`Stop`) should be reserved for crash scenarios.

Coordinating Errors and Shutdown

A robust server loop waits for **either** a shutdown signal **or** a fatal serving error:

```
select {
case <-sigCh:
    grpcServer.GracefulStop()
case err := <-errCh:
    return err
}
```

This pattern ensures that

- External shutdown is intentional and clean.
- Internal failures are surfaced immediately.
- The process exits with a clear cause.

From an operational perspective, this clarity is invaluable for debugging, alerting, and automated restarts.

Enterprise Tip Graceful shutdown must be *bounded*. A server that waits forever is not being polite—it is unsafe. Always enforce timeouts so slow streams or misbehaving clients cannot stall deployments. In mature systems, shutdown deadlines align with client timeouts, load-balancer drain windows, and orchestration limits to ensure the system keeps moving forward.

Design for Testability

In production code, never hard-code logic inside the adapter. Instead, use a constructor and pass in dependencies such as

- Domain services
- Data repositories
- Logging or metrics interfaces
- Caches or message brokers

For example:

```
func NewVehicleService(repo VehicleRepository, logger Logger)
*NewVehicleService {
    return &Service{
        repo: repo,
        logger: logger,
    }
}
```

This approach keeps your gRPC adapter simple and lets you test domain logic independently using mock interfaces.

When done right, this pattern gives you a clean separation of concerns—Protobuf for contracts, gRPC for transport, and domain services for core logic.

Using Interceptors in gRPC

So far, you've implemented specific RPC methods in your gRPC service. But what if you want to add behavior that applies to all methods—like logging, authentication, metrics, or tracing? Writing that logic into each function would be error-prone and hard to maintain.

That's where interceptors come in.

Interceptors in gRPC act like middleware. They let you wrap each RPC call with shared logic, without touching the business code of individual handlers. This makes them ideal for cross-cutting concerns that apply to every request.

What Can You Do with Interceptors?

Interceptors are commonly used for

- Structured logging of requests and responses
- Metrics collection (e.g., count, duration, status codes)
- Authentication and authorization enforcement
- Deadline checks and context validation
- Tracing and correlation ID propagation
- Request shaping or validation

In short, if you've ever written the same code across multiple handlers, an interceptor might be the better place for it.

Interceptors in Go

The Go `google.golang.org/grpc` library supports two kinds of server-side interceptors:

- **Unary Interceptors:** For standard request/response RPCs
- **Stream Interceptors:** For server, client, or bidirectional streaming

Let's start with a simple unary interceptor that logs the method name and how long it took:

```
import (
    "context"
    "log"
    "time"

    "google.golang.org/grpc"
)
```

```
func LoggingUnaryInterceptor(
    ctx context.Context,
    req any,
    info *grpc.UnaryServerInfo,
    handler grpc.UnaryHandler,
) (any, error) {
    start := time.Now()
    res, err := handler(ctx, req)
    duration := time.Since(start)

    log.Printf("method=%s duration=%s error=%v", info.FullMethod,
    duration, err)
    return res, err
}
```

This function wraps any unary RPC and logs useful information after the handler runs.

Registering the Interceptor

To attach an interceptor, pass it into your grpc.NewServer() setup:

```
grpcServer := grpc.NewServer(
    grpc.UnaryInterceptor(LoggingUnaryInterceptor),
    grpc.ConnectionTimeout(5 * time.Second),
)
```

Now every unary RPC—such as FindAvailableVehicle or GetVehicleInfo—will automatically go through your logging layer. No changes needed inside the method implementations.

You can register both unary and stream interceptors if your service uses streaming calls:

```
grpcServer := grpc.NewServer(
    grpc.UnaryInterceptor(LoggingUnaryInterceptor),
    grpc.StreamInterceptor(LoggingStreamInterceptor), // Optional
)
```

Enterprise Tip Use interceptors to centralize logging and metrics. This avoids expensive logging calls in hot paths and makes profiling easier with tools like pprof or OpenTelemetry.

Writing a Stream Interceptor

Stream interceptors follow a similar pattern but operate on the stream level. You can log connection starts, monitor traffic volume, or inject tracing metadata:

```
func LoggingStreamInterceptor(
    srv any,
    ss grpc.ServerStream,
    info *grpc.StreamServerInfo,
    handler grpc.StreamHandler,
) error {
    log.Printf("stream=%s started", info.FullMethod)
    err := handler(srv, ss)
    log.Printf("stream=%s ended with error=%v", info.FullMethod, err)
    return err
}
```

This is useful for cases like `StreamAssignments`, where gRPC maintains a live connection.

Now your VehicleService is more than functional—it's observable, maintainable, and ready for production workloads. Interceptors help enforce that every request is traced, validated, and logged—without diluting your business code.

Implementing a gRPC Client in Go

Connecting to the gRPC server is so easy. As follows:

```
conn, err := grpc.NewClient(target, opts...)
```

What matters is how to make it production grade and how to handle performance problems, network errors, credentials, timeouts, etc. In Go, using `grpc.DialOption`, you can easily apply policies.

Resilience and Error Handling

A production-grade gRPC client must expect failures. Network problems, temporary overload, and rolling deployments are normal in distributed systems. A client that treats every failure as an exception will not survive in production. gRPC provides built-in retry support with exponential backoff. This mechanism helps clients recover from temporary failures such as short network interruptions or brief service unavailability. For real systems, you must explicitly enable retries using a **ServiceConfig**.

A retry policy defines

- How many attempts are allowed
- How long to wait before retrying
- How the delay grows between retries
- Which error codes are retryable

In Go, this policy is usually passed using `grpc.WithDefaultServiceConfig`. The configuration is written in JSON.

```
grpc.WithDefaultServiceConfig(`
{
  "methodConfig": [{
    "name": [{ "service": "my.pb.Service" }],
    "retryPolicy": {
      "MaxAttempts": 5,
      "InitialBackoff": "0.2s",
      "MaxBackoff": "5s",
      "BackoffMultiplier": 1.6,
      "RetryableStatusCodes": ["UNAVAILABLE", "RESOURCE_EXHAUSTED"]
    }
  }]
}
`)
```

This configuration allows gRPC to retry failed calls up to five times, with exponential backoff between attempts.

Retries must always be used carefully. Too many retries during long outages can overload already unhealthy services. For this reason, retries should always be combined with timeouts, backoff, and monitoring.

For longer or repeated failures, retries alone are not enough. A **circuit breaker** is often added at the client boundary. Here is a simple example using Sony Gobreaker; you can use other libraries or implement your own as well:

```
gobreaker.NewCircuitBreaker(gobreaker.Settings{
        Name:        "vehicle-client",
        MaxRequests: 1,
        Interval:    30 * time.Second,
        Timeout:     30 * time.Second,
        ReadyToTrip: func(counts gobreaker.Counts) bool {
              if counts.Requests < 10 {
                    return false
              }
              failRate := float64(counts.TotalFailures) /
              float64(counts.Requests)
              return failRate >= 0.5
        },
        IsSuccessful: func(err error) bool {
              if err == nil {
                    return true
              }
              if st, ok := status.FromError(err); ok {
                    switch st.Code() {
                    case codes.InvalidArgument, codes.Unauthenticated,
                    codes.PermissionDenied:
                          return true
                    }
              }
              return false
        },
    })
```

As you can see, some errors like InvalidArguments are considered successful because the next request can be successful, and we don't need to break requests. When failure rates become too high, the circuit breaker stops outgoing calls and fails fast. This protects the rest of the system and allows time for recovery.

After implementing the circuit breaker, this is the method that we can use:

```
CircuitBreaker) Execute(req func() (interface{}, error))
(interface{}, error)
```

Here is an example:

```
_, err := c.cb.Execute(func() (any, error) {
        resp, err := client.FindAvailableVehicle(ctx, req)
```

Graceful degradation is the final layer. When a service is unavailable, the client may return cached data, partial results, or a controlled fallback instead of blocking or crashing.

Client-Side Load Balancing

In gRPC, load balancing can be done client-side. Using a client-side load balancer, the client does not connect to a server. It connects to a logical target that resolves into multiple addresses. A load-balancing policy then selects which address to use for each call. This policy can initially be configured in loadBalancingConfig. Example in vehicleServiceConfig:

```
{
   "loadBalancingConfig": [ { "round_robin": {} } ],
   "methodConfig": [{
     "name": [{ "service": "vehiclepb.VehicleService" }],
     "retryPolicy": {
       "MaxAttempts": 4,
       "InitialBackoff": "0.2s",
       "MaxBackoff": "5s",
       "BackoffMultiplier": 1.6,
       "RetryableStatusCodes": ["UNAVAILABLE", "RESOURCE_EXHAUSTED"]
     }
   }]
 }
```

The subsets of grpc load balancing policies are: round_robin, pick_first, weighted_round_robin, ring_hash, outlier_detection, and least_request. Here is the official resource about gRPC load balancing that can help you learn more:

`https://grpc.io/docs/guides/custom-load-balancing/`

The simplest approach is DNS-based round-robin. When multiple IP addresses are returned, a round-robin policy distributes calls across them.

Authentication

Security is mandatory in production systems. Never use insecure connections outside local development. Instead, configure TLS using `grpc.WithTransportCredentials`. Here is an insecure example:

```
grpc.WithTransportCredentials(insecure.NewCredentials()),
```

You can replace TLS or any other credentials that implement `credentials.TransportCredentials` interface. As we decided to use gRPC in service-to-service, you need to follow company-defined policies for service-to-service communications. Most of the companies have their own policies for this type of communication.

Enterprise Tip Always test failure paths. Authentication errors should fail fast and clearly, not silently degrade into retries.

Observability

In enterprise systems, a gRPC server is not an isolated component—it is part of a larger, distributed execution flow. When something goes wrong, the first question is rarely *what failed*, but *where* and *why*. Without observability, a gRPC service becomes a black box that is difficult to operate, debug, and evolve.

At a minimum, every production-grade gRPC server should expose **logs, metrics, and traces**. Logs help explain *what happened* during a request. Metrics reveal *how often* it happens and *how long* it takes. Traces show *how a request moves* across service boundaries. Together, they turn runtime behavior into something you can reason for.

Interceptors are the natural integration point for observability concerns. They allow you to capture request counts, latency distributions, and error rates consistently across all RPCs, without polluting business logic. In mature systems, these signals are exported to centralized platforms such as Prometheus, OpenTelemetry collectors, or vendor observability stacks, where they can be queried, visualized, and alerted on.

The key principle is intent: if a gRPC service is important enough to run in production, it is a must to be observable. Treat observability as part of the server's contract with operators—not as an afterthought added during incidents.

Exercises

1. Add a new RPC to your `vehicle.proto` file:

   ```
   rpc GetRouteVehicles(RouteRequest) returns (RouteResponse);
   ```

   Then define the request and response messages. Regenerate the code using `protoc`, and implement a stub in your gRPC service that returns dummy data. This will help reinforce how to evolve contracts safely and update the Go adapter.

2. Create a server-side unary interceptor that logs the full method name and how long each call takes. Use this pattern:

   ```
   func LoggingUnaryInterceptor(...) { ... }
   ```

   Then pass it to `grpc.NewServer()` using `grpc.UnaryInterceptor(...)`. Run your service and verify the output in your logs when calling an RPC like `GetVehicleInfo`.

3. Modify a field name or add a new optional field to one of your existing messages. Regenerate the code and inspect the generated `.pb.go` files. Observe how the code reflects the schema change, and confirm that your adapter still compiles.

4. Try removing a field from a Protobuf message without reserving its number. Regenerate the code and reflect on the risk. Then, update your `.proto` to use `reserved` and regenerate again. This will help you internalize why contract safety is crucial in real systems.

Summary

In this chapter, we explored how gRPC enables fast, structured, and maintainable communication between services in enterprise systems. You learned how it differs from REST, when to use each, and how Protobuf brings strong typing and compact messages to your architecture. We walked through defining Protobuf contracts, generating Go code, and implementing service adapters that keep business logic clean. You also learned how to use interceptors for logging and observability without repeating code. With these tools, you're now equipped to design reliable internal APIs that scale and evolve with confidence.

What's Next

In the next chapter, you'll explore design patterns that help you write clean, testable, and maintainable Go code in enterprise systems. You'll learn how Go's simplicity leads to powerful abstractions and how to structure your services for flexibility, clarity, and long-term scale.

CHAPTER 20

Design Patterns in Go: Building Maintainable Enterprise Systems

> *Patterns mean that we don't have to reinvent the wheel; we just have to learn how to drive.*

When we speak about design patterns in Go, we are not copying the *Gang of Four* book into a language that does not use inheritance. Go solves the same design problems that Java or C# developers face, but it uses different tools. It prefers small interfaces, functions as values, simple composition, and a concurrency model built into the language.

Because of these choices, many classical patterns become smaller and easier to use. They do not disappear, but they become lighter. The idea of the pattern stays the same, but the Go version is clearer and easier to understand.

Go Idioms for Maintainable Code

Enterprise Go is not only about classic design patterns. It is also about small techniques and habits that make systems easier to understand and safer to change. These idioms shape how we design boundaries, manage resources, and protect shared state. They are simple on the surface, but they have a deep impact on reliability and long-term maintainability. In this section, we explore the idioms that experienced Go developers rely on every day and see how they apply to our transport system.

S. Shahsavan, *Building Enterprise Projects with Go*, https://doi.org/10.1007/979-8-8688-2370-1_20

Small Interfaces, Big Wins

Go encourages us to build software from small parts that fit together well. Interfaces are one of the clearest examples of this idea. In languages based on inheritance, interfaces often become large because they try to describe a full identity. In Go, an interface is much smaller. It should describe only the behavior that a consumer depends on. When interfaces stay focused, the whole system becomes easier to understand and easier to change.

A small interface answers one simple question:

What can you do? Not What are you?

This difference reduces coupling and creates room for flexibility as the system grows.

Why Small Interfaces Matter

Large interfaces often look attractive. They gather many operations in a single place and make an API appear complete. But as soon as an interface becomes too large, every implementation must support every method, even the ones it does not need. This creates pressure across the system. A small change in one method can force many adapters, mocks, and services to update.

Go avoids these problems by letting interfaces stay small and focused. Instead of describing an entire role on the implementation side, you describe only the behavior that a single consumer requires. This matches how enterprise systems grow in real life. Different services often need different slices of the same domain.

Example in the Transport System

Our transport system works with assignments in several services. Each service needs a different capability.

- The booking service saves new assignments.
- The dashboard lists existing assignments.
- The scheduler counts assignments to make planning decisions.

It is better to express these needs with small interfaces:

```
type Saver interface {
    Save(ctx context.Context, a Assignment) error
```

```
}

type Finder interface {
    FindByID(ctx context.Context, id string) (Assignment, error)
}

type Lister interface {
    FindAll(ctx context.Context, status *string) ([]Assignment, error)
}

type Counter interface {
    Count(ctx context.Context) (int, error)
}
```

Each service imports only what it needs. This makes the system easier to extend without breaking existing code.

Small Interfaces in the Go Standard Library

This design is not unique to our domain. It is common in the standard library. The `io` package uses minimal interfaces:

```
type Reader interface {
      Read(p []byte) (n int, err error)
}

type Writer interface {
      Write(p []byte) (n int, err error)
}

type Closer interface {
      Close() error
}
```

These can be combined into larger abstractions when needed:

```
type ReadWriter interface {
      Reader
      Writer
}
```

This gives maximum flexibility without losing clarity.

When Composition Helps

Sometimes a larger view is useful. Go supports this by allowing interfaces to be composed:

```
type AssignmentRepository interface {
    Saver
    Finder
    Lister
    Counter
}
```

This provides the complete set of operations only when a consumer needs it.

Interface Discovery Instead of Interface Design

Developers from an OOP background often design interfaces before writing concrete code. This usually leads to many interfaces with a single implementation. These interfaces add work but give no real flexibility.

Go encourages the opposite. Start concrete. Build the real code first. Introduce an interface only when more than one consumer appears or when testing needs a mock.

When an Interface Appears Naturally

Imagine our scheduler must save assignments, but we want to test it without a real database. This is the perfect moment to introduce a minimal interface:

```
type AssignmentRepository interface {
    Save(ctx context.Context, a Assignment) error
}
```

Now we can create a simple mock:

```
type MockAssignmentRepository struct {
    Saved []Assignment
}
```

```
func (m *MockAssignmentRepository) Save(ctx context.Context, a
Assignment) error {
    m.Saved = append(m.Saved, a)
    return nil
}
```

The interface appears when it is useful, not before.

A Common Anti-pattern

Below, you can see an example of a common mistake about interface design:

```
type AssignmentRepository interface {
    Save(ctx context.Context, Assignment) error
}

type AssignmentRepositorySQL struct {
    db *sql.DB
}
```

If `AssignmentRepositorySQL` is the only implementation, the interface adds ceremony without adding value. Remove it. Introduce the interface only when a second implementation or test requires it. This keeps the design clean and avoids unnecessary layers.

Resource Management with defer

Reliable services depend on careful resource management. Every request that enters a system opens something: a database connection, a file, a network stream, or a lock. Each of these resources must be closed or released. If even a small number of them remain open, the service slowly loses capacity. Over time, this leads to connection pool exhaustion, unpredictable performance, and hard-to-trace failures.

Go provides a simple and safe mechanism to prevent these issues. The `defer` keyword attaches cleanup to the end of a function. Once the function returns, no matter how it returns, all deferred actions run. This protects the service from forgotten cleanup, early returns, and unexpected errors.

The Problem Without defer

Consider a service that loads assignment data:

```
rows, err := db.Query("SELECT * FROM assignments")
if err != nil {
    return err
}

// process rows
for rows.Next() {
    // ...
}
rows.Close() // must not forget
```

This code looks correct, but it becomes fragile under real conditions.

- If the function returns early, cleanup is skipped.
- If iteration stops due to an error, the resource may stay open.
- If this happens often, the connection pool becomes empty, and new requests are blocked.

Modern systems can perform thousands of database operations per second. Even a small number of forgotten closes can create significant pressure on shared resources.

How defer Solves the Problem

The idiomatic solution in Go is to attach cleanup immediately after acquiring the resource:

```
rows, err := db.Query("SELECT * FROM assignments")
if err != nil {
    return err
}
defer rows.Close()

for rows.Next() {
    // process row
}
```

Here, the intent is clear. As soon as the connection is opened, its cleanup is scheduled. It does not matter if the loop runs to the end, if the function returns early, or if an error interrupts processing. The connection is returned to the pool as soon as the function ends.

This predictable cleanup behavior is one of the reasons Go is used for long-running back-end services. A small leak per request may seem harmless, but over hours or days, it becomes a serious operational problem. In enterprise projects where your service should run for a long time, adding `defer` at the right moment stops the leak entirely.

Transport System Example

In our transport system, the assignment repository loads data from the database. Each query returns a `rows` object that must be closed. Forgetting to close even a few of these can exhaust the connection pool during busy hours. The safe way is to attach cleanup immediately after the query:

```
rows, err := r.db.QueryContext(ctx, q, args...)
if err != nil {
    return nil, err
}
defer rows.Close()
```

This single line protects the service. No matter how the function exits, the database cursor is released on time. In high-traffic systems, this predictable cleanup prevents slowdowns and avoids hard-to-diagnose connection leaks.

Enterprise Lessons

- Place the `defer` statement immediately after acquiring the resource. This makes the intent visible and reduces the chance of missing cleanup in complex functions.
- Use multiple `defer` statements when a function manages several resources. Deferred calls run in last-in, first-out order, which makes layered cleanup predictable and easy to reason about.

Immutability by Convention

Go gives us the `const` keyword, but it applies only to values known at compile time, such as numbers, strings, or fixed durations. It does not protect struct fields, slices, maps, or other complex data. These types remain mutable by default, and Go does not offer a `final` or `immutable` keyword. In many enterprise systems, especially those that use concurrency, this mutability becomes a source of subtle bugs. A shared slice or map can change while another goroutine is reading it, which leads to data races and broken invariants.

Experienced Go developers solve this problem through design rather than language features. They build APIs that treat data as immutable even when the language does not enforce it. This includes returning defensive copies, hiding internal state, and designing data flow so that values move forward through the system rather than being modified in place.

Why Immutability Matters

Concurrent programs often read the same data from many places. If one goroutine updates a value while another is using it, the results can be unpredictable.

By treating shared data as immutable, you remove these risks. When no part of the program can modify a value, no race condition can occur. This leads to safer and more predictable behavior, especially during high load.

Example: Safe Snapshots

Imagine a registry that stores active routes in memory. The simplest version might return the internal slice directly:

```
func (r *RouteRegistry) ActiveRoutes() []Route {
    return r.routes
}
```

This exposes the internal slice, allowing callers to modify it by accident. A small change in one part of the program could corrupt the entire registry.

A safer approach is to return a copy:

```
func (r *RouteRegistry) ActiveRoutes() []Route {
    cp := make([]Route, len(r.routes))
    copy(cp, r.routes)
    return cp
}
```

The caller can now modify the returned slice freely without affecting the original data.

File Embedding for Portability

Most applications depend on small but important files. These may include schemas, templates, default configuration files, or seed data that the service needs at startup. In the past, these files had to be shipped beside the binary. A missing file in a container image or a wrong file path during deployment could cause a service to fail immediately.

Go solves this problem through the `embed` package. With this feature, you can include files directly inside the compiled binary. The result is a self-contained application that behaves the same in development, testing, and production. This reduces the number of moving parts and makes deployment more predictable.

Embedding also improves portability. A single binary can travel through different environments without relying on the file system. This is especially useful in container-based systems where directory structures and mount points can vary.

The Pattern

To embed a file, you import the `embed` package and place the `//go:embed` directive above a variable. The Go compiler loads the file at build time and stores its contents in that variable.

The variable can have any of the following types:

- `string` for text files
- `[]byte` for binary files
- `embed.FS` for embedding entire directories or multiple files

This gives flexibility while keeping the API simple.

Transport System Example

In our transport system, services use Avro schemas to encode and decode messages. The schema version must always match the version of the code. Embedding the schema inside the binary removes the risk of reading the wrong file at runtime.

Here is the pattern we use:

```
// Assignment holds the embedded Avro schema for assignments.
//
//go:embed assignment.avsc
var Assignment []byte
```

This schema is now part of the binary itself. When the service runs, it reads the schema directly from memory. There is no dependency on external file paths, container volumes, or runtime configuration. This also simplifies testing because the schema is always available during tests.

Memory and Performance Note

Embedded files increase the binary's size. They are loaded into memory at startup and stay available for the lifetime of the process. For typical service assets, the memory cost is small. The reliability gain far outweighs it. Large assets such as images, video files, or large datasets should not be embedded. These are better stored in external object storage or loaded on demand. For everyday service files, including Avro schemas in our transport system, embedding is the recommended approach.

Creational Patterns

Creational patterns help us build and configure values clearly and predictably. In languages with heavy class hierarchies, this often means factories, builders, and many constructor variants, but Go takes a simpler path. It prefers clear construction code, sensible defaults, and small extension points instead of layers of abstraction.

Functional Options

Configuring a service often becomes harder as the system grows. A constructor that starts simple may become overloaded with parameters for timeouts, caching, retries, metrics, security, or logging. Long parameter lists make code difficult to understand, and optional values force callers to pass placeholders they do not care about. Functional options give Go developers a cleaner way to handle this complexity. Instead of creating many constructor variants, we define small option functions that modify the initial configuration in a controlled and readable way.

How Functional Options Work

Functional options remove configuration details from the constructor. Instead, we define simple functions that apply specific changes to the service. Each option focuses on one behavior, and the constructor applies all provided options before returning the final object. Defaults stay inside the constructor, where they belong.

This keeps the API simple while allowing flexible configuration.

Example from the Transport System

Our transport system exposes a gRPC service. Different teams have different needs. The booking team may require strict timeouts. The monitoring dashboard may want detailed logging around streaming requests. The assignment service may need connection-level settings.

Using functional options, the configuration becomes clear and easy to read:

```
grpcServer := grpc.NewServer(
      grpc.UnaryInterceptor(LoggingUnaryInterceptor),
      grpc.StreamInterceptor(LoggingStreamInterceptor),
      grpc.ConnectionTimeout(5*time.Second),
)
```

Each argument in `NewServer` is a functional option. The caller chooses only what it needs. All other defaults are handled internally by the gRPC library. This makes the code expressive, predictable, and simple to extend later.

When a new feature is added, you simply write another `WithX` option. Existing code continues to compile without change.

Builder Pattern

The builder pattern appears in many languages as a way to construct complex objects step by step. It is often used when a value needs many optional settings or when the construction process has several stages. In Go, the builder pattern can be useful, but it is less common than in languages with heavy class hierarchies. Go already provides simple struct literals and functional options that address most configuration needs. Even so, there are situations where a builder improves clarity, especially when building a value that requires many related steps or when you want to guide the order in which those steps happen.

A Simple Builder in Go

Let us imagine we want to build a `RoutePlan` for our transport system. A route plan may include the vehicle, the list of stops, a schedule, and optional safety rules. Setting these values directly in a struct literal can become confusing, especially as more features appear. A builder can guide the caller and keep the code readable.

```
type RoutePlan struct {
    VehicleID string
    Stops     []string
    StartsAt  time.Time
    Notes     string
}

type RoutePlanBuilder struct {
    plan RoutePlan
}

func NewRoutePlanBuilder() *RoutePlanBuilder {
    return &RoutePlanBuilder{
        plan: RoutePlan{
            StartsAt: time.Now(), // safe default
        },
    }
}

func (b *RoutePlanBuilder) WithVehicle(id string) *RoutePlanBuilder {
    b.plan.VehicleID = id
    return b
}

func (b *RoutePlanBuilder) WithStops(stops []string) *RoutePlanBuilder {
    b.plan.Stops = append([]string{}, stops...)
    return b
}

func (b *RoutePlanBuilder) WithNotes(notes string) *RoutePlanBuilder {
    b.plan.Notes = notes
    return b
}

func (b *RoutePlanBuilder) Build() RoutePlan {
    return b.plan
}
```

Using the builder is straightforward:

```
plan := NewRoutePlanBuilder().
    WithVehicle("BUS-42").
    WithStops([]string{"Central", "Museum", "Park"}).
    WithNotes("Peak hours route").
    Build()
```

This style helps when readability matters or when constructing the value takes several steps.

When to Use a Builder

The builder pattern is not the first tool to reach for in Go. Start with a simple constructor or functional options. Choose a builder when those approaches no longer keep the code clean.

Builders work well when

- The object has many related fields that need to be set in a clear order.
- The value must be validated while being built.
- You want to make the construction process easy to follow for new team members.
- You want to avoid exposing internal fields directly to callers.

Builders are also useful in domain-heavy areas like scheduling, planning, and workflow creation. These areas often involve several decisions that must be applied step by step.

Builder vs. Functional Options

Both patterns help with configuration, but they solve different problems.

- Use functional options when you want flexible, optional behavior.
- Use a builder when construction requires a sequence of steps or when readability improves by clearly showing each part.

In many enterprise services, you may mix both approaches. For example, a builder may create a configuration object, which is then passed into another constructor that supports functional options.

Lazy Initialization and Singletons

Some parts of a system must exist only once. Examples include a shared HTTP client, a schema decoder, a configuration store, or a cache that all components rely on. Many languages solve this with the Singleton pattern, often using private constructors or global classes. Go takes a simpler and safer path. Instead of forcing global objects, Go encourages clear ownership and lazy initialization. This means a resource is created only when the program needs it for the first time.

Lazy initialization helps in situations where the initialization is expensive, depends on the environment, or may not be needed in every execution path. Go provides a dedicated tool for this through the `sync.Once` type. It guarantees that the initialization function runs exactly one time, even when many goroutines call it at the same moment.

How sync.Once Works

`sync.Once` has one method called `Do`. The function you pass to `Do` runs on the first call. All later calls return immediately. This gives you a predictable and thread-safe way to create a shared value.

```
var once sync.Once
var client *http.Client

func Client() *http.Client {
    once.Do(func() {
        client = &http.Client{
            Timeout: 5 * time.Second,
        }
    })
    return client
}
```

The first call builds the client. Every other call reuses it. There is no need for manual locks or checks. For many systems, this is enough to guarantee safe and lazy initialization.

Note that this is not the classical Singleton pattern from object-oriented design. Go does not force you to hide constructors or create private types. Instead, lazy initialization is used only when the architecture truly needs a shared object that is identical everywhere. In most services, you still prefer constructor injection.

When to Avoid Singletons

Lazy initialization is helpful, but global singletons can introduce real problems if they are used without care:

- They are harder to replace in tests.
- They create a hidden coupling between packages.
- They remove flexibility for future versions.

A practical rule is

Use lazy initialization only when a resource truly has a single correct instance across the entire service and when constructor injection does not provide a better structure.

Typical examples where lazy initialization makes sense:

- A schema parser that is shared everywhere
- A heavy configuration loader
- A long-lived HTTP client
- A cache that is safe to share across goroutines

In these cases, you are not hiding the global state. Instead, you are protecting the system from repeated, expensive initialization.

Structural Patterns

Structural patterns help us shape how parts of a system fit together. They let us adapt external libraries, add cross-cutting behavior, and organize dependencies without changing the core logic. In Go, these patterns stay simple because interfaces are small and easy to implement. The goal is not to build complex hierarchies but to create clear boundaries that make systems easier to test, extend, and maintain.

Decorator Pattern

In real systems, a single handler or service often needs extra behavior around it. A request may need logging, metrics, retries, authentication, or timeouts. These features are important for operating a system, but they should not live inside the business logic. When too many concerns are mixed into one place, the code becomes difficult to test and slow to change.

Go provides a simple way to keep these concerns separate: the decorator pattern. A decorator wraps an existing implementation and adds behavior before or after the main action. Because Go's interfaces are small and easy to implement, decorators fit naturally into the language.

The idea behind a decorator is simple. It uses the same interface as the original component, adds its own behavior, and then forwards the call to another implementation. This creates clean and flexible layers around the core logic without changing it.

In enterprise systems, this pattern keeps services observable and safe under load while keeping business rules clean and clear.

How Decorators Work in Go

In classic object-oriented design, a decorator is an object that shares the same interface as the thing it decorates, forwards all calls to it, and adds behavior before or after those calls. Go keeps the same idea, but replaces inheritance with small interfaces and composition.

In Go, a decorator usually has three parts:

- **A Small Interface or Handler Contract**

  This defines the behavior you want to extend, such as `ServeHTTP`, `Handle`, or `Save`.

- **A Concrete Implementation That Does the Real Work**

  This is the component that talks to the database, sends an HTTP response, or executes the core business logic.

- **A Wrapper That Holds a Reference to the Interface and Forwards Calls**

  The wrapper has a field like `next` of that interface type. Its method implementation runs extra logic, then calls `next.Method(...)`, then optionally runs more logic.

Because Go has no inheritance, all of this is done through composition. The result is simple and flexible:

- Each decorator is just another implementation of the same interface.
- You can stack multiple decorators at runtime to combine behaviors as needed.
- You can extend behavior for one object or one handler without touching others, which matches the Single Responsibility and Open/Closed principles in a very natural way.

Gin Middleware Example

Gin's middleware system is a practical example of the decorator pattern. A middleware receives a request, adds behavior, and then lets the next handler continue.

Here is a simple timing middleware that measures how long each request takes:

```
func RequestTiming() gin.HandlerFunc {
    return func(c *gin.Context) {
        start := time.Now()

        c.Next() // call the next handler

        duration := time.Since(start)
        log.Printf("request to %s took %s", c.FullPath(), duration)
    }
}
```

Adding it to the router is easy:

```
router := gin.Default()
router.Use(RequestTiming())
```

Now every handler in the service is wrapped with timing logic. The business code does not change. The decorator adds value around it:

- Before the handler, record the start time.
- After the handler, write a log entry.

Gin's built-in Logger and Recovery middlewares work in the same way. They wrap handlers, add behavior, and call the next handler through `c.Next()`.

This pattern can be extended easily. You can create decorators for logging, metrics, rate limiting, authentication, tracing, or caching. Each decorator stays focused on one responsibility, and you can stack them in any order.

Why This Pattern Fits Go

Decorators fit naturally into Go because

- Interfaces and handler functions are small.
- Wrapping logic is easy to read and test.
- Go encourages composition instead of inheritance.
- Pipelines of behavior are simple to build and extend.

Decorators also help with testing. You can wrap a mock handler to observe its behavior or count how many times it was called without changing the mock itself.

Decorators help you build modular and maintainable systems. They allow you to add cross-cutting features such as tracing, retries, or validation without touching the business logic. As the system grows, you add new decorators instead of rewriting existing handlers.

This pattern also supports team collaboration. Infrastructure teams can build decorators for logging or metrics while domain teams focus on the correct business rules. The boundaries remain clean and easy to manage.

Behavioral Patterns

Large systems do not succeed only because their structure is correct. They succeed when their components *behave* correctly as they interact under real load, real failures, and constantly changing conditions. Behavioral patterns focus on these interactions. They help you shape how services decide, coordinate, notify, and adapt. In Go, these patterns take on a practical, lightweight form. By understanding these patterns in a Go-specific way, you can guide complex systems with clear rules for communication and decision-making, without introducing unnecessary architecture or abstraction.

Strategy Pattern in Go

Many enterprise systems need to switch between different ways of performing the same operation. A payment service may choose between several gateways. A routing engine may compute paths using different algorithms. A search service may decide between exact match, prefix match, or fuzzy match depending on the query. All these variations are strategies: alternative behaviors that solve the same problem in different ways.

The strategy pattern provides a structured way to keep these variations separate and choose between them when needed. In classical object-oriented languages, this is usually done with interfaces and subclasses. Go supports interfaces, too, but the language offers something more flexible: you can use either interfaces or simple function values. This allows Go developers to implement strategies with less ceremony and better testability.

A strategy should focus on one clear responsibility. The caller decides which strategy to use, and the strategy performs the work without depending on the rest of the system. This keeps the code easy to read, avoids complex conditionals, and prevents features from becoming tightly coupled.

Strategies As Interfaces

A common way to express a strategy in Go is with a small interface that defines one operation. For example, imagine our Routing strategy:

```
type RouteStrategy interface {
    Compute(from, to Location) Route
}
```

You can implement different routing rules as separate types:

```
type FastestRoute struct{}

func (f FastestRoute) Compute(from, to Location) Route {
...
```

```
}

type ShortestRoute struct {
}

func (s ShortestRoute) Compute(from, to Location) Route {
...
}
```

The caller chooses the strategy at runtime:

```
func Compute(from, to Location, strategy RouteStrategy) float64 {
    return strategy.Compute(from, to)
}
```

This keeps the routing logic independent of priorities. New strategies can be added without changing the existing code; that's what the Open/Closed principle asks you to do.

Strategies As Functions (The Go-Native Style)

In many cases, an interface is more structured than you need. Go developers often use function values as strategies. A function can represent a strategy directly:

```
type RouteFunc func(from, to Location) Route
```

Now you can define strategies as simple functions:

```
var Seasonal = func(from, to Location) RouteFunc {
    ...
}

func EcoRoute(from, to Location) RouteFunc {
    return func(from, to Location) RouteFunc {
        ...
    }
}
```

And the compute function becomes

```
func Compute(from, to Location, compute RouteFunc) Location {
    return compute(from, to)
}
```

This approach reduces boilerplate and makes tests shorter and clearer. It also aligns with Go's philosophy of preferring small, explicit abstractions.

Choosing Between Strategies

A strategy is most useful when the application must choose behavior dynamically. Common reasons include

Configuration: Select faster or more accurate behavior depending on the environment.

User Input: Choose fuzzy search when the query looks misspelled.

Runtime State: Use a fallback strategy when a service is unreachable.

Gradual Rollout: Activate a new algorithm for a percentage of requests.

Keep strategy selection near the edges of your system. When selection happens too deep inside the code, it becomes harder to test and maintain.

Strategy and Testability

The strategy pattern improves testability by separating behavior. Each strategy becomes a small, predictable unit:

```
func TestShortestRoute_ComputeReturnsConsistentRoute(t *testing.T) {
from := Location{Lat: 48.2082, Lon: 16.3738} // Vienna (example
coordinates)
to := Location{Lat: 48.2100, Lon: 16.3630}

var s ShortestRoute
got := s.Compute(from, to)
```

```
if got.From != from {
t.Fatalf("expected From=%+v, got %+v", from, got.From)
}
if got.To != to {
t.Fatalf("expected To=%+v, got %+v", to, got.To)
}
if got.DistanceMeters <= 0 {
t.Fatalf("expected positive DistanceMeters, got %d", got.DistanceMeters)
}
}
```

The logic that selects strategies can also be tested independently. This leads to clearer tests and better coverage.

Observer Pattern in Go (Using Channels)

Modern systems generate a constant stream of changes: configuration updates, background job completions, new messages from a broker, or network failures. Other components often need to react to these events. The observer pattern provides a structured way to broadcast updates without tightly coupling producers and consumers. Instead of calling each dependent component directly, the subject emits events, and observers respond independently.

In class-based languages, observers commonly use interface callbacks. Go supports that model, but the language offers a more natural alternative: channels. Channels give the observer pattern a clear communication path, asynchronous delivery, and built-in concurrency. Observers process events at their own pace, and they stop cleanly when the system shuts down or when a context is canceled.

The core idea is simple: broadcast information without dictating how it must be consumed. Channels make this pattern explicit, composable, and suitable for both small services and large event-driven systems.

Why Channels Fit the Observer Pattern

Channels provide several advantages when implementing observers.

Asynchronous Delivery

Observers receive events independently. Slow observers do not block the publisher.

Backpressure Visibility

If an observer cannot keep up, the channel exposes that slowdown. You can decide whether to drop, buffer, or block based on your system's requirements.

Loose Coupling

The publisher does not know who is listening or how many observers exist. It only sends events to channels.

Graceful Shutdown

Observers exit naturally when their channel closes or when the context is canceled. No extra signaling is required.

Support for Many Observers

Broadcasting becomes simple: each observer receives its own channel or subscribes through a shared event router.

Channels turn the observer pattern into a concurrency pattern tailored to Go.

A Simple Broadcasting Observable

The following example shows a minimal observable that delivers events to multiple observers:

```
type TransportEvent[T any] struct {
    Name string
    Data T
}

type TransportObservable[T any] struct {
    subs []chan TransportEvent[T]
}
```

```
func (o *TransportObservable[T]) Subscribe() <-chan TransportEvent[T] {
   ch := make(chan TransportEvent[T], 16) // small buffer for short bursts

   o.subs = append(o.subs, ch)

   return ch
}

func (o *TransportObservable[T]) Publish(evt TransportEvent[T]) {

   for _, ch := range o.subs {
        select {
        case ch <- evt:
        default:
            // observer is slow; choose drop, block, or log
            // depending on transport system requirements
        }
   }
}

func (o *TransportObservable[T]) Close() {
   for _, ch := range o.subs {
        close(ch)
   }
}
```

A key design choice is that **each observer receives its own channel**. This prevents one slow observer from delaying another and allows independent processing and cancellation.

Observers As Independent Goroutines

Most observers run in their own goroutine and react to events until the channel closes or the context ends:

```
func StartObserver[T any](ctx context.Context, id int, events <-chan
TransportEvent[T]) {
    go func() {
         for {
```

```
            select {
            case evt, ok := <-events:
                if !ok {
                    return
                }
                fmt.Printf("observer %d received: %s\n", id, evt.Name)

            case <-ctx.Done():
                return
            }
        }
    }()
}
```

This approach makes the system easy to scale, and the resulting system is easy to understand and modify.

Graceful Shutdown in Go

Modern enterprise systems must not only start reliably, but also stop reliably. **Graceful shutdown** is a system-lifecycle pattern that ensures a service can terminate predictably, coordinately, and safely—even while concurrent work is still in progress. In practice, graceful shutdown means the service stops cleanly: goroutines complete their work, resources are released, and no operations are abandoned halfway.

In production systems, this is not optional. Without a well-defined shutdown strategy, services risk data corruption, leaked goroutines, half-written responses, or broken client interactions. In enterprise Go systems, graceful shutdown is an architectural concern, not a cleanup detail.

Why Graceful Shutdown

We treat graceful shutdown as a **design pattern** because it provides a reusable behavioral rule for managing service termination across many systems. Each component—servers, workers, schedulers—follows the same contract. This consistency localizes complexity and avoids subtle failures during deploys, restarts, or infrastructure-initiated termination.

In cloud and container environments, graceful shutdown is essential. Orchestrators such as Kubernetes send a termination signal (typically `SIGTERM`) and allow only a short grace period before forcefully killing the process. A service that ignores this window may be terminated mid-request or mid-transaction. The graceful shutdown pattern exists to ensure that this never happens silently.

Architecturally, shutdown mirrors startup. Just as services have a structured initialization phase, they require a structured teardown phase. That phase is governed by a few recurring responsibilities.

Core Responsibilities of a Graceful Shutdown

Shutdown begins with an external signal—most commonly `SIGINT` or `SIGTERM`. In Go, these signals are translated into application-level intent using `signal.Notify` or `signal.NotifyContext`. Separated goroutine is a listener to these signals, and Go channels are the backbone to transfer these signals to running services.

A **root context**, tied to these signals, represents the lifetime of the service. When this context is canceled, the shutdown intention propagates through the entire system. Any goroutine, server, or worker observing `ctx.Done()` knows it must stop. This shared cancellation signal is the backbone of coordinated shutdown.

Refuse New Work

Once shutdown begins, the system must refuse new work immediately. Servers stop listening for new connections; schedulers stop pulling new jobs. This prevents the shutdown window from extending indefinitely.

Go's standard servers support this model directly. HTTP servers stop accepting new connections and wait for active handlers to finish. gRPC servers follow the same principle, allowing in-flight RPCs to complete while rejecting new ones. The detailed mechanics of these behaviors are covered elsewhere in this book. For gRPC server graceful shutdown, *Chapter 19*, and for HTTP server graceful shutdown, *Chapter 13*.

Finish In-Flight Operations

Graceful shutdown does not mean "stop instantly." Ongoing work should be allowed to complete—within reason. This is typically enforced using contexts with deadlines.

Well-designed handlers and workers already respect `context.Context`. When shutdown begins, cancellation signals flow naturally, allowing database operations to roll back, loops to exit, and background tasks to conclude cooperatively.

Resource Cleanup

After work completes (or times out), resources must be released: network listeners, database connections, file handles, and message consumers. Many of these cleanups occur naturally when goroutines exit and deferred functions run. Others require explicit shutdown steps.

The key principle is simple: **goroutines must be allowed to exit normally**. Abrupt termination prevents defers from running and leaves the system in an undefined state.

Concurrency Patterns

Modern Go services do not run in a straight line. They serve many users at the same time, call external systems, process streams of data, and often wait for network or disk operations. To keep these workloads efficient, Go gives us goroutines, channels, and context. These tools are simple, but the way we combine them shapes the reliability and performance of the whole system. Concurrency patterns capture the proven structures that experienced Go developers use to organize concurrent work safely. They help you avoid common pitfalls such as goroutine leaks, uncontrolled parallelism, and unpredictable shutdown. By learning these patterns, you gain a toolbox for building scalable and stable enterprise systems that behave correctly under real traffic.

Context Pattern

Starting work is easy; the real challenge is knowing when to stop. Modern Go services spend much of their time waiting: waiting for HTTP responses, waiting for database responses, waiting for other services. A client may disconnect, a deadline may pass, or the server may need to shut down. If goroutines continue running after that point, they consume resources and make the system unstable.

The context pattern gives Go developers a safe way to control this behavior. A `context.Context` carries three important signals across your call graph:

- A cancellation signal

- An optional deadline or timeout
- A small set of request-scoped values

Using context correctly cannot be optional. It is the foundation of clean shutdown, safe cancellation, and predictable behavior in concurrent programs.

The pattern is simple:

1. Every blocking or long-running function accepts a `context.Context` as its first argument.
2. The caller creates or derives the context.
3. The callee checks `ctx.Done()` and exits quickly when it is closed.

This cooperation allows the entire service to stop work at the right time.

Core Ideas

The `context.Context` interface provides four methods:

- `Done() <-chan struct{}`
- `Err() error`
- `Deadline() (time.Time, bool)`
- `Value(key any) any`

These methods support three important capabilities.

Cancellation

`Done()` returns a channel that closes when work should stop. Long-running tasks and loops should select on this channel and exit immediately when it closes.

Deadlines and Timeouts

`Deadline()` tells you if the context has a fixed point in time when it must stop. Go provides two helpers that build child contexts with limited lifetimes.

- `context.WithTimeout` cancels the context after a duration. For example, cancel this work if it takes longer than 200 milliseconds.
- `context.WithDeadline` cancels the context at an exact moment in time. For example: stop all requests at 12:00:30 because the batch window ends.

Both functions return a new context and a cancel function. The difference is simple:

Use **WithTimeout** when you know how long the work may run.

Use **WithDeadline** when you know the exact moment when the work must end.

Both cancel the context automatically when the limit is reached. It's important to consider configurations to use them; it makes your application flexible.

Request Scoped Values

`WithValue(key,val), Value()` allows you to attach a small amount of data that must travel with the request, such as a user ID or correlation ID. These values must be safe for concurrent use.

Contexts form a **tree**. Canceling a parent context cancels all of its children. This makes it easy to stop a whole branch of work with one signal.

Context in the Transport System

Our graceful HTTP server in transport service builds its root context from operating system signals:

```
sigCtx, stop := signal.NotifyContext(
    context.Background(),
    os.Interrupt,
    syscall.SIGTERM,
)
defer stop()
```

This root context represents the entire lifetime of the service. All long-running goroutines should eventually respect it. When the service receives a termination signal, we use a child context with a timeout to shut the server down gracefully:

```
ctx, cancel := context.WithTimeout(context.Background(), 3*time.Second)
defer cancel()

if err := server.Shutdown(ctx); err != nil {
    log.Printf("graceful shutdown timed out: %v", err)
    _ = server.Close()
}
```

The pattern looks like this:

- Create a root context tied to OS signals.
- Cancel it when a signal arrives.
- Use a child context for shutdown with a fixed timeout.
- If the shutdown cannot finish in time, force close.

Handlers inside the HTTP server can also read their own request contexts through `r.Context()`. If a client disconnects or a timeout expires, the handler stops immediately.

How to Use Context in Your Code

Throughout this book, whenever a function may block or run for a noticeable amount of time, we follow a consistent rule: accept `context.Context` as the first parameter and pass it downstream.

Accept Context First

Having a standard method signature helps the code to be clear and maintainable. It applies to all programming languages. Let's first see the code example:

```
func (s *assignmentService) Save(ctx context.Context, a models.Assignment)
(models.Assignment, error) {
    // use ctx for database, RPC, or external calls
}
```

Placing `ctx` first makes the intent clear and keeps the signature consistent across the code base.

Pass Context to All Downstream Calls

Any function that receives a context must pass the same context, or its child, to other calls it makes. This allows deadlines and cancellations to propagate through the entire chain.

```
assignment, err := s.assignmentRepo.FindByID(ctx, id)
if err != nil {
    return err
}
```

Never create a new root context inside a function. Doing so disconnects the work from the caller's lifetime. As we said, the main function is a perfect place for wiring; you can use it to create a root context.

Use `select` with `ctx.Done()` in Loops

If a function listens on channels or processes work in a loop, it must stop when the context is canceled.

```
for {
    select {
    case msg := <-incoming:
        // handle message
    case <-ctx.Done():
        return ctx.Err()
    }
}
```

This prevents orphaned goroutines from running after a client disconnects or a shutdown begins.

Derive Child Contexts Only When the Function Needs a Different Lifetime

Sometimes a specific part of a function needs a stricter timeout than the parent context. In these cases, create a child context and cancel it when finished.

```
dbCtx, cancel := context.WithTimeout(ctx, 200*time.Millisecond)
defer cancel()

rows, err := db.QueryContext(dbCtx, q, args...)
```

A child context is still tied to the parent. If the parent is canceled, the child is canceled as well.

Store Only Essential Request-Scoped Values

A context may carry small pieces of data required by downstream layers. Good examples include

- Correlation ID
- Authenticated user identity
- Locale
- JWT token (if needed)

These values help with logging, authorization, and tracing.

Avoid storing

- Configuration
- Optional parameters
- Large structs or slices
- Anything that does not need to travel through the entire request path

Context should not be used as a general-purpose key/value store. Overusing it makes the code harder to understand and breaks the intended design. Keep in mind: it heaps memory as it travels between methods!

Context As a Pattern, Not Just a Type

Think of context as an architectural rule.

- The edge of your system creates the root context.
- Every function on the request path accepts and forwards that context.
- Goroutines exit when `ctx.Done()` closes.
- Shutdown uses cancellation to signal all components.

This approach provides strong guarantees.

- The caller decides when work must stop.
- No goroutine remains alive longer than necessary.
- Database connections and file handles are released on time.
- Timeouts and cancellations provide natural backpressure under load.

In our transport system, this means

- HTTP handlers use request contexts for all work.
- Internal workers listen for server shutdown through context.
- Shutdown is coordinated across the whole service with `WithTimeout`.

You can think of context as a behavioral pattern for concurrency in Go. This consistency allows large teams to work together, even on complex systems. As long as each function respects `ctx.Done()`, features like timeouts, cancellation, and graceful shutdown can be added without rewriting the entire service.

Context is a small interface. But if used correctly, it becomes one of the strongest and most important patterns in Go.

Pipeline Pattern

Many real systems do not process data in one step. Information enters the system, is transformed, enriched, validated, filtered, and finally stored or sent somewhere else. When these steps must happen in sequence and when the data can be processed as a stream, the pipeline pattern becomes a powerful tool. It lets you build concurrent, modular flows that are simple to understand and easy to scale.

Go is an excellent language for pipelines because channels and goroutines make it natural to build independent stages. Each stage reads values from a single channel, performs its operations, and sends output to the next stage. When connected, the stages create a clear chain of responsibility.

A well-designed pipeline reduces latency, increases throughput, and keeps code maintainable even as systems grow.

What a Pipeline Is

A pipeline is a structured way to pass data through a sequence of steps, where each step works independently and communicates only through channels. This structure helps you build systems that are easy to reason about, easy to test, and naturally concurrent.

A pipeline is based on three core ideas.

Stages

A stage is a function that receives values from an input channel, performs one focused operation, and sends the result to an output channel. Each stage has a single responsibility. This makes the code easier to maintain and allows each step to be improved or replaced without affecting the others.

Channels As boundaries

Channels connect stages. They act as clear boundaries that define how data moves through the system. Because stages only read from one channel and write to another, they remain loosely coupled. This separation makes the flow of data visible, simplifies debugging, and allows each part of the pipeline to be tested in isolation.

Completion and Cancellation

A pipeline must shut down safely. Two rules make this possible.

- When the upstream channel closes, the stage finishes its remaining work and closes its own output channel. This prevents goroutines from running forever.
- When the context is canceled, the stage stops immediately. This avoids leaks, helps with graceful shutdown, and ensures that all goroutines respect the overall lifetime of the request.

These rules apply to every stage in the pipeline. When they are followed consistently, cancellation travels from the entry point of the system to the entire chain of workers.

More Than One Pattern

A pipeline is not a single design pattern. It is a combination of simple pieces: small functions, clear boundaries, and predictable shutdown rules. When you connect these pieces, you create a processing flow that is both powerful and easy to understand.

You can also find some successful, famous products that fully follow this pattern; *Elasticsearch* and *Logstash* are just some of them that I like.

A Simple Pipeline Structure

Below, you can see a simple example of a pipeline in our transport project; first, we need to define pipeline stages:

```
// StageSelectVehicle simulates matching ride requests to available
vehicles.
func StageSelectVehicle(ctx context.Context, in <-chan RideRequest) <-chan
Assignment {
   out := make(chan Assignment)
```

```
    go func() {
        defer close(out)
        for req := range in {
            asg := Assignment{
                RequestID: req.RiderID,
                VehicleID: fmt.Sprintf("vehicle-%s", req.RiderID),
                Route:     fmt.Sprintf("%s -> %s", req.Pickup, req.Dropoff),
            }

            select {
            case out <- asg:
            case <-ctx.Done():
                return
            }
        }
    }()
    return out
}

// StageFormatMessage renders an assignment as JSON ready for publishing/
logging.
func StageFormatMessage(ctx context.Context, in <-chan Assignment) <-chan
string {
    out := make(chan string)
    go func() {
        defer close(out)
        for asg := range in {
            payload, _ := json.Marshal(asg) // ignore error in this
            small demo

            select {
            case out <- string(payload):
            case <-ctx.Done():
                return
            }
```

```
        }
    }()
    return out
}
```

After defining pipeline stages, you need to connect them to each other. As you can see below, pipeline stages can be connected using the returned channels of each stage (function):

```
ctx, cancel := context.WithTimeout(context.Background(), 5*time.Second)
    defer cancel()

    in := make(chan RideRequest)
    go func() {
        defer close(in)
        requests := []RideRequest{
            {RiderID: "alpha", Pickup: "airport", Dropoff: "hotel"},
            {RiderID: "bravo", Pickup: "downtown", Dropoff: "station"},
            {RiderID: "charlie", Pickup: "harbor", Dropoff: "conference"},
        }
        for _, req := range requests {
            in <- req
        }
    }()

    assignmentStream := StageSelectVehicle(ctx, in)
    messageStream := StageFormatMessage(ctx, assignmentStream)

    for msg := range messageStream {
        fmt.Println("assignment ready:", msg)
    }
```

Each stage runs in its own goroutine and processes values independently. All stages respect context cancellation to ensure safe shutdown.

Why Pipelines Matter in Real Systems

Pipelines address several practical challenges that appear in large and growing applications. They offer a clear structure for handling streams of data and make concurrency manageable instead of chaotic.

Concurrency Without Complexity

Instead of building one large function that performs many operations, a pipeline breaks the work into small stages. Each stage has a single purpose, is easy to read, and can be tested in isolation. This keeps the overall design simple while still allowing the system to run many operations concurrently.

Natural Backpressure

Channels naturally limit how many values can move through the pipeline. If a downstream stage becomes slow, the upstream stage stops sending new work because the channel buffer fills up. This behavior protects the system from overload and provides a built-in way to slow down gracefully during traffic spikes.

Easy Parallelism

A pipeline can run several workers inside the same stage. This allows higher throughput without changing the rest of the pipeline. It is a structured form of fan-out and fan-in and keeps parallel work predictable instead of relying on unbounded goroutines.

Stages Evolve Independently

Each stage can be replaced, extended, or optimized without touching other parts of the pipeline. This makes long-lived systems easier to maintain, especially when different teams own different parts of the processing flow.

Safe and Predictable Shutdown

Every stage listens to `ctx.Done()`. When the service shuts down or a request is canceled, the entire pipeline stops immediately. Goroutines exit cleanly, channels close in order, and no part of the system continues running in the background.

Fan-Out and Fan-In

Modern services often need to process many small units of work at the same time. A request may trigger hundreds of database lookups, message decodings, or API calls. If all this work runs in a single goroutine, the system becomes slow and cannot use the full power of multi-core CPUs. The fan-out and fan-in pattern gives you a simple way to spread work across several goroutines and then collect the results in a controlled and predictable way.

- Fan-out means sending work to several goroutines so they can run in parallel.
- Fan-in means collecting all results from those goroutines into a single place.

The pattern is one of the most useful concurrency tools in Go, especially when you need to speed up CPU work, handle many I/O operations at once, or create worker pools for background jobs.

Fan-out and fan-in work well with Go because channels and goroutines are lightweight, and the select statement gives you natural control over cancellation using contexts.

Why This Pattern Matters in Real Services

Enterprise systems often have tasks like

- Parsing thousands of messages or CSV records
- Transforming or validating many records
- Fetching data from several remote services
- Reading files or objects from object storage
- Running batch jobs for analytics

These tasks are independent of each other, so running them sequentially wastes CPU time. Fan-out lets you start multiple workers, so the work is divided automatically. Fan-in gives you a clean point for combining the results, handling errors, or applying any final rules.

The pattern reduces latency, increases throughput, and keeps the code readable.

Core Idea of Fan-Out

Fan-out means several goroutines read from the same input channel.

```
func worker[T any, R any](id int, in <-chan T, process func(T) R)
<-chan R {
    out := make(chan R)
    go func() {
        defer close(out)
        for n := range in {
            time.Sleep(150 * time.Millisecond) // simulate work
            fmt.Printf("worker %d handling %v\n", id, n)
            out <- process(n)
        }
    }()
    return out
}
```

As it's implemented generic, you can use it for other types of data, and by function as a parameter, you can apply the required job. You can see the creation of multiple workers below:

```
jobs := make(chan int)

// Fan-out: start several workers consuming from the same jobs channel.
worker1Output := worker(1, jobs, processDelivery)
worker2Output := worker(2, jobs, processDelivery)
worker3Output := worker(3, jobs, processDelivery)
```

All three workers pull from `jobs`. Go schedules them fairly, so the workload is spread naturally without any extra logic.

DeliveryRequest type and processDelivery function can be defined separately like below, and it's not coupled to the pattern:

```
type DeliveryRequest struct {
    ID      string
    Pickup  string
    Dropoff string
```

```
}
func processDelivery(req DeliveryRequest) string {
    // Simulate planning a route or printing a ticket for the delivery.
    return fmt.Sprintf("ticket %s: %s -> %s", req.ID, req.Pickup, req.
    Dropoff)
}
```

Core Idea of Fan-In

Fan-in means combining the outputs of multiple workers into a single channel.

The classic merge function looks like this:

```
func merge[T any](inputs ...<-chan T) <-chan T {
    var wg sync.WaitGroup
    output := make(chan T)

    for _, ch := range inputs {
        wg.Go(func() {
            func(c <-chan T) {
                for v := range c {
                    output <- v
                }
            }(ch)
        })
    }

    go func() {
        wg.Wait()
        close(output)
    }()

    return output
}
```

In the merge function:

- Each worker writes to its own output channel.
- Merge copies values from all of them into one place.
- Merge closes the final channel only after all workers finish.

Enterprise Lesson Most probably, in your project, you need the usage of patterns multiple times. Using generic types helps you to reuse code.

This gives a clean, single stream of results. Using generics makes this pattern more readable and flexible in Go.

Putting Fan-Out and Fan-In Together

Here is an example of usage:

```
requests := []DeliveryRequest{
      {ID: "A1", Pickup: "Central Depot", Dropoff: "North Hub"},
      {ID: "B2", Pickup: "Warehouse", Dropoff: "Airport"},
      {ID: "C3", Pickup: "Port", Dropoff: "City Station"},
      {ID: "D4", Pickup: "Downtown", Dropoff: "University"},
      {ID: "E5", Pickup: "East Yard", Dropoff: "Harbor"},
  }
  jobs := make(chan DeliveryRequest)

  worker1Output := worker(1, jobs, processDelivery)
  worker2Output := worker(2, jobs, processDelivery)
  worker3Output := worker(3, jobs, processDelivery)

  // Feed work and then close the input channel.
  go func() {
      defer close(jobs)
      for _, req := range requests {
          jobs <- req
      }
  }()

  // Fan-in: merge worker outputs into a single stream.
  results := merge(worker1Output, worker2Output, worker3Output)

  for result := range results {
      fmt.Printf("completed: %s\n", result)
  }
```

This pattern uses more CPU cores when available and reduces overall processing time.

Integrating Context for Cancellation

Real systems must stop work when the request is canceled or when the system is shutting down. A worker should check the context and exit quickly:

```
func worker[T any, R any](ctx context.Context, id int, in <-chan T, process
func(T) R) <-chan R {
    out := make(chan R)
    go func() {
        defer close(out)
        for {
            select {
            case <-ctx.Done():
                return

            case n, ok := <-in:
                if !ok {
                    return
                }
                time.Sleep(150 * time.Millisecond) // simulate work
                fmt.Printf("worker %d handling %v\n", id, n)
                select {
                case <-ctx.Done():
                    return
                case out <- process(n):
                }

            }
        }
    }()
    return out
}
```

This makes the worker safe for shutdown and avoids dangling goroutines.

Worker Pool Pattern

Go makes goroutines easy to start, but creating too many goroutines can overload the service: CPU usage spikes, memory grows without control, and downstream systems receive more traffic than they can handle.

A scalable service needs **controlled concurrency**, not unlimited concurrency. The worker pool pattern is a simple and reliable way to achieve this. It creates a fixed number of workers that stay alive, receive tasks through a channel, and process them one at a time. This keeps resource usage predictable and allows the system to handle traffic safely, even under load.

Worker pools are a practical extension of the fan-out/fan-in pattern, but designed for long-running production systems.

Why Worker Pools Matter in Real Systems

Worker pools appear simple, but they solve several important challenges in production systems. When traffic grows or external dependencies slow down, uncontrolled concurrency can damage the entire service. A worker pool gives you a predictable and safe way to run tasks in parallel.

Controlled Concurrency

Without limits, every request may start new goroutines. Under heavy load, this can create thousands of goroutines that all compete for CPU time and memory. A worker pool defines exactly how many tasks may run at the same time. This protects resources such as

- System resources (CPU cores, memory, disk)
- Database connection pools
- External APIs with rate or concurrency limits

By setting a stable number of workers, you make throughput predictable and keep the system healthy even during peak load.

Natural Backpressure

When all workers are busy, new tasks wait in the job channel. This queue acts as a natural safety valve. Instead of the system collapsing during spikes, it slows down in a controlled way. This makes overload visible and prevents cascading failures.

Stable Memory and CPU Usage

Workers stay alive and reuse the same goroutine stack and internal buffers.

This makes the system predictable and helps

- Reduce short-lived allocations.
- Reduce garbage collection pressure.
- Keep memory usage predictable.
- Keep CPU scheduling predictable.

A stable worker pool consumes far less memory than creating new goroutines for each task.

Clear Separation of Responsibility

The producer of the work does not need to understand how the work is processed. It only sends tasks to the job channel.

Workers focus only on executing tasks. This creates a clean and testable design:

- Producers generate tasks.
- Workers process them.
- The pool controls the flow between them.

This separation makes the system easier to maintain and allows each part to evolve independently.

A Simple Worker Pool in Go

A worker pool always follows the same structure. You create a fixed group of workers, you send tasks through a channel, and each worker processes tasks one by one. This gives you controlled concurrency without creating unbounded goroutines.

A worker pool has three basic parts:

- A worker function
- A channel for incoming jobs
- A channel for results (optional, but useful for error handling or metrics)

Worker Function

Worker function is the core part of the pattern; it calls the business logic function and handles context, cancellation, and everything; you implement what your system is supposed to do and just use it in the worker.

Here you can see an example; suppose this is what your business logic looks like:

```
type RideJob struct {
    ID      int
    Rider   string
    Pickup  string
    Dropoff string
}

type JobResult struct {
    JobID   int
    Vehicle string
    Err     error
}

func assignRide(job RideJob) JobResult {
    time.Sleep(100 * time.Millisecond) // simulate routing/dispatch time

    if job.Pickup == "maintenance-yard" {
        return JobResult{JobID: job.ID, Err: errors.New("no vehicles
        available at yard")}
    }

    return JobResult{
```

```
        JobID:    job.ID,
        Vehicle: fmt.Sprintf("vehicle-%02d", job.ID%4+1),
    }
}
```

In this example, you can run the worker function **assignRide** without any effort, but the problem is that it takes time (time.Sleep); it makes your system slow. On the other hand, if you use call it in another goroutine, then you don't have any control over the number of running goroutines in your system.

Worker

The solution to run a predictable number of goroutines and call your defined function **assignRide** in this pattern is worker; here is an example:

```
func worker(ctx context.Context, id int, jobs <-chan RideJob, results
chan<- JobResult, wg *sync.WaitGroup) {
    defer wg.Done()

    for {
        select {
        case job, ok := <-jobs:
            if !ok {
                return // channel closed, worker stops
            }

            fmt.Printf("worker %d dispatching rider %s\n", id, job.Rider)
            results <- assignRide(job)

        case <-ctx.Done():
            return // graceful stop when context is canceled
        }
    }
}
```

A worker listens for jobs until the jobs channel is closed or the context is canceled. This makes the worker cooperative during shutdown and prevents goroutine leaks.

Starting the Pool

After defining the worker function, we need to start with the specific number of workers. I highly recommend you to put the workerCount in configs; this helps you to make your system easy to tune based on the system load and hardware spec:

```
func StartPool(ctx context.Context, workerCount int) (chan<- RideJob,
<-chan JobResult) {
    jobs := make(chan RideJob)
    results := make(chan JobResult, workerCount)

    var wg sync.WaitGroup
    wg.Add(workerCount)

    for i := 0; i < workerCount; i++ {
        go worker(ctx, i, jobs, results, &wg)
    }

    go func() {
        wg.Wait()
        close(results)
    }()

    return jobs, results
}
```

This function creates

- A **jobs channel** where callers send work
- A **results channel** where workers return errors or metrics
- **workerCount** goroutines that wait for tasks
- Workers that stop automatically when `ctx.Done()` closes

Where Worker Pools Fit in Enterprise Systems

Worker pools become valuable when tasks arrive faster than they can be processed. They give the service a stable level of concurrency and prevent spikes from overwhelming downstream components.

Message Consumers (Kafka, Pulsar, NATS)

A single goroutine reads messages from the broker, and the worker pool processes them in parallel. This protects the database, caches, and external APIs from sudden bursts.

Batch Operations

Worker pools are ideal for tasks that can be divided into many small pieces, such as

- Recalculating assignments
- Importing or processing large CSV files
- Rebuilding search indexes or caches

They keep CPU usage predictable even when processing thousands of items.

External API Calls

Many external services apply rate limits. The worker count becomes a natural limit on concurrency, preventing accidental overload.

High-Throughput Pipelines

Worker pools help systems stay responsive during bursts of traffic. They make the system predictable and tunable by controlling how many tasks run at the same time.

Anti-patterns in Go

In large Go code bases, some mistakes tend to recur, leading to resource exhaustion or hung processes. We examine key anti-patterns below, each illustrated with code examples and guidance on how to avoid them.

Goroutine Leaks

A **goroutine leak** happens when a goroutine starts but never stops. The program continues to run, but some goroutines remain alive forever and keep holding resources. Over time, this leads to higher memory usage, more open file descriptors, and unnecessary CPU work. In long-running services, this problem slowly degrades system stability.

Goroutine leaks usually appear when background work has **no clear stop condition**. This often happens with infinite loops, blocking channel operations, or missing cancellation logic.

Consider the following example:

```
func leakyDispatcher() {
    fmt.Println("goroutines before leak:", runtime.NumGoroutine())

    routes := make(chan string)

    // Dispatch loop that never stops sending.
    go func() {
        for i := 0; ; i++ {
            routes <- fmt.Sprintf("route-%02d", i) // blocks when no
            receiver exists
        }
    }()

    // Consumer stops early, leaving the dispatcher goroutine blocked
    on send.
    for r := range routes {
        fmt.Println("assigned:", r)
        if r == "route-05" {
            break
        }
    }

    time.Sleep(time.Second)
    fmt.Println("goroutines after leak:", runtime.NumGoroutine())
}
```

At first glance, this code looks harmless. The main loop stops after printing a few values. However, the goroutine sending values to `routs` never exits. Once the receiver stops reading, the send operation blocks forever. That goroutine remains alive until the process exits.

This type of leak is dangerous because it is **silent**. The program does not crash. Tests may pass. But in production, repeated leaks slowly consume resources and make the service unstable.

How to Avoid Goroutine Leaks

Having a checklist helps avoid goroutine leaks. To prevent goroutine leaks, apply these rules consistently.

Use Cancellation Signals

Every long-lived goroutine should listen to a stop signal. The most common approach is `context.Context`.

A loop should regularly check for cancellation:

```
for {
    select {
    case <-ctx.Done():
        return
    case v := <-ch:
        process(v)
    }
}
```

Ensure Clear Exit Conditions

Do not write infinite loops without a clear way out. Loops should exit when

- A channel is closed.
- A sentinel value is received.
- The context is canceled.

Always Call cancel()

When you create a cancellable context using `context.WithCancel`, `context.WithTimeout`, or `context.WithDeadline`, always call `cancel()`:

```
ctx, cancel := context.WithTimeout(parent, time.Second)
defer cancel()
```

Calling cancel helps the child context or functions called with the current function to understand they need to stop. Forgetting this keeps internal timers and goroutines alive longer than needed.

Close Channels When Producers Finish

If receivers use `for range` on a channel, the channel must be closed when sending is done. Otherwise, receivers will block forever.

Observe Goroutine Growth

In production systems, monitoring `runtime.NumGoroutine()` can help detect leaks early. A steady increase over time is often a warning sign.

Goroutines are cheap, but they are not free. Every goroutine must have a clear start, purpose, and end. In well-designed Go systems, goroutines are treated like managed resources, not fire-and-forget tasks. Careful lifecycle management is what separates reliable concurrent systems from fragile ones.

Channel Deadlocks

A **channel deadlock** happens when one or more goroutines wait on channel operations that can never be completed. When this occurs, the program stops making progress. In some cases, Go detects this situation and panics. In other cases, the program simply hangs forever.

Deadlocks are not caused by channels themselves. They are caused by **missing coordination** between goroutines.

Sending Without a Receiver

A very common deadlock happens when a value is sent on an unbuffered channel, but no goroutine is ready to receive it.

```
func deadlockExample() {
	ch := make(chan int)
	ch <- 42 // blocks forever: no receiver
}
```

An unbuffered channel requires a sender and a receiver to meet at the same time. In this example, the send operation blocks immediately. Since there is no other goroutine that can receive from ch, the program cannot continue. Go will panic with this message:

```
fatal error: all goroutines are asleep - deadlock!
```

Receiving from a Channel That Is Never Closed

Another common deadlock appears when using for range on a channel that is never closed.

```
func rangeDeadlock(tasks []int) {
	ch := make(chan int)

	go func() {
		for _, t := range tasks {
			ch <- t
		}
		// channel is never closed
	}()

	for v := range ch {
		fmt.Println(v)
	}
	// blocks forever waiting for more values
}
```

Here, the sender goroutine finishes its work, but the channel remains open. The receiver loop waits for more values that will never arrive. This goroutine blocks forever, and the program never terminates. Again, you will receive the same fatal error:

```
fatal error: all goroutines are asleep - deadlock!
```

Why This Happens

Channel deadlocks usually occur for these reasons:

- A send happens before any receiver exists.
- A receiver waits on a channel that no goroutine will ever write to.

- A channel used with `for range` is never closed.
- Termination logic does not clearly define who closes the channel.
- Multiple producers or consumers assume someone else is responsible.

In enterprise systems, these issues often appear in pipelines, worker pools, or fan-out/fan-in designs, especially when ownership of channels is unclear.

How to Avoid Channel Deadlocks

To prevent channel deadlocks, follow these rules:

- **Match Sends and Receives**

  For every send, there must be a receiver. If timing is uncertain, consider buffered channels or starting the receiver goroutine first.

- **Close Channels Intentionally**

  If a receiver uses `for range`, the channel must be closed when sending is finished. Closing a channel is a signal that no more values will arrive.

- **Define Channel Ownership**

  The goroutine that creates a channel should usually be responsible for closing it. Avoid closing channels from multiple places.

- **Use `Select` to Avoid Permanent Blocking**

  A `select` with a timeout or a cancellation case allows a goroutine to exit instead of blocking forever.

- **Coordinate Shutdown Explicitly**

  In multi-stage pipelines, make sure producers finish before consumers exit. Context cancellation helps ensure correct ordering.

A Safer Pattern

Here are two simple ways to avoid a blocking send:

```
func fixedExample() {
        // Buffered channel
        ch := make(chan int, 1)
        ch <- 42

        // Dedicated sender goroutine
        ch2 := make(chan int)
        go func() {
                ch2 <- 42
        }()
        value := <-ch2
        fmt.Println(value)
}
```

Buffered channels reduce the need for exact timing. Dedicated sender or receiver goroutines make coordination explicit.

Context Misuse

In Go, `context.Context` defines **how long work is allowed to live**. It carries cancellation signals, deadlines, and request-scoped boundaries across goroutines. When context is used well, concurrent code stays stable and responsive. When it is used poorly, failures appear in slow and frustrating ways: goroutines that never exit, requests that wait forever, and resources that are released too late.

Context bugs show up often in production systems. The reason is not complexity. The reason is that context errors are usually **small** and the consequences appear **later**, often only under real traffic.

Forgetting to Cancel a Context

A classic mistake is creating a cancellable context and never calling its cancel function.

```
func runTimedTask() {
        ctx, _ := context.WithTimeout(context.Background(), time.Second)

        go func() {
                <-ctx.Done()
                fmt.Println("background task stopped")
```

```
    }()

    // function exits without canceling the context
}
```

Internally, a context created with `WithTimeout` sets up timers and related management state. Below, you can find the cancel private method of context:

```
func (c *timerCtx) cancel(removeFromParent bool, err, cause error) {
   c.cancelCtx.cancel(false, err, cause)
   if removeFromParent {
       // Remove this timerCtx from its parent cancelCtx's children.
       removeChild(c.cancelCtx.Context, c)
   }
   c.mu.Lock()
   if c.timer != nil {
       c.timer.Stop()
       c.timer = nil
   }
   c.mu.Unlock()
}
```

If `cancel()` is never called, those resources stay alive until the timeout triggers, or until garbage collection happens to clean them up. If this occurs repeatedly in a high-throughput service, the cost becomes visible: higher memory usage, more goroutines, and increasing scheduler overhead. On the other hand, functions/methods that are called with this context can't be aware about what is going on, because cancel was not called.

The rule is strict and easy to remember: **If you create a cancellable context, you must cancel it.**

```
ctx, cancel := context.WithTimeout(parent, time.Second)
defer cancel()
```

This applies even when the timeout is short. Calling `cancel()` early is cheap, and it frees internal resources immediately. This simple call can save a lot of resources in enterprise projects, where you might have millions of function calls.

Ignoring Context in I/O Operations

Another common misuse happens when a function performs blocking I/O without passing a context. In transport systems, this often appears when services call each other to fetch route or vehicle data.

```
func loadRoute(routeID string) (*Route, error) {
	resp, err := http.Get(fmt.Sprintf(
		"https://routing.service/api/routes/%s", routeID,
	))
	if err != nil {
		return nil, err
	}
	defer resp.Body.Close()

	return decodeRoute(resp.Body)
}
```

This function has **no deadline and no cancellation path**. If the routing service becomes slow or unresponsive, this goroutine can block indefinitely. In a real transport system, this leads to request backlogs: schedule calculations wait, vehicle assignments stall, and goroutines accumulate under load.

Modern Go libraries are context-aware by design. The correct approach is to pass context explicitly and use APIs that respect cancellation, such as `http.NewRequestWithContext`, database methods like `QueryContext`, and RPC calls that accept a context. This ensures that when a request is canceled or times out, **all dependent transport operations stop together**.

How to Avoid Context Misuse

Follow these rules consistently:

- **Always Cancel Cancellable Contexts**

  Call `defer cancel()` immediately after creating them.

- **Pass Context Explicitly**

  Accept `context.Context` as the first parameter and pass it down the call chain. Do not store context in global variables or long-lived struct fields.

- **Use Context-Aware APIs**

  Prefer APIs that accept context, especially for network, database, and RPC operations.

- **Respect Cancellation in Long-Running Work**

  In loops or background tasks, watch `ctx.Done()` and exit as soon as cancellation is requested.

Excessive Concurrency

Go makes it very easy to start goroutines. This is one of its strengths. However, **using concurrency too early** or **too aggressively can hurt performance instead of improving it**. More goroutines do not automatically mean faster code.

Each goroutine has a cost. It needs stack space, it must be scheduled, and it competes for CPU time. When a program starts thousands of goroutines for very small tasks, the runtime spends more time managing concurrency than doing real work.

Consider this transport-related example:

```
func printVehicleIDs(vehicleIDs []string) {
   fmt.Println("goroutines before run:", runtime.NumGoroutine())
   for _, id := range vehicleIDs {
       go fmt.Println(id) // one goroutine per vehicle
   }
   fmt.Println("goroutines after run:", runtime.NumGoroutine())
   time.Sleep(time.Second) // fragile and unreliable
}
```

At first glance, this looks efficient because everything runs in parallel. In reality, printing a string is extremely cheap. If `vehicleIDs` is large, the program creates many goroutines that mostly wait to be scheduled. The overhead of scheduling dominates the actual work.

The result is higher memory usage, more context switching, and unpredictable execution. Under load, this pattern can slow the system instead of speeding it up.

Summary

In this chapter, we explored how Go supports design patterns in a way that is practical, lightweight, and aligned with its core principles. From idioms like small interfaces and deferred cleanup to structural and behavioral patterns such as decorators, strategies, observers, pipelines, and worker pools, we saw how Go encourages clarity over complexity. Instead of copying classical patterns directly, Go developers use interfaces, functions, and concurrency primitives to solve the same problems in simpler ways. These patterns are not about rules—they are about reliable habits that help teams scale systems safely and keep code maintainable as business requirements evolve. Understanding them deeply gives you the power to shape robust, testable, and performant enterprise software in Go.

What's Next

You've reached the end of the book, but this is just the beginning of your journey. We've explored not only Go-specific design and concurrency patterns, but also how to work better as a team—writing clearer code, designing safer systems, and communicating through structure.

Now the stage is yours. Apply what you've learned to real projects. Refactor one service with a worker pool. Add context cancellation to a background job. Improve team collaboration by sharing teamwork ideas.

If this book helped you, consider recommending it to others, telling us what worked for you, and commenting on links. Every shared insight keeps the Go community moving forward.

Keep building. Keep improving. Wishing you success in building enterprise projects you're proud of.

APPENDIX

Further Reading

- **Lencioni, Patrick.** *The Ideal Team Player: How to Recognize and Cultivate the Three Essential Virtues.* Jossey-Bass, 2016.
- **Cook, Curtis R.** *Just Enough Project Management: The Indispensable Four-Step Process for Managing Any Project, Better, Faster, Cheaper.* McGraw-Hill, 2004.
- **Maxwell, John C**. *The 21 Irrefutable Laws of Leadership.* Thomas Nelson, 1998.
- **Skelton, Matthew, Manuel Pais.** *Team Topologies: Organizing Business and Technology Teams for Fast Flow.* IT Revolution, 2019.
- **Gumus, Inanc.** *Effective Go: Elegant, Efficient, and Testable Code.* MEAP v5. Manning Publications, 2023.
- **Tsoukalos, Mihalis.** *Mastering Go: Harness the power of Go to build professional utilities and concurrent servers and services.* 3rd ed. Birmingham, Packt Publishing, 2021.
- **Harsanyi, Teiva**. *100 Go Mistakes and How to Avoid Them.* Manning Publications, 2022.
- **Cockburn, Alistair.** *Hexagonal Architecture (Ports & Adapters).* HaT Technical Report 2005.02. Salt Lake City: Humans and Technology, 2005.
- **Evans, Eric.** *Domain-Driven Design: Tackling Complexity in the Heart of Software.* 2003.
- **Martin, Robert C.** *Agile Software Development: Principles, Patterns, and Practices.* 2002.

S. Shahsavan, *Building Enterprise Projects with Go*, https://doi.org/10.1007/979-8-8688-2370-1

- **Martin, Robert C.** *Clean Architecture: A Craftsman's Guide to Software Structure and Design.* Addison-Wesley, 2018.
- **Martin, Robert C.** *Clean Code: A Handbook of Agile Software Craftsmanship.* Pearson, 2008.
- **Newman, Sam.** *Building Microservices: Designing Fine-Grained Systems.* 2nd ed. O'Reilly Media, 2021.
- **The Go Programming Language Specification.** Accessed [2026 January]. `https://go.dev/ref/spec`
- **Go Documentation.** Accessed [2026 January]. `https://go.dev/doc/`
- **gRPC Documentation.** Accessed [2026 January]. `https://grpc.io/`
- **Go by Example.** Accessed [2026 January]. `https://gobyexample.com/`
- **Refactoring Guru.** Accessed [2026 January]. `https://refactoring.guru/design-patterns/go`
- **A Guide to the Go Garbage Collector.** Accessed [2026 January]. `https://go.dev/doc/gc-guide`
- **The Green Tea Garbage Collector.** Accessed [2026 January]. `https://go.dev/blog/greenteagc`
- **Benchmarking Go: two ways of comparing slices.** Accessed [2026 January]. `https://www.mihail-ivanov.com/posts/benchmark-go/benchmark-go/`
- **Go Runtime Code.** Accessed [2026 January]. `https://go.dev/src/runtime/runtime2.go`
- **Scalable Go Scheduler Design Doc.** Accessed [2026 January]. `https://golang.org/s/go11sched`
- **More powerful Go execution traces.** Accessed [2026 January]. `https://go.dev/blog/execution-traces-2024`
- **Software Testing Guide.** Accessed [2026 January]. `https://martinfowler.com/testing/`

- **Understanding the API-First Approach to Building Products.** Accessed [2026 January]. `https://swagger.io/resources/articles/adopting-an-api-first-approach/`
- **GORM Guides.** Accessed [2026 January]. `https://gorm.io/docs/`
- **Testcontainers for Go.** Accessed [2026 January]. `https://golang.testcontainers.org/`
- **On the Diverse And Fantastical Shapes of Testing.** Accessed [2026 January]. `https://martinfowler.com/articles/2021-test-shapes.html`
- **Pulsar package documentation.** Accessed [2026 January]. `https://pkg.go.dev/github.com/apache/pulsar-client-go/pulsar`
- **Anton Zhiyanov.** Accessed [2026 January]. `https://antonz.org/`

Index

S. Shahsavan, *Building Enterprise Projects with Go*, https://doi.org/10.1007/979-8-8688-2370-1

D

E

F

G

H

I

P

Q

R

S

T

GPSR Compliance
The European Union's (EU) General Product Safety Regulation (GPSR) is a set of rules that requires consumer products to be safe and our obligations to ensure this.

If you have any concerns about our products, you can contact us on

ProductSafety@springernature.com

In case Publisher is established outside the EU, the EU authorized representative is:

Springer Nature Customer Service Center GmbH
Europaplatz 3
69115 Heidelberg, Germany

www.ingramcontent.com/pod-product-compliance
Lightning Source LLC
LaVergne TN
LVHW082010200926
848481LV00010B/2831
9798868823695